P9-DHF-019

INSIDE
MUSIC

For Joanne

with best wishes,

KARL HAAS

INSIDE MUSIC

HOW TO UNDERSTAND, LISTEN TO, AND ENJOY GOOD MUSIC

Drawings by Mona Mark

ANCHOR BOOKS
DOUBLEDAY
NEW YORK   LONDON   TORONTO   SYDNEY   AUCKLAND

AN ANCHOR BOOK
PUBLISHED BY DOUBLEDAY
a division of Bantam Doubleday Dell Publishing Group, Inc.
666 Fifth Avenue, New York, New York 10103

ANCHOR BOOKS, DOUBLEDAY, and the portrayal of an anchor
are trademarks of Doubleday, a division of Bantam Doubleday
Dell Publishing Group, Inc.

Inside Music was originally published in hardcover by
Doubleday in 1984. The Anchor Books edition is
published by arrangement with GuildAmerica Books.

Library of Congress Cataloging-in-Publication Data
Haas, Karl.
Inside music.
Bibliography: p.   Includes index.
1. Music appreciation.   I. Title.
MT90.H14   1984   780'.1'5   78-22614
ISBN 0-385-41774-8

Copyright © 1984 by Karl Haas
ALL RIGHTS RESERVED
PRINTED IN THE UNITED STATES OF AMERICA
FIRST ANCHOR BOOKS EDITION: OCTOBER 1991
1   3   5   7   9   10   8   6   4   2

Preface

IS THERE A NEED for another book on the makings of music? Indeed, can one hope to put into so many words the meaning of myriads of aspects of an art that has been expressed by its creators far more eloquently in its original medium than through words?

Following my publisher's request that I write such a book, a lengthy period of self-searching yielded an affirmative answer to these questions. In more years of broadcasting and performing than I am willing to admit, it has become abundantly clear to me that there exists a far greater number of music lovers than those who comprehend what it is they love. I believe it is safe to state that music is the best loved and least understood of all the arts.

As for myself, I have been completely and irrevocably addicted to music professionally, emotionally, and intellectually. Ever since early childhood there was never any doubt that I wanted to be a musician. The road to reaching that goal was by no means always smooth. But I have been fortunate to have been given the opportunity of devoting my entire life to music – and much of it to sharing that devotion with others. I am not at all sure whether this qualifies me to author that which follows. No one can be sure enough to put into print what so often defies such concreteness.

Making no claim to completeness, I have tried to describe some aspects of music making that may be of particular interest to the sincere music lover looking for answers to specific questions. At times these descriptions may be found distributed in various chapters according to the desired context. (For instance, the sonata will be discussed in the chapters on Form, Categories, and Periods of Music.) In addition, I thought it important to focus the reader's attention on the time and the circumstances that prompted the creation of certain categories of music in general, and some of the great masterworks in particular, by relating them to history and to other arts. If in the process I may be found to be somewhat subjective at times, I beg my reader's indulgence. Being an active musician and not a musicologist, I admit to the passions of the former and to a respect for the learnedness of the latter.

It is my fervent hope that this book will afford more than just a mere glimpse at the infinite realm that is "inside music."

Acknowledgments

THIS BOOK was written during a period filled with heavy broadcast commitments and performance engagements. It often occurred to me how much easier it might have been had I written it during a sabbatical. But this was not to be. All the more do I appreciate the understanding, encouragement, and assistance that I had the good fortune to receive throughout the time required to complete this volume.

First, I wish to thank my wife, Maria, who with thought and deed was always at my side, and without whose persistent empathy my task would have been a far more difficult one. My gratitude goes to my daughter, Alyce, for her most helpful and intelligent research assistance and her always warmhearted support.

If it had not been for the convincing approach and long-suffering patience of Marjorie Goldstein, managing editor, I would have never thought of conceiving this book in the first place. It is she who is responsible that it came into being.

My special thanks go to Mary Sherwin, my editor, whose editorial skill and humane understanding guided me through the crucial stages of my task with compassion and remarkable tact.

Last, but by no means least, I wish to thank my friend Hans Heinsheimer, distinguished scholar, author, and publisher, for his astute criticism and invaluable counsel; and Henry Krawitz, copy editor, for the admirable dispatch and interest with which he discharged his duties.

Contents

ix

CONTENTS

PART ONE

THE MAKINGS OF MUSIC

CHAPTER ONE

THE INFINITE PLEASURES OF LISTENING TO MUSIC

DO YOU EVER sing in the shower, whistle a tune while you tie your shoelaces, or hum bits of a melody while you comb your hair? It could be any melody you heard somewhere, sometime, that somehow seeped into your memory. If your answer is yes, chances are that you enjoy music, that you have the makings of a true music lover. Maybe you can't read a note of music, have never had a music lesson or attended a music appreciation class; maybe you've never been present at a concert or an opera performance. It doesn't matter. Humming, whistling, or singing tunes – even without knowing their names – show that you take to music instinctively.

One doesn't need a formal, or even informal, education to be able to enjoy music thoroughly. Music is for everyone because it is a natural part of daily living. There are enough kinds of music to suit every taste, fill every need, match every mood, "send us" in any particular direction. All of it is valid as long as it gives us satisfaction and pleasure. Because music mirrors life and its daily happenings, joys, sorrows, and frustrations, it appeals either to our senses or to our intellect – ideally to both. Our reaction to the music is spontaneous, not planned. So much the better. I applaud anyone who is capable of being moved, who can respond to something as vague and abstract as musical sound.

Let's consider painting, sculpture, or architecture, for example. You can actually touch the canvas, the bronze or terra-cotta, the stone – the raw material is concrete in each instance. The same is true of literature. You can hold a book in your hands, see and read the words with your own eyes, even though their meaning may not always be easily understood. In the case of music, its raw material is sound, and it seems to come from nowhere. Although you can see the instrumentalists and singers perform, you are unable to touch the sound that they produce, which, in all its multicolored splendor, brings to life the flights of the composer's fancy and imagination. All of this can create one of man's greatest and noblest experiences.

The sources of sound and the role of the performing musician will be discussed a little later on in this book. Let us now look at what we can expect to gain from listening to music.

FIRST. We seek relaxation and a change from the chores of our daily existence. Is there a better way to achieve it than by listening to, say, Mozart's *Eine kleine Nachtmusik* or Bizet's Symphony in C? This is music of a positive nature, bubbly and effervescent in most parts, like a vintage champagne. If you are looking for a spiritual, moral, or emotional lift, then try Beethoven's Symphony No. 3 ("Eroica"); or his "Emperor" Piano Concerto No. 5; or perhaps Brahms' Double Concerto for Violin and Cello. These are examples of great sweep and exalted musical content and fiber.

SECOND. We can derive a physical lift from listening to music. Think of some of the irresistible passages found in opera, such as the triumphal scene in Verdi's *Aida*, the soldiers' chorus in Gounod's *Faust*, or the entrance of the masters in the final scene of Wagner's *Die Meistersinger*.

However, it is not always elation or sheer thrill that we expect to experience. Sometimes listening to music can become an emotional outlet, as with the deeply moving closing scene of Puccini's *La Bohème* or Verdi's *La Traviata;* or, perhaps a bit less emotionally but by no means less dramatically, Tchaikovsky's Symphony No. 6, the "Pathétique." We can be visibly moved by the tragic impact of these masterworks. Even the emotional pain that they convey can bring satisfaction of a psychological sort.

THIRD. We can reap intellectual rewards from listening to great music. Is it not a challenge to learn more about the makings of a superb symphony – how it is constructed, how motifs and phrases fall into line, what its creator's aim or purpose was? What are some of the infinite secrets of composition and performance that enable them to conjure up a vivid picture in our minds or an unforgettable experience in our hearts? There is also the thrill of witnessing the superior execution, insight, and virtuosity of great performing artists.

These are only a few of our expectations when we allow ourselves to enter into a partnership with the process of music making. If you just sit passively at a concert or an opera, expecting to be entertained, you will miss a great part of what music can give you. If, on the other hand, you become a knowledgeable listener and a true partner of the composer, sharing his emotions and intentions and those of the interpreter, then you close the link and complete the cycle of music's purpose – the transmission of a composer's immortal message, delivered by outstanding interpreters for the express delight of you, the receptive listener.

This brings us to a consideration of the subject of listening itself. Let's start with the questions of *who, why, when, how,* and *where* to listen to music.

Anyone and everyone can and should listen to good music. No formal training is required for its enjoyment.

Listening is a great source of relaxation and a singular challenge to our emotions, our intellect, even our physical well-being. We come away from music satisfied, fulfilled, refreshed, elated, even sensually provoked.

Obviously, the mood in which we find ourselves at a given moment determines the degree of our receptivity. If you have a mercurial nature, you may not appreciate the lighthearted gait of Prokofiev's "Classical" Symphony when you are unhappy. Perhaps something noble, yet poignant, like the *Adagio for Strings* by Samuel Barber, or the elevating *Adagio for Strings and Organ* ascribed to Tommaso Albinoni, might be more appropriate to your mood. If, on the other hand, you are feeling euphoric and want to calm down, you might like to hear Handel's *Water Music,* the third movement of the Symphony No. 6 by Tchaikovsky, the second movement of the Symphony

5

No. 5 by Prokofiev, or the Symphony No. 8 by Beethoven. Of course, there are many in-between choices for in-between moods that you will discover as a matter of personal preference. But, generally speaking, listen whenever the spirit moves you. You will soon find yourself gravitating toward the appropriate choice at any given time, as your repertoire of compositions begins to widen.

Let me urge you to listen alertly, with all your faculties, to whatever music you select. Only then will it remain ever fresh for your fullest enjoyment.

I might add that I find it difficult to be a lover of good music and, at the same time, to tolerate that deterrent to true musical enjoyment known as "background music." In effect, this is tantamount to a continuous spray inflicted upon our subconscious just about everywhere we go: in markets, dentists' offices (medical doctors do not seem to succumb to the practice as easily), restaurants, banks, drugstores, on airplanes, trains, ships, and even in homes. (In some cases your hosts may take offense if you ask them to turn off or lower the volume because they like to show off their stereo equipment, even though the music intrudes upon conversation and plays on while no one listens.) This wall-to-wall intrusion is designed with the questionable purpose of making us feel "pleasant." In theory I suppose there is really nothing wrong with "background music," and many people actually enjoy it. However, the problem is that this consistently bland, innocuous music becomes habit-forming and can adversely affect our capacity to listen attentively to what I like to call "foreground music."

The people responsible for "programming" background fare in public places take great care in selecting inoffensive, nonchallenging pieces and ditties. Continuous exposure to this musical chatter dulls our ability to listen undividedly to more challenging musical fare. My advice: Avoid background music whenever possible.

Listen wherever you find the most beneficial ambience for doing so – in the privacy of your home, your car, at musical gatherings (many music lovers organize regular listening sessions, followed by a spirited discussion of what they have heard), and at concerts or recitals. Try to be as undisturbed as possible. The great masters deserve no less, notwithstanding the fact that Haydn and Mozart were often called upon to supply new scores for mere entertainment purposes. Luckily, the fruits of their genius transcend the original reason for their creation.

WHAT TO LISTEN FOR IN MUSIC

The contents of this book will furnish you with some of the many answers to and facets of this important question. Meanwhile, our discussion here will be rather practical and easily accessible, though perhaps more simplistic.

Depending upon how vivid your imagination is, music usually conjures up a mental picture, or at least a state of mental or emotional awareness. Never attempt to suppress or hamper that natural urge. You may even be ahead of the composer or the interpreting artist, for, more often than not, neither may have had any image in mind at the time the piece was conceived or studied for interpretation. Arturo Toscanini, the legendary conductor, was once asked, "Maestro, do you agree that those pregnant opening notes

of the Fifth Symphony by Beethoven represent fate knocking at the door?" The maestro's answer was typical and revealing. With his lovable Italian touch he said, "By me, is *Allegro con brio* [fast, with verve]." Still, if in your imagination these notes do become pictorial in any way, then I, for one, prefer *your* reaction to Maestro Toscanini's.

Do not hesitate to have a reaction or opinion as you listen to music, and do not feel apologetic about forming or even uttering them (except, of course, while a concert is in progress). When attending a concert, never be intimidated by your neighbor's opinions and do not ever wait to read a critic's review before formulating your own judgment. Trust in your own critical abilities, even if you happen to be proven wrong later. Don't suddenly assume the role of a self-appointed musical expert, though. Increased listening experience and a mounting absorption of information and learning will sharpen your faculties of perception and judgment.

Above all, beware of "definitive" or "authoritative" explanations of music and performance. There is no such thing; the more you learn or think you know, the more you will realize how much there is left to explore. No single lifetime can begin to suffice to get to know it all, for music is as infinite in its ways as it is individual in eliciting responses.

When I was a student, my classmates and I often were the lucky recipients of tickets to pairs of concerts with the same program. As I remember, these concerts were on Thursday and Friday evenings of the regular season. The first night we would be seated, score in lap, dissecting, marking, listening for all kinds of clues to wisdoms of form and interpretation that we had studied in class. The second night we would leave behind all scores and reference materials, and we would just listen, often with eyes closed, yielding completely to the flow of musical sound that welled up from the orchestra, and through it, ultimately, from the composer's heart, soul, and mind. Needless to say, our way of listening had become somewhat more knowledgeable by the second night's performance. How much more we enjoyed that second night, with its complete freedom from analyses, syntheses, and anticipation of predictable things to come!

So, by all means allow yourself as often as possible the luxury of listening with the fiber of your being rather than with the acquired learning of your faculties. Naturally, the ideal condition is a proper mix of the two. But do not look for such a mix to happen overnight. It will take a while, and even then it is rather difficult to come by.

Here are some aids that you will find helpful to enhance your listening experience.

• Often the descriptive captions at the start of a composition or at the beginning of the individual movements of a symphony or sonata – representing tempo markings, with or without conditioning adjectives – afford a good clue to the spirit and character of the music. You find them frequently given in the printed program of a concert or on the jacket of a record. They are most often in Italian, the traditional language of musical directions, although German, French, and English have been used increasingly in the nineteenth and twentieth centuries. You will find some translations of these markings in the Glossary. Thus, *andante* ("walking") indicates a leisurely, fairly slow pace. *Adagio* ("slow") is much more measured than *andante;* and if the word *cantabile* ("singing") is added, we know that we can expect music of an introspective, deeply felt nature. The second movement of Beethoven's "Pathétique" Sonata, Op. 13 – the beginning portion of which serves as the "live" theme of my radio program "Adventures in Good Music" – surely justifies that heading. On the other hand, the notation *allegro con brio* ("fast, with verve"), with which Beethoven's Fifth Symphony is introduced, can only hint at the excitement that ensues. Tempo markings and interpretative guidelines that composers provide in terse language constitute broad suggestions as to what we may expect to hear.

• The titles that preface many compositions may be easier to understand than tempo notations, but they are usually just as tersely expressed. We do not expect a piece called "nocturne" ("night piece") to sound upbeat (unless the writer intends to convey a nightmare), whereas the caption "gigue" ("jig") prepares us for an active listening experience.

One-word titles can be amazingly revealing, especially when they describe a specific "happening." Aaron Copland tells us an entire story when he uses "Hoedown" as the last episode of his ballet score *Rodeo,* replete with the tuning of fiddles and barn dancing; for a few brief moments even the sound of the band "running out of steam" can be heard. Similarly, a colorful ebullience is conjured up with the one-word geographic description "España" that the French composer Emmanuel Chabrier used for his Spanish rhapsody. Castanets punctuate the Spanish dance tunes of *jota* and *malagueña.* You can even hear the traditional stomping of heels as simulated by the sudden outbursts of percussion.

Of course, the more explicit and elaborate the titles, the less is left to our imagination as we listen. Here are several examples of titles that aid us immensely in following the action of the music as it progresses.

Pictures at an Exhibition, by the Russian composer Modest Mussorgsky – in its original version for solo piano or in orchestrations by several musicians of stature, the most famous being Maurice Ravel

9

– calls for a pictorial approach to listening, with our mind's eye, as it were. Mussorgsky was particularly explicit in labeling each of his "pictures," such as "Tuileries" (the famous Parisian gardens), "Ballet of Unhatched Chicks," "Marketplace at Limoges," "Catacombs," or "The Great Gate at Kiev." A connective musical link is provided among all of these, a recurring melody called "Promenade," suggesting our footsteps as we walk from one picture to another while viewing the exhibition. We can allow ourselves to be joyfully led by the composer's hand in literally seeing the drawings and sketches by his artist friend Victor Hartmann, to whose memory he pays tribute in this colorful work.

Another example of vivid listening prompted by descriptive titles is the three-part tone picture called *La Mer (The Sea)* by the French composer Claude Debussy. Possessed by a passion for the sea, Debussy filled this score with impressions of various aspects of undulating waves – a prototype of impressionist music conceived by its most distinguished exponent. *La Mer* has three highly suggestive and specific subtitles, each of which gives us a mental image of the composer's intentions: "From Dawn to Noon at Sea," "Play of the Waves," and "Dialogue of the Wind and the Sea." There is no question here as to what to listen for. Everything is spelled out for us in detail; all we need to do is let the tonal waves engulf our senses.

• Some composers supply a detailed account of the action by describing the music as it unfolds. Interestingly enough, such thorough guidance is not restricted to any one period of music history. Thus, we find it in the Romantic age (the late eighteenth and early nineteenth centuries), when elaborate directions were used with considerable frequency, as in the *Symphonie Fantastique* by Berlioz or, even later, in the tone poems by Richard Strauss; it is also much in evidence during the first half of the eighteenth century, during Johann Sebastian Bach's time, when there were usually no directions of any kind other than the notes themselves. Bach provided us with a gem with his "Capriccio Written on the Departure of a Favorite Brother" on the occasion of his brother Johann Jakob's imminent journey to Poland. In this delightful score for the harpsichord we find a blueprint for what Bach had in mind as he wrote each part: his friends entreating Johann Jakob not to embark on the journey;

a recital of the dangers that might befall him on the way; the ensuing lament over his resolve to go; then the sound of the horn of the postilion, followed by a remarkable fugal treatment of the horn motif.

Somewhat earlier, in 1700, the German composer and keyboard artist Johann Kuhnau conceived an interesting set of pieces entitled *Biblische Historien nebst Auslegung in sechs Sonaten (Biblical Stories with Interpretation in Six Sonatas)*. The scenario of the first sonata follows the story of David and Goliath, with subtitles such as "Bravado of Goliath," "Terror of the Israelites and Their Prayer," and "Paeans of Victory by the Israelites." The music is replete with sound effects, such as the fierce staccato chords simulating the stamping and ranting of Goliath. This score is so real that it would be difficult for even an inexperienced listener to be unable to follow the plot as conceived by the composer.

In Chapter Nine we will see how composers became more and more involved with extramusical associations, outside sources from which they derived inspiration and from which they utilized descriptive directions that were appended to their scores. They delved freely into the fields of literature and religion, as with Tchaikovsky's *Romeo and Juliet* or Berlioz's *Requiem*; politics and current events, such as Sibelius' *Finlandia* or Shostakovich's "Leningrad" Symphony, No. 7; history and geography, as in Verdi's *Un Ballo in Maschera (A Masked Ball)*, which deals with the assassination of King Gustav III of Sweden, Rossini's *William Tell*, or Skalkottas' colorful *Greek Dances*.

Such interrelationships between music and the extramusical are limited only by the extent of the composer's talent and imagination. Listening under these circumstances becomes a guided tour; we are being told exactly what to listen for.

• The challenge to our listening experience can be greater when the music exists for its own sake. We are left to listen – to savor the flow of melodies, the orchestral colors, the richness of harmonies, the fascination of rhythmic patterns – without any predetermined ideas imposed upon us. Most symphonies, sonatas, and most categories of chamber music and concertos offer little, if anything, to shape our consciousness in advance. In the long run, the less cluttered our

11

minds are with listening aids, the more directly the music will manifest itself and speak to us.

• A brilliant scheme of musical form applies to most large-scale works. Once we become acquainted with some of the aspects of form and construction – with their architectural, harmonic, and melodic implications – these can easily take the place of a detailed plot. For well over two hundred years symphonies, concertos, string quartets, sonatas, and most chamber music compositions have been "blood relatives." Needless to say, their outward appearance and musical content are as different as facial features and personality traits of brothers and sisters. However, there are similarities in the shape of their components and the course of their harmonic and thematic development. All of this serves as a means to an end for the listener: a more knowledgeable *enjoyment* of music.

• One of the great joys of increasing your listening experience is being better able to listen for differences in interpretation of the same work as performed by various artists. In Chapter Five we will find that there are untold varieties of nuances and subtleties with which to express the same musical thoughts. One way will probably appeal to us more than another. Thus, the groundwork is laid for that inexplicable, unteachable, elusive, indispensable, indisputable, often overbearingly stated possession: musical taste. It allows us to realize that there are many ways to be right when it comes to the performance of a masterwork, but there is only one way to be wrong, namely, when the music does not "come across" to us. The possession of musical taste becomes a great lesson in tolerance and humility rather than a franchise for snobbishness and overbearingness.

• Listening for instrumental and vocal timbres or tone colors becomes a rich frosting on the cake of listening achievement. What fun and exhilaration there is in being able to listen to the voices of various instruments in a score, both individually and in a variety of combinations! Their tonal idiosyncracies and characteristics of musical speech as produced by different artists are as numerous and as personal as the many hues and timbres of the human voice. And why should this not be so! They are produced by human efforts, and the instruments are merely the channels through which these efforts are realized and conveyed to us.

Whether it be a matter of untutored, natural perception or the result of carefully cultivated and increasingly sophisticated knowledge, listening to music is unlike most other sensory experiences. We may see something new and extremely worthwhile every time we look at a favorite painting or sculpture; we may discover a new substantiation of truth with every rereading of a favorite book; but can this compare with the immeasurable pleasures of listening to, relistening to, and even reliving a cherished symphony or concerto that is interpreted differently every time? It is for you, the reader and listener, to answer. I, for one, believe in giving them all equal time, not by way of slides of artwork, nor musical recordings, but "in the flesh" as it were.

There is available today an abundance of fine recordings and tapes, plus outstanding reproduction equipment of the latest technological achievement. It makes available at the flip of a switch or the turn of a dial a constant flow of your favorite music, to be relived over and over, in the absence of a "live" performance, or long after the memory of a concert has faded.

However, it is my ardent belief that none of this can ever take the place of a "live" performance. Music is an unsurpassed form of human expression and can never be more fully enjoyed than under human, not mechanical, conditions. Partaking of a musical performance in progress assures us of that extra flow of adrenalin to uplift and enable us to literally breathe the music with the performers. Conversely, the performers also benefit from the reverse flow of adrenalin, back across the footlights from the audience, a phenomenon that can be matched neither in the listener's den or living room nor in the musician's recording studio.

Of equal importance is the fact that even the finest recordings capture only the conception of a given moment, while interpretations change from one performance to another. Imprisoning nuances and moods in any one recording is depriving the music of the undulating flow of its lifeblood. Reproductions are second-best. Arthur Rubinstein put it so aptly when he told me, "I make records with great enthusiasm. Often, when I listen to a playback I say to myself,

13

'Oh wonderful! That really came out so well!' Invariably two or three months later I cannot stand listening to it anymore; for I change and the record doesn't. And so we are divorced."

Far be it for me to inhibit you in the acquisition of a fine record library – today's music world is unthinkable without it. You will find some helpful suggestions on this subject in a special appended section, "Suggestions for Building a Music Library." However, I would be remiss in fulfilling the purpose of this book if I did not urge you vigorously to attend "live" concerts and recitals whenever possible; or, if it is in your power, to make music yourself, alone or with others. There'll be no splicing out here of possible errors or mistakes, with its resultant antiseptic perfection.

Of course, no artist can perform with machinelike precision every time. Modern recording techniques can deal easily with any contingencies, but listening under "live" conditions adds the welcome human touch to music's infinite pleasures.

CHAPTER TWO

MUSIC'S MAIN INGREDIENTS

WE TAKE THE sound of music quite for granted. It is all around us. All we need to do is put a record on our stereo or flip the switch of our radio or television set and music enters our ears. We are not witnessing the performance itself; only our attendance at a concert or other gathering of performing musicians enables us to both hear and see the process of music making. We can observe the bowing or plucking of strings, the blowing into mouthpieces of wind and brass instruments, the beating of percussion surfaces, the striking of keys, and the emission of musical sound from human throats. But none of this explains how sound – music's raw material – originates in the first place, in order then to be transformed into music by the performer.

The field of physics shows us that sensations of sound result from the vibrations of elastic objects. These sensations enter our consciousness through our sense of hearing, transmitted via the eardrum to the auditory nerves in the inner ear. When the vibrations are irregular, fitful, sporadic in time and duration, or oppressive in intensity, they excite our hearing nerves and are perceived as mere noise. When the vibrations are regular, continue uniformly and unaltered, and return in measured periods, they enter our awareness as organized musical sound. So it is the sound of ordered wavelengths, or definite pitch, that emerges as the primary raw material of music – a far more abstract substance than stone, wood, and mortar in the case of architecture, or paint materials, bronze, and terra-cotta in the visual and plastic arts.

As we examine music's main ingredients, there is a danger of oversimplification. I am not even sure if the dissection of music into its main components should serve any purpose other than to provide a more informed understanding of a work of art. I am reminded of a delectable meal. In consuming it we savor the delicious flavor in its totality. Only gourmets and experienced cooks are interested in knowing the exact preparation and application of each individual ingredient. However, for the sake of cultivating our musical taste buds, let me invite you into the "kitchen."

In order of importance and indispensability to the art of musical composition, the main ingredients of music are:

RHYTHM   MELODY   HARMONY   COLOR   FORM

These are completely interdependent – at least in any traditional musical work. For the purpose of our discussion here, let us look at each of these ingredients separately, define them, and select some typical compositions in which each plays a dominant role.

RHYTHM – THE PULSE OF MUSIC

"In the beginning there was rhythm." This is an oft-quoted dictum derived from the story of Creation itself. Although we do not know with certainty exactly how music began, we can safely assume that percussion instruments – drums of various shapes, as well as other primitive "noisemakers" – played a large role in accentuating per-sistent rhythms of varying degrees of regularity. Pictures and draw-ings of early civilizations support that assumption, and its manifes-tation still exists today in primitive cultures. Whether music had its inception as a kind of singsong or as an imitative byproduct of spoken words or language, rhythm became an intrinsic element.

Different rhythms seem to have evolved for various aspects of daily routine: to accompany all kinds of work; during festivals, wed-dings, funerals; or for worship, ritual, dancing, even lovemaking. Rhythms were used to evoke rain and plentiful harvest, and to urge men into war. To this day rhythms can exist by themselves as a means of conveying a musical message. For the creation of a lasting masterpiece, none of the other musical ingredients are conceivable without the presence of rhythm.

In the context of today's music, rhythm is the discipline that regulates the flow of music. It orders tones into patterns of duration through the use of accents, impulses, stresses, and releases. Rhythm creates the regularity or irregularity of the "beat." It is often identified as "meter," a regular recurrence of the beat. This, in turn, establishes the succession of measures into musical phrases, and ultimately into entire sections of a composition. Bar lines – drawn vertically through the five lines of the music staff – divide one measure from the next, once the exact size and extent of that measure has been determined by means of rhythmical description. The following verses from Act 4, Scene 2 of *The Two Gentlemen of Verona* by William Shakespeare may serve as a visual illustration:

> Who is Sylvia? what is she?
> That all our swains commend her?
> Holy, fair, and wise is she;
> The heaven such grace did lend her,
> That she might admired be.

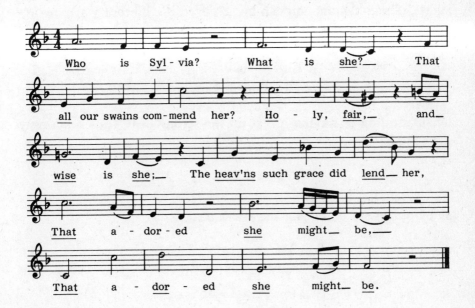

Translated into the musical notation that Franz Schubert used in his famous setting of this text, the flow of rhythm is shown in the previous example. (The German translation is by Eduard von Bauernfeld, an acquaintance of Schubert's.)

The underlined words or syllables and the corresponding notes denote the strong beats of the measure, even though the phrases of the poem are halved in the metric scheme chosen by Schubert. We react to these strong beats naturally. We feel the impulse to tap our feet or snap our fingers. Musical examples of strong rhythmical predominance are found among perennial favorites such as Sousa's "Stars and Stripes Forever" for march rhythm and Johann Strauss's "On the Beautiful Blue Danube" for waltz rhythm.

The remaining, unmarked beats of the measures shown above are obviously the weak ones. Normally we would give them less emphasis, just as we would the second syllable in the name Sylvia, or the first syllable in the word commend when speaking these words.

Irregularities such as the stress of a weak beat can have a very special charm all their own. In fact, the pleasant physical shock that we receive from an "off-beat" accent forms the heart of the characteristic idiom of the blues, ragtime, jazz, and the Negro spiritual. We call it syncopation, a word derived from the Greek, meaning "cutting short." This phenomenon can be achieved in different ways: by anticipating the strong beat or holding on over it;

by suspending or having a rest on the strong beat, thus seemingly ignoring it;

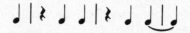

or by purposely accenting the weak beat.

"Limehouse Blues,"* written by Philip Braham, with lyrics by Douglas Furber, offers a combination of the first and last of the above possibilities:

Oh! Lime-house kid___ Oh! Oh! Oh! Lime-house kid

It is "Fascinating Rhythm," as George and Ira Gershwin so aptly described it in words and music. Another Gershwin classic, "I Got Rhythm," is also an excellent illustration of syncopation.

The regular recurrence of the accented beat is governed by metric units, or measures, which are divisions of time in a musical composition. Let's consider the following analogy. In an effort to stay on the right road when driving along the countryside, we are guided and comforted by a shield bearing the highway's route number. This shield is generally erected at regularly measured distances, and particularly at intersections, to keep us from veering off the chosen road. The same guide in music is provided by the posting of a double number at the beginning of a composition, resembling a mathematical fraction. It shows us at a glance the metric order that underlies the work. It is known as a *time signature.* In the Schubert selection "Who is Sylvia?" $\frac{4}{4}$ denotes four beats to a measure and also that a fourth or quarter note receives one beat. Similarly, waltz time is $\frac{3}{4}$ time; the upper numeral indicates the number of beats to the measure – or "bar," in the vernacular – while the lower numeral tells us the kind of note that receives one beat (quarter note, eighth note, etc.). If the beat is divisible by two, such as in $\frac{2}{4}$ or $\frac{4}{4}$, we speak of "simple duple time." The time signature $\frac{3}{4}$ is known as "simple triple time"; $\frac{6}{8}$, $\frac{9}{8}$, and $\frac{12}{8}$ are known as "compound time."

These examples point up the variety of directions or signatures that indicate the metric units of "time." The spice of rhythmic life is found within these measures.

Now let's apply the tried and true definition of *relativity* to how

*© 1922 (Renewed) ASCHERBERG, HOPWOOD & CREW, LTD. All Rights Reserved. Used by Permission of WARNER BROS. MUSIC.

we perceive the passage of time. Most of us have experienced a week at work that was utterly tedious, when time seemed interminable; but we could spend a week's vacation and feel as if time passed much faster. By the same token, we can fill a few measures of $\frac{4}{4}$ time with sustained, even notes and the resultant look is one of placidity and little excitement.

("CHILDREN'S PRAYER" FROM HUMPERDINCK'S *HANSEL AND GRETEL*)

In the following example you can readily see the agitation created by a far more active flow of rhythmic patterns within the same space of time.

(TCHAIKOVSKY'S SYMPHONY NO. 4, FOURTH MOVEMENT)

The variety of rhythmic patterns, created by the use of metric units or time, are limited only by the extent of the composer's inventive power.

Also, you should note that the pace of the second example is considerably faster than that of the first. The pace of a composition and its performance is known as *tempo,* a word derived from the Italian, meaning "time." Simply stated, meter or time determines the space in which rhythm moves; the rhythmic pattern furnishes the vehicle of movement; and tempo denotes the speed or pace of a piece. (Most compositions are captioned with a tempo designation either in Italian, the original language of music, or in the native language of the composer. The Glossary includes some of these markings together with their English meaning.)

Since the time of Beethoven, markings of numerical measurement have been used to guide performers with quasi-mathematical precision of tempo. They refer to the slide rule of an instrument called the metronome, invented by Johann Nepomuk Maelzel in 1816 to ensure the regularity of beats. A marking such as MM (Maelzel's Metronome)

$$\quarternote = 120$$

means that a quarter note must be played at the setting 120 on the metronome, or 120 quarter-note beats per minute. Beethoven adopted this device one year after its invention, but not without poking good-natured fun at the inventor in the third movement of his eighth symphony.

Keep in mind that tempo and metronome markings constitute only a general guide for the performer, who ultimately must be the judge of them. Fortunately for all of us, interpreters of a given work of music seldom reach metronomic agreement about the exactness of its tempo. Creativity, as well as re-creativity, defies metronomic or any other pedantic sameness.

Rhythm emerges from all this as a multifaceted, life-giving ingredient of music, completely indispensable for its existence. When Gershwin said musically, "I got rhythm," he surely spoke for every composer.

THE BUILDING BLOCKS OF MELODY

How shall I define a melody? One definition is a group of tones sounded one after another to make a meaningful entity. Although this may sound simple, it's not. To compose a memorable melody requires a touch of genius; there is no formula for success.

Basically, a melody is constructed of smaller units, such as motifs and phrases. These components can follow the notes of the scale in any conceivable order, beginning with as small a motif as two tones. (The cuckoo call is such a unit. In fact, its imitation has been woven into the fabric of some fine works by various music masters for centuries. An example appears on page 41.) A composer can employ the tones of a melody in scale fashion;

(TCHAIKOVSKY'S SYMPHONY NO. 5, THIRD MOVEMENT)

or omit every other note of the scale in skipping or bugle-call order.

(MOZART'S SYMPHONY NO. 39, THIRD MOVEMENT)

A melody can be constructed so that one phrase omits every other note of the scale, while another phrase follows the scale's tones in succession. This famous section of the final movement of Beethoven's Fifth Symphony serves as a case in point:

Anyone wishing to invent an original melody faces a constant challenge. The traditional diatonic system consists of only eight tones. You can use them in sequence, interchange them, or skip entire intervals. The options seem endless – until you proceed to compose and then reflect upon the work of so many great masters and so many lesser ones who came before you.

Although rhythm can exist without melody, the latter is unthinkable without some rhythmic structure or division. Sometimes rhythmic patterns can change within the thematic development of a piece of music. For example, listen to *The Rite of Spring (Le Sacre du Printemps)* by Igor Stravinsky and you will soon realize how the rhythmic stress changes from one note to another. Although the actual tones employed may be repeated over and over, the challenging rhythmic irregularity adds ever new dimensions. Rhythm in partnership with melody can expand the arrangement of sounds from which a composer can choose without adding tones per se.

Let's look at a simply constructed melody and see how it can mirror an entire little drama. The music in the following example was written by one of the most outstanding inventors of great melodies, Wolfgang Amadeus Mozart. In the first act of his opera *Don Giovanni* the notorious Don Juan attempts to add the charming peasant girl Zerlina to his long list of conquests by seducing her. At first she is reluctant to yield and listens with a mixture of fear and anticipation as the Don sings to her:

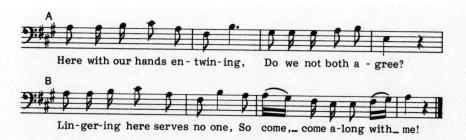

Here with our hands en - twin-ing,   Do we not both a - gree?

Lin-ger-ing here serves no one, So come,_ come a-long with_ me!

This simple melody is built so naturally that its greatness could easily escape us. There are two phrases, A and B, that are similarly constructed. Each has four measures; the first two are identical. The next two measures of A end with a sort of question mark – the note E begging for an answer, as it were, since it represents the fifth step, or "dominant," of the scale of A, in which the melody is written. The second two measures of B bring us the answer – a return to the center of the "tonality" of A, or "tonic." (See the following section on "Harmony.") Thus, all is well. We have barely left home, and we return immediately. If I were to mirror the motion of this melody, it might look like this:

That question mark constitutes the dramatic high point of the musical sentence; and the return to the starting "key," A, provides a release from that dramatic buildup. In *Don Giovanni* Zerlina then repeats the melody, the musical sentence, but intensifies it by expressing her dilemma of willingness versus hesitation:

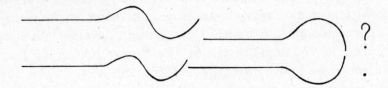

My heart is more than will-ing, I trem-ble to de - part,

Yet fear you may de - ceive me, should I— o - bey my—

heart— should I— o - bey my— heart.

This time the motion of the melody registers more excitement and agitation:

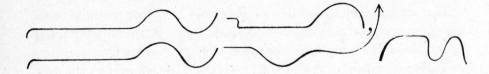

Each of Zerlina's phrases has a quick upbeat, showing a faster pulse rate than that of the suave Don. Her added two measures follow the frantic, almost panic-stricken upswing of the words "my heart," which makes us realize how worried she is.

Any melody of substance must arch toward an emotional zenith. Once a climax is reached, the carefully prepared musical phrases must lead to a natural release. Here is a well-known example to further illustrate my point:

Long before the words of Friedrich Schiller's "An die Freude" ("Ode to Joy") became attached to these notes, Beethoven, in the magnificent Finale of his Symphony No. 9, introduces the melody in the orchestra in all its simplicity and inexorable correctness. Symmetrically there are four phrases consisting of four measures each. Within the first eight measures the genius of Beethoven invented little arches of tone and emotion in every two measures, a remarkable intuitive achievement. The sentence would be complete at the end of phrase B, but Beethoven felt the urge to further heighten the excitement by introducing a thematically and rhythmically new phrase C, upon which the return to B becomes all the more satisfying.

Melody has the musical flow of poetry. As previously shown, it subscribes to the same urges of symmetry and rhythmical division,

and is governed by the same impulses of emotional stress and release. However, prose-based melody, derived from the tradition of
Gregorian chant (see p. 261), unfettered by rhythmical restrictions,
can also be utilized with dramatic effect. Gian Carlo Menotti, in his
popular one-act opera *The Telephone,** combines talk and song
like this:

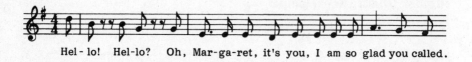

Hel-lo! Hel-lo? Oh, Mar-ga-ret, it's you, I am so glad you called.

In opera and oratorio the technique of the musically recited word
is further employed to great advantage in the "recitative." This is
a style of melody writing in which the voice follows the natural
inflections of the spoken word, taking the place of both an elaborate
melody and a measured beat. Very often it employs a fast, patterlike
repetition of the same note, which, when used in rapid dialogue,
often creates the impression of excited chatter. The recitative can
have the support of some occasional chords played on a keyboard
instrument, such as a harpsichord or piano. This is referred to as
recitativo secco ("dry recitative"). In contrast, the recitation over an
orchestral support of more elaborate scope is known as *recitative
accompagnato* ("accompanied recitative") or *recitative stromentato*
("instrumental recitative"). I suggest that you listen to recitatives,
which often precede arias or vocal ensembles, in the operas of Mozart and Rossini, the oratorios of Haydn, and the works of their
contemporaries.

Fundamentally, music is melody, the overriding importance of
rhythm notwithstanding. But I must also stress the great importance of the proper rendition of a melody. This may seem quite
obvious. I am not referring to such aspects of interpretation as dynamics and expression. Rather, the art of phrasing (which I like to
call "musical punctuation") can make or break the message of a
melody.

*Copyright © 1948 by G. Schirmer, Inc. All rights reserved. Used by permission.

Take the common occurrence of a spoken sentence. The omission or the placement of commas in a sentence can change or even obliterate its meaning.

Johnny says his mother is six years old.
Johnny, says his mother, is six years old.

Similarly, a melody must have a flow of natural inflection that renders its meaning intelligible. This is called *phrasing* in music. The printed page can go only so far in indicating it. The responsibility rests with the interpreter to endow his rendition of the melody with the kind of "punctuation" that conveys its message readily to the listener. A rise toward the climax of a sentence, a slight letup at the end of a phrase, a reaffirmation of the close of a musical thought, a suspension of a line signaling the importance of an ensuing portion – all of these components of "punctuation" can be utilized to achieve the same nuances that commas, semicolons, question marks, exclamation points, or periods do in a book. The following example, taken from the second movement of Tchaikovsky's Symphony No. 5, supplied with both musical and linguistic punctuation marks, serves as an illustration.

To summarize: While rhythm induces a sense of order and often even a physical sense of well-being, if not actual excitement, a melody is what we seek for aesthetic satisfaction. There are few true music lovers who do not respond to it. Many people are unable to appreciate music that is completely devoid of a melody. Provided that it is memorable, the melody is the only element of music that lives on when all else about the piece has been forgotten. Examples of memorable (hence predominant) melodies as part of large-scale compositions can be found in slow movements of sonatas, concertos, and symphonies by such masters as Mozart, Beethoven, Schubert, Chopin, Brahms, Tchaikovsky, and Mahler.

HARMONY – SYNCHRONIZATION OF SOUND

It is quite apparent that melody, endowed with a rhythmic order, is most often what we want to carry away from a musical experience. Yet we may sense that something is missing in our recall of a composition. It is the element in music underpinning the melody, called *harmony*, which adds depth to a melody, much like perspective adds depth to a painting. At the very least, it can be an accompaniment to the melody; ideally it can become a true partner, supporting, guiding, and challenging the melody for listening supremacy.

Harmony is the simultaneous sound of two or more tones. It can be achieved by two or more voices (a vocal ensemble, a choir); by two or more instruments (as in chamber music); or by the capacity of an instrument to produce simultaneous tones (as do stringed instruments, the piano, organ, harpsichord, accordion, or harmonica).

Play any key of the scale on a piano, then play another key, and you create a spanned distance between them known as an *interval*. That distance is measured by the number of steps between keys,

ranging from a "unison" (repetition of the same pitch), a "second" (two adjacent keys), and a "third" (a span of three keys) to an "octave" (a span of eight keys).

Intervals become harmony when the tones involved are sounded simultaneously. Superimpose one interval upon another and you have a "chord." Chords are the most solid building blocks of harmony. A chord made up of three tones is known as a "triad."

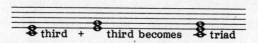

The interval of E to G (a span of three keys, hence a "third") built on top of the interval of C to E (another "third") becomes the basic chord in music, the triad known as a "tonic chord." The empty spaces between the audible tones of C, E, and G help produce both the peculiarly hollow sound and the spaciously sonorous quality of the chordal structure.

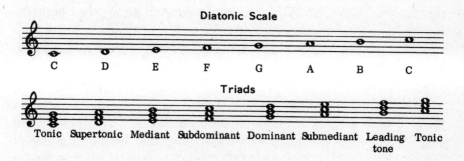

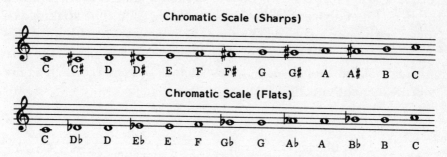

A tonic chord is always built on the first step of the scale, no matter which scale is chosen as the basis of a composition. A chord, or in this instance a triad, can be constructed on any of the twelve keys that constitute both the diatonic and the chromatic systems. A *diatonic scale* consists of the notes that are whole or half steps apart. The latter are also called semitones. A *chromatic* (from the Greek word for "color") *scale* refers to all the keys in the diatonic scale plus the use of "accidentals," namely, sharps and flats.

The tonic chord affords emotional and even physiological contentment. Reasons for this are found in the law of physics that says that no tone we perceive is heard by and of itself alone. Every musical tone sets into motion a set of "overtones," produced by a physical phenomenon known as *sympathetic vibration*. For example, it is a common occurrence to hear a metal or pewter vase vibrate audibly when a certain key on a nearby piano is struck. This indicates that the metal is on the same wavelength as some strings in the piano, and it vibrates when the corresponding key on the piano is sounded. Only the identical wavelength (the same number of vibrations produced by the vibrating body) will make this occur. Strike a G on the piano, for instance, and you can hear it. An A or an F – the neighboring keys – will not cause such magic.

Conversely, certain strings in the piano will vibrate sympathetically when a lower key is struck and the pedal depressed. As an experiment, hold down the piano's right pedal. Depress the key of C, one octave below middle C, without striking it. Now strike the next lower C (two octaves below middle C) quickly and vigorously. You will clearly hear the higher C, whose key you are holding down. Proceed to depress G below middle C, then middle C itself, followed by E, G, B-flat above middle C in succession, each time striking the low C with your left hand. You will hear a clear, if perhaps somewhat weaker, sound of each of these tones. This will not be the case with any of the "in-between" tones, such as D, F, or A, which do not vibrate sympathetically.

C   G   C   E   G   B♭

The tones that respond in sympathetic vibration are shown on page 30. These are known as harmonics, overtones, or upper partials.

The physical cause for tones responding in sympathetic vibration is as follows: A vibrating body (in this case a string) does not only vibrate uniformly the whole of its length but simultaneously in sections of a half, a third, or a fourth of its length. No matter which key is struck, the intervals of the overtones will always be proportionately the same. The overtones, then, are an integral part of every note that we hear, though our ear does not discern them as clearly as the basic tone itself.

All we need to do now is to rearrange the overtones in the order of their equivalent notes on the staff closest to the bass note rather than in the order of their audible appearance. The result looks like this:

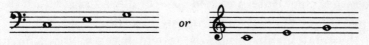

which, when sounded together, becomes a tonic chord.

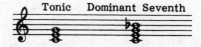

The tonic chord emerges all the more true and welcome now that we realize that nature itself, through the phenomenon of overtones, has created it. The dominant seventh chord (shown above) is formed by topping the tonic chord with the note B-flat, which is part of that row of overtones previously described. Actually, the contrasting consonance and dissonance of the tonic and dominant seventh chords are very closely related.

Play the dominant seventh chord (below, left) on the piano and you will find yourself reaching for a new chord of repose, a tonic chord.

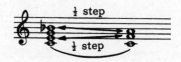

31

This new chord, when rearranged, becomes a subdominant chord, built on the fourth step of the scale.

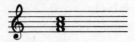

The countermovement of the two half steps (bottom, p. 31) progresses from B-flat down to A, and from E up to F. (A half step is the closest distance between two keys.) The original basis of the chord, C, remains constant. The chord finally emerges as an inversion, with C as the top note of this chord of resolution.

In traditional music a minidrama unfolds regularly by means of the tension created by the interchange of dissonance and consonance. Without it music would remain static and uninteresting. Just as suspense constitutes the real spice of life, so dissonance furnishes the ingredient of excitement in our favorite music.

In the relationship of chords, to which the study of harmony is applied in the broadest sense, the tonic chord plays the most basic role. Proof of this can be found in a fundamental example of chordal relationship, the so-called cadence (derived from Latin, meaning "a falling"). The word's derivation indicates a return to the tonic chord at the end of a composition, a section, or just a phrase. We customarily know the cadence as an ending composed of primary chords. In traditional musical writing such endings can vary in character. Below are examples of the most frequently used cadences:

1. Authentic Cadence 2. Plagal Cadence 3. Mixed Cadence

The *authentic cadence* (authentic here meaning convincing or satisfying) or full cadence is most commonly found in compositions. It consists of the simple progression of a dominant seventh chord to a tonic chord. Note that the chord's differing tones are in close proximity, while the common tones remain in a stationary position. If the interval between the differing tones is a half step, the lower of the two becomes the "leading tone," which assures the smoothest transition from one chord to the next. In the first example illustrated above, the top note B literally rises to "lead" to the tonic chord, with C as the top note.

A *half* or *imperfect cadence* occurs when the progression of chords moves from tonic to dominant, creating an incomplete ending.

The *plagal cadence* derives its name from a Gregorian mode. The progression is from subdominant to tonic. Play this cadence on the piano and it will remind you of the final "amen" of a hymn. For this reason it is also referred to as a "church cadence." Here again, inversions of chords are used to show the closest relationship and smoothest transition between them.

The *mixed cadence* has both the majesty of the plagal cadence and the urgency of the authentic cadence. In each instance the tonic chord emerges as the dominating force, the tonal center to which we move for comfort and reassurance.

I am reminded of the lovely anecdote in which King Frederick the Great once asked his friend Voltaire, the renowned French writer-philosopher-dramatist, "You are such a wise and learned man! Tell me, where is the center of the universe?" Voltaire, without a moment's hesitation, stuck his cane into the ground in front of him, saying, "Right here, Your Majesty!" The king, astonished by this immediate answer, demanded a more explicit explanation. "What concerns me at this very moment," Voltaire offered, "*that*, for me, assumes the importance of the center of the universe." Thus, the tonic chord, no matter where it is found, becomes the center of the tonal universe.

It stands to reason that if harmony is created by the simultaneous sound of two or more tones, then individual tones of horizontal melodies can coincide, if only fleetingly, to form a harmonic link. Consider the individual voices of a duo or a string quartet. Each follows its own horizontal course:

(BEETHOVEN'S STRING QUARTET, OP. 59, NO. 1)

Yet if we stop at any point along this simultaneous flow of melodies, we arrive at a vertical interval. Thus, the common concept of "harmonizing" – as in barbershop quartets – becomes an avenue for vertical harmonies.

This brings us to *counterpoint* (meaning literally "point for point"), an imitation of melodic components, which, when superimposed upon one another, yield consonances and dissonances at any given time. Counterpoint is the art of fitting various independent melodies or voices simultaneously into a self-sufficient harmonic unit.

(SCHUBERT'S "O GENTLE MAY")

The round (shown above) or canon is a typical, if primitive, form of counterpoint. (For a more comprehensive account of counterpoint see pp. 224–28.)

In this section we have seen how harmony is the foundation of melody, the house in which music thrives. It concerns the relationship of tones and chords, the family that gives strength to its members. It is the network of transitions, progressions, and modulations. Perhaps most importantly – and contrary to the generally accepted meaning of the word – harmony is the flow of tension and relaxation in music, looking after the listener's emotional well-being.

TONAL COLOR – A MUSICAL KALEIDOSCOPE

Of all the ingredients that constitute music, tonal color or timbre is of the most varied derivation. A composition without one or more of its varieties is like a meal without spices. It may be wholesome enough, but it lacks the kind of richness that affords us an ultimate measure of satisfaction. In this connection, the sense of hearing can be just as discerning and demanding as the sense of sight, with which the word color is usually associated.

Let's start off by examining some of the sources from which tonal color is derived.

PERIOD OF ORIGINATION

It takes very little experience to distinguish contemporary music from eighteenth-century baroque sound (e.g., Stravinsky's *Rite of Spring* from Handel's *Water Music*), or highly romantic music from that of the Renaissance (e.g., a Chopin nocturne from a Dufay mass). Analogous examples can readily be found in music's "sister arts" – literature, painting, and architecture. The language employed by Shakespeare in his plays leaves little doubt as to their approximate time of origin. We can say the same about the costumes of Rembrandt's "The Syndics," the porticos, facades, and columns of the palace at Versailles, and the Gothic majesty and vaulted glory of the cathedrals of Reims or Canterbury. Each example conveys a distinctive "color" all its own, which, because of its timeless greatness, transcends its timebound origin.

Similarly, music of any given period bears the imprint of the tonal color of that time. The greater the creator, the more enduring and continually valid his work becomes. We readily recognize the color of the baroque period, during which compositions by Johann Sebastian Bach, Georg Friedrich Handel, and Domenico Scarlatti were written. Yet their timeless worth by no means relegates them to that period alone.

In fact, the validity of such period color is proven countless times by the desire of composers of later periods to recreate it. They often enhance their efforts by fusing their personal stylistic traits and those of their own time in their compositions. Some famous examples are Prokofiev's "Classical" Symphony; Ravel's *Le Tombeau de Couperin,* Stravinsky's *Pulcinella,* Poulenc's *Suite Française d'après Gervaise,* and Grieg's *Holberg Suite.*

Great listening experiences can also be found in many selections that evoke the stylistic color of a composer's work of a bygone era. For instance, there are compositions whose names honor a master by tagging the ending "iana" or "iano" onto his name: Tchaikovsky's *Mozartiana,* Casella's *Paganiniana,* Respighi's *Rossiniana,* or, in an extramusical sense, Respighi's *Trittico Botticelliano* and Schumann's *Kreisleriana.* The Brazilian composer Heitor Villa-Lobos created a colorful series of compositions entitled *Bachianas Brasileiras* that evokes the spirit of Bach set against a background of Brazilian folklore.

The Composer's Individual Style

For the most part, everyone has a distinctive speech pattern and an individual manner of talking. So it is with the style of a composer. Much color can be derived from a creative musician's style of writing. This is conditioned by many influences: social background, temperament, behavior, age, experience; musicians who influenced him; and his own personal musical preferences. It is easy to see that a Beethoven style yields tonal color completely different from a Stravinsky style.

The Artist's Performance

The style of an artist's performance is formed by his talent, training, experience, and knowledge of all the facets of the music to be performed. When we speak of the immensely colorful style of a Horowitz, a Stern, a Rostropovich, or a Fischer-Dieskau, we mean the sum total of the myriad factors that make up the artist's manner of performing.

NATIONALISM IN MUSIC

One of the most enjoyable sources of tonal color in music is found among the rich treasures of various nations, the influence of their folklore upon composers, and their tonal and rhythmic idiosyncracies (e.g., the way in which a phrase is shaped, an accent placed, a major and minor mode interchanged, a dance rhythm employed). These coloristic effects reveal the country's identity. A detailed discussion of this brilliant harvest of hues and colors and their application in musical composition will be found on pages 323–30.

THE SOUND OF INSTRUMENTS AND VOICES

What a never-ending pleasure and challenge can be realized from the choice of instrumental and vocal colors! Just as a composer's or a performer's personal style can be likened to individuality of speech, the timbre of an instrument or voice can be compared with that same highly personal element. Chapter Three reveals the infinite variety of tonal colors inherent in the many shapes and forms of objects that produce musical sound.

Like choosing colors on a painter's palette, the selection of instruments for the purpose of coloristic tonal production represents a special art for which many skills are required. For instance, no other timbre can take the place of an oboe to produce that plaintive sound in the second movement of the Symphony No. 4 by Tchaikovsky. Can you think of any timbre other than the low register of the clarinet to represent the bleak opening of the Symphony No. 1 by Sibelius, or the nobility of the horn solo that opens the overture to *Oberon* by Carl Maria von Weber?

Choosing combinations of tonal colors to achieve certain effects of an extramusical nature is even more challenging to the listener. In the "Tuba mirum" section of his Requiem, Berlioz combines the massive sound of the entire brass section with the unison chorus to give us his vision of the Day of Judgment. It is difficult to imagine such an effect of utter awe with any other combination of sound. In a less pictorial sense, although no less effective, Beethoven combines three wind instruments (clarinet, bassoon, horn) and four string instruments (violin, viola, cello, bass) to bring us a color spectrum in his Septet, Op. 20, that no other combination could match. Similarly, Stravinsky in *L'Histoire du Soldat* gives us the complete range of pitch of each family of instruments by choosing the highest and lowest capabilities of each group: violin and double bass for strings; clarinet and bassoon for wind instruments; trumpet and trombone for brass; plus percussion. Although economic necessity may have been a causative factor – the work was written on a minimum budget during World War I – the result is a miracle of coloristic imagination.

Almost any listening experience – at a concert, via radio or records – provides plentiful examples of color combinations. The ones cited above are meant to guide you in the right direction. Multiple joys await the seeker.

TONAL RESOURCES OF AN INSTRUMENT OR VOICE

Consider the organ – in effect, a one-instrument orchestra – which is capable of producing almost any sound imaginable, from a bare whisper of a muted stop to the physically overwhelming composite sound of the full organ. Or think of the remarkable variety of technical resources that a talented violinist uses to evoke cascades of spiccato, or light staccato, sound in a Paganini caprice, or a dazzling array of double and triple stops in Bach's Chaconne, scored for solo violin; from the unearthly sound of harmonics in the third movement of Paganini's Concerto No. 1 to the prayerful legato of the second movement of the Beethoven Violin Concerto. Vocally, consider the coloratura acrobatics of the "Bell Song" from Delibes' *Lakmé,* and then listen to the same soprano voice sustaining a lyrical quality in the aria "O moon, high up in the deep, deep sky" from Dvořák's opera *Rusalka.* The same pianist and piano that can soothe the listener with the deceiving simplicity of Schumann's "Träumerei" are also capable of thrilling us with the thundering chords of Tchaikovsky's Piano Concerto No. 1. These are just a few examples that illustrate individual tonal resources and the resultant colors produced.

ACOUSTICS

Comments never cease as to how much better orchestral color comes across in New York's Carnegie Hall or in Amsterdam's Concertgebouw than in a brand new auditorium constructed with the latest acoustical devices. How different Bach's Toccata and Fugue in D Minor sound in the magnificence of London's Westminster Abbey than in the vastness of the Washington, D.C., National Shrine of the Immaculate Conception, even though the instruments used are similar and the organist might even be the same person.

Reverberation of sound is an element that, along with other acoustical properties, can play an important role in producing tone color via radio, recordings, or television. The color of a Toscanini performance with the NBC Symphony Orchestra differs vastly according to the place of performance. NBC's Studio 8H in New York, where many of the Toscanini broadcasts and recordings originated, was completely devoid of any reverberation. The resultant dry, colorless sound, both live and recorded, was a gross injustice to a great artist. Listen to a Toscanini performance recorded in Carnegie Hall and you will hear the difference, the state of recording techniques of the time vis-à-vis those used today notwithstanding.

Tonal color is truly the spice of musical life. Our awareness of its infinite ways of origination and emanation heightens our enjoyment of music as few other factors can.

FORM – THE UNIFYING FORCE IN MUSIC

Each of music's main ingredients discussed thus far has its own degree of importance and significance, each lending its own individual peculiarities to a musical creation. What is needed now is an overriding order within which each of the elements of composition can function best, a benevolent discipline embracing them all for the good of the whole. Such a unifying force is found in the various principles of musical form.

Just as symmetry of features can be essential to a beautiful face, shapeliness and proper proportion to an attractive body, various aspects of form are indispensable for the aesthetic, emotional, and intellectual well-being of a traditional work of art such as music. (I use the word traditional here because it is in this context that regularity as a general concept is most readily applicable.) Think also of the untold shapes of symmetry found in the forms of nature: the noble beauty of a tree whose branches aspire to the perfection of a well-rounded crown; the slender grace of a well-proportioned pine; or the vertical thrust of a desert palm, with its evenly spaced branches and leaves reaching upward. Think of the unending succession of day and night, of season after season, of year upon year. There is form, shape, and logic in these phenomena of nature, just as there is in the anatomy of its creatures.

Interestingly enough, the regularity inherent in nature is dependent upon contrast and change, with which it is interlaced. The aesthetics of form depends upon such recurring change. This interchange between the familiar and the new constitutes the essence of musical form.

A variety of patterns contributes to larger concepts of musical form. A natural evolution has advanced them from embryonic beginnings to the highly elaborate stage in which we experience them today. Basic molds have prevailed, adjusting to the flexibility of the individual composer's approach and needs.

Again, the parts of the human anatomy can serve as an analogy. Nature has arranged the components of every face – eyes, ears, nose, mouth – in exactly the same order, yet no two faces are exactly alike.

So it is with the shapes of music. No two sonatas, symphonies, or string quartets are alike, even though they adhere to the same principles of form. Even more exciting is the variety of such works from the pen of one master, whether it is the 4 symphonies of Brahms or Schumann, the 9 symphonies and 32 piano sonatas of Beethoven, the 41 symphonies of Mozart, or the 104 symphonies of Haydn. The individuality with which each composition is endowed by its creator is as remarkable as nature's handiwork in fashioning an infinite variety of heads, faces, and torsos within the same species.

The smallest unit of form is a *motif,* which can be as brief as the two-note call of the cuckoo. In order to establish a rhythmical regularity, the motif generally consists of two measures. Beethoven used it in this way at the beginning of the last movement of his Piano Concerto No. 2:

An extension of the motif – either by way of repetition or thematic development – is known as a *phrase.* This may be self-contained, ending with a full cadence (see p. 32); or open-ended, through the use of a half cadence (analogous to a comma in punctuation). Two phrases form a musical *sentence,* and the doubling of a sentence can become a *section.*

This famous melody from Haydn's "Surprise" Symphony begins in the key of C and ends in the key of G. Haydn repeats the sentence (see below); the second time the G ending is reiterated with a sudden resounding G chord marked fortissimo (as if to wake up any would-be sleepers in the audience; hence the nickname "Surprise," for which single incident the entire symphony has become known).

The above sentence, even in its powerful repetition, is left open for a continuation that generally culminates in a return to the "home" key, in this instance C.

The previous two sentences are structurally interdependent. The first moves to a related key (the dominant); the second returns home (the tonic), forming a logical completion. This scheme of A-B is known as *binary form*, meaning of two parts or twofold. A continuous form, it does not allow for complete contrast, and often lacks the kind of emotional excitement found in more complex forms. Examples of binary construction can be found in dance movements of seventeenth- and eighteenth-century suites, such as gavottes, allemandes, and courantes by Bach and Handel.

One of the most satisfying forms in music is the A-B-A scheme known as *ternary form*, meaning of three parts or threefold. This form consists of an initial melody (often repeated once so as to be impressed upon our consciousness), a completely contrasting melody, followed by a return to the opening melody. Here is a basic example:

(STEPHEN FOSTER, "OLD FOLKS AT HOME" OR "SWANEE RIVER")

As can easily be seen, the first line presents both a statement and a reiteration (A and A¹), while the second line offers a new melody (B). The last line leads us back to the second phrase of the first line (A¹). We have been provided simply and well with a musical statement, contrast, and restatement.

It is fascinating to witness the elevation of this basic A-B-A principle of form to more and more sophisticated types of musical structure. Consider the minuet of Mozart's *Eine kleine Nachtmusik*. The first part ("A") consists of a statement and reiteration, contrast, and briefer restatement:

Here is the second portion ("B") of this minuet, known as a trio:

We now feel the instinctive compulsion to return to the body of the minuet ("A"), and we do so verbatim, except for the repetition of each component. (It is customary to omit the repeats upon returning to the main part.)

An interesting occurrence has taken place here. Not only are the minuet and trio each conceived in A-B-A fashion, but the first part as a whole (i.e., the minuet) becomes a large A. This is contrasted by the entire trio, which becomes a large B. And the return to the first part becomes a large A^1. Thus, the dimensions of the modest principle have grown. You can now marvel at a further expansion of it by listening to Chopin's Nocturne in G Minor, Op. 37, No. 1. First listen to the A-B-A pattern in the main section of this haunting work, then again in the prayerlike middle part. With a return to the main section, it is easy to realize that you have traversed a large A-B-A^1 form composed of three small A-B-A^1 patterns.

In the case of the *rondo form*, it can be represented by the notation A-B-A-C-A or extended to A-B-A-C-A-D-A. The basic premise of the rondo is that the main portion, A, appears at least three times, interlaced with contrasting parts. A fine example is the Rondo, Op. 51, No. 1 by Beethoven. The rondo form is applied quite often to the last movement of a large-scale work, such as a sonata, concerto, symphony, or chamber music work. (See also pp. 223–24.)

The natural steps of a marvelous evolution have now brought us to the threshold of the fulfillment of the three-part form, namely, the *sonata form*. This grand design is the unifying force that rules over the first movement of the sonata, symphony, concerto, trio, quartet, and most other forms of chamber music. Of course, there are some notable exceptions. Perhaps the most famous is the first movement of Beethoven's "Moonlight" Sonata, one of two sonatas he wisely called "quasi una fantasia," as if to explain his departure from custom. All this is easier to state than to illustrate, for examples are legion and the individual modifications literally without limit. In fact, the greater the genius who writes in the sonata form, the more the form is modified to suit the unfathomable ways and intuitions of the composer. Therefore, any description of the "ground rules" or design of sonata form can only be general in nature.

The word *sonata* is derived from the Italian verb *sonare* or *suonare* ("to sound"). This simple linguistic derivation poses a responsibility for the composer from the start. The goal of writing such a work should be beauty of sound, guided by a traditional structure, rather than the form imposing the execution of a cerebral exercise.

Enlarging upon the A-B-A¹ principle, the sonata form consists of three large sections: exposition, development, and recapitulation. The three-part concept, or ternary form, we have examined so far has imposed no conditions other than contrasting thematic material, at times enhanced by contrasting rhythmic and harmonic treatment. In the case of the sonata form we encounter far more specific and explicit prerequisites in the three subdivisions. These concern primarily the themes or melodies and their tonality or key.

The first part, or *exposition,* consists of two themes that must be completely different from one another. The themes can differ in various ways: modes (generally minor and major); dramatic complexion (agitated to lyrical); rhythmic structure (from dotted rhythms to smoothly spaced patterns); manner of performance (from staccato or otherwise detached ways of tone production to caressing legato); dynamics (from determined forte to whispering piano); and pace of performance (from strict adherence to the tempo to the freedom of rubato).

The composer's choices in combining these contrasting ingredients reveals his style, his musical personality, and even the time of origin of a work (both within his own career and, in a broader sense, with regard to his place in history). While that choice is as wide as his ingenuity, the one irrevocable attribute peculiar to the form is the tension of contrast that exists.

The second theme of the exposition must appear in a different key from that of the first theme. Traditionally, the two tonalities are related to one another harmonically. The second theme is usually in the dominant or subdominant key, with the first theme established in the tonic. If the first theme is presented in a minor mode, its opposite generally appears in the relative major key.

In most instances composers link the two themes with an intermediary section or transition known as a *bridge.* This affords the opportunity to move smoothly from one tonality to another. At times the bridge represents new thematic material. Most composers are not satisfied by ending the exposition with the completion of the second theme. An extension of it, a passing reference to an earlier melody, or even a brand new theme may be added. The musician refers to it as the *coda* (Italian for "tail"). Just as sometimes the tail will wag the dog, so the coda can become as elaborate as the whole portion to which it is attached. However, the coda must eventually return to the key of the second theme.

The shifting of tonality during the exposition creates a feeling of tension that prepares us to enter the middle section of the three-part form, the *development*. This section presents the greatest challenge to the composer. Here no limitations exist. The composer can give free reign to his fantasy. He may restate the first or second theme, or that of the bridge or the coda, in its entirety or in bits and pieces. He may move from key to key or intermingle them at will. He may even include a melody never heard before.

Consequently, the development can easily become the most exciting part of the entire sonata; and the greater the composer, the more drama he can develop. Indeed, purists feel that unless the development is truly different and does not restate previously heard material, the form cannot be considered A-B-A but rather a modified and compounded A-B.

After these new thematic and harmonic departures, the composer ultimately prepares for a return to the original opening theme to satisfy the listener and himself emotionally and intellectually. In doing so he intensifies even further the impact of the development.

This is accomplished most effectively by ending the journey of the development in the dominant or dominant seventh position. The composer may then choose to quote his original melody verbatim or modify it slightly. At times he may even lengthen it in order to justify what will follow. The bridge, second theme, and coda must now relinquish the dialectic struggle of contrasting tonality in order to return to the gravity of the tonic.

Therein lies the important difference between the exposition and *recapitulation* sections of sonata form. They are made of the same thematic fabric – the two contrasting themes – yet their tonalities, and hence their emotional impact, differ sharply. In the recapitulation the two themes coexist peacefully in the same key, unlike the opposition of themes in the exposition.

When we realize that the sonata form underlies only the first

47

movement of a work associated with the sonata concept, we gain a bit of insight into its scope. Other movements may also follow this type of form. Quite often the forms known as theme and variations, rondo, and fugue appear among the movements of large-scale works. These will be discussed in Chapter Eight.

Our examination of music's main ingredients – rhythm, melody, harmony, color, and form – leaves us with an acute realization that their application is as infinite as the stars. New vistas open up for the listener with every step of the pleasurable journey of musical discovery and rediscovery.

CHAPTER THREE

THE INSTRUMENTS AND THEIR PRINCIPAL USE

As WE HAVE seen in the previous chapter, sound is the result of vibrations in the atmosphere that excite our auditory nerves by impinging on the eardrums. What causes these vibrations in the first place, and how they are disseminated, is a story of never-ending fascination, for it parallels the evolution of human expression. Man has always been known to utter sounds that spontaneously accompany his feelings and emotions. To this day we clap our hands, snap our fingers, stamp our feet, whistle, and use an endless variety of vocal sound formations as a response to a myriad of causative factors. A personal recollection may serve as a vivid illustration.

Paul Paray, the great twentieth-century French conductor, was leading the Detroit Symphony Orchestra during a recording session. The orchestra was playing the Prelude to the third act of Wagner's *Lohengrin,* an exhilarating piece of music that precedes the famous bridal chamber scene. It happened to be one of Maestro Paray's favorites. His anticipation of and reaction to the opening of the Prelude was so powerful that he jumped vertically off the podium to give the downbeat, which coincided with a loud thump as he landed again. The chief engineer assigned to the session by the record company interrupted the proceedings, saying, "I am sorry, sir, but your exuberance will be audible on this record for generations to come. Please try to curb or control it." Whereupon Maestro Paray, with his inimitable French accent, answered, "Oh, I am sorry. I did not notice it. Tomorrow I will do much better!" Tomorrow came and Mr. Paray appeared in his bedroom slippers. Not being sure whether he could suppress his spontaneity, he at least wanted to assure a more muted landing.

Natural, uncontrollable reactions such as this show that man is given to spontaneously producing sounds. Through the ages he created various devices and mechanical contrivances to imitate or reinforce these sounds. Early carvings and drawings show these devices progressing from the primitive and purely functional to more sophisticated stages, gradually evolving to resemble the wind and percussion instruments we know today.

The capacity to set in motion the vibrations of a stretched, suspended string is a natural phenomenon of ancient origin that ultimately gave birth to the concept of stringed instruments of many shapes and forms. This culminated in the matchless creations of Cremona, where an early school of violin makers developed in the sixteenth and seventeenth centuries. Far more sophisticated than other instruments in their way of enhancing human sound, stringed instruments became a basic addition to the ever-increasing number of contrivances with which to produce musical sound.

According to the materials of construction and the manner of tone production, instruments today are identified as members of the following families: string, wind (subdivided into woodwinds and brass), and percussion. Although the human voice and keyboard instruments could be included among the wind and percussion instruments, each deserves a classification of its own. Let us take a closer look at each of these instrument groupings, the history and evolution of their constituent members, their tonal capabilities, and their principal uses during various stages of music history.

Grouping the instrumental families in this way is by no means the definitive, scientific, or artistic "last word." Some instruments seem to defy classification. For instance, since the piano has strings that produce its sound, does this make it a stringed instrument? Or, since hammers operated by the keys strike the strings, is the piano in the percussion family? Another example is the saxophone. This instrument has elements of the clarinet in its use of a free single reed, yet its tube is made of brass, not wood. Is it then a brass instrument or a woodwind?

The important factor in classifying an instrument is whether the vibrations that generate sound are activated by the beating of elastic surfaces (as in percussion instruments), by the bowing, plucking, or striking of stretched strings (as in stringed, plucked, or certain keyboard instruments), or by the moving of air columns contained in woodwind and brass instruments and the organ. It is the shape of the tubes, the length of the strings, the form and components of the mouthpiece, and the overall size and thickness of the instrument that gives each member of an instrument family its own individual, characteristic sound, provided that the instrumentalist can make it speak with categorical eloquence.

THE HUMAN VOICE

Let us focus our attention first on the human voice, our most natural, completely self-contained instrument. Aside from speech, singing is one of the most natural ways in which to express oneself. Even if you can't "carry a tune," singing surely fills an emotional need and should be encouraged.

As is the case with other instruments, ability and perseverance are necessary for the finest possible production of musical sound. In fact, with the voice there are added difficulties. It is not only a tone-generating mechanism, but it also has the power to couple tones with words and their components, vowels and consonants. Because of these multidimensional uses, it is all the more necessary to care for the voice properly.

Leo Slezak, the *Heldentenor* ("heroic tenor") and famous wit of the early 1920s, was seen strolling in the streets of Vienna on a balmy day in May, his neck wrapped in a heavy scarf with the collar of his overcoat raised to his ears. One of his many fans stopped him and asked, "Herr Kammersänger, pardon the intrusion, but aren't you feeling well? It is such a beautiful warm day and you are dressed for winter weather." With great dignity Slezak responded, "I am quite well, thank you; but, you see, I have a concert in October!" While this was perhaps overdoing things a bit, it does show the importance of great foresight, at least on the part of most professional singers.

How does the voice function? The two vibrating strips of flexible or elastic connective tissue, known as cartilage or vocal cords, emit the actual vocal sound, like a vibrating metal strip does in an organ's reed pipe. The vocal cords, enclosed in the larynx, vibrate by means of the wind supplied by our lungs via the windpipe or trachea, which in turn branches out into the bronchial tubes connecting each of the two lungs. Wind is supplied by the bellows of the chest, to which the windpipe is connected, and sound is projected by way of the cavities of the mouth, nose, and throat. If this sounds complicated, it is. However, since nature has supplied it all for us, we use this apparatus with comparative ease and are relatively unaware of its great complexity.

Whereas people need to have their wind supply renewed at regular intervals, an organ pipe's wind supply can continue indefinitely, as long as the bellows remain operative. A voice running out of breath is as critical to a musical performance as is the breaking of a violin string in the middle of a concerto. The flow of the performance has been interrupted disturbingly. Hence, breath control becomes equal in importance to vocal tone production itself.

Vocal tone production is a challenge to music teachers and students alike. It must be based upon knowledge of the physiological realities, personal needs, and vocal characteristics of an aspiring singer – and, above all, a lot of common sense.

Since the voice is both a tone- and word-producing apparatus, proper diction, irrespective of the language used, is very important. Diction involves enunciation and intelligibility of words. It is difficult to achieve while speaking, let alone singing, yet its absence is unacceptable, artistically speaking. Unfortunately, some of our finest singers – whose vocal instrument may be unmatched, wisely trained, and developed – cannot project to an audience the message of their song because of poor diction, or no diction at all. In such cases the question of substituting a translation versus singing in the original language of the text, which is so frequently contested by music lovers and musicians – myself included – becomes an academic one, since frequently not a word can be understood in any language.

The voice is capable of all the nuances, innuendos, and expressive and interpretive details of any other instrument. Achieving this requires the insight, devotion, knowledge, experience, patience, and that constant "must" of any would-be performer – ability, if not talent – all of which apply to anyone wishing to become a musician. In the case of a singer, literally having to live with the instrument can be a mighty advantage.

The following pages classify categories of voices, along with illustrative selections and roles.

SOPRANOS

Dramatic, a fairly heavy-textured voice with declamatory, almost rhetorical ability, yet flexible enough to shift into many moods with complete identification.

Princess Turandot in Puccini's *Turandot:* "In questa reggia"
Elisabeth in Wagner's *Tannhäuser:* "Dich, teure Halle"

Lyric, a voice of lighter quality, capable of a flowing cantabile ("singing") style, and particularly suitable for the interpretation of lieder.

Countess in Mozart's *Marriage of Figaro:* "Dove sono"
Mimi in Puccini's *La Bohème:* "Mi chiamano Mimì"

Coloratura (literally "colored"), a voice of particular flexibility and agility, capable of negotiating demanding feats of vocal acrobatics, such as rapid trills, extended intervals, and skips.

Queen of the Night in Mozart's *Magic Flute:* "Der Hölle Rache"
Zerbinetta in Strauss's *Ariadne auf Naxos:* "Grossmächtige Prinzessin"
Lakmé in Delibes' *Lakmé:* "Bell Song"

CONTRALTOS AND MEZZO-SOPRANOS

The same dramatic and lyric attributes as for sopranos apply. A sharp distinction must be made between a true contralto of deep, often dark, hues and a mezzo-soprano (literally, "half soprano") with a wide range approximating both the soprano and contralto registers. Both can be artistically satisfying, but each has its own convincing role in the repertoire.

Dramatic Mezzo-Soprano:
Carmen in Bizet's *Carmen:* "Habanera"
Dalila in Saint-Saëns' *Samson et Dalila:* "Mon coeur s'ouvre à ta voix"

Lyric Mezzo-Soprano:
Artaxerxes in Arne's *Artaxerxes:* "Oh, too lovely!"

Dramatic Contralto:
Arsace in Rossini's *Semiramide:* "Ah, quel giorno"
Azucena in Verdi's *Il Trovatore:* "Stride la vampa"

Lyric Contralto:
Orfeo in Gluck's *Orfeo ed Euridice:* "Che farò senza Euridice?"
Angel in Mendelssohn's oratorio *Elijah:* "O rest in the Lord"

TENORS
Dramatic (often *tenore robusto* in Italian or *Heldentenor* in German), a voice suited for roles of great vocal power and passion.
Lohengrin in Wagner's *Lohengrin:* "In fernem Land"
Radames in Verdi's *Aida:* "Celeste Aida"

Lyric, a voice that corresponds to the lyric requirements of the soprano voice of that persuasion.
Nadir in Bizet's *Pearl Fishers:* "Serenade"
Assad in Goldmark's *Queen of Sheba:* "Magische Töne"

BARITONES
For dramatic characters the prerequisites are power and passion.

Dramatic Baritone:
Iago in Verdi's *Otello:* "Credo in un Dio crudel"
Scarpia in Puccini's *Tosca:* "Ella verrà"

Lyric Baritone: Many roles call for more philosophical insight and depth of feeling; hence the voice is often called upon to project compassion and tenderness.
Figaro in Rossini's *Barber of Seville:* "Largo al factotum"
Hans Sachs in Wagner's *Die Meistersinger:* "Wie duftet doch der Flieder" (may be sung by a bass voice)
Germont in Verdi's *La Traviata:* "Di Provenza il mar"

BASS
The bass voice is ideal for deep register and depth of sonority.
Colline in Puccini's *La Bohème:* "Vecchia zimarra, senti"

Dr. Bartolo in Rossini's *Barber of Seville:* "A un dottor della mia sorte"

Mephistopheles in Gounod's *Faust:* "Le veau d'or est toujours debout"

Sarastro in Mozart's *Magic Flute:* "O Isis und Osiris"

These categories are meant to serve only as a general guide. Further subdivisions are commonly found in large mixed choirs, as well as in all-female or all-male ensembles. As for personal idiosyncracies, it is difficult to find two identical voices. It is not uncommon for a female singer to change from soprano to mezzo-soprano, or a male singer from tenor to baritone after some experience with their tonal register, or as a result of getting older. It is not necessarily due to the fact that certain tones are too high or too low for their comfort, but that the general texture of the voice may not be quite comfortable with the placement of those tones anymore. This important aspect of singing is known as *tessitura,* the Italian word for "texture." This applies to the average prevailing pitch rather than to a few isolated notes found to be of extreme border range.

"Head tones" and their opposite, "chest tones," are special effects that characterize vocal sound. These terms denote the higher and lower ranges of the voice as they are produced with characteristic shades of tonal color. Tone production is hardly affected by a concentration on the head or chest as the "location" for the sound. However, a sensation that can be associated with either part of the body is discernable.

When a male voice produces tones by activating only the edges of the vocal cords, it results in a "falsetto." These high-pitched sounds are emitted with soft head tones.

Here I would like to interject a reference to the "castrato." This was an adult male singer with a soprano or contralto voice resulting from his castration before the age of puberty. The singer thus retained the larynx of a youth as he matured, but he also possessed the insight and power of an adult. Castrati were famous for the exceptional beauty of their voice in sixteenth-century church music and particularly in Italian opera of the seventeenth and eighteenth centuries. Special parts were written for them. Mozart created the role of Idamante in his opera *Idomeneo* for a castrato.

Almost all music conceived before 1500, and most of the music of the sixteenth century, is music for voices – including Gregorian chant of the eighth to the thirteenth centuries, songs of the troubadours, motets, early masses, and madrigals of the ensuing centuries. The baroque period saw the rise of instrumental music to a position of equal prominence. Around the middle of the eighteenth century, during Bach's lifetime, there was a decline in the dominance of vocal music. However, the increasing importance and variety of instrumental music began to suggest new ways to merge the sounds of man-made instruments with those of the human voice, thus creating a continuing challenge for composers.

First, let us look at the instrumental family most similar in tone production to the human voice, namely, wind instruments, which include woodwinds and brass. To show their comparative structure, an illustration of each instrument is provided, along with its approximate tonal range.

THE WOODWIND FAMILY

As I have already indicated, woodwinds is a general term that includes some instruments not made of wood at all but whose prototypes were so constructed. Some of them, like recorders, are enjoying renewed popularity. All woodwinds have one important fact in common: Their tone is generated by setting in motion a column of air within them. There are three ways of accomplishing this:

• You can blow air directly into the instrument through an opening at its end (recorder) or through a hole in its side (flute).

• The air column can be activated by the breath entering the instrument and causing a single reed to beat directly against the side of the opening (clarinet and saxophone).

• The air column can be moved by means of double reeds vibrating against each other as the breath enters (oboe, English horn, and bassoon).

To digress for a moment, I might mention the lifelong preoccupation that wind players have with reeds. Most of them readily admit to spending a great deal of time cutting and shaping their own reeds. Often a reed will suit the quality of a certain composition better than another, and so a constant supply of reeds becomes a necessity.

I remember preparing for a voyage to France shortly after World War II, when several of my musician friends approached me with the fervent plea to purchase some uncut cane for them in the South of France, where the best bamboo cane is grown. I was told that it could not be just any cane, though I professed to have a bit of an eye for it. It turned out to be a kind of Alfred Hitchcock adventure, complete with having to climb some back stairs in a tiny village, pronounce the password, and then receive a carefully packed bundle containing the precious cane, which I guarded with my life for the rest of the journey and handed over to my eager friends upon my return. Even today good cane for reed cutting is not easy to come by.

As with the voice, it is human breath that provides the power needed to produce tone in most of the wind instruments. The old expression "don't waste your breath" becomes more than an economy measure, it becomes a necessity. When singing, you use your lung power instinctively to emit soft or loud tones. Just as instinctively, the willpower of your mind can dictate the pitch or the exact position of a tone on the scale. The same principle applies to the playing of wind instruments. However, there is a difference: You now have to channel your lung power or breath directly into the instrument, where the air column within takes the place of the vocal cords in your larynx. You must control consciously what often comes more naturally with the voice. The pitch now depends on the length of the air column, and on the diameter of the opening through which your breath is emitted.

To alter the pitch there are holes placed in the bore of the instrument, according to exact requirements. You can cover or "stop" these holes individually or in combination, partly with your fingers (especially in the case of less sophisticated instruments such as the tin whistle), or, more frequently nowadays, with an elaborate apparatus consisting of a series of padded keys that fit over the holes. In addition, modern wind instruments are provided with an arrangement of metal trackers, rollers, and finger pieces designed to stop or unstop the holes, activating parts or the entire length of the air column.

To help you understand the principle, tie a little weight to the bottom of a long string; hold the string at the top and swing it back and forth. Then grasp the string at its midpoint. Given the same swinging motion, this homemade pendulum should now swing twice as fast as it did at the string's full length. The speed of the swinging body is in direct proportion to the length of the string. The same is true in the case of the sound-producing air column. The shorter its length, the faster its vibrations; the longer its length, the slower its vibrations. Conversely, the faster the vibrations, the higher the pitch; the slower the vibrations, the lower the pitch. Covering and uncovering the holes of the instrument serve the same function as does holding a string at various points of its length. The section on the string family in this chapter will reveal the secrets of tonal "string power."

Although this may all sound simple, it takes infinite patience and diligent practice to call forth beautiful sound, no matter what the instrument.

Before discussing each woodwind instrument individually, I'd like to mention the very rewarding literature of music written for woodwinds – alone, in chamber ensembles, and in combination with strings and piano. For those interested in this veritable treasure, suggestions for building a basic record library appear in Chapter Eight.

RECORDER

The ancestors of the flute are the recorders, which date back to medieval times and are derived from even earlier folk instruments. Today we can observe the rebirth of these ancient instruments – ranging in size from the penny whistle to that of a modern bassoon – and their reinstatement to a status of great vitality as the object of contemporary composers' interests and ingenuity. Their names have differed according to time and country, from the fipple flute of sixteenth-century England, blown with a beak-shaped mouthpiece, to the Italian *flauto traverso* ("traverse flute"), played through a hole in the side much like today's elaborate orchestral flute.

RECORDER

In Germany the recorder has been called *Blockflöte* when played vertically or straight out from the player's mouth, or *Querflöte* when held horizontally and side blown. The French equivalents are *flûte à bec,* named after the beak-shaped mouthpiece, and *flûte traversière.* The tone is somewhat woody but greatly diverse in character, according to the size of the instrument. The recorder's tonal range is approximately two octaves, starting at F for soprano and tenor sizes and an octave above middle C for alto and bass recorders.

The literature for the recorder is quite extensive, traversing centuries of flute music, and is now being enriched by contemporary composers.

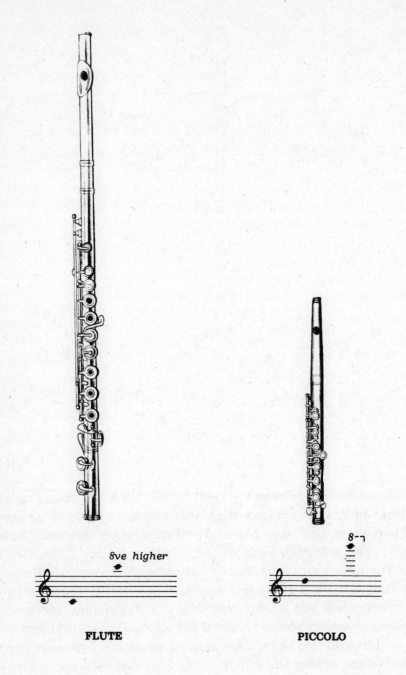

FLUTE

PICCOLO

FLUTE

The modern flute can be considered the soprano of the woodwind family. Its air column vibrates sideways since it is held horizontally and to the right of the player's mouth. The range of the flute is wide, three full octaves upward from middle C. Its tonal characteristics range from a rather thick and velvety low register, through a beautifully melodious middle range, to a very bright, sometimes piercing upper limit.

There is a large repertoire of flute music available – larger than for any other wind instrument – from very easy pieces to elaborate compositions, from early baroque music to contemporary works.

Flutes today are usually made of silver, or silver alloy, and sometimes even precious metals such as gold and platinum. Incidentally, in answer to a frequent question, both "flutist" and "flautist" are correct when referring to the player of this instrument.

For an amazing variety of flute tone, listen to Claude Debussy's *Afternoon of a Faun,* in which the flute represents the main protagonist.

PICCOLO

This small flute's name is derived from the Italian word for little, the full name being *flauto piccolo.* Piccolos can be used for high-tone solo effects or as high-pitched support for wind instruments' tones. Its effect can be provocative, humorous, shrill, and piercing. Its full, workable range is about two and one half octaves. Notes for the piccolo are written an octave lower than their actual sound.

For your listening enjoyment I recommend a lovely piccolo concerto by Antonio Vivaldi in order to get an idea of the tonal texture and range of this highest pitched of all instruments. You might also listen to the famous piccolo choir in Sousa's "Stars and Stripes Forever," which (since Toscanini started the tradition) is usually played at concerts with the piccolo players standing.

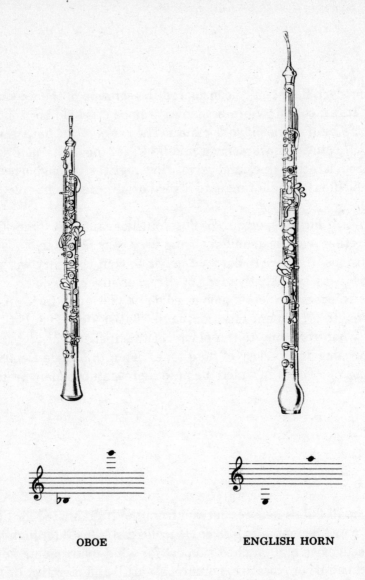

OBOE   ENGLISH HORN

OBOE

The oboe produces the most haunting sound of all the wind instruments. It combines plaintiveness with nostalgia, nobility with lyricism. To play this instrument an oboist forces his breath through the almost invisible space between two thin slivers of cane that are bound together and fit into a narrow piece of metal tubing known as the staple. The breath then passes into a small conical pipe – usually made of ebonite, rosewood, or cocuswood – with a bell-shaped opening at the end. The instrumentalist's red face and bulging cheeks are an indication of the physical demands made upon the player in exercising the utmost breath control.

The oboe's ancestry dates back to such medieval instruments as the German *Schalmei* and the English pommer and bombard. The range of the modern oboe is approximately three octaves. Its best register – where its most singable, direct tone quality is produced – lies in the middle of this span. Just before a concert begins the orchestra's concertmaster has the oboist sound an A by which all the other instruments are tuned. The reason for this is the fidelity of pitch found to be most constant in the oboe.

For an example of the finest oboe tone, listen to the second movement of the Symphony No. 4 by Tchaikovsky. There are many opportunities to hear the peculiarly nasal and reedy sound of the oboe, since it performs in a solo capacity in orchestral concerts more frequently than any other instrument.

ENGLISH HORN (COR ANGLAIS)

While the oboe may be considered the mezzo-soprano of the woodwind family, its relative, the English horn, can be considered the contralto. It originated in France and, like the oboe, consists of a wooden pipe. However, that pipe is longer than an oboe's (hence, its capacity for lower tones); and it is also wider. Unlike the oboe, the English horn's upper end, or staple, which holds the double reed, curves backward and away from the body, while the opposite end merges into a somewhat larger, more globular bell than an oboe's.

The instrument's range extends upward approximately two and one quarter octaves. The English horn has a poignant, beautifully deep-throated tone color. The most famous example of its fairly limited use in the orchestral repertoire is the largo movement of the "New World" Symphony by Antonin Dvořák (upon which the popular song "Goin' Home" is based).

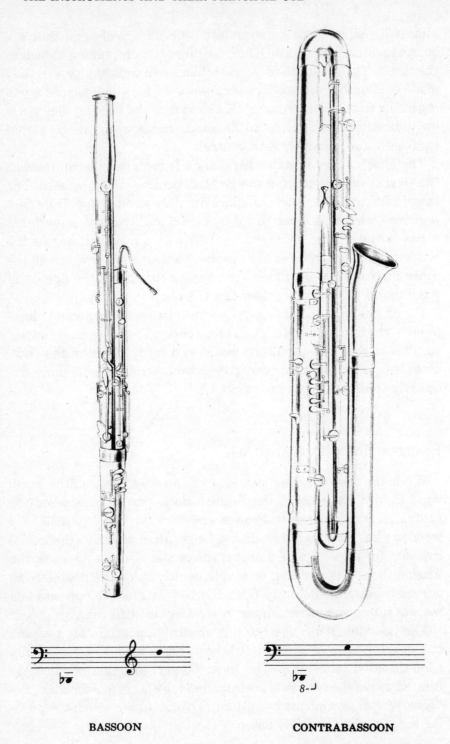

BASSOON   CONTRABASSOON

BASSOON

Another double-reed member of the woodwind family is the bassoon (*fagotto* in Italian, *Fagott* in German), derived from the bass of the shawm family of the sixteenth century. It's easy to spot because it rises above the other instruments of the orchestra like a ship's funnel. The bassoon is the masculine voice of the woodwind choir, capable of both baritone and bass functions. The bassoon has a truly extensive tonal range, about four and one half octaves. The length and breadth of its tonal texture is ideal for the performance of great skips and jumps, which, when used in staccato fashion, create humorous effects. Thus, the bassoon is sometimes described as the clown of the orchestra.

This rather unwieldy instrument consists of a conically bored pipe that is so long that it is doubled back upon itself, and even then it measures approximately four feet. The funnel you see is the top of a diagonally held mechanism of keys, finger pieces, and trackers located near the player's fingers. The crook, a separate attachment consisting of a thin metal tube holding the double reed, is located near the player's mouth.

To appreciate the bassoon's distinctive middle register, listen to its solo in the first movement of Tchaikovsky's Symphony No. 5. The grotesque lower register can be heard in the "March to the Scaffold," the fourth movement of the *Symphonie Fantastique* by Hector Berlioz, and in the role of the broom in *The Sorcerer's Apprentice* by Paul Dukas. For overall scope and ingenuity of color, by all means listen to the Concerto in B-flat for Bassoon, K.191, by Mozart in its entirety. In fact, ever since Mozart, this intriguing instrument has been put to artistic and virtuosic use not easily apparent from its complicated construction.

CONTRABASSOON

The *basso profundo* or lowest toned woodwind instrument is the contrabassoon, or double bassoon. Its tonal range starts an entire octave below the regular bassoon, and it serves to reinforce the bass foundation of that instrument.

The finest bassoons and contrabassoons are made by the firm of Heckel in Biebrich, Germany. The contrabassoon consists of a conical wooden pipe, usually made of hard maple. It is more than sixteen feet long; hence it has to be doubled back on itself four times, with a metal bell at the end of the pipe pointing downward.

For all practical purposes, Beethoven was the first composer to make significant use of this immense instrument. In the opera *Fidelio*, its low, threatening tones describe the digging of Florestan's grave. More happily, the contrabassoon accompanies the bassoon very effectively in parts of Beethoven's Ninth Symphony. A grotesque example of its use is found in the fourth section of Ravel's *Mother Goose* Suite ("The Conversations of Beauty and the Beast"). The contrabassoon even inspired twentieth-century American composer Gunther Schuller to write a concerto.

CLARINET

The clarinet is one of the most popular of all instruments. It is capable of producing a very versatile, and at best an aesthetically liquid, sound. Composers call upon it frequently for significant solo passages and, because of its distinctive timbre, for special blending effects within the texture of instrumentation.

Its prototype in medieval times was the *chalumeau*, which is related to the *Schalmei*, the oboe's ancestor. Unlike the oboe, the clarinet has a cylindrical bore and a single reed.

The clarinet is built of wood or ebonite, and is about two feet long. Like most wind instruments, it can be disassembled into the barrel joint, the top joint, the lower joint, and the bell for easy storage in a carrying case.

The most commonly used clarinets today are B-flat and A clarinets. The E-flat clarinet, smaller in size, is used in bands to strengthen the higher tonal register. Its role (but not the height of its pitch) is somewhat similar to the piccolo vis-à-vis the flute.

The clarinet is a "transposing instrument," as are the trumpet, horn, and saxophone, among others. In each instance their sound is different from the way their music is written; in other words, the music is written in a higher or lower key than the notes that the instrument actually plays.

Generally speaking, *transposing* means moving a melody or an entire compositional structure from one key, or tonality, to another. This is usually done for the sake of convenience of performance or rendition. Before the use of an apparatus such as padded finger pieces was possible, if a composition was written in D or E-flat only those wind instruments whose natural tones would match that particular tonality could complement the stringed instruments. Now, as then, the tonality that is easiest for a wind player to use is dependent upon the size of the instrument, today's added mechanical devices notwithstanding.

In the case of the clarinet, the sizes normally used today are those that function most easily in the key of B-flat or A. For the clarinetist this means that B-flat (in the case of the B-flat clarinet) is the equivalent of C for the pianist. When the clarinetist sees the note C in his music, the tone actually produced comes out B-flat. Conversely, if a composer wishes to write a work in the key of B-flat (or two flats), he provides the clarinet part with no flats at all, as though it were written in the key of C.

All this is helpful for the instrumentalist. He or she plays just what is written. It is for the composer to see that the transposing instrument's tones match the rest of the orchestral sound. It is far more difficult for the conductor, however. His full score shows each of the instruments in its proper tonality, with its pertinent key signature. It must be part of the training of a conductor to match, hence transpose on sight, in order to be able to correct the pitch of each player in the orchestra in his very own tonal habitat, as it were.

Fine examples of diversified clarinet sound are found in orchestral literature. For a mellow, almost mysterious low register, listen to the first movement of Tchaikovsky's Fifth Symphony. In the opening of the Symphony No. 1 by Sibelius the solo clarinet appears in a bleak, brooding low register. A beautifully lyrical mid-register passage is found in the andante cantabile section of Tchaikovsky's *Francesca da Rimini;* and a friendly, expressive clarinet passage occurs in the overture to the opera *Oberon* by Carl Maria von Weber.

CLARINET   BASS CLARINET   BASSETT HORN

Incidentally, Weber highlighted the clarinet in his concertos, as did Mozart, whose clarinet concerto should become dear to every music lover's heart. First, it is an unexcelled masterpiece that calls for exceptional virtuosity by the clarinetist. Second, it was Mozart's friend Anton Stadler, a master clarinetist, whose skill and beauty of tone so inspired Mozart that he wrote the concerto, as well as other works involving the clarinet, with him in mind. Stadler, in turn, played a very important role in the evolution of the instrument. In fact, the clarinet had only scant use before Mozart's time, after which it came to prominence in orchestral writing.

Featured use of the E-flat clarinet can be found in Richard Strauss's tone poem *Till Eulenspiegel's Merry Pranks.* The rogue Till Eulenspiegel utters his last gasp as he is being hanged for his misdeeds, depicted with throat-gripping faithfulness by the E-flat clarinet. Actually, Strauss prescribed a clarinet in D, which is not generally used outside the borders of Germany.

Bass Clarinet

The bass clarinet, a fairly regular member of the modern orchestra, produces a rich tone one octave below that of the regular clarinet. Its basic shape is an enlarged version of the clarinet, with two curved metal additions at either end; one holds the mouthpiece with the single reed, while the other has a wide metal bell that points upward and slightly outward.

The bass clarinet, like the regular clarinet, is a transposing instrument, usually in B-flat. Its voice of authoritative assurance can be heard in the "Dance of the Sugarplum Fairy" section from Tchaikovsky's *Nutcracker Suite,* or in an elaborate passage in the *Sinfonia Domestica* by Richard Strauss.

Bassett Horn

This is in effect a tenor clarinet and looks like a smaller version of the bass clarinet. The bassett horn and the alto clarinet are heard very rarely in concert halls, although there has been a welcome revival of original bassett horn compositions on records recently.

ALTO SAXOPHONE

Saxophone

Of mixed derivation, the saxophone has a tube like an oboe yet looks like a bass clarinet. It has the metal body of a brass instrument yet acts like a woodwind. It has the single reed of the clarinet family yet it can produce nasal sounds like a double reed bassoon.

The saxophone generally comes in five varieties: soprano, alto, tenor, baritone, and bass. There are two additional extremes extant in France and Belgium: the sopranino and the contrabass. All except the soprano saxophone are similar in appearance to the bass clarinet. Their collective tonal range is about two and one half octaves. All are transposing instruments. Middle C written for each of these instruments will sound as indicated in the musical illustration.

Sopranino   Soprano   Alto   Tenor   Baritone   Bass   Contrabass

The tone of the saxophone is a curious, distinctive mixture of horns and woodwinds. The saxophone has remarkable expressive powers capable of a string vibrato or a combined string and wind cantabile. Listen to a saxophone quartet or quintet and you will realize its broad potential.

This provocative instrument is of fairly recent vintage. It was invented in 1841 by a Belgian, Adolphe Sax. No other instrument has spread the fame of its inventor's name to such an extent, notwithstanding the far less well known sousaphone, named after John Philip Sousa, and a brass instrument – the sarrusophone – named after the French bandmaster Sarrus. Both are used in bands.

The saxophone's increase in popularity in just under one hundred and fifty years is phenomenal. Even though it is today mostly associated with jazz, there are between three and four thousand works that employ the saxophone in "concert music." The first of these was a "Hymne Sacrée" by Hector Berlioz, dated 1844. Richard Strauss has an interesting quartet of saxophones in his *Sinfonia Domestica*, and a lovely alto saxophone solo occurs in the adagietto section of the suite extracted from the incidental score that Georges Bizet wrote for Alphonse Daudet's play *L'Arlésienne (The Woman of Arles)*.

THE BRASS FAMILY

Brass instruments, although not originally made of brass, are among the oldest instruments. They probably were first made from the horns of animals, or possibly from tusks. Such a horn, with some sort of mouthpiece attached, undoubtedly was used for all kinds of functions – religious, ceremonial, or utilitarian.

The ancient ram's horn (*shofar* in Hebrew), which dates from biblical times, is still used today in religious observances. On Rosh Hashanah, the Jewish New Year, the shofar proclaims the sovereignty of God, just as, according to Exodus 19:16, the revelation of Yahweh at Mount Sinai was introduced by the sound of the shofar, "causing all the people who were in the camp to tremble." Although used with a mouthpiece in reform temples and synagogues, the shofar is still frequently blown as in ancient times, without the help of a mouthpiece, simply by blowing into the smaller end of the ram's horn. An awesome, ancient sound issues forth from the larger opening.

It is an interesting matter of evolution how, in addition to animal horns, metal horns of all sizes and forms, provided with cup-shaped mouthpieces, began to be used by hunters and medieval watchmen. These metal horns were embellished and handsomely decorated for use by members of medieval guilds, such as those Wagner glorified in *Die Meistersinger*.

The more elaborate these ceremonial horns became, the more unwieldy they were to play. The old alphorn, which is still used today in Switzerland to call cattle to pasture, is so huge that the bell – the tubular opening at the end of its length – must be rested on the ground while the mouthpiece is lifted high for playing. In the case of a hunting horn, it became necessary to wind its body into a circle so that the player could carry it under his arm, with the bell-shaped opening protruding over his shoulder. You can see pictures of this horn, or bugle, in reproductions of English hunting scenes. It is also mentioned in many British literary masterpieces. In France it became known as *cor de chasse* ("hunting horn"). It then returned to England during the early eighteenth century and became known as a French horn, a name that persists even today, although instrumentalists wish to be known simply as hornists. (The German designations of *Jagdhorn* ("hunting horn") and *Waldhorn* ("forest horn") offer a clearer distinction of purpose.

It is a fallacy that all brass instruments are of the horn variety (the word horn being attached to all wind instruments in the vernacular). Both the trumpet and the trombone have medieval prototypes known as the *Claro* or *Clario* (remember the expression "clarion call"?), and *buysine,* respectively. For linguists it may be of interest to note that in German *Buysine* became *Buzaun,* then *Posaune,* which to this day is the German designation for trombone.

Except for the mouthpiece, the various types of instruments mentioned thus far are natural ones, unadorned by valves or pistons. Only the position of the lips and the volume of the breath upon the mouthpiece, known as *embouchure* (French for "lipping"), produced and altered the pitch. Subsequent stages of development brought forth "crutches" that we now take for granted, such as valves, crooks, slides, and at times even human fists inserted into the bells to increase one's control of pitch. It is therefore safe to say that none of the brass instruments used today looks or acts like its historical predecessor.

FRENCH HORN

The French horn has assumed a pivotal position between woodwinds and brass because of its beautiful, pliable timbre, which enables it to blend easily with both or either group of instruments. It is one of the most difficult of all wind instruments to play.

An ancestor of the ancient hunting horn, today's French horn has the appearance of a brass tube of considerable length, coiled in a spiral and expanding into a large opening or bell. Unlike the other brass instruments, which have cup-shaped mouthpieces, the French horn's mouthpiece is funnel-shaped. With its added tubing, or crook, the horn attains the enormous length of almost twelve feet. Valves control the extra portions of tubing, and tuning slides aid in finely regulating the pitch. All this enables the French horn to have a considerable tonal range of about three octaves.

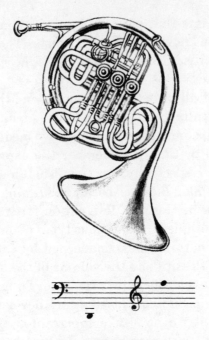

FRENCH HORN

The French horn can sound uncommonly distant in soft passages or brilliantly majestic when played full force. Skilled artists can make deft use of their hand or fist when inserted into the bell of the instrument, resulting in a lowering or raising of any given pitch, as well as in "stopping" or muting the tone. In addition, a pear-shaped metal mute can be inserted into the instrument for effects prescribed in the score.

Among the finest examples of horn sound in orchestral music are a melodious opening solo in the second movement of Tchaikovsky's Fifth Symphony and the throbbing sighs in the "love theme" passage of the same composer's *Romeo and Juliet* Overture Fantasy. For double horn examples listen to the trio section of the minuet in Mozart's Symphony in G Minor, No. 40, which is reminiscent of

Horn Fifths

etc.

hunting music because of its frequent use of the interval of a fifth, known as a "horn fifth" (see example on previous page). Other memorable double horn passages are found in the opening of the Symphony No. 2 by Johannes Brahms, which is bucolic in character, or in the passage underlying the entrance of the solo violin in Beethoven's Violin Concerto, which is actively exciting in spirit.

For a triple horn sound listen to the mounting agitation of the three horns in the trio section of the scherzo in Beethoven's "Eroica" Symphony, No. 3; or the gentle opening of Weber's overture to *Der Freischütz*. There is also a clarion call of three horns answering two trumpets at the beginning of Tchaikovsky's Symphony No. 4.

As for horn concertos, nothing can take the place of Mozart's four masterworks in this category. Composed for his friend Ignaz Leutgeb, who must have been an exceptional hornist, these concertos were written for a valveless instrument. For a more modern sound, try the two horn concertos by Richard Strauss, who grew up knowing the horn well since his father, Franz Strauss, was a renowned solo hornist and a professor at the Academy of Music in Munich. The *Konzertstück* for Four Horns and Orchestra by Robert Schumann is a most unusual example of multiple horn sound in concerted form (see pp. 312–13). For some other distinctive uses of the French horn in chamber music, see pp. 218–19.

TRUMPET

If your child wants to learn how to play the trumpet, count your blessings. This used to mean untold hours of suffering for the child, for you, and for your neighbors. Only a most diligent and well-trained student could master a tune on the old natural trumpet. That trumpet was much smaller than today's valve trumpet, and the embouchure was so small that proper breath control was extremely difficult.

The natural trumpet dates back to the beginning of the seventeenth century, but it did not come into regular use until the time of Bach and Handel, who wrote for the high C and D trumpets some brilliant bravura roles. For a thrilling experience listen to the high trumpet in the orchestral introduction to Bach's Magnificat in D

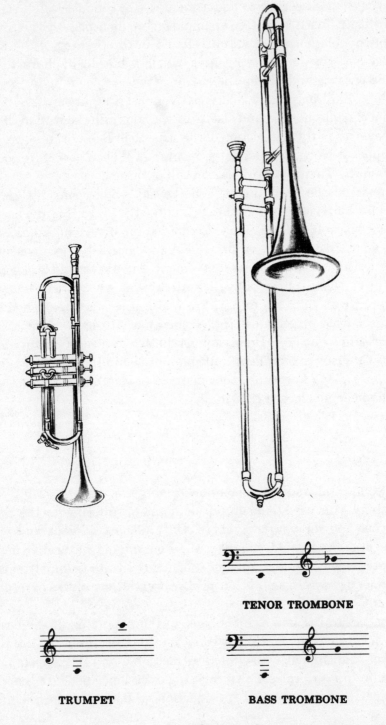

TENOR TROMBONE

TRUMPET

BASS TROMBONE

Major or the aria "Sound an Alarm!" in Handel's oratorio *Judas Maccabaeus*. They are as breathtaking to listen to as they are difficult to play.

The eighteenth century saw a decline in this kind of tonal acrobatics. The age of the classical symphony called for a less abrasive trumpet sound. Crooks or additional pieces of brass were inserted into a larger trumpet, which, because of its compatibility with the rest of the orchestral sound, became a regular part of the symphonic repertoire. The creation of the valve trumpet in the early nineteenth century provided a tonal range of over two octaves.

Trumpets vary in size according to the length of the added crooks and the resultant change of the instrument's basic tonality. All are transposing instruments. Because it possesses the highest pitch in the brass section, as well as a very positive, prominent brilliance, the trumpet is called upon to cap the orchestral ensemble in passages of great majesty. The offstage trumpet call in Beethoven's Leonore Overture No. 3 is a fine example of trumpeting nobility. In its more modest moments the trumpet is muted with the aid of a pear-shaped object inserted in its bell. Some of our great jazz performers have achieved endless interesting effects and hours of pleasure by means of such mutes.

TROMBONE

I'd like to relate a lovely story about the trombone that focuses on the instrument's unique physical makeup. A rather resolute but musically poorly versed lady sat in a side gallery of a concert hall with a good view of the trombone section. With great amazement she watched the first trombonist perform a solo passage requiring a good deal of slide manipulation. Impatiently she rushed to see him right after the performance, tore the trombone from his unsuspecting hands, exclaiming, "Give me that thing. I'll get it out for ye!" And with that she tore the slide loose from the trombone.

This supposedly true incident focuses on the U-shaped slide that takes the place of valves to vary the pitch of the trombone by shortening or lengthening the air column vibrating within the instrument. In other words, the trombone has no preset tones; they must be produced by embouchure and by moving the slide into the right places.

Trombones are transposing instruments with a reach of about two octaves.

Today's orchestra generally calls for three trombones. Formerly that meant an alto, a tenor, and a bass trombone; today we have two tenors and a bass trombone. The trombone's ancestor, dating back to the Middle Ages, was known as the sackbut; the highest pitched instrument was known as the zinke. In medieval times there existed a larger variety within this category of instruments; these can be seen in old prints of "tower musicians" performing chorales from the church steeple before services. Happily, there is currently a rebirth of this colorful kind of music making; trombone ensembles play works by masters in both original and contemporary arrangements.

Today's trombones are expected to lend emphatic support to the orchestral texture. Both martial and eloquent effects can be obtained, such as their repeated use in an inherently stately work like Tchaikovsky's *Marche Slave.* The size of the cylindrical tube and the conical bell are vital, but it is the player's lips and his mastery of the slide mechanism that are all-important in tone production.

Aside from managing absolutely correct intonation in the absence of predetermined pitch of any given tone – much as is the case with stringed instruments – trombonists often have the opportunity to "slide around," both in jazz and in humorous moments of "serious" music. Listen to the "Humoresk" movement of the Symphony No. 6 by the Danish master Carl Nielsen and you will enjoy the yawning effects of the trombones, connoting the composer's alleged boredom with modern trends.

For your further listening pleasure, there is a rare Concerto for Trombone and Military Band by Rimsky-Korsakov. For your own record library, I suggest the innovative Sonata for Trumpet, Horn and Trombone by Francis Poulenc, the gifted French master.

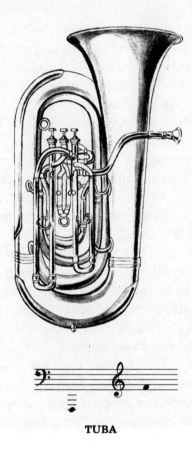

TUBA

TUBA

What Tubby did for the tuba in the delightful narrated piece "Tubby the Tuba," by George Kleinsinger, the tuba could hardly have done for itself. There it sits, way back in the orchestra, oom-pah-pahing a bass foundation in its supporting role and sporting a bright cylinder like an old-fashioned formal high hat for a mute when needed, very visible and often amusing to the audience.

The tuba player, more often than not, is hidden behind the instrument. While conducting an orchestra not long ago, I was reminded that someone was actually playing the instrument only by a pair of cheeks protruding when the instrumentalist exhaled into the tuba.

Good lungs are surely an important asset in order to be a successful tuba player, since the instrument's bore is enormous.

There are some truly outstanding tuba players in our orchestras today. Of special note is the finest tuba virtuoso of our time, Harvey Phillips, who has raised the instrument to solo rank almost single-handedly because of his artistry and devotion. There are also fine freelance instrumentalists. Since there is generally only one tuba in the orchestral repertoire, few openings for players ever exist.

Richard Wagner was the first composer to envision horns that would complement, and at the same time outdo, trombones in their depth of tone. Thus, the first true tuba was employed in *Der Ring des Nibelungen* to simulate tonally the descent to the bottom of the Rhine. Today's tuba gives the player the option of producing pitch with the help of four valves (dividing the air column into various sections), as well as by using the bore alone (i.e., removing the valve mechanism coiled within the bend of the bore). Today's concert and marching bands sport a variety of tubas, including one called a euphonium for added low brass tones.

Wagner's Prelude to *Die Meistersinger* has a significant solo part for tuba that is shared with its stringed cousins the double-basses, in which the main theme is pronounced ponderously, befitting the pompous character of the occasion. There is also a demanding Concerto for Bass Tuba and Orchestra written by the imaginative English composer Ralph Vaughan Williams. Listen to it and your respect for the tuba will be greatly increased.

THE STRING FAMILY

Strictly speaking, stringed instruments is a broader designation for this large family, for it immediately reminds us that there are many instruments whose strings are not bowed but plucked or even struck. Today's orchestral string section consists of violins, violas, cellos, and double bases. Each of these instruments will be discussed in detail on the following pages, with additional mention being made of some of their distant cousins of the past.

VIOLIN

By means of an introduction to this section, I would like to relate an interesting encounter that took place after I played a joint recital with the violinist and pedagogue Josef Gingold, for many years concertmaster of the Cleveland Orchestra (when George Szell was its conductor) and now Distinguished Professor of Music at Indiana University. Mr. Gingold had just purchased a magnificent Stradivarius violin, a fact that was publicized in great detail in the local newspapers. After the recital a well-dressed gentleman came to our dressing room backstage and questioned Joe. "I read that you are playing a very old fiddle," he began. "How old did they say it is?" Gingold replied, "Well, sir, I have papers proving that it was made in 1709." The visitor responded, "Isn't it a shame that an artist in your position can't afford a new fiddle!" For a moment we were both utterly speechless, since we were convinced of our visitor's complete seriousness in the matter. But then Joe Gingold broke into a broad, benevolent smile and launched into one of his priceless discourses, informing the man of the proper state of affairs.

I mention this incident to emphasize a remarkable historical fact. Of all the instruments used in music today, the violin has not undergone any real, appreciable changes since the time of Antonio Stradivari and his fellow Cremonese master craftsmen some three hundred to four hundred years ago. Can you name any other instrument with such unchanging longevity? To be sure, some minor adjustments have been made in order to accommodate the stringent demands exerted upon today's artists by the works of modern composers. So perfect were the concepts of construction of the masters of Cremona, so unique were their specifications for the use of materials and their shapes and dimensions, that the passage of time has not only failed to erode but has even shown that it may be impossible to surpass their creations. Actually, the only eroding factors are misuse or no use at all. Never buy a Stradivarius for the sake of monetary investment without having it used by a highly competent violinist.

It is believed that a bowed, stringed instrument, predecessor of the present-day violin, originally came from Central Asia to the Far East and to Europe. The violin's current form is the result of multiple changes, from simple round sound boxes in ancient China to bottle-shaped ones in early Europe. During the sixteenth century its present shape emerged as a prototype for the violin. From c. 1550 to about 1760 Cremona, a little town in northern Italy, was the center where the great violin makers created their masterpieces. There were other well-reputed artisans in Germany, Austria, England, and France during this time, but the Cremonese masters were the most renowned.

Among these craftsmen were Andrea Amati (1500?–75?) and his grandson Nicolò (1596–1684); Andrea Guarneri (1625–98) and Giuseppe Guarneri del Gesù (1698–1744); and, above all, Antonio Stradivari (1644–1737). Their craft was passed on from generation to generation, from master to apprentice. For example, Andrea Guarneri and Antonio Stradivari were students of Nicolò Amati.

It is believed that the Stradivari, Guarneri, and Amati families of Cremona and the Testore and Grancino families of Milan together created some twenty thousand masterpieces of the violin maker's art. Add to this the magnificent products of Gasparo da Salò in nearby Brescia, Domenico Montagnana in Venice, Francesco Ruggieri and Lorenzo Storione of Cremona, and you gain some idea of the immense musical importance of this tiny region. It is well worth your while to explore further the skills of instrument construction, the secrets of wood, the mysteries of varnish, and the mixtures of colors. The Bibliography will suggest some pertinent books for your perusal.

Although the violin's outward appearance is familiar, we may not realize the innumerable details of its construction. Some sixty to seventy pieces of wood are fitted together so skillfully by a great violin maker that the resultant instrument appears to be seamless. Various categories of wood are employed, such as pine, maple, and sycamore, depending upon the instrument's areas of greatest friction. The violin's overall length is approximately fourteen inches.

The body of the violin consists of the soundboard or table, the back, and the side walls or ribs. Attached to the body are the fingerboard, merging into a box holding the pegs, and the scroll. The tailpiece holds the strings that traverse the bridge between the F-shaped soundholes, on their way up the full length of the fingerboard to the strings' terminals, the pegs.

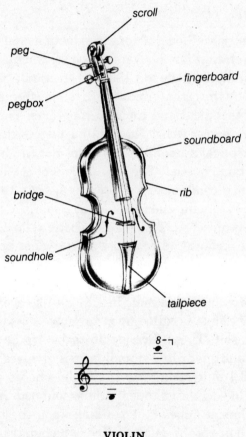

VIOLIN

If you could look inside a violin, you would find a strip of wood glued inside the table, known as a bass-bar. Its function is to distribute the vibrations of the bridge over the sounding board as the strings activate them. You would also notice small blocks of wood glued to the side walls and the back for reinforcement. In addition, you would see the all-important soundpost, a small wedge of pine-wood, placed between the table and the back, which coordinates the various vibrating parts of the instrument.

The four strings of the violin are tuned in intervals of fifths:

There are many methods of tone production and countless nuances of interpretation for this versatile instrument. Some of these involve the technique of the left hand upon the fingerboard, while the bow, guided by the right (or bowing) arm, performs an incredibly wide variety of technical and musical functions. The coordination between the two arms, wrists, hands and fingers may well be described by the biblical admonition: ". . . let not thy left hand know what thy right hand doeth." The four fingers of the left hand press down any one or a combination of strings against the fingerboard, with the thumb balancing the instrument under the neck, to which the fingerboard is attached. This pressing action shortens the vibrating length of the strings and produces all the tones according to the swinging weighted-string principle previously described (see p. 58).

The music lover usually thinks of the violin as an ideal instrument with which to produce single melodies, much like a singer does. But frequently the violinist is called upon to "sing" duets, trios, or even quartets by himself. These formidable tasks are accomplished by double-, triple-, and quadruple-stopping. This involves playing either two, three, or all four strings so that solid chords and arpeggios (broken chords in successive tones) can be sounded. All this is even more difficult than it appears, depending upon the position of the fingers for the choice of the desired pitch (which may include the use of open, unstopped strings), the proximity of strings involved, and the pressure exerted on the strings by the bow and the resultant volume of tone.

For an excellent example of single and multiple tone that can be achieved by one player, I urge you to listen to the famous Chaconne from the D Minor Partita for unaccompanied violin by Johann

Sebastian Bach. While marveling at the technical as well as intellectual challenge of this ingenious masterwork, you should experience great emotional satisfaction.

Another method of tone production involves lightly touching the strings rather than pressing them down on the fingerboard. The resulting tones are known as harmonics. Their eerie sound is difficult to attain in perfect intonation due to the indeterminate pressure of the finger. It should be emphasized that the string player produces every single tone himself. No "preset" arrangements, such as a specific sequence of keys on the piano, or valves or keys on a wind instrument, are there as aids. The only "constant" tones are those produced by the open strings G, D, A, E. Even this constancy is relative, for a perfect ear and a thorough know-how in tuning are a good violinist's – or any string player's – absolute prerequisites. Beyond this, the burden placed upon the instrumentalist to be solely responsible for proper intonation is enormous.

In addition to the string player's left-hand technique, it takes proper use of the bow and what the right hand and arm and wrist do with it for complete mastery of the instrument. One must complement the other. I might add that the art of violin playing has been more determined by the bow at various stages of its evolution than by the violin itself.

The superb creations of the masters of Cremona predate the finest bows as we know them today by as much as a century. The modern bow for the violin, as well as for the viola and the cello, was perfected by the Parisian craftsman François Tourte (1747–1835), who was born ten years after the death of Stradivari and sixty-three years after the death of Nicolò Amati. It staggers the imagination to realize that these masters never knew the true potential of the sound of their finest instruments because the development of the modern bow lagged so far behind. The Italian violinist-composers of the seventeenth and eighteenth centuries – such as Corelli and Tartini – as well as the greatest composers of that time – such as Bach, Handel, and even the young Haydn and Mozart – used the kind of bow

85

that resembled the weapon of the same name. All they would have needed, had they been so inclined, was an arrow, and the bow that helped express the beauty of their works to their admirers could have doubled to still the venom of their critics.

The appearance of the bow has changed markedly, from a plain stick of wood strung with strands of horsehair to various curvatures of the wood – first away from the hair and later to an inward position. Today's bow, according to Tourte's principles, is made of flexible wood called Pernambuco, just under thirty inches in length. The hair is fastened onto it from the top (called the point) to the lower end (known as the heel, or nut, or frog) and threaded into a ring-shaped holder. Below is a head, often beautifully ornamented, which in some valuable bows is made of mother-of-pearl. This head contains a screw that fits into the holder, thus enabling the player to tighten or slacken the hair. Perhaps you have observed how a violinist will tear loose from the bow a stray hair that has become unfastened through vigorous use. The average bow is provided with approximately one hundred and fifty strands of hair, all taken and processed from horses' tails. Bows need to be restrung periodically by a highly experienced, talented craftsman.

The basic principle of bowing is to induce the strings to vibrate and keep them in a constant state of oscillation so the left-hand stopping action can vary the pitch. By way of oversimplification, what matters most is where and how the bow touches the strings. The area for the exact point of contact is very small – only the few inches between the bridge and the termination of the fingerboard. However, we find a variety of tone here. The strings respond most readily and are tonally most acceptable when the bow touches them about halfway between these two terminal points. The closer to the bridge, the harder the sound; the nearer to the fingerboard – or at times even above it – the more airy the sound. A composer can call for either tone color with such specific instructions as *sul ponticello* ("on the bridge") or *sul tasto* ("on the fingerboard").

How does one set the bow on the strings? The following list gives a sense of the complexities of string playing:

• You can bring the bow in partial contact, sideways as it were, and then turn it upon contact to a full confrontation. The amount of pressure by the fingers and bowing arm and the speed of execution play a large role in the resulting tone, from a lovely legato (smooth and closely connected tones) to a carefully sustained single sound.

• The bow can be brought down in a quasi-frontal attack, which in turn can elicit any number of tonal responses from the strings, with the most minute collaboration of arms, wrists, and fingers. The results can range from a sharp but brief initial attack and immediate release of pressure, known as *sforzando,* to an abrupt hammerblow, known as *martellato* in Italian and *martelé* in literal French translation.

• The strokes can be delivered by drawing the full length of the bow across the strings, separating one tone from another. This is referred to as *détaché.*

• The bow can be bounced lightly to produce quick, individual tones, called *sautillé;* or it can be made to dance on the strings so as to produce entire patterns of tone, known as *jeté.*

• With a very loose wrist one can make the middle of the bow produce a light staccato known as *spiccato* ("clearly articulated").

• Some scores call for the bow to be turned over so that the wood touches the strings instead of the hair. Such extramusical sounds are marked *col legno* ("with the wood"). The overture to Rossini's *Il Signor Bruschino* contains a fine example of this.

• The direction *a punta d'arco* denotes lowering the bow on the strings at its point.

• The designation *au talon* calls for the bow to be held at the end nearest the hand (known as the bow's heel or nut).

• A rather colorless tone can be produced by playing the bow very gently near the fingerboard, designated by *flautando* ("like a flute").

• There are various kinds of *tremolo,* achieved by rapid movements of the bow and/or fingers of the right hand.

• *Vibrato* is a fast movement of a finger of the left hand as it "pinches" or stops any given spot on a string.

• The strings of the violin can be plucked with one or more fingers of the bowing hand. This is known as *pizzicato,* which is indicated in the score by the abbreviation *pizz,* followed by the word *arco* (Italian for "bow") when regular bowing is to be resumed. This applies not only to the violin but to the playing of all stringed instruments.

When playing pizzicato the string player can hold the bow in the palm of the hand while using the first and second fingers (not counting the thumb) for plucking; or in extended pizzicato passages the player may put the bow in his lap or on the music stand. Pizzicato can be applied singly or in chordal fashion. The classical example of an extended pizzicato is the scherzo movement of Tchaikovsky's Fourth Symphony; the slow movement of his Fifth Symphony contains some sonorous strumming pizzicato passages.

Orchestral literature is filled with many other fine passages containing the distinctive pizzicato sound. In some instances of special virtuosic effects pizzicato is executed by the overtaxed left hand plucking one string with one finger while bowing other strings simultaneously. A perfect example for such left-hand acrobatics is found in parts of *Zigeunerweisen* ("Gypsy Airs") by Pablo de Sarasate.

The artist must know when and how to use any of the above devices, in compliance with the demands of the score, and when they best suit any given style of composition.

I recall rehearsing Brahms's Concerto for Violin, Cello, and Orchestra, known as the Double Concerto, with two superb artists. The violinist was trained in the German tradition of string playing and the cellist in the French school. Thus, the cellist was accustomed to a faster vibrato, which sounds very elegant when applied, for example, to the Cello Concerto by Édouard Lalo or the one by Camille Saint-Saëns. Brahms, on the other hand, benefits from a more moderate vibrato. My violinist friend requested that we stop the rehearsal for a moment. Turning to the cellist, he whispered for me to hear, "Georges, for goodness' sake, Brahms was born in Hamburg, not Cherbourg. Let's settle on a slower vibrato!"

I relate this delightful incident in order to illustrate how the intangibles of taste and style enter into the manner of application of technical means. The vibrato happens to be one of the important ways of lending a particularly expressive quality to playing any stringed instrument. It must not become second nature for the player, but should be applied judiciously according to the artistic requirements of any given work.

The mute is a special accoutrement used to soften the string tone in a very distinctive way. Playing even the softest pianissimo without a mute will not produce a muted tone, whose quality is one of utter privacy as well as eerieness at times. The mute of the violin looks like a tiny comb whose three prongs fit firmly on the bridge of the instrument and dampen the vibrations of the strings. It is generally made of wood and sometimes even of ivory or metal. The composer calls for its use by prescribing in the score *con sordino* ("with the mute"), followed by the direction for lifting it, *senza sordino* ("without the mute").

Here I would like to share another personal experience with you. Upon the request of a dear friend, I once asked my favorite bakery to make me a mute of dark brown sugar so it would resemble the real thing. This violinist-friend of mine remembered that I had brought a cake to a party following his performance of the Beethoven Violin Concerto, with the frosting representing the opening timpani notes of the concerto. Now he insisted on having the sugary mute so that he could surprise his desk partner in the orchestra by attaching the mute, then lifting it and swallowing it before his partner's disbelieving eyes! Who says serious music can't be fun?

In conjunction with the violin, one should realize that the same instrument is used to perform first and second violin parts of orchestral or chamber music works. Playing the second violin does not imply any inferiority of ability or musicianship. Quite the contrary, playing the inner part of a score requires perhaps more sensitivity, and hence even greater musicianship, as well as the not-to-be-underestimated temperamental quality of being content with providing very often an accompanying part to the melodies of the first-violin section.

The conductor Georges Sebastian relates how as a very young orchestra leader he was conducting in one of the Hollywood studios. Upon completion of a rehearsal session, the conductor's attention was directed to an imposing figure standing in the doorway, thumbs in his vest with fingers protruding and pointing at him threateningly. It was a world-renowned film producer, a long cigar in his mouth, beckoning the young maestro: "Come here, boy, I want to talk to you." The frightened young musician did as he was told. "Very good, boy, very good," said the tycoon, patting the maestro on the shoulder reassuringly. "Just one thing. Did I hear you say something about second violins?" Georges responded, "Yes, sir, I corrected them in one place at rehearsal." To which the movie executive quipped, "That won't do. You see, at this studio I want only firsts, not seconds! Understand?"

VIOLA

The alto member of the string choir is the viola. The French actually call it *alto,* while the Germans refer to it as *Bratsche.* This latter term is derived from the instrument's Italian name during the seventeenth century, *viola da braccio,* an instrument held with the arm (*bras* in French, *braccio* in Italian), rather than with the knees or legs (*jambe* in French, *gamba* in Italian) as with the *viola da gamba,* which became the cello.

The viola is larger than its soprano cousin the violin; but it is not as large as the difference in pitch would indicate, which is a fifth lower than that of the violin. Of all the stringed instruments, the viola has differed the most in size over the years, from very large

VIOLA

older models to their smaller modern counterparts, with a corresponding difference in technique needed to manage the reaches of the fingerboard.

Much of the music written for the viola uses the alto clef, which facilitates writing notes of the predominantly lower register on the staff. Thus, the following notation indicates middle C.

The four strings of the viola are tuned in intervals of fifths:

91

The viola's timbre is particularly rich in the middle and lower registers, displaying great warmth and depth.

By all means listen to Mozart's Sinfonia Concertante for Violin, Viola and Orchestra, one of the great masterpieces of all time; you will be thrilled by the dialogue between the youthful pronouncements of the violin and the wise, sobering answers of the viola. In Berlioz's *Harold in Italy* the viola becomes the unforgettable protagonist of Byron's famous epic *Childe Harold* upon which the music is based. The two sonatas for viola (originally for clarinet) and piano by Brahms will give you an idea of the range and the tonal diversity of the instrument. Listening to some string quartets that are representative of the viola's range, such as No. 12, Op. 127 in E-flat by Beethoven or any of the Brahms quartets, will help train your ear to single out "inner voices." You will also discover that the viola's upper register – especially the top string – has a nasal quality some composers use for special effects. It should also be mentioned that the two low strings, C and G, wear a covering or spun-metal substance over the usual catgut. This adds weight to the tone quality in the lower range.

The bow of the viola is somewhat heavier than the violin's bow, but it is just as versatile – except perhaps for some of the lighter strokes, which, due to the greater weight, are not as effective. Much of the discussion of left-hand and bowing techniques of violin playing also applies to the viola as well as other stringed instruments.

It is only since the early seventeenth century that the viola as we know it has become a full-fledged member of the orchestra. Its use in chamber music coincides with the development of the string quartet, dating from the time of Haydn. To a musician the voice of the viola is especially dear as the ideal inner voice supporting and balancing the overall tonal structure. Personally speaking, I can never quite hear enough of it.

CELLO

Until the seventeenth century the cello was called upon mainly to provide the bass foundation in orchestral works as well as in chamber music. Today its noble, distinguished tone is enjoyed not only in

CELLO

these two categories but particularly in such masterful works as the cello concertos by Antonin Dvořák, Camille Saint-Saëns, and Édouard Lalo, and the Hebrew rhapsody *Schelomo* by Ernest Bloch. Richard Strauss makes effective use of both the viola and cello as solo instruments in his tone poem *Don Quixote*.

The name cello is really an abbreviation of violoncello, the bass of the violin family. This is a derivation from the early *Violone*, or double-bass viol, so that cello ("small") would imply the small bass violin.

93

The cello is tuned like the viola, but each of the four strings is an octave lower in pitch:

In appearance the cello looks like an oversized viola that rests on the floor, supported by a peg or pin protruding from the bottom of the instrument to give it greater support. Playing in a seated position, the cellist is obliged to move his left hand away from his body on the fingerboard for the higher notes rather than toward it, as in the case of an instrument held under the chin. The bow tends to move upward toward the higher tones rather than the reverse incline when playing the violin or the viola.

Music for the cello is written in three clefs: for the low register (left); for the middle register (center); and for the upper register (right).

The cello's bow, even though it is shorter and heavier than the one used for the violin, can perform all the special bowing techniques described earlier for the violin. As for its tone, the cello is versatile and authoritative in the middle and upper registers and awesomely majestic in the lower register. When played well, the cello is one of the most satisfying of all instruments, both for the cellist and for the listener.

In addition to the examples mentioned above, the cello plays a particularly graceful role when combined with other stringed instruments. Do listen to Brahms's Double Concerto; its second movement yields some rapturous moments. Beethoven, Brahms, Mendelssohn, Rachmaninoff, and Debussy all wrote most rewarding sonatas for cello and piano. My choice for a prime listening experience would be the third of Beethoven's five such sonatas, Op. 69 in A Major. Also of special interest are the Bach suites for unaccompanied cello and the works by Zoltán Kodály and Maurice Ravel for solo cello and for cello and violin.

DOUBLE BASS

Double Bass

The double bass, sometimes called the contrabass or simply the bass, differs from the other stringed instruments not only in size but in shape (e.g., in its sloping shoulders). Because of its very low sound,

95

music for the double bass has to be written one octave higher than the pitch you hear; otherwise the composer would run out of ledger lines below the regular staff.

Before Beethoven's time the number of strings and the function of the double bass were quite different in orchestral music than they are today. The bass used to have only three strings, and it was used almost exclusively to support and deepen the cello line by simply playing the same notes as the cello one octave lower. For example, in the choral movement of Beethoven's Ninth Symphony there is a famous declamatory section headed "In the manner of a recitative but in tempo," with the double bass adding a sagacious voice to the youthful zest of the cello's tones. Other well-known examples of this technique come to mind readily, such as the opening measures of Schubert's "Unfinished" Symphony and Mozart's opera *Don Giovanni,* and the primary theme of Wagner's overture to *Die Meistersinger,* where basses, cellos, and tuba combine to do battle with the rest of the orchestra for thematic supremacy.

The double bass of Mozart's time was tuned in intervals of fourths:

During Beethoven's lifetime a fourth string was added to enlarge the tonal compass downward:

This tuning is still in use today. The modern instrument is even occasionally used with five strings, with a low C string added; alternatively, a special mechanism can be attached to the E string at the tailpiece to enable the bassist to lengthen it in order to produce the low C when needed.

Since the early part of the nineteenth century, the double bass has become an increasingly self-sufficient, independent member of the orchestra. Listen to the opening of the third movement of Gustav

Mahler's First Symphony for an effective and eerie bass solo against the background of muffled kettledrums; or the spine-tingling part played by the bass section in Verdi's opera *Otello,* just before the murder of Desdemona. Conversely, the double bass has entered the field of chamber music as an equal partner, the best known example being Schubert's "Trout" Quintet for Piano, Violin, Viola, Cello, and Double Bass.

This diversity of musical assignments is due, in large measure, to some outstanding musicians who have displayed their extraordinary virtuosity. Leading this group were Domenico Dragonetti of Venice and London (he knew both Haydn and Beethoven), Giovanni Bottesini of Cremona (1821–89) and, more recently, Serge Koussevitzky of conducting fame, who started his illustrious musical career as a double bass virtuoso. This tradition is carried on in our own time by the American bassist Gary Karr, among others.

The bass bow has a history all its own. While the early bow looked and acted more like a weapon with which to attack the strings, the modern bass bow, known as the Bottesini bow, looks more like the one used for the cello. However, it is shorter, heavier, and "wears" black hair far coarser in texture than regular bow hair. The resultant tone quality is quite different. A long, sustained passage is impossible to achieve because of the shortness of the bow. The player must change bow strokes repeatedly and judiciously in order to keep the tone from fading. However, short and energetic strokes can yield incisive effects called for in the score.

Pizzicato, or plucking the strings with the fingers, is a frequent device for producing the kind of pungency for which the bass tone is ideally suited. This is true in symphonic music as well as in jazz, where the prominence of pizzicato is also of great rhythmical significance. The bow is rarely used here at all.

HARP

The harp is one of the stringed instruments that is activated exclusively by plucking. No one knows the exact century of its origin, but it is mentioned in Psalms in the Bible. Its original shape is uncertain, although ancient murals and drawings depict it in various images. Scandinavia, England, and Ireland claim that it originated in their country. In fact, it became the national instrument of Ireland and was even elevated to the status of a national emblem.

Basically, the principle of the harp's operation has not changed over the centuries. Strings are stretched across a frame, constructed at an angle so that they are of varying lengths, hence of different pitch. The plucking action of the fingers of one or both hands causes the strings to vibrate according to the pitch of their particular length.

To relieve and alter the rigidity of pitch imposed by immovable strings, mechanisms were invented to alter and tune each of the strings to comply with the demands of a melody or composition, and to enable it to accompany other, more flexible instruments. At first attachments were built for each string, which led to a pedal. This pedal could shorten the length and pitch by as little as a half tone.

Some ingenious steps were taken by the Alsatian-born Frenchman Sébastien Érard (1752–1831), one of the most important instrument manufacturers of the nineteenth century. Realizing the need for greater flexibility of tone, he invented the double-action harp, whose principles of construction became lasting guidelines for all future models. In essence, Monsieur Érard's invention consisted of an apparatus that would shorten each string both one or two degrees, tantamount to changes of both half or whole tones in pitch. He also provided the harp with seven pedals, each serving to alter any string of the same pitch among the eight tones of the diatonic scale. If you pushed down one pedal to the first notch, all the C's became C-sharps; if you depressed the pedal to the second notch, all C's became D's, or C-double sharp, known as "enharmonic unison" with D. Eventually a third notch was added to the pedal mechanism. By pushing the pedal down and into a sideways position, any one pitch and all its corresponding octaves could be lowered a half step as well. This triple action afforded the harpist the full range of the chromatic scale.

Sébastien Érard also made sure that the aesthetic beauty of the harp was preserved despite all the new mechanical improvements. A vertical pillar was provided, often with elaborate embellishments. This column merged into an equally graceful neck, with an attach-

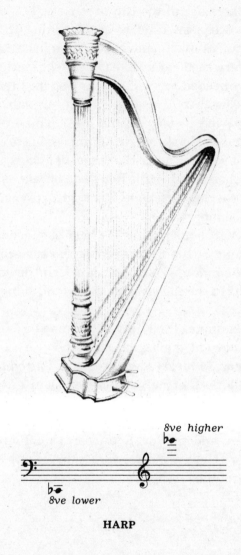

8ve higher

8ve lower

HARP

ment known as a comb, which cleverly concealed all of the mechanical apparatus. The sound board, or resonator, emerged from the
comb, descending diagonally downward and attached to the lower
end of the vertical pillar by way of the pedal box. Generally two
different colors, such as red and blue, distinguish strings of one basic

pitch from another. The longest strings are spun with a metal layer, while all the others are of the catgut variety.

Much of the harpist's time is spent tuning those forty-seven strings; this requires much endurance, both before and during the concert, and a very good ear attuned to the slightest flaws of intonation. The agility needed to span so many strings renders the little finger quite useless. As a result, only the thumb and first three fingers are employed in playing the harp. This influences a composer's writing for the harp, making it impossible to score big chords or arpeggios that would require the use of all fingers, as on the piano. Although solid chords and single notes can be very effective, most of the playing of the harp is done in rapid arpeggio, or successive broken-chord fashion.

Another striking component of the harpist's technical equipment is the rapid sliding of the fingers across the surface of the strings. This is known as *glissando* ("sliding"), a colorful device that can vary greatly according to the choice of scales and the many ways of tuning the instrument.

A delightful example of the harp's tone may be found in the colorful cadenza for harp at the beginning of the overture to *Mignon* by Ambroise Thomas. Maurice Ravel wrote an *Introduction and Allegro* for Harp, Flute, Clarinet, and String Quartet, which is a fine showpiece for the harp. My further recommendations for listening are the Sonata for Flute, Viola, and Harp by Claude Debussy, one of his last works, and the lovely Concerto for Flute and Harp by Mozart. Another Debussy masterwork is his *Danse Sacrée et Danse Profane* for Harp and Orchestra.

LUTE

The lute is among the oldest of plucked instruments. Its origin is in antiquity; in the year 2000 B.C. lutes were pictured on Mesopotamian pottery. The lute is often mentioned in English literature, particularly in the works of Chaucer and Shakespeare. Bach used the instrument in his *Saint John Passion,* and he also wrote some remarkable scores for solo lute, including four suites and two fugues.

LUTE

All lutes have a round back, beautifully pear-shaped, and are represented in innumerable paintings of the sixteenth and seventeenth centuries. The strings are strung along the entire body, uninterrupted by any bridge. There is no set number of strings.

Their basic tuning is accomplished as follows:

A   D   F   A   D   F

Raised lines on the fingerboard, known as frets, show the instrumentalist the location of half tones. The head of the lute is bent backward from the neck and contains the box for the pegs.

101

A rebirth of the lute has occurred in our time, and it now lends welcome authenticity to the accompaniments of early English and French songs.

MANDOLIN

GUITAR

MANDOLIN

The mandolin bears a strong family resemblance to the lute, although its tone is not as sonorous. It is also pear-shaped, though less full, and has a fretted neck. Most mandolins today have eight strings, arranged in four pairs, which are tuned exactly like the strings of the violin:

They are set in motion by a small piece of bone, tortoiseshell, or ivory, known as a plectrum, for plucking. While this does not constitute plucking in the truest sense of the word, it does give the player the advantage of a sustained sound that continues as long as the plectrum is in motion. This distinguishes the sound of the mandolin from that of the lute and the guitar.

A fine example of a mandolin playing is found in the serenade in Act II of Mozart's opera *Don Giovanni*, where the lecherous Don makes his servant Leporello coax Donna Elvira in his behalf. Beethoven wrote several memorable pieces for mandolin and piano.

Guitar

The guitar, like its distant relative the lute, has a fretted fingerboard, and its strings are plucked with the fingers. Instead of a pear-shaped back the guitar's back is flat. Inward curves at the sides of the body, known as the resonance chamber, make the instrument look like a member of the viol family.

The guitar's six strings are tuned in intervals of fourths except for the one between the second and third strings, which is a third:

The fingers of the right hand are used for strumming or plucking the strings, while only four fingers of the left hand stop the tones on the fretted fingerboard, with the thumb supporting the long neck from underneath.

Although the popularity of the guitar knows no national borders, it has always been in vogue in Spain and Italy. In fact, the guitar is descended from an instrument in Spain known as the *vihuela*, which was used in aristocratic circles and has some features in common with the lute.

Quite a few composers have featured the guitar in their compositions, among them Fernando Sor of Spain, a very fine guitarist and contemporary of Beethoven. As a very young man Paganini gave up violin playing for three years in order to concentrate on the guitar. It is said that the reason for this was not so much a fascination with the instrument as a love affair with an aristocratic lady who played the guitar well and in whose country home quite a few duets resulted. The outcome of the episode was of lasting benefit to the music world. During that period, Paganini composed six lovely sonatas for violin and guitar, and an equal number of quartets for violin, viola, cello, and guitar, in addition to other miscellaneous works involving the guitar.

In our own time the superb guitarist Andrés Segovia, born in 1893 in Spain, brought about almost single-handedly a renaissance of the art of classical guitar playing on the highest level. The power of his artistry has been so great that it has inspired a number of significant scores written expressly for him by the following masters: Manuel de Falla, Joaquín Turina, and Rodolfo Halffter of Spain; Albert Roussel of France; Manuel Ponce of Mexico; Heitor Villa-Lobos of Brazil; and Mario Castelnuovo-Tedesco of Italy, among others. Listen to the Castelnuovo-Tedesco Guitar Concerto, for instance, to appreciate the beauty of this instrument's sound.

Balalaika

The balalaika may be considered the Russian counterpart of the guitar. It is of ancient Tartar origin, has a triangular shape, and usually has only three strings.

Balalaikas come in a number of sizes, ranging from the popular type, which is held in the player's lap, to an oversized one that has to be rested on the ground. The sizes generally in use are tuned to these intervals:

E   E   A

A cousin of the balalaika, also Russian in origin, is the dombrā, which is similar in appearance and is often artistically carved and embellished. There are some exciting recorded examples of the playing of both these instruments by fine Russian soloists and ensembles. The Armenian oud has a similar sound but a charm all its own.

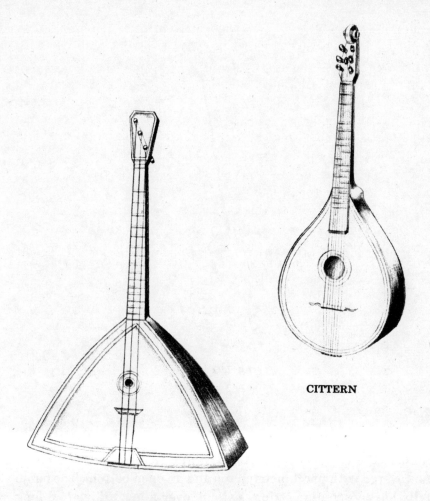

CITTERN

BALALAIKA

CITTERN

The cittern (also called cither or cithern) was a popular instrument in sixteenth- and seventeenth-century England and is referred to in the literature of that time. A cross between the lute and the guitar, the cittern could be played with either a plectrum or the fingers.

BANJO

Banjo

The banjo is a very distant member of the guitar family and is very popular in the United States. Its body, in effect, consists of a metal drum covered with parchment on top and an open bottom. The banjo usually has five to nine strings passing over a low bridge to a long neck and it is played with or without a plectrum. The tuning of the banjo's strings is as follows:

D   B   G   C   G

Said to be of African origin, the banjo was brought to the United States by black slaves, and thus found its way onto southern plantations. Subsequently minstrels as well as jazz and folk musicians used it with great effect. Today examples of good banjo playing are plentiful and quite accessible.

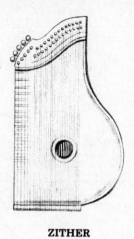

ZITHER

ZITHER

Another plucked instrument is the zither. It is very popular in the Bavarian and Austrian countryside, mountain regions, and inns. This instrument consists of an elaborately carved, often artistically ornamented wooden box strung with as many as forty-five strings. Some of these are "open" strings used for accompanying, which are stopped with the thumb of the left hand on a fretted board and plucked by the fingers of the left hand. The melody is played by the right thumb covered with a ring plectrum, while the other fingers of the right hand play the accompaniment. The zither's melodic strings are tuned as follows:

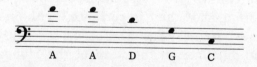

A   A   D   G   C

The zither is usually played while it rests on a table, unless your knees are big and steady enough to be of service for smaller models. If you listen to a recording of the unshortened version of the famous Strauss waltz entitled "Tales from the Vienna Woods," you can hear an enjoyable zither solo in the introductory section. A more expensive alternative is to journey to the outskirts of Vienna and sample a Heuriger, a recent vintage wine, in a Grinzing courtyard, where a zither is almost always in evidence.

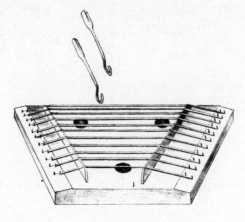

DULCIMER

Dulcimer and Cimbalom

The dulcimer dates back to medieval times and is an ancestor of today's piano. It consists of a closed box of narrow depth strung with metal wires. The instrument is known as a psaltery if its wires are plucked. It is known as a dulcimer if its wires are struck with wooden hammers. From the late fourteenth to the late seventeenth century these two kinds of instruments were quite popular. However, the rise of the early keyboard instruments, operating on the same basic principles, diminished their importance – with one noteworthy exception. The countries of Eastern Europe, especially Hungary, have retained the dulcimer in the form of the Hungarian cimbalom, which is still enthusiastically enjoyed to this day. It is the undisputed national instrument of the Hungarian people.

As with the ancient dulcimer, the cimbalom consists of metal strings fastened to pegs set in a wooden box. The player activates the strings with padded sticks or wooden hammers. To hear its distinctive sound clearly I suggest you listen to the thrilling "Intermezzo" portion of the orchestral suite extracted from the ballad opera *Háry János* by Zoltán Kodály. Interestingly, Igor Stravinsky employs the cimbalom in his *Ragtime* for Eleven Instruments.

Lyre and Hurdy-Gurdy

In the days of Greek, Hebrew, and Assyrian antiquity the word "lyre" was applied to a small harp played with a plectrum. In parts of Europe (and with different spellings), it became one of the earliest bowed instruments.

In medieval times an early stringed instrument called the hurdy-gurdy was played. Existing in a variety of shapes, it was known as *Lyra* or *Leier* in Germany, *vielle* in France, *symbal* or *symphony* in England, and *lira organizzata* in Italy. This stringed instrument had some unusual attachments. The right hand operated a handle that, in turn, moved a rosined wheel, while the left hand played some keys controlling a mechanism to stop the strings, as on a violin's fingerboard. In some parts of France, Spain, and Scandinavia you can still hear this instrument played at folk gatherings. Haydn legitimized the *lira organizzata* by writing some concertos for it to please one of his noble patrons.

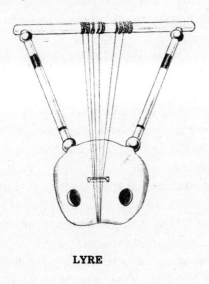

LYRE

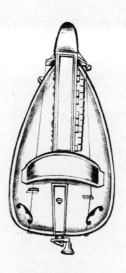

HURDY-GURDY

THE PERCUSSION FAMILY

Some members of the percussion family may well be considered the oldest of all instruments. Since the dawn of human history, rhythms beaten out on primitive surfaces or makeshift instruments have served to express sentiments and feelings. They have also been used on a wide variety of ceremonial occasions. Indeed, rhythmical patterns might have evolved so as to differentiate one occasion from another, making such events recognizable by the respective sounds of the percussive beats.

Throughout the ages man has displayed a physical reaction to percussive sound. The delight seen on a baby's face when banging away with a kitchen spoon, the snapping of fingers, the swaying of hips, the shuffling of feet, the clicking of heels, the nodding of the head to the rhythm of a percussive beat – all these manifest the physical force not only of rhythm itself but particularly of the sources that reinforce its presence, namely, percussion instruments of varied types.

The phrase percussion instruments is generally applied to objects that are activated by striking other objects or by shaking. The resulting sound can articulate and otherwise enhance not only the rhythm but also the color, tonal complexion, and dynamic impact of any vocal or instrumental music of which they are a part; certain types of percussion instruments can contribute to the melodic and harmonic components of an ensemble as well.

Percussion is generally classified either as instruments of definite, fixed pitch or of indefinite pitch. Some instruments are made of wood and metal, which produce sound by themselves, while other instruments have a stretched skin as a sound-producing agent. In more technical language, we call them idiophones (from the Greek *idios*, "self") and membranophones (from the Greek *membrana*, "skin"). Idiophones are instruments that are struck, such as the gong, triangle, bell, chime, glockenspiel, cymbal, castanet, celesta, xylophone; or shaken, such as the tambourine or rattle. Membranophones encompass all the varieties of drums.

PERCUSSION INSTRUMENTS OF DEFINITE PITCH

Let us first discuss several of the percussion instruments whose capacity of producing definite pitch puts them in the ranks of true musical instruments.

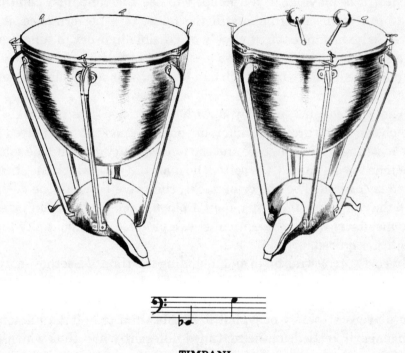

TIMPANI

TIMPANI

Of greatest importance and of most frequent use in the orchestral literature for percussion instruments are the kettledrums or timpani. In German the kettledrum is referred to as *Pauke;* in French *timbale* or *timballe.*

Timpani consist of a bowl-shaped "shell" or kettle made of metal, usually copper or some alloy, with a skin or membrane (the "head") stretched over the entire open end. The membrane or parchment is made of calfskin. Great care must be taken to select skins of unblemished quality and even thickness. Once properly stretched, the head is fastened to a wooden ring ("flesh hoop") which in turn is firmly attached to a circular iron rim. Screws with T-shaped heads, spaced evenly around the circumference, enable the timpanist to increase or lessen the tension of the skin in order to produce a number of definite musical notes, as called for in the score. This method of tuning is a painstaking task that must often be performed while the orchestra is playing. If you happen to see the timpanist bend his head low to his instruments in the midst of a performance, it is because he has to listen as closely as possible in order to tune them to a desired pitch. Some scores are better served by pedal timpani or machine drums whose pitch can be altered instantly by way of a foot pedal.

The kettledrums are played with two sticks. The materials of which the heads are made differ, depending upon the role played by the instruments in the score and the tonal quality desired. The softer the tone to be attained, the softer the material with which the stick's head is covered. The choice of sticks, the place between the center and the rim where the instrument is played, and constant tuning are the means by which the timpanist can produce just about any tone quality required.

In early orchestras up to and including the time of Beethoven, two kettledrums were called for. This number has grown to from three to five, all played by one timpanist in modern orchestras. This keeps the player extremely busy, but it enables him to enlarge his tonal range, each kettledrum being tuned differently and thus widening the tonal spectrum. A composer can specify in the score to which keys the timpani are to be tuned, thereby guiding the player in this all-important effort.

There are many examples of prominent timpani passages in orchestral works, from muffled funereal rolls to thunderous crashes. The reader's attention is called to the following:

Sibelius – Symphony No. 2, scherzo movement

Berlioz – *Symphonie Fantastique,* "March to the Scaffold" section of the fourth movement

Strauss – *Till Eulenspiegel's Merry Pranks,* arrival of the jury in the finale

Beethoven – Symphony No. 4, allegro vivace section of the first movement

The study of timpani is extremely involved, given the myriad gradations of tone, incisiveness or imperceptibility of attack, exactitude of intonation, and absolute reliability of rhythm, irrespective of pattern changes or special effects. Outstanding timpanists grace our major orchestras and conductors count upon their artistry for rhythmic support and coloristic variety.

BELLS OR CHIMES

Actual bells are too heavy for orchestral use, though Giacomo Meyerbeer (1791–1864) requested the Paris Opéra to install large, theatrical bells for the St. Bartholomew alarm in his opera *Les Huguenots*. As a practical and acceptable substitute tubular bells evolved. In French they are referred to as *cloches tubulaires* and in German they are known as *Röhrenglocken*.

Tubular bells is a set of metal tubes suspended from a wooden frame. These tubes are struck with one or two wooden mallets. The sound simulates that of church bells. Examples are found in the Symphony No. 2 by Mahler and, most prominently, in the finale of Tchaikovsky's *1812 Overture*, where they underscore the Russian victory over Napoleon's forces.

GLOCKENSPIEL

This popular instrument is known in English by its German name (in French it is called *carillon;* in Italian *campanetta*). The glockenspiel was originally meant to be a toy imitation of the Flemish church carillons, and it has retained that name in French. Today's glockenspiel is composed of twenty-seven to thirty-seven steel plates or bars of different lengths, mounted like a stepladder in two parallel rows. If resonators are used, they are of tubular shape and are placed beneath each plate. When tuned accurately, the tone quality of the

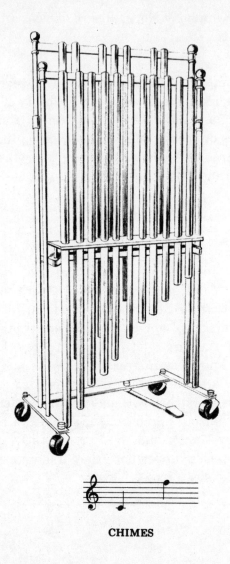

CHIMES

instrument is greatly enhanced, making it considerably more brilliant. The glockenspiel requires from two to four small-headed mallets, in performance. The plates are arranged in chromatic order in a range of about two and one half octaves.

The glockenspiel can be heard in such works as the "Dance of the Apprentices" in Wagner's *Die Meistersinger,* the "Chinese Dance" in Tchaikovsky's *Nutcracker Suite,* and in Mozart's opera *Die Zauberflöte,* among many others.

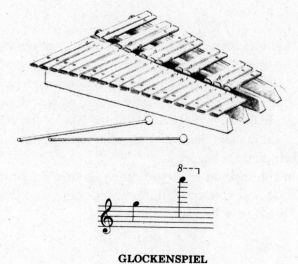

GLOCKENSPIEL

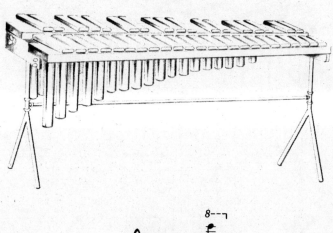

XYLOPHONE

XYLOPHONE

This remarkable instrument consists of twenty-seven bars made of hard wood arranged in two rows, somewhat like the glockenspiel. A set of resonators tuned to their respective notes and located under the bars amplifies the sound. The bars are played with light beaters that are either made of willow and shaped like a spoon or, more often, with a head made of boxwood. Good xylophonists can perform formidable technical feats.

Examples of the instrument's prominent sound are found in the tone poem *Danse Macabre* by Camille Saint-Saëns and the *Scottish Strathspey and Reel* by Percy Grainger.

MARIMBA

MARIMBA

This instrument of African and South and Central American origin is built much like the xylophone. The tone is more mellow because the wooden bars are struck with mallets whose heads have a rubber or felt surface. The underlying metal resonators (in more primitive instruments, they are made of gourd) are tuned to the respective plates or bars. Marimbas of many sizes are found in Central America, and it is Guatemala's national instrument. While in orchestras in the United States the marimba is generally played by one person, Central American marimbas can be so large that they require as many as seven players.

The instrument can be heard to best advantage in the 1940 Concertino for Marimba and Orchestra by the American composer Paul Creston and in a 1949 Concerto for Marimba and Vibraphone by the Frenchman Darius Milhaud.

PERCUSSION INSTRUMENTS OF INDEFINITE PITCH

These are the noisemakers of the orchestra, indispensable for the rhythmic and dynamic life of countless compositions. The psalmist's admonition to "make a joyful noise unto the Lord" is only a part of their numerous functions. The percussionists of the symphony orchestra exhibit the diverse artistry involved in playing a wide variety of instruments.

SIDE DRUM OR SNARE DRUM

In Italy this small drum is referred to as *tamburo militare*, in France *caisse claire* or *petit tambour*, in Germany *kleine Trommel*. The snare drum is cylindrical in shape, with two heads of parchment stretched over a metal shell. The upper head ("batter") is struck with two drumsticks. The lower head has strings of gut or silk ("snares") that are stretched tautly across the surface. The snares may be muted by placing a wooden wedge between the snares and the parchment. A lever serves to shut off the snares completely. The vibrations of the parchment against the snares produce the brilliant sound for which the snare drum is known. Many patterns of sound can be produced: the roll, which is of varying length; the flam, consisting of two notes; and the drag, which consists of a series of from two to six strokes fused into a roll and ending with an accented note.

SNARE DRUM

Snare drum playing is a difficult art. Its technique differs from other percussion instruments because it is based on double alternate strokes with each hand rather than the usual single strokes. To put it another way, the strokes are not left-right-left-right, but left-left, right-right, left-left, right-right – a rebound stroke controlled by the player, somewhat like a spiccato in violin playing. Listen to Rossini's overture to *La Gazza Ladra* for some fine snare drum effects.

TENOR DRUM

The size of this drum falls midway between the snare and the bass drum. Its shell is made of wood instead of metal and it is deeper and larger than that of the snare drum. Snares are absent in the tenor drum, so its use in the orchestra is limited. Outdoors it often forms part of the traditional "drums and fifes" military band.

Bass Drum

In Italian the bass drum is known as *cassa grande,* in French *grosse caisse* or *tonnant,* and in German *grosse Trommel.* This is the largest of the conventional drums. It varies in size from an enormous instrument built for very special effects to the smaller size encountered in concert halls. Even here the depth of sound is in direct proportion to the drum's diameter. The heads are stretched over hoops with leather braces, tags, or thumbscrews, enabling the player to tighten or loosen the heads. The bass drum is played with a heavy stick, which has a large felt-padded knob at its end. For certain special effects a birch broom (*Rute* in German) replaces the stick.

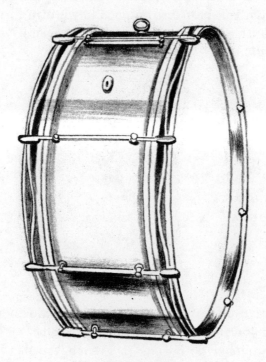

BASS DRUM

The variety of the bass drum's special effects are colorful indeed, as are the resultant moods. A pianissimo attack will sound like distant thunder or far-off artillery fire. A regular stroke will resemble the deepest thirty-two-foot pipes of a great organ. When the drum is played fortissimo, run for the hills!

It is easy to realize that quick rhythmical figures are difficult to negotiate on such a large drum. The bass drum's pitch is indefinite, resulting in a noise rather than recognizable, fixed tones; slow, irregular vibrations set in motion a very low rumble. This, in turn, triggers sympathetic vibrations, making it impossible to articulate rapid sound patterns. However, drum rolls on the instrument are entirely feasible and very effective. An example of a pianissimo bass drum roll occurs in the opening of Liszt's symphonic poem *Ce Qu'on Entend sur la Montagne,* also known as *Bergsymphonie* or *Mountain Symphony.* The sound of the instrument can be made mysterious by muffling it with a cover or by loosening the parchment.

The bass drum can be heard to good advantage in the finale of Beethoven's Ninth Symphony and in Mozart's opera *The Abduction from the Seraglio.*

TAMBOURINE

TAMBOURINE

This distinctive instrument, approximately two thousand years old, is called *tamburino* in Italian, *Schellentrommel* or *Tamburin* in German, and *tambour de Basque* in French. It looks like a small, shallow drum with one or two heads and pairs of circular metal disks or jingles hanging loosely in the wooden rim or shell. The tambourine can be played in different ways, depending upon the effect desired: striking the head with knuckles, back of hand, fist, or knee for detached sounds and simple rhythmical patterns; shaking it firmly for a roll of the jingles, often heard in Spanish and Arabic music; rubbing the thumb along the rim of the head for a tremolo effect of the jingles. You can even put the tambourine in your lap and play it like a drum, with fingers or drumsticks.

Examples of the tambourine sound can be found in various types of Spanish and Gypsy folk music. Classical music examples can be heard in the *Roman Carnival* Overture by Berlioz or the "Arabian Dance" in Tchaikovsky's *Nutcracker Suite.*

TRIANGLE

TRIANGLE

This instrument consists of a cylindrical steel bar bent into the shape of a triangle and struck with a beater made of the same metal. Simple and clear groups of notes in basic rhythms are particularly effective on this instrument. A roll on the triangle, achieved by beating quickly to and fro between its sides, can top off an orchestral crescendo to great advantage. But brief groups of notes can have an equally satisfying result when played at the beginning of a new section, such as Wagner prescribes in the overture to *Die Meister-singer.*

For additional examples, listen to the "Turkish" effect in Mozart's *The Abduction from the Seraglio;* Haydn's "Military" Symphony, No. 100; and the Piano Concerto No. 1 in E-flat by Liszt, who was taken to task by a critic for inserting something "as strange as a triangle" in a formal work.

CYMBALS

CYMBALS

In Italian they are known as *piatti* or *cinelli;* in French *cymbales,* in German *Becken.* Cymbals consist of two large brass circular plates with a convex depression, so that the contact between them is only around the edges rather than the entire surface. The cymbals are held by straps attached through a hole in the center of the saucer-shaped plates.

Sound can be produced in different ways: clashing them together edge-to-edge with a brushing movement; clashing them together in quick repetition with a rotating motion at the edges; striking a single plate with a soft kettledrum stick or a hard snare drum stick; hanging up a single plate and playing a roll on it with kettledrum sticks or a wire brush. In any of these cases the dynamics can be varied all the way from pianissimo (pp) to fortissimo (ff). The cymbals can be used alone or, as is often the case, in combination with the bass drum. Berlioz favored the latter in some of his overtures, as did Tchaikovsky in his *Marche Slave.*

GONG

GONG OR TAMTAM

This broad, round disk made of metal is hung vertically and struck in the center with a soft-headed mallet. The instrument is of oriental origin. Its effect can be solemn, terrifying, or mysterious. Puccini's

Madama Butterfly and *Turandot* feature it prominently, as does Respighi's *Church Windows*.

CASTANETS

Castanets

This instrument consists of two small hollow pieces of hardwood, called clappers, connected with a string passing over the player's thumb and first finger. When clacked together they lend a special rhythmic verve to dances, especially those of a Spanish character, such as the fandango and the bolero. Portions of Bizet's *Carmen* contain passages for the castanets.

Other Instruments

Chinese block, claves, bongo drums, vibraphone – these are just some of the many other possible instruments to which the percussionist can apply his skill. Also deserving special mention are the rattle, a wooden cogwheel that makes a rattling noise when whirled, used by Richard Strauss in his tone poem *Till Eulenspiegel's Merry*

Pranks; and the anvil, consisting of small steel bars made to simulate the sound of an iron block, eighteen of which can be heard in the Anvil Chorus of Verdi's *Il Trovatore.* The anvil is also called for in the score of Berlioz's opera *Benvenuto Cellini.*

Employing the instruments in the percussion family is the conventional means by which composers can stress, amend, reiterate, or otherwise underline and support passages demanding special attention. The art of orchestration calls upon percussion instruments as part of a palette of special tonal colors, individually or in ingenious combination with other instruments, for the enjoyment of the listener. Thus, often primitive uses of some of the varieties of percussion instruments become ennobled by the mental agility of talented orchestrators.

THE KEYBOARD FAMILY

Today many instruments constitute the Keyboard Family. They are called keyboard instruments regardless of the sound produced by depressing keys, as long as it is the keys that activate the sound mechanism. That mechanism differs widely from one instrument to the next, as we shall presently see.

Historically, until approximately 1750, the time of Bach's death, little distinction can be discerned between compositions written for harpsichord, clavichord, fortepiano, and organ. The collective designation of "clavier" appears often, denoting any of these instruments. From 1750 on, with the gradual appearance of additional keyboard-operated instruments, the family has grown ever larger.

The following is a detailed description of the most commonly known members of the Keyboard Family.

CLAVICHORD

The clavichord is the true forerunner of the modern piano. It has been in existence since the beginning of the fifteenth century. Small

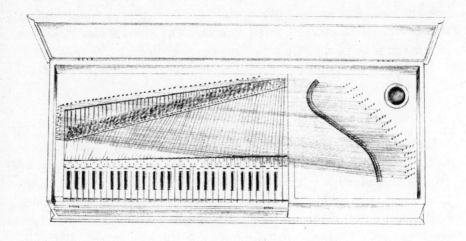

CLAVICHORD

in appearance, the clavichord consists of an oblong box with a series of strings stretched across it, parallel with its front. The keyboard player's bible, the monumental set of preludes and fugues (two sets of twenty-four each, in all major and minor keys) known as *The Well-Tempered Clavier,* by Johann Sebastian Bach, was conceived primarily on and for this diminutive instrument. An aside: "Well-tempered" means to divide an octave into twelve equal half tones so as to avoid inaccuracies of pitch between certain intervals, and to accord all intervals the same value in all tonalities. This tuning method of keyboard instruments is referred to as equal temperament. It was universally adopted in the eighteenth century, hence Bach's colossal work may be considered as a major demonstration of its true value.

This instrument's method of tone production suggests its relationship to the piano in the early stages of the latter's development. When a key on the clavichord is depressed, a tiny piece of thin brass, known as a tangent, presses against the string, which is not unlike the action of the hammer in a piano. This divides the string into two parts or lengths – one part is free to vibrate, while the other is damped by a piece of felt.

Early clavichords equipped with two tangents enabled the player to elicit two tones from one string, activated by adjacent keys, rather than by only one key. This little instrument was known as a "fretted" clavichord. The German word *gebunden* ("tied") is revealing; it indicates that strings were probably tied up at certain points of their length to produce a desired pitch.

The next stage of development saw the rise, in the early eighteenth century, of the "unfretted" clavichord (*bundfrei* in German), with one string and one tangent for each note. Its tone quality was very soft and light, almost luminescent, and was better adapted for a small, intimate room than a recital hall.

The clavichord has one all-important idiosyncracy that makes it resemble the modern piano more than the harpsichord, as we shall soon see. The clavichordist's touch can produce nuances of tone that the harpsichordist cannot achieve to the same extent. Putting pressure on the key in vibrato fashion not only achieves the slight variations of pitch associated with the vibrato but also controls minute differences in volume. When sustaining a tone for a brief while (*Bebung* in German literally means "vibration"), the clavichordist approaches the enviable ability of the string player to express himself, to emote in a modest way.

It is no wonder that the clavichord became very popular among musicians. Bach's commitment to it is common knowledge. His son Carl Philipp Emanuel Bach was highly esteemed as a clavichordist. Even Beethoven felt that the clavichord served the "control of tone and expression" best among keyboard instruments. This opinion was obviously expressed before the advent of the Hammerklavier. The word *clavier* simply means keyboard. It is restricted, in general usage, to keyboard instruments with strings attached, such as the clavichord, the harpsichord, and the piano. However, a clavier is also used in organ playing; hence we have to include all clavier-operated instruments in this discussion.

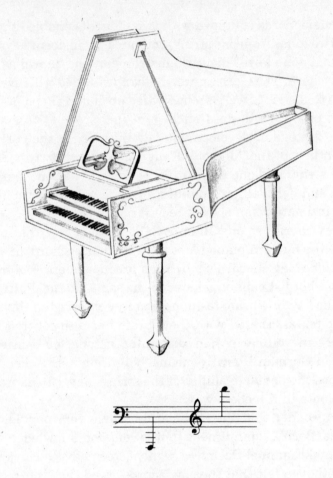

HARPSICHORD

HARPSICHORD

The harpsichord is derived from the psaltery in the manner of its tone production. It is known in French as *clavecin,* in German as *Kielflügel,* in Italian as *clavicembalo* or *cembalo,* and in English first as virginal, then as spinet, and finally as harpsichord. While in the clavichord the tangent gently hits the string, in the harpsichord the string is plucked by a quill or a leather tongue activated by the key by means of a piece of wood rising vertically from the end of the key, known as a jack. Look inside an upright piano and you will find the action to be similar, except that the mechanism culminates with the hammer striking the string rather than the quill plucking it.

The harpsichord comes in many shapes: square, upright, wing-shaped, grand, triangle. The model seen most frequently these days looks like a slender, lower, and much smaller relative of a grand piano. It can have one, two, or, in rare instances, three keyboards that are used for transposing or for contrasting tone colors. Both changes of color and special tonal effects are obtained on the more elaborate models by "stops" similar to those found on the console of an organ. Some harpsichords are equipped with a pedal board for added sonorous possibilities. Indeed, an elaborate harpsichord of Bach's or Mozart's time could easily exceed the early pianos of the day, both in range and in volume. A truly overwhelming sound could be produced by this instrument of the later seventeenth and most of the eighteenth centuries – the most advanced keyboard instrument after the organ.

As we immerse ourselves in the billowing waves of sound of the present-day concert grand piano, we should remember that some of the greatest works being played on it were first entrusted to the harpsichord. How can we imagine the keyboard masterpieces created by Bach, Handel, Scarlatti, Couperin, Rameau, or the early Haydn and Mozart without identifying them with the harpsichord? Johann Sebastian Bach owned six harpsichords made to his own specifications. Johann Christian Bach, Johann Sebastian's youngest son, played a harpsichord in recital for the first time in England in 1764. In 1802 Beethoven provided for his Sonata No. 12, Op. 26 ("Funeral March") and No. 14, Op. 27, No. 2 ("Moonlight") the caption "For Harpsichord or Pianoforte." Even if this was done on the advice of an enterprising publisher, it is still proof of the harpsichord's popularity at that time.

The entire baroque period depended upon the harpsichord not only as the dominating keyboard medium for solo and ensemble music but also as an important guide for vocal music in all its forms. Conductors would lead performances of oratorios and cantatas from their seat at the harpsichord. To this day recitatives in eighteenth-century opera are kept on pitch with the help of chords, arpeggios, and modulations played on the harpsichord.

The harpsichord is important in the realization of the "figured bass," also known as *basso continuo* ("thorough bass"). A single line of notes is provided with figures according to which the harpsichordist, or very often the organist, constructs the harmonic background for the guidance of the other participating instruments or voices. For the student of music this amounts to a language all its own, a kind of musical shorthand, and to learn to decipher it is part of any professional preparatory process.

The emergence of the piano in particular and the evolution of ensemble music in general meant the decline of the harpsichord for all its above-mentioned roles. The renaissance of this unique instrument in our time has been so complete, and its new musical challenge so real, that significant works have been and are being written by contemporary composers. Their search for the utilization of its special timbre has led them to explore new dimensions and combinations of sound.

As a result, some remarkable scores have emerged from the pens of leading twentieth-century masters, such as Jean Françaix, Darius Milhaud, Manuel de Falla, Francis Poulenc, Walter Piston, Hans Werner Henze, and Paul Ben-Haim. The American composer Elliott Carter wrote a Double Concerto for Harpsichord, Piano and Two Chamber Orchestras. Thanks to artists of the stature of Wanda Landowska, Ralph Kirkpatrick, Igor Kipnis, Gustav Leonhardt, and Robert Veyron-Lacroix, the art of the harpsichord remains vividly alive. I find it to be a great comfort to witness this linkage in the continuity of keyboard music, enabling the musician and the music lover alike to get close to its sources in the midst of ongoing revolutionary developments.

It is an equal thrill for the devotee of visual art to sample some of the magnificent embellishments, paintings, carvings, and color combinations that appear on the exterior, including cases and legs, of clavichords and harpsichords. Outstanding instrument makers of the baroque period were the Ruckers family of Antwerp and members of the Silbermann family of Germany; of more recent vintage and eminently worthy of mention are Dolmetsch of England, Pleyel and Gaveau of France, Challis of the United States, and Neupert and Sperrhake of Germany.

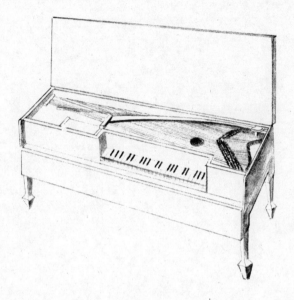

VIRGINAL

Virginal

The virginal is an early relative of the harpsichord and resembles the clavichord in shape, consisting of an oblong box that easily fits on a table. There is only one string for each note and its range is approximately four octaves. The name virginal supposedly comes from the fact that young ladies usually played this instrument. The music written for the virginal forms an indispensable link in the history of keyboard music. Leafing through the *Fitzwilliam Virginal Book*, generally available in libraries and better music stores, one can encounter some real gems by such early English masters as William Byrd, Christopher Gibbons, and Giles Farnaby.

131

SPINET

Spinet

The spinet (*épinette* in French) is differently shaped than the virginal. Its strings run diagonally from left to right of the player in a wing-shaped frame. In this way some strings can be longer and possess greater sonorities. The origin of the name spinet is unclear, but it may refer to the quills that pluck the strings, which are derived from a thorny material. Another possibility is that the name is derived from the Venetian musician and instrument maker Giovanni Spinetti.

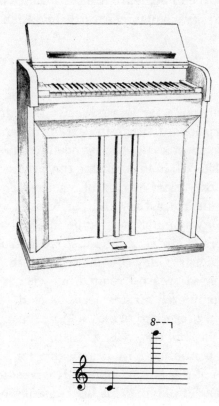

CELESTA

CELESTA

A fairly recent invention (1886), this graceful-sounding instrument resembles a tiny upright piano and its playing action approximates that of a horizontal glockenspiel. The steel bars are struck with hammers, which are activated by keys like those on a piano keyboard. Under each steel bar is a wooden resonator, and this combination produces the clear, transparent, fairylike quality for which the tone of the celesta is known. It is the only keyboard instrument guaranteed never to go out of tune! Among the works in which the celesta can be heard are the "Dance of the Sugarplum Fairy" in Tchaikovsky's *Nutcracker Suite* and Richard Strauss's *Der Rosenkavalier*.

PIANO

The early piano was a far less powerful instrument in terms of tone than the harpsichord. Much important research has been conducted in order to reconstruct the piano since its beginnings.

In 1956 I was asked to help celebrate the two hundredth anniversary of the birth of Mozart as part of a series of worldwide events involving many musical artists and performing groups. I had the ardent desire to play a pianoforte that John Challis, one of the great instrument makers of our time, had just reconstructed with all the specifications of Mozart's day. I went to see him in his New York studio and with bated breath I related my wish to him. Graciously pointing to the completed masterpiece, he said, "Please be seated and be my guest." I proceeded to play a Mozart sonata very gingerly and with a great deal of awe. He interrupted me, saying, "Wait a moment, you are pounding!" My heart sank, for I felt I was barely touching the keys of the Mozart pianoforte. Needless to say, I realized that a full year of playing this instrument would be necessary before I would dare to use it in concert. So my contribution to the Mozart celebration was conducted at the keyboard of the modern grand piano, praying that it would not be offensive stylistically, both to me personally as well as to my public.

This fragile pianoforte as Mozart knew it already constituted a pace-setting improvement over the original model. It was in 1709 (as far as can be established) that a harpsichord maker from Padua, Italy, by the name of Bartolommeo Cristofori, decided to replace the jacks and quills used in harpsichords with little hammers. Thus a new instrument was born, which Cristofori called *gravicembalo col pian e forte* (harpsichord with soft and loud). Although the change seemed rather insignificant, it turned out to be a far-reaching development. For the first time the player was able to call forth at will a gradation of tone by his own application of greater or lesser pressure to the keys.

The new name of this Cristofori invention, pianoforte or fortepiano, indicated to the world that the instrument could be played both *piano* (soft) and *forte* (loud). The forte was eventually dropped from the name. The fallacy of abbreviating pianoforte as piano is illustrated by the sarcastic musician who suggested that most pianists should be called fortists. He had a point. On the other hand, how can we possibly call a Vladimir Horowitz a pianofortist? In trying to be this faithful to the original concept, we become aware of how even this designation ignores the endless shades and nuances that lie between piano and forte, which so distinguish the art of any great pianist.

In regard to in-between shades of expression, the need for a gradation of tone must surely have been an important matter to the sensitive creators of harpsichord music. While they most probably reveled in that instrument's brilliance and volume, they may also have anticipated a more elaborate use of the nuances of touch that were available, however slightly, in the clavichord. In his early keyboard works Bach must have craved a semblance of a singing touch, a cantabile, which was unachievable on any of the instruments available to him. I am thinking, for instance, of the lament comprising the third part of his wondrously descriptive "Capriccio Written on the Departure of a Favorite Brother," composed on the occasion of his brother Johann Jakob's journey to Poland. Very few of the five generations of Bachs ever left their native Thuringia, hence this expression of anxiety by Johann Sebastian.

Cristofori's invention marked a giant step toward combining the virtues of the clavichord with those of the harpsichord. This ingenious Paduan craftsman, who spent many years of his life serving the famed Medici family in Florence, succeeded not only in implementing the idea but also in inventing the most essential mechanism of the pianoforte, at least in embryonic form, namely, a device we call escapement. As soon as a hammer strikes a string, the hammer must fall back to its starting position so that the string is free to vibrate and its sound can be heard. Cristofori also provided dampers that would touch the string as soon as the key was released, thereby terminating vibrations and sound. His principle of construction still prevails to this day. The earlier of two original Cristofori creations, built in 1720, is housed in New York's Metropolitan Museum of Art. It represents one of the great landmarks in the history of music.

Having the same basic outer shape, this early pianoforte evolved into what we now refer to as a grand piano. Two other early shapes became known as the square or table piano and the upright piano. In a square piano the strings are fastened horizontally, as with the clavichord. In the upright piano they are strung vertically. Quite a few additional shapes of the piano have come and gone over the years, but from the beginning the grand piano exhibited marked advantages over the others. The dampers fall naturally on the strings, and the soundboard is in the most advantageous position – horizontal and at a distance from the closest surrounding solid substance, namely, the floor, so as not to interfere with reflecting vibrations. The soundboard is of the utmost importance, for it reflects the sound and amplifies it much as the belly of the violin does. Subsequent stages of development of the piano have prompted innumerable experiments to overcome the inherent inflexibility of the soundboard.

The use of seasoned wood, a rare commodity in this age of mass production, is of special significance in the construction of the soundboard. Even the distribution of string vibrations in properly regulated volumes of sound depends upon this material. It is this substance that converts the energy of the action created by the fingers of the player into the sound that the listener perceives. Here is the nerve center that ultimately makes possible nuances of touch, volume, duration of tone, and intention of expression. Unfortunately, modern piano manufacturers often admit to the use of green wood that has not been allowed to season. Even substitutes, such as plastics and light metals, have been used with questionable results.

Sound travels best along the grain of the wood and at great speed, about fifteen thousand feet per second (many times the speed at which sound travels in air). Only carefully selected wood, skillfully prepared and sufficiently seasoned, ought to be used for piano construction. Erect-growing trees, such as pine, silver fir, and spruce gathered from the dense part of a forest where there is little sunlight, have been used most successfully. Ideally the wood is processed from these sources into narrow planks, of which about twenty to twenty-five are carefully matched to form the soundboard.

Another important element with regard to material is the bridge, which is responsible for transmitting the string vibrations to the

soundboard. Maple or Swiss pine is used, which is sturdy enough to bear the enormous pressure exerted upon the soundboard.

Starting with Cristofori's pianoforte, the length of the keyboard and the number of strings have increased. It staggers the imagination to conjecture how today's full complement of eighty-eight keys or seven and one quarter octaves (some grand pianos have as many as eight octaves) might have affected the creative output of the great masters centuries ago. The fact that with each generation another octave was added serves to show that composers of the previous group must have longed for additional space on the keyboard. One of Cristofori's two surviving originals has four octaves; the other has four and one half octaves. Mozart's grand piano, as can be seen in Salzburg's Mozarteum museum, has a compass of five octaves. Over the next fifty years or so the length of the keyboard grew to six and one half octaves. When you examine the compositions of the masters of successive periods, you will find that even the composers of the romantic age, such as Chopin and Schumann, were amply served by this range. However, this same size keyboard cannot, at times, contain the flights of fantasy, the breadth of conception, and the logic of thought that are inherent in the monumental thirty-two sonatas by Beethoven. Some suggest Beethoven's wish to expand a passage beyond the available keyboard limits. It is easy to imagine his delight if he had at his disposal the freedom of today's span of eighty-eight or more keys.

Keys, as a means of conveying whatever physical energy is needed to produce sound, have been in use for about six hundred years. They have been made of various materials: ivory, bone, porcelain, even mother of pearl. Some pictures show artistic carvings on the front of the keys; sometimes they are even adorned with precious metals. Today various kinds of wood are used that can withstand the varying climatic conditions in different locations around the globe. Plastic substances that have been used for reasons of economic expediency do not seem to "feel" right under the fingers, at least not those of this pianist.

The material of which the strings are made also plays a role in determining tone quality; the density of the metal used has to withstand the enormous tension exerted upon it when activated. To ease the pressure the later harpsichords and the early pianofortes were

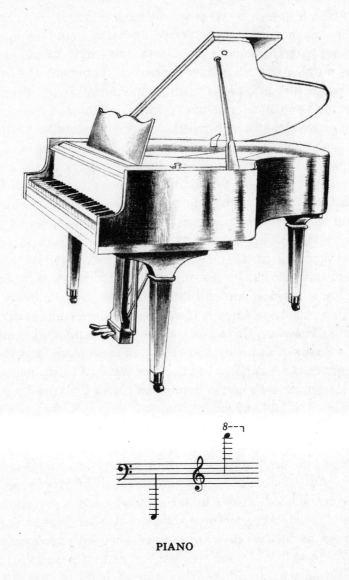

PIANO

provided with two strings for each note and hammer. Today's instrument has one string for each low tone, two for each of a group of high tones, and three for the majority of tones, from about an octave below middle C on upward. The lower strings are spun with copper coiling to aid sonority. The length of the string helps determine the

pitch of tone, along with such factors as thickness, tension, and quality of metal.

In terms of the tension of the strings, exerted individually and collectively upon the soundboard, it stands to reason that the frame of the instrument was increasingly in need of strengthening. From the middle of the nineteenth century on, the wooden frame was replaced by an iron frame, the casting of which is one of the most important operations of modern piano manufacture.

Hammers are made of soft wood covered with wool felt. It takes special skill to build felt hammers properly and then to "voice" them with highly specialized tools when worn.

The modern piano has at least two pedals. Some uprights and all grand pianos have three pedals. The most frequently used of these – and, in fact, generally overused – is the one on the right, known as the sustaining pedal. To call it the "loud pedal" is a gross misnomer. Its function is to remove all dampers simultaneously from all the strings. As a result, you can take your finger off a key and the sound continues. More importantly, all strings are now free to produce sympathetic vibrations, bringing into play all the overtones in the fashion explained on pages 30–31. When handled properly, both volume and sonority can be increased most effectively. This pedal should not become a mere footrest. The result is an intolerable blurring of sounds that makes musical intentions unintelligible. It takes a good deal of study to learn to either change the pedal with changing harmonies or manipulate it to merge certain common components of changing harmonies. At times a technique known as half pedaling is needed to accommodate a prolongation of lower tones.

On the grand piano the left, or piano, pedal moves the keyboard and hammers sideways into a position where only two instead of three strings are struck. On the upright piano the soft pedal moves the hammers closer to the keys. In either case the result is a softer tone. This does not imply, however, that all that is needed to soften the tone is the use of the soft pedal. Depending upon the overall effect desired for a given composition, the pianist may be better advised to perfect his finger and key control so that a gradually softer tone can be achieved without the help of the soft pedal.

The middle, or sostenuto, pedal of the grand piano has a very special function. With the help of a special mechanism it sustains only certain notes and chords played immediately before it is depressed; all other tones are discontinued as the dampers return to their rest position on the strings, thus terminating their vibrations. It takes a good deal of know-how as to *when, why,* and *how* to utilize this pedal. Effects of sustained common tones for the sake of harmonic continuity can be quite remarkable, such as befits the performance of some impressionist music in particular. Careful and judicious practice is of the essence.

The piano is the sum total of many components and many governing factors – all of which have been subject to, and continue to undergo, constant changes and improvements. The history of the piano parallels the development of public concerts as an institution and the growth of auditoriums and concert halls. Since the piano had to serve ever larger audiences, it had to become increasingly more powerful in terms of its sound-producing capacity. Not only greater volume but also greater subtleties were expected of it which Cristofori could not possibly have foreseen. Composers during subsequent centuries took up the challenge of exploring and expanding its resources; and performing artists demanded the kind of equipment that would favor their virtuosic prowess. A case in point is the double escapement action that facilitates a pianist's ability to play repeated notes at great speed and with undiminished articulation. Before falling all the way back after striking the string, this mechanism allows the hammer to come to rest in an intermediate position from which it can be returned to the string more quickly and repeatedly.

Today the concert grand piano stands at the zenith of its power. If used wisely, it can serve as a vehicle of great strength as well as of limitless interpretive resources for the transmission of the richest and most multifaceted repertoire of any single instrument or combination of instruments. More than any other instrument, it is completely self-contained, a confidant of composers in the expression of some of their noblest thoughts and emotions, and an endless challenge for the musical resourcefulness and interpretive abilities of the practicing musician, provided that he is equipped physically and intellectually to master its capabilities.

The piano in general, especially in its smaller forms, has been the mainstay of pleasurable music making, both professional and amateur, the kind that the Germans so aptly call *Hausmusik.* This word conjures up some of the great joys of music, both during solitary hours as well as in the company of kindred souls (e.g., the incomparable piano duets written by the masters for the sheer love of entertainment). If only the television set did not usurp the time that ought to be devoted to such rewarding activities. For the music student the piano is invaluable. Not only is there a wealth of good teaching material available, but the piano (more than any other instrument) offers facilities for the study of keyboard harmony, a study that is indispensable for the understanding of compositional structure.

Among the great makers of the pianoforte and its descendants over the years, the following names should be mentioned. Gottfried Silbermann (1683–1753), a contemporary of Bach in Germany, was famous for his stature as clavichord maker and organ builder. When Bach performed at the Potsdam court of Frederick the Great in 1747, he played a Silbermann pianoforte. The very music-minded king had already added three Silbermann instruments to his household inventory.

By 1800 the name of John Broadwood in England was one of the most prominent in the field. The manufacture of pianos in England became a flourishing enterprise. Sébastien Érard became equally famous, establishing his own firm in Paris and London. In Germany Bechstein, Schiedmayer, Steinway, Ibach, and Blüthner all started to build their justly renowned products during the first half of the nineteenth century.

The oldest American firm for piano making was founded by Jonas Chickering of Mason Village, New Hampshire. First known as Stewart & Chickering, its fame spread rapidly. In 1848 it changed its name to Chickering & Sons. Steinway & Sons had its origin not in America but in the Harz Mountains of northern Germany. There a young boy named Heinrich Steinweg (1797–1871) turned out to be the only survivor of a forester family of sixteen children. Despite the ravages of war and tragic deaths within his family, young Heinrich pursued his bent for instrument making, in due time seeking his fortune in the New World. He settled in New York and subsequently changed his name to Henry Steinway. His children and their descendants have continued a tradition of building the finest pianos.

In addition to Steinway & Sons, the Baldwin Piano Company of Cincinnati, Ohio, and Mason & Hamlin Company of Rochester, New York, are among today's leaders. Bösendorfer of Vienna has always been a pianist's piano and has been making significant inroads in England as well as in the United States. The firms of Chappell & Company, and Broadwood & Sons in England, and Pleyel and Gaveau in France continue to have the confidence of the piano-loving public. Yamaha of Japan, with a large production and the latest methods of construction in its favor, has also received worldwide attention.

ORGAN

If the criterion of a keyboard instrument is the fact that the tone production is set in motion by a set of keys, the organ also fits this description. But this is just about the only justification for its inclusion in this category. It is surely more precise to describe the organ as possessing certain characteristics of other instrumental families, as we shall presently see.

The organ's forerunners predate the Christian era. The first likeness appears to be the hydraulos, or water organ, created by Ktesibios of Alexandria, Egypt, who lived in the third century B.C. Aristotle described it as a wind instrument whose airflow was regulated by a mechanism operated by water pressure. Its sound must have been formidable, for it was used in open-air arenas, presumably for secular occasions.

Both ancient Roman and Greek accounts suggest that the pneumatic organ was in use since the early second century A.D. The wind supply was furnished by simple bellows rather than by means of water pressure. The earlier crude pipes were often replaced with ornamented pipes of silver and other metals.

There is ample evidence that organs of primitive construction existed in the early Middle Ages. The playing mechanism consisted of pipes being sounded by simple slides that were pulled out or pushed in to open or close them. In time these slides were hinged to a key mechanism that enabled the player to strike the keys or levers with his fists, as had been customary in the playing of carillons.

In the tenth century a powerful English instrument was erected at Winchester Cathedral. It was so large that it required two players to perform on two keyboards of twenty keys each, activating twenty-six bellows operating four hundred pipes. As yet there were no ranks of pipes that could furnish a harmonic background for a melody. All the volume of this organ poured forth in unison plainsong for congregational guidance.

Up to the fifteenth century most instruments were provided with only one set of pipes. Additional pipes, arranged in ranks, were added gradually as increasing demands for church use necessitated larger organs. In the fourteenth century the concept of the wind-chest (see p. 144) provided a reservoir of air for all the pipes mounted upon it. Multiple keyboards that were less unwieldy in size made it easier for the organist to vary tonal colors, which were limited at first to a simple gradation of volume and timbre.

It was also during the fourteenth century that the positive organ was conceived. This was a separate, completely self-contained instrument, small enough to be moved around in order to serve a small group of singers stationed in different locations throughout the church. Some of these organs were placed in or near the chancel to serve the clergy in the use of plainsongs. The organist positioned them within easy reach of his bench at the main organ, thus permitting him to obtain softer effects than the large instrument could produce. The German name *Rückpositiv* indicated that the small organ was placed behind the player's back and connected to a separate keyboard of the main organ.

In addition, a portative organ evolved that enabled a person to walk while playing it, depressing the keys with one hand and manipulating the bellows with the other. This instrument was secured around the player's neck during processions. A smaller instrument was the regal organ, the forerunner of the harmonium, a fixture in the nineteenth-century parlor.

From the sixteenth century on, national schools of organ building evolved and advanced at a steady pace in northern Germany, the Netherlands, France, and Scandinavia. Meanwhile, England suffered a serious setback due to the destruction of existing instruments because of Puritan attitudes toward the use of music in church services.

Organs in America date back to the turn of the seventeenth century. The Swedish Gloria Dei Church in Philadelphia is said to have installed an organ as early as 1694. King's Chapel in Boston followed suit in 1714; Christ Church in Philadelphia did so in 1728; and Trinity Church in Newport, Rhode Island, in 1733. These instruments were imported from England. Early eighteenth-century German colonists in and around Pennsylvania imported small organs from their native land. In 1737 John Clemm constructed the first American instrument for Trinity Church in New York; it had three manuals and twenty-six stops.

Subsequently two schools of organ building emerged in New York and Boston. Among the prominent North American organ designers of the nineteenth century were Hilborne Roosevelt in New York, George Hutchings in Boston, and the Casavant brothers in Montreal. These were followed by John T. Austin, Ernest M. Skinner, and the English-born Robert Hope-Jones, the father of the "theater organ" of the early 1900s.

A basic description of the organ, including its major components and their function, is in order here. A series of pipes of various sizes are placed on a box known as a wind-chest. This chest is provided with valves linked to a keyboard, or a number of keyboards, played with the organist's hands and feet. The keyboard upon which the feet play is referred to as the pedal board. The connecting valves are operated by air delivered to the wind-chest by means of electrically operated bellows.

The organ's pipes are arranged in several rows or ranks. Each rank is composed of pipes of the same tonal color or character, known as registers. Stops are the mechanical devices by which such ranks or registers can be activated. Depending upon the construction of the console, the case that encloses the keyboards and stops, these devices can be in the form of knobs to be pulled or tabs to be pressed down.

Some of the stops that add to the dimensions of sound of the organ include: mutation, mixture, diapason, bourdon, vox humana, vox angelica, reed (marked trombones, trumpets, etc.), flute, and string-toned (marked cello, viola, etc.). In the latter cases the tone qualities of these instruments are emulated on the organ. For a detailed explanation of the functions of these and other stops, I suggest that you refer to a general encyclopedia such as Westrup and Harrison's *The New College Encyclopedia of Music* (see Bibliography).

Under each rank of pipes there is a slider, a thin strip of wood or plastic with holes inserted at regular intervals. When a stop is drawn the slider moves into a position where each hole fits under the opening of each pipe, readying it to sound when the keys of the keyboard are depressed. The pushing back of the stop moves the slider's holes away from the pipes' "mouths" or openings, and shuts off the sound. Leaving the stop open and pulling additional stops enlarges and mixes the tonal colors of different ranks of pipes by means of the system of sliders.

Most organs have at least two keyboards, each for a separate division of five or six ranks, and a pedal board operating from two to five ranks. Some organs are much larger, with four or five manuals and a pedal board serving anywhere from fifty to one hundred ranks of pipes. There are instruments so large that the sound can easily drown out even Mahler's, Bruckner's, or Richard Strauss's grandiose orchestral effects. Think of the awesome power that the organist of the Chicago Stadium has under his fingers and feet when he pushes the button marked "full organ." That organ has six manuals, operating close to one thousand ranks of pipes.

The divisions of an organ are generally named great, choir, swell, solo, echo, and pedal organ. The great organ has the loudest and most basic stops. The choir organ activates softer sounding pipes and is used primarily for the accompaniment of voices.

The swell organ takes its name from a box fronted with shutters that can be opened and closed gradually by means of a special foot pedal. When properly controlled, this creates crescendo and diminuendo effects. The swell organ shares qualities of both the great and choir organs.

The solo organ employs stops whose tonal colors are particularly suited for solo purposes with the accompaniment of another division,

ORGAN

such as the choir organ. The sound of these pipes comes close to that of certain orchestral instruments, such as the oboe, trumpet, flute, and viola da gamba.

The echo organ contains ranks of pipes of a more delicate nature. These pipes are often located in a part of the church edifice far removed from the main organ so as to create an echo atmosphere.

The pedal organ is to the main organ what the bass strings are to the orchestra, furnishing a foundation for the general sound spectrum. The pipes of the pedal organ are larger than the corresponding pipes of other divisions; hence their pitch is generally one octave lower. Other low-pitched pipes can be added by pulling appropriate stops.

Most organs have a separate keyboard for each of the divisions described above. At the discretion of the organist, they can be played singly (e.g., the great organ for a postlude or the choir organ to accompany a choir), or in combination (e.g., the right hand playing a solo effect on the solo organ while the left hand accompanies on the swell or echo organ).

To facilitate such combinations organs are provided with couplers. These are mechanical devices that make it possible to play the pipes of one division on the keyboard of another, adding them to the pipes of the keyboard presently being used. For example, the coupler marked "swell to great" enables the organist to use the ranks of pipes of the swell organ on the manual of the great organ, so that the tonal resources of both divisions can be used simultaneously.

A special skill needed for playing the organ is the use and combination of organ registers, known by the general term registration. Much like a talented painter uses various colors of his palette singly or in combination to obtain a proper mix, a masterful organist chooses his tonal color combinations by grouping pipes of different divisions. This calls for deft manipulation in terms of pulling the right stops quickly at the right time. Thumb buttons located within easy reach under the keys, and toe studs pressed by nimble feet just above the pedal board, provide the controls needed for fast changes of registration. These devices are collectively known as pistons.

Having examined the keyboards of the organ, let us now examine briefly the nature of the instrument's various pipes. They are of two basic classes, flue and reed pipes. Flue pipes are like tin whistles in their manner of tone production. They consist of tubes of wood or metal in which air is set into motion and produces sound through the mouth, a rectangular opening in the body of the pipe. The length of the pipe and the speed of the vibration produce the pitch of sound associated with the pipe. Reed pipes are named after tongues of metal that vibrate against the opening of a brass tube at the bottom of the pipe.

The normal length of a pipe that sounds its pitch as written is eight feet. Those pipes of half or quarter that length sound one and two octaves higher, respectively. Similarly, some pipes are two or four times as long – sixteen and thirty-two feet – and render sound one and two octaves lower than written.

It is not without justification that the organ is often called the king of instruments, for it embodies within its vast and complicated playing mechanism the total power, as well as many individual qualities, of a symphony orchestra. Yet it lacks many of the personal touches with which a pianist can execute his or her art. A swell box cannot compensate for a crescendo or diminuendo carefully controlled by the gradually applied pressure of the pianist's hands and fingers. However, the challenges for the able organist are every bit as great, and his ability to coordinate the myriad sources of tone and volume must be even more demanding.

Many of the great masters wrote for and performed some of their finest works on the organ, including the Italian Girolamo Frescobaldi, the Englishman John Bull, the Dutchman Jan Pieterszoon Sweelinck, the Dane Dietrich Buxtehude, the Germans Georg Philipp Telemann and Georg Friedrich Handel, and the Frenchmen François Couperin and Louis Nicolas Clérambault. The baroque era abounds with some of the noblest organ works of all time, especially the compositions of Johann Sebastian Bach. Among his outstanding creations are chorale preludes, toccatas, fugues, and sonatas.

Each subsequent generation of composers confided its thoughts to the organ, which was generally less limited in tonal capacity than other instruments. The freedom of the romantic age found unbridled expression in the organ creations of the French, Belgian, and German schools, notably César Franck, Camille Saint-Saëns, Alexandre Guilmant, Charles Widor, Max Reger, Louis Vierne, and many others. The concert literature of the organ, including solo pieces, concertos, symphonies, and chamber music, offers great challenges to the organist above and beyond the duties germane to his ecclesiastical post.

A Final Note

The story of the musical instruments unfolds as one of the most colorful phenomena in the history of civilization, a history that it helped create and that it mirrors eloquently. These tools of the art of music making, from their most primitive beginnings to their present-day counterparts in the modern symphony orchestra, have proved to be an extension of human thought and artistic endeavor. Therein lies their everlasting charm and potential as sources of human achievement.

CHAPTER FOUR

THE ORCHESTRA AND ITS EVOLUTION

OF ALL THE musical riches with which our lives are blessed, the orchestra affords us the most varied source of genuine listening pleasure. Countless communities look upon their local orchestra, whether small or large, as their most treasured cultural possession. Many of the larger orchestral ensembles maintain fairly extensive travel schedules that bring them to towns and cities without a regular orchestra of their own.

In addition, the great orchestras of the world can now reach remote areas and even the most modest homes due to a profusion of recorded performances, as well as through radio and television broadcasts. An enormous musical repertoire is available for anyone who cares to listen. Works in this repertoire run the gamut, from early orchestral literature for chamber orchestra to grand creations written for the classical orchestra by major symphonists, from the giant Wagnerian and Straussian orchestral masterpieces to the avant-garde complexities of modern times.

Without a doubt, the orchestra has become the most important vehicle for the transmission of musical thought. In fact, the orchestra may well be considered the musical conscience of a town. Within it dwell the forces for the execution of chamber music. The musicians within the orchestra's ranks enrich their community immeasurably by ensuring that new generations of would-be musicians, or simply music lovers, are given the kind of superior instruction that only an actively engaged, practicing musician can impart. In Europe orchestras usually enjoy either direct or indirect government or municipal support. In the United States – where there are today close to one thousand orchestras of all sizes and of varying importance – it is more a matter of civic consciousness and pride for the people to rally to the cause by supporting their orchestras, thereby getting personally involved in individual as well as group efforts in behalf of music.

Both in a musical and sociological sense, the orchestra today occupies a central position in our cultural life. A look at the evolution of the orchestra not only provides us with invaluable insight into the development of music but also affords us a capsule history of the patronage of the arts.

EARLY HISTORY

The term orchestra is of Greek derivation and connotes "a place for dancing." In the ancient Greek theater a semicircle was reserved for both the dancers and instrumentalists, and the chorus also stood between the audience and the stage. Later the name was identified with a similar position of the instrumental ensemble in the early opera house. Even in biblical times groups of instrumentalists performed on both religious and secular occasions. These groups were composed of players of various instruments, depending upon their availability at any given time rather than according to any musical logic. In the Scriptures combinations of harp, flute, trumpet or cornet, psaltery, sackbut, and various stringed instruments are mentioned. How they sounded is difficult to conjecture.

During the Middle Ages such motley instrumental groups were used to accompany, or at least add diversity to, worship services. The history of the Cathedral of Notre Dame in Paris included instrumental participation during the late twelfth and early thirteenth centuries, under the leadership of two of the earliest known composers, Leoninus (Léonin) and Perotinus (Pérotin). It seems reasonable to assume that instrumental functions were limited to keeping the singers on pitch; but I can imagine that it might have been difficult at times to know who tried to keep whom in tune.

From the mid-thirteenth century on, instrumental ensembles of a pre-orchestral nature began to assume considerable prominence. These groups were known as "town musicians" or "waits" in England. Their duties were manifold: patrolling the city streets at night, alerting the populace to extinguish lamps and fires before retiring in the evening (a famous musical watchman appears in Wagner's *Die Meistersinger*), performing during ceremonial occasions and dances. It was an honor for a young musician to be admitted to the "guild of waytes," a prerequisite of which was the ability to play a number of instruments.

In Germany the guilds of town musicians were very highly respected. Foremost among their professional activities was *abblasen*, which consisted of marking the hours with musical signals or performing entire chorales on the hour. This took place from the galleries of church steeples or town hall towers, or at the top of staircases leading up to official edifices; hence the linguistic concept of playing down from a high place, or *herab-blasen*. Noted composers wrote for such groups, and the occasions often resembled a regular performance, especially during holidays, when townspeople and visitors alike were proud and inspired by such offerings from on high.

THE BAROQUE ORCHESTRA

The early baroque period of the sixteenth century saw a marked development of musical groups, from small brass and woodwind ensembles to increasingly larger groups of musicians. For instance, the glory of sixteenth-century Venice was emphasized and enriched by such great masters as Andrea Gabrieli and his nephew Giovanni Gabrieli, both of whom created unique music for Saint Mark's Cathedral by utilizing the rare acoustical properties of that multidomed edifice. Their works were performed polyphonically by groups of musicians moving solemnly across Saint Mark's Square, later being joined by their colleagues inside the cathedral, a practice that still occurs today. The resounding echoes are as splendid and awe-inspiring as they surely are taxing to coordinate.

Not all the compositions of the Gabrielis were intended solely for use in the cathedral. With the advent of stringed instruments of the viol family, composers began to write for larger, more diversified musical groups, as well as for occasions of a more general character. For example, such enlarged instrumental groups served the cause of opera in its infancy. They also performed appropriate music between the component parts of the mass for the edification and the delight of worshipers.

From the mid-seventeenth century on we find the string orchestra to be the staple musical group. Such an orchestra, however, produced a sound far different than that which our sophisticated ears expect to hear. For instance, gut strings were used exclusively and tuning was more haphazard than it is today. In addition, the bridge as well as the bow of the stringed instruments were constructed differently. Composers did not yet score their works to exploit the full range of string capabilities. Bowing and fingering techniques were not nearly as developed and demanding as modern string players find them to be. During the mid-1600s wind instruments were even less developed, and in certain cases nonexistent.

The achievement of this age becomes all the more impressive when we consider the brilliant creations the great baroque composers produced in the light of the sparse forces both qualitatively and quantitatively at their disposal. They were able to transport themselves into regions of sound far ahead of their time. Johann Sebastian Bach's bold and ingenious instrumental and orchestral creations – as exemplified by his four suites for orchestra and the six Brandenburg concertos, so called because they were written for a Brandenburg prince – show the unbelievable breadth and depth of his inventive power given the instrumental forces available to him. He and composers before him, such as Vivaldi, Corelli, and Torelli, knew how to satisfy their quest for richer and more varied sound by adding other instruments to the usual string complement, which resulted in the development of the concerto grosso (see pp. 213–14).

Some royal and princely courts of the time employed and encouraged string and wind ensembles of various sizes. Larger works, using multiple instruments, permitted more ambitious effects, such as musical dialogues between groups of instruments, interspersed between the full orchestral sound. The individual use of the constituent instruments and the gradual growth of each instrument's technical and tonal capabilities naturally contributed to the growth of the orchestra.

Although the baroque orchestra was still significantly dependent upon the basso continuo, or figured bass for harmonic support, its gradual decline was in direct proportion to the growing self-sufficiency of the instrumental families within the orchestra. Other reasons also help explain why the basso continuo was found to be increasingly unsatisfactory. Frequent outdoor performances, as was the custom of the time, pointed up the tonal inadequacy of the keyboard instrument – usually the harpsichord – to supply an audible harmonic structure. Thus, composers gradually allotted a more expressive, harmonically binding role to wind and stringed instruments. These instruments now furnished all the "inner voices" that had previously been supplied by the chordal structure played on the harpsichord, with only cello or bassoon lending extra support to the bass line.

Before long, series of concerts were organized – performed not only at court, where they remained the privilege of the aristocracy, but also in places accessible to the increasingly music-hungry and knowledgeable general populace. New facilities were built to replace the taverns, the military drill rooms, and other places that had previously been used for musical performances. Obviously, the groups that performed there varied in size and instrumentation according to the availability of town musicians or the willingness of town authorities to satisfy the musical director's or leader's demands. For performances of compositions with a more ambitious score, extra players were added for each occasion. In many instances young and inexperienced students were called upon to assist. The smaller the remuneration offered them, the more questionable the quality of their musical contribution, a fact that must have added many a gray hair under the serene wig of the harassed composer.

It boggles the imagination to realize how great creations of the period, such as Bach's sublime Mass in B Minor, could have been rehearsed and performed by groups of inadequate size, in musical disarray, and often of amateurish ability. We know, for instance, that many of Bach's works were first performed by amateurs whose ensemble training consisted of the "blood, sweat, and tears" exerted by the harried composer during insufficient rehearsals. Fortunately for posterity, the vision and the imagination of the great composers overcame the tremendous obstacles imposed on them. Thanks to composers such as Bach and Handel, the orchestras, such as they were, flourished and multiplied.

In Germany the Collegium Musicum enjoyed great popularity among both amateur and professional aspirants. Many of its members were recruited from German universities. The Collegium Musicum of Leipzig was particularly noteworthy, for it later became the famed Gewandhaus organization. One of its co-founders was Bach's distinguished contemporary Johann Friedrich Fasch (1688–1758).

In a more general sense, the Musik Gesellschaft (Music Society) became a regular institution in many German cities and towns. Its realm of activity and performance was restricted only by the musical and technical limitations of its members.

The Music Society's counterpart in Italian towns was known as Accademia. Ostensibly created to answer the musical needs of local musicians, the Accademia also became the center for the town's general artistic efforts.

Another source of musical performances was the conservatorios, which were dedicated to training illegitimate children and orphans for a future in music. The conservatorio was often part of a foundling hospital. The most famous such institution was the Conservatorio dell' Ospedale della Pietà in Venice. For almost forty years the great composer Antonio Vivaldi created hundreds of compositions for the foundling girls under his tutelage while he was music master of the conservatorio. The most varied and inventive combinations of instruments and voices, for which Vivaldi's works were conceived, bear witness to the fertile mind of one of the greatest masters of the baroque. His choice of composition was contingent upon the availability of instruments and voices at any given time. Can you imagine how these young girls must have sounded trying to perform Vivaldi's *Concerti for Diverse Instruments* requiring two mandolins, two flutes, strings, organ, and harpsichord?

It was a common practice of the period for noble households or communal institutions to maintain a small nucleus of instrumentalists for regular services, to which extra instruments could be added for special occasions. The impetus for expansion depended either upon the provision of extra funds by wealthy patrons or upon the determination and perseverance of the musician in charge – in most instances upon both.

REPRESENTATIVE ORCHESTRAS –
SEVENTEENTH AND EIGHTEENTH CENTURIES

To illustrate the orchestra of the late Renaissance and early baroque, I would single out the group assembled in 1607 by the Italian composer Claudio Monteverdi (1567–1643) to perform his *favola per musica* ("fable for music") *L'Orfeo*. It was the first "opera" ever to be produced, utilizing two harpsichords, two double-bass viols, ten viols, one harp, two violins, two bass lutes, two organs (with wooden pipes), three bass viols, four trombones, one regal, two cornets, one small recorder, one high trumpet, three "soft" trumpets, and kettledrums. Obviously none of these instruments should be judged by their present-day counterparts. Except for parts of the overture, all the instruments were not called upon in the score to perform at the same time. This implies that quite a few players could double on two or even three instruments. The cost for the thirty-seven instruments was paid by the Duke of Mantua, in whose employ Monteverdi wrote this pace-setting work.

During the mid-seventeenth century the orchestra at the Court of Versailles – which Jean Baptiste Lully (1632–87) assembled under the title Les Vingt-quatre Violons du Roi ("The Twenty-four Violins of the King") – was exemplary. The designation proved to be misleading, for woodwinds were soon added. By 1700 Louis XIV was listening to and paying for a standard orchestra of about thirty-six players. Lully soon organized his own ensemble.

Some fifty years later, during Louis XV's reign, the illustrious French composer Jean Philippe Rameau (1683–1764) became the first truly orchestral composer in the sense that he presided over a well-defined orchestra of approximately forty-six players. Thus, he did not have to be concerned with fitting his music to whatever instruments happened to be available at the time since he had the instruments with which to serve his musical fancy. Incidentally, Rameau is also credited with the early occasional use of the forerunner of the clarinet, the chalumeau, in the ranks of the orchestra.

Turning our attention to Johann Sebastian Bach's orchestral requirements in Germany, it is difficult to find a representative orchestra, for the genius of Bach miraculously succeeded in suiting every musical need even within the same composition. Here are two examples of orchestras assembled during the year 1723. A cantata composed on the occasion of the election of the Leipzig City Council called for four trumpets, two timpani, two flutes, three oboes, two oboes da caccia ("hunting oboes"), first and second violins, violas, and figured bass played and executed by cellos and an organ. The number of strings was optional, depending upon availability. The famous Magnificat in D Major, on the other hand, required first and second violins, violas, cellos, double basses, two flutes, two oboes, two oboes d'amore, three trumpets, drums, and a keyboard instrument (harpsichord or organ). This orchestra resembled the burgeoning standard orchestra of the eighteenth century (see p. 162).

Georg Friedrich Handel's (1685–1759) orchestra – active during the same period as that of Bach – already reached the respectable size of thirty-four regulars. The strings formed the basic group, with winds and brasses added for special sonorities or coloristic effects, depending upon the opera or oratorio involved. The score of the *Messiah* calls for trumpets in various choruses, which create some memorable effects. In his oratorio *Saul* Handel employed timpani, trumpets, and trombones or sackbuts to paint tonal scenes of biblical events. The orchestra was also divided into sections or choirs for greater dramatic effect. These are just a few examples to illustrate the "instruments-as-needed" custom for occasions not entirely of an orchestral nature. Only twenty-five years after Handel's death England's Handel festivals would employ an orchestra consisting of 152 strings, 59 woodwinds, 30 brass instruments, organ, and drums, with a choir of over 250 voices performing "For unto Us a Child Is Born."

THE CLASSICAL ORCHESTRA

On the previous pages we witnessed the growth of the orchestra from a small group of players, occasionally enlarged in number for functional purposes, to an ensemble of increasingly professional members with standard numbers of instruments and musical duties. The late 1700s were marked by significant developments, as various musical centers in Europe gained prominence.

For instance, Salzburg emerged with a fairly large orchestra assembled by the ambitious Archbishop Colloredo. Up to sixteen violins and multiple oboes, flutes, horns, and bassoons enabled Mozart to develop more elaborate orchestral ideas, although his relationship with the philistine clergyman was short-lived. Among the fruits yielded up by the brief, hapless association of Mozart and the Archbishop of Salzburg – and the finest of such entr'acte efforts – are the sonatas for organ and small instrumental ensemble, often referred to as church or epistle sonatas, performed between parts of the service of worship.

An equally remarkable orchestra was available at the Court of Vienna and at Milan's famed La Scala opera house founded in 1778. The latter boasted a nucleus of thirty-six strings. Each category of wind instruments had two representative members. Depending upon the requirements of certain scores, some orchestras would muster as many as five or six oboes.

The orchestra of Mannheim, a city on the Rhine in southwestern Germany, emerged as the first of true virtuosic quality. In fact, its achievements were so great that it spawned an entire school of orchestral playing, known to this day as the Mannheim school.

The story of how Mannheim attained this stature is rather typical of this stage in the development of the history of patronage. Historically it had been the custom until the mid-eighteenth century for the emperors of the Holy Roman Empire to be chosen by princes from various regions, known as electors. In the 1740s Mannheim happened to be the residence of a remarkable prince, Karl Theodor, the Elector Palatine. He was not only an extraordinary music lover but also provided funds to induce some of the finest musicians to come to Mannheim in order to form a first-rate orchestra. It was he who put Mannheim on the musical map.

Karl Theodor obtained the services of the Bohemian Johann Stamitz (1717–57) as leader and composer-in-residence. His reputation enabled him to assemble some of the finest instrumentalists from various parts of Europe, specifically from Italy, Germany, Austria, and his native Bohemia. Some of them were also notable composers. Together they developed by precept and example a technique and precision of orchestral playing previously unknown.

The Mannheim orchestra was credited with evolving such interpretative innovations as completely disciplined collective crescendos and diminuendos, which, even today, can only be achieved with the utmost collaboration and single-mindedness of every member of the orchestra. Other Mannheim hallmarks that presaged the highest degree of orchestral professionalism were an absolutely unanimous attack, a sustained pianissimo, and a style of interpretation that illumined every possible nuance of the score. We can appreciate the magnitude of these achievements by realizing that up to that time composers had only provided a bare minimum of markings (or none at all) in their scores to reveal their intentions and expectations. Obviously this entailed an ability on the part of the player to read between the lines and demanded the kind of training that orchestral players had hitherto rarely enjoyed.

The standards of the musicians assembled in Mannheim must have been of such high quality that the group's fame as the first virtuoso orchestra spread far and wide. Not only were visitors to the city impressed by their concerts but Mannheim's musicians, traveling to other posts, spread word of the uniqueness of their musical involvement. The disciples of Johann Stamitz, led by his sons Karl and Anton, and his successor, the violinist Christian Cannabich, carried on his tradition. Some of the world-famous conductors of our own age who furthered their conducting careers in this Rhenish city are Artur Bodanzky, Wilhelm Furtwängler, and Erich Kleiber – an indication of the Mannheim orchestra's continuing stature.

As for the structure of the Mannheim orchestra, since most of its members had distinguished themselves as string players, the body of the group was string-oriented. The number of strings fluctuated, finally stabilizing at twenty-five. Woodwinds and brasses were added as needed. During the year 1747 there were thirty-six players, among them eleven wind and brass musicians. Such a group could undertake performances of most of the repertoire extant at the time.

In their quest for the best possible renditions, the Mannheim artists were concerned with such problems as faulty intonation of the stringed instruments, which to this day requires constant vigilance. I remember Pablo Casals, the renowned cellist, telling me on more than one occasion how he remembered tuning to be practically nonexistent in the orchestra during the early part of his solo career, and how painful he found performing a concerto with orchestra because of this.

The brass family was used sparingly, depending upon the acoustical exigencies of the halls. For example, trumpets were called upon primarily for brilliant climaxes, while trombones could be employed only in large rooms, particularly in churches. Limitations often resulted because of the inaccurate construction of instruments, many of which were still at an early stage of evolution.

Another ensemble that attained considerable fame at this time was the Gewandhaus orchestra of Leipzig, Germany, named after the hall of the clothiers' guild in which it performed toward the end of the eighteenth century. It consisted of twelve violins (six first and six second violins), three violas, two cellos, and two double basses. The nineteen players performed in a hall that could hold about eight hundred people, with rows of seats facing each other across a center aisle. This must have made it considerably easier for concertgoers to admire each other's new clothes while catching a strain of the music here and there. There seems to be no other precedent for the accommodation of an audience of this size, other than the customary church seating arrangement.

In terms of precedents, although in a different vein, the publishing house of Breitkopf & Härtel of Leipzig, founded in 1719, was the first to issue catalogues of musical scores and parts initially for the convenience of the Leipzig orchestra, eventually supplying them to other orchestras and conductors to keep them abreast of new materials.

From the latter part of the eighteenth century on, it is very rewarding to witness the expansion of orchestras to accommodate the growth of the symphony, from the standpoint of design, thematic development, and harmonic structure. More and more ambitious compositional concepts led, quite naturally, to the need for more musicians and a greater variety of instruments. The popularity of outdoor concerts led to such typical "open-air" works as serenades, divertimentos, partitas, and suites, which called for greater numbers of woodwinds in order to create a more satisfying aural balance. Emancipation from the figured bass challenged composers to construct scores allowing various choirs of instruments to meet their harmonic needs without the use of the hitherto omnipotent device of the basso continuo.

Meanwhile, some instruments had to overcome certain inadequacies in order to fully participate in these new opportunities. Trumpets, for instance, had to await valve mechanisms to allow them greater tonal versatility. Horns, which were now called upon for harmony-filling roles, had to be provided with additional tubing, crooks, and a greater facility to manually alter the pitch within the bell of the instrument.

While no single composer can be credited with any particular stage of an ongoing evolution, there is one master who brought about significant changes by virtue of an exceptionally large output of original compositions made possible through the generosity of an enthusiastic family of patrons, the Esterházys. The composer was Franz Joseph Haydn (1732–1809), who was in the service of the Esterházy family in the small town of Eisenstadt, near Vienna, for nearly thirty years. The court orchestra over which he first presided included a flute, two oboes, two bassoons, two horns, and timpani, in addition to a very small contingent of strings. However, Haydn seemed to have little difficulty in convincing his wealthy and music-minded employers to add instruments when necessary. Extra players were recruited from the local church or from the *Stadtpfeifer,* the town musicians. Later on free-lance musicians were readily available. In addition, virtuoso instrumentalists were attracted to Haydn's sound and stable musical establishment.

About eighty of Haydn's 104 symphonies were composed while he was in the employ of the Esterházy family, and the form of the symphony evolved by virtue of Haydn's prolificacy. His fruitful efforts and experience also brought about the standardization of an orchestra that served as the classical model for some time to come: one or two flutes, two oboes, two bassoons, two horns, timpani, six first violins, six second violins, three violas, two cellos, and two double basses. The double basses echoed one octave lower the parts played by the cellos, thus creating a formidable underpinning of sonorous bass parts. Early Haydn symphonies call for a harpsichord to perform the duties of the figured bass, with Haydn himself presiding over the orchestra from his seat at the instrument. In his later symphonies trumpets in pairs were added, particularly in the symphonies written for Paris and London performances (Nos. 82–87, most of the intervening Nos. 88–92, and then Nos. 93–104).

There are hardly any clarinets in the general lineup of this model orchestra. However, Haydn's Symphony No. 99 does call for two clarinets (the clarinet appears in only 6 of Haydn's 104 symphonies). Mozart did not utilize the clarinet as an important instrument to provide tonal color until he visited Mannheim in 1778 while en route to Paris. Haydn, in turn, became more interested in the clarinet when he began to see Mozart more often after the latter's departure from Salzburg. How inspiring it is to credit forty-six-year-old Haydn with the open-mindedness that allowed him to profit from the genius of twenty-two-year-old Mozart!

I should like to reiterate here the great debt that the history of instruments owes to some of the virtuosi-performers, in whose hands certain instruments gained elevated stature. The clarinet is a good case in point. It was the artistry of Mozart's friend Anton Stadler that made Mozart fall in love with the clarinet, its tonal color and capabilities, musical phenomena first encountered in Mannheim's acclaimed orchestra.

As for Mozart's use of the orchestra, he added little to the dimensions established by Haydn, except for certain effects in his opera orchestra. His most remarkable innovation is not the number of instruments he employed or the instrumental structure of the orchestra, but rather the ingenious and infinite variety of its use. The woodwinds, in particular, are given roles of rapturous melodic beauty, both individually and in choirs, which no one had ever conceived before. While this is true in his later symphonies and concertos, it is strikingly evident in the partnership that Mozart created between the orchestra and the stage action in his operas. Here the orchestra is no longer used merely to produce beautiful sound, but is now engaged in tonal characterization of the dramatic behavior of the singers onstage.

This is not to belittle the sheer dramatic magic that Mozart is able to evoke from the orchestra in such works as the Symphony in G Minor, No. 40, or the "Jupiter" Symphony, No. 41; the Piano Concerto in C Minor, K. 491, No. 24, or the Sinfonia Concertante in E-flat for Violin, Viola and Orchestra, K. 364. Mozart and Haydn set the stage for the great symphonists of the future to shape the orchestra into a multiple instrument of such impact that no nuance of the instrumental palette and no dramatic detail of the composer's fancy were outside the power of orchestral execution. However, conductors must bear in mind that the acoustical proportions of the rooms used in the eighteenth century were more modest than some of the out-size halls of today. Since it would probably be financially disastrous for our modern orchestras to try to play a Haydn or Mozart symphony in a hall seating from two to three hundred people, modern acoustics do allow for a Haydn or Mozart-size orchestra of about nineteen strings and nine wind, brass, and percussion instruments to recreate at least a semblance of the sound for which these masters strove.

THE ORCHESTRA OF BEETHOVEN'S TIME

Crossing the threshold into the romantic age, we find that Ludwig van Beethoven inherited an orchestra completely self-sufficient and free of the figured bass. He had at his disposal an orchestral balance to serve any desired tonal need: a five-voiced string choir, with first violins serving as sopranos, second violins as mezzo-sopranos, violas as altos, cellos as tenors and baritones, double basses as basses; a pair each of flutes, oboes, clarinets, bassoons, trumpets, and horns; and kettledrums (timpani). This was sufficient for Beethoven's first four symphonies, although he did call for a third horn in his Symphony No. 3, "Eroica".

In Beethoven's Fifth Symphony, the best known of all symphonies, he added a piccolo, a contrabassoon, and three trombones. The fact that Beethoven reserved these newcomers for the symphony's triumphant final movement deserves special attention. He seemed quite content to bend the traditional forces to do his dramatic bidding in the first three movements. But in the finale the regular group could no longer contain the power of his jubilation. So he called on the piccolo and contrabassoon to reinforce the extreme ranges of pitch, while the trombones provided their own special power.

Incidentally, this was the first time that the trombones took their place within the orchestral family on the concert stage. Beethoven knew that he could not depend only upon horns and trumpets to play all the notes required by the harmonic structure. The trombones could fill the gaps, since their slides could produce the missing tones.

In the "Pastoral" Symphony, No. 6, Beethoven again used extra instruments, but this time he only selected the piccolo and two trombones to help work up the famous thunderstorm in the fourth movement. In his seventh and eighth symphonies Beethoven used only traditional instrumental forces, albeit for new tonal schemes. The Ninth Symphony thrusts us into hitherto unexplored orchestral regions. Not only did Beethoven re-employ the piccolo, contrabassoon, and three trombones; he also introduced the triangle, cymbals, bass drum, and timpani. These extra instruments are not used throughout but rather for special effects.

Beethoven's Ninth Symphony should be placed in a proper historical perspective so that we may fully appreciate its greatness. This symphony was completed during the winter of 1823–24, and only thirty-five years separate it from Mozart's three last symphonies, including the G Minor and the "Jupiter." Haydn's last symphonic opus, No. 104, was written only twenty-eight years before Beethoven's Ninth. Listen to them side by side and you will be awed by what happened in such a brief span of time.

To be sure, Beethoven's last symphony took years to germinate. His notebooks, now available in facsimile, show sketches for the Ninth as early as 1815; we know that he began actual work two years later. This proves that for approximately eight years Beethoven was occupied with the work, notwithstanding the fact that he also wrote other compositions during this time. In sharp contrast, Mozart created his last three symphonies within an unbelievably short period of six weeks during the summer of 1788. Suffice it to say that the development period of the Ninth Symphony would seem to indicate that something extraordinary was in the making.

Indeed, Beethoven's Ninth Symphony became a landmark of unique proportions, and its use of the orchestra remains unsurpassed. From the foreboding opening tremolo in the strings, growing inexorably into a mighty and defiant unison threat proclaimed by the entire orchestra, the first movement is fraught with agitation, relieved only by a gentle episode shared by flute and clarinet. Never before had an orchestra been called upon to hurl such dramatic thunderbolts. The fleet-footed scherzo follows with an uncanny theatrical sense, punctuated by a persistent dotted rhythm pattern of timpani, and interspersed with a sunny trio section shared by winds and strings. The ensuing slow movement, marked *Adagio molto e cantabile* ("very slow and songlike"), transports us into a world of pure and ethereal serenity, with an orchestration pointing the way to a thematic expansiveness that has become a model for generations of composers. A piercing dissonance blared forth by the entire orchestra shocks us back into reality. Now Beethoven presents us with brief options for the finale, as he has the orchestra recall for us a thematic germ of each of the preceding movements. None quite seems to suffice anymore as Beethoven prepares us for the nobility of his setting of Schiller's "Ode to Joy," one of man's immortal creations. The orchestra now shares the stage with four solo voices and a four-part choir, confronting us with enough innovations to affect our psyche for a long time to come. Together these forces afford us a glimpse of Beethoven's vision of a better world.

It is by no means solely the extra instruments – piccolo, contrabassoon, trombones, triangle, cymbals, bass drum, timpani – that create the symphony's new dimensions. After all, Mozart used trombones in his opera *Don Giovanni* and again in *Die Zauberflöte*. Rather, it is Beethoven's innovative use of orchestral forces as a means to shape and give expression to his dramatic needs which proved so powerful that he is now credited with ushering in the modern orchestra and its limitless tonal spectrum. His principles of orchestral use still prevail today, notwithstanding further amplification and utilization of basic orchestral techniques.

Beethoven's orchestral innovations were not born exclusively of his genius as a visionary and brilliantly inventive force. They are illuminated by extramusical facts which occurred only because of Beethoven's mighty presence at that point in time. First of all, Beethoven was not beholden to any employer since he never had one. Hence, he could write for the kind of orchestral forces that his titanic spirit dictated, unfettered by the budgetary considerations that constantly beset his predecessors. If he needed extra players, he did not have to go to a prince to ask, "May I have them?" If necessary, he paid for them himself, hoping to recover any losses from the proceeds of his concerts or the sale of his music. If the need arose, he could coerce one of his supporters to supply extra musicians; they fully recognized his stature. Also, unless his music was performed as written, Beethoven would threaten to cancel the concert – and his devoted friends knew that the loss would be theirs. It was the irresistible force of Beethoven's stature as an artist and as a man that was not to be bargained with, which, in the end, got him what he asked for. Thus, the orchestral group as he first inherited it was enlarged.

Beethoven's symphonies and concertos were considerably larger in scale, longer in duration, and stronger in sheer dramatic power than those of his predecessors. In addition, there was increasing thematic and dynamic involvement of the orchestra, specifically in Beethoven's last three piano concertos, his Violin Concerto, and his Concerto for Violin, Cello, and Piano. The orchestra no longer accompanied and echoed the solo themes in tutti passages. Beethoven's concerto orchestra became a democratic symphonic partner of the solo instrument, projecting an interdependence that is evident in later romantic concertos.

There was also the necessity for more massive sound occasioned by larger halls. A performance of Beethoven's Ninth Symphony would have been a deafening experience for the listener in the Esterházy chapel in Eisenstadt, although Vienna's Kärthnertor Theater, where the Ninth was premiered in 1824, was not much larger by today's standards. Beethoven's constant search for a more massive sound became evident as he moved from one hall to another in Vienna, in accordance with the requirements of the scores to be performed. It was the orchestral tail chasing the acoustical dog, and each became larger in the process.

One should also understand that Beethoven's creations put far greater demands on the playing ability of every member of the orchestra, both in terms of individual dexterity as well as physical endurance. A twofold problem appeared, as instruments were pushed to their limits to achieve the master's often unorthodox requirements of volume. Here I am referring to intonation, or the ability to play exactly on pitch, as contrasted with tonal balance and proportion. The former is the responsibility of the individual player, while the latter is primarily the task of the conductor.

Again, let us bear in mind that instruments were not what they are today; hence intonation was very often an insurmountable problem. In certain instances it was only the composer's ingenuity that made things a bit more bearable. An example is Beethoven's use of trombones. In the case of his Piano Concerto No. 3, it is reputed that

Beethoven transposed the entire concerto from C Minor to C-sharp Minor because the piano he had to use was so badly out of tune that the orchestra could not tune accordingly.

SOME NINETEENTH- AND TWENTIETH-CENTURY MILESTONES

The considerations mentioned above show that the story of the orchestra is conditioned by many interconnected factors. We have seen that there has never been a clearly defined number of instruments required to structure an orchestra. Especially after Beethoven the balance between stringed and wind instruments appears to have been neglected. The so-called classical orchestra had from twelve to sixteen violins, about ten lower-pitched stringed instruments – violas, cellos, and double basses – and woodwinds, horns, and trumpets in pairs. Beethoven demanded more strings, but winds more or less remained the same in number.

Most composers, from Berlioz and Wagner on, have had thirty-two violins – sixteen first violins and sixteen second violins – in order to ensure a well-balanced tone and proper volume. Very little, if anything, was done to add winds proportionately, individual demands for a third bassoon, an English horn, a contrabassoon, a bass clarinet, or one or two extra basses notwithstanding. While this generally accepted balance of sound serves quite adequately most of the nineteenth- and even the early twentieth-century repertoire – provided that the conductor is judiciously attuned to it and knows how to balance his forces – it is a matter of musical common sense to reduce the strings to approximate eighteenth-century conditions when performing Haydn, Mozart, their contemporaries, or even early Beethoven. Thirty-two strings would simply negate their conception of thematic and harmonic balance.

The transition from the orchestra as Beethoven knew it to one of larger dimensions in the late romantic and postromantic eras was accompanied by the emergence of new instruments, which lent extra tonal colors to the orchestral spectrum.

First, let's consider the harp. While it was used in early Italian opera, in an occasional Handel work, and in Gluck's *Orfeo ed Eur-idice,* neither Bach, Haydn, nor Mozart included it in their orchestral writing. Mozart, however, did feature the harp in a double concerto for flute and harp. Beethoven's only orchestral use of the harp occurs in his rarely performed ballet score *The Creatures of Prometheus.* Later composers of the romantic age used the harp only sparingly, except for Berlioz, Liszt, and Wagner. Wagner used as many as six harps in *Das Rheingold* and in the famous "Magic Fire Music" from *Die Walküre.* The harp served the impressionist composers exceedingly well, blending with and complementing the vague coloristic scheme of their intoxicating fantasy. Today's standard orchestra for large-scale postclassical works has two harps in its ranks.

Wagner added to his orchestra what is referred to as Wagner tubas. These are really more akin to horns, and the name "tuba" is misleading. "Tubes" would be a truer translation of Wagner tubas, in case you should hear them in the subterranean orchestra pit of Wagner's Bayreuth Festival Theater in Germany. There the orchestra magnifies every nuance and detail of the often highly complex stage action, just as Wagner had envisioned it within the framework of his *Gesamtkunstwerk,* his all-encompassing "total art" concept. Gabrieli had created remarkable multiple sound effects at St. Mark's in Venice three hundred years earlier.

It was no longer unusual in the nineteenth century to find orchestras performing highly specialized sound effects. For instance, in the "Dies Irae" section of his Requiem, Berlioz impresses upon us the awe of the Last Judgment by placing four groups of heavy brass instruments in a different corner of the hall, answering one another above the orchestra, with the timpani rolls heralding the frightful final day. The first performance of this mammoth work took place in Paris in 1837 at the church that three years later became Napoleon's tomb, namely, Les Invalides. In addition to the brass extras, there were 110 musicians in the orchestra and 400 voices competed or collaborated, depending upon where in the huge edifice you found yourself.

The proliferation of percussion instruments opened up many new possibilities for tonal color within the orchestra. Here, too, Berlioz broke new ground by creating very descriptive effects in his *Symphonie Fantastique.*

Equally stimulating, from the standpoint of tonal coloration, is the challenge of nationalist music (see pp. 323–30). As will be demonstrated, additional instruments indigenous to certain countries played an important role in achieving distinctive picturesque effects. Although the nationalist masters of the nineteenth and twentieth centuries did not make any new inroads regarding the size of the orchestra, they did produce scores of a highly specialized flavor utilizing an unconventional palette.

In order to make the reader aware of subsequent phases of the orchestra's evolution, I would like to single out some milestones of the repertoire that show both the utilization of instruments and the flexibility inherent in orchestral growth. In doing so, I do not wish to create the impression that beauty and artistic values are in direct proportion to an increase in the number of instruments. Quite the contrary, some of the finest musical creations of the last 150 years were designed for smaller, or at least traditional, orchestras. Even the great master Johannes Brahms was perfectly happy with the instrumental forces bequeathed to him by Beethoven when writing his symphonies and concertos.

The following list presents some major works, in chronological order, with comparative orchestration.

1830–31
Berlioz *Symphonie Fantastique:*

> 2 Flutes (1 interchangeable with Piccolo),
> 2 Oboes (1 interchangeable with English Horn),
> 2 Clarinets (B-flat and E-flat), 4 Bassoons,
> 4 Horns, 2 Trumpets, 2 Cornets, 3 Trombones,
> 2 Tubas, 4 Timpani, Small and Large Drums,
> Cymbals, Glockenspiel in C and G, 2 Harps,
> 30 Violins, 10 Violas, 11 Cellos, 9 Basses.

1884–90
Bruckner *Symphony No. 8:*

> 3 Flutes, 3 Oboes, 3 Clarinets,
> 3 Bassoons (1 interchangeable with Contrabassoon),
> 8 Horns, 3 Trumpets, 3 Trombones, Tuba,
> 3 Timpani, Cymbals, Triangle, 3 Harps,
> 60 Strings as above.

1890–94

Mahler   *Symphony No. 2:*

4 Flutes (2 interchangeable with 2 Piccolos),
4 Oboes (2 interchangeable with 2 English Horns),
5 Clarinets (2 in E-flat, 3 in B-flat, 1 interchangeable
with Bass Clarinet),
4 Bassoons (2 interchangeable with Contrabassoons),
10 Horns (6 onstage, 4 offstage),
6 Trumpets, 4 Trombones, Tuba, 6 Timpani,
Several Side Drums, Bass Drums, Cymbals,
2 Tambourines, Triangle, Głockenspiel,
3 Tubular Bells, Switch of Birch Twigs,
2 Harps, Organ, 60 Strings as above, 2 Solo Voices,
Large 4-Voiced Choir.

1903

R. Strauss   *Sinfonia Domestica:*

Piccolo, 3 Flutes, 2 Oboes, Oboe d'Amore,
English Horn, 4 Clarinets, Bass Clarinet,
4 Bassoons, Contrabassoon, 4 Saxophones,
8 Horns, 4 Trumpets, 3 Trombones, Tuba,
3 Timpani, Bass Drum, Cymbals, Triangle,
Tambourine, Glockenspiel, 2 Harps,
60 Strings as above.

1906

Mahler   *Symphony No. 8:*

Piccolo, 4 Flutes, 4 Oboes, English Horn,
5 Clarinets, Bass Clarinet, 4 Bassoons,
Contrabassoon, 8 Horns, 4 Trumpets, 4 Trombones,
Tuba, 9 Timpani, Bass Drum, Cymbals, Triangle,
Tam-tam, Glockenspiel, 2 Sets of Tubular Bells,
2 Harps, Celesta, Piano, Harmonium, Organ,
Mandoline, 60 Strings as above.
Offstage: 4 Trumpets, 3 Trombones, 6 Solo Voices,
2 large 4-Voiced Choirs, Children's Choir.

1907–12

Ravel *Daphnis and Chloé, Suite No. 1:*

Piccolo, 2 Flutes, Alto Flute, 2 Oboes,
English Horn, 2 Clarinets, Bass Clarinet,
3 Bassoons, Contrabassoon, 4 Horns, 4 Trumpets,
3 Trombones, Tuba, 3 Timpani, Side Drums,
Bass Drum, Cymbals, Tenor Drum, Triangle,
Tam-tam, Castanets, Glockenspiel, 2 Harps, Celesta,
60 Strings as above.

1912–13

Stravinsky *Le Sacre du Printemps:*

Piccolo, 3 Flutes, Alto Flute, 4 Oboes,
English Horn (Oboe interchangeable with a
second English Horn), 4 Clarinets,
2 Bass Clarinets, 4 Bassoons, 2 Contrabassoons,
8 Horns, Cornet, 4 Trumpets, 3 Trombones,
2 Tubas, 15 Timpani, Bass Drum, Cymbals,
Tambourine, Tenor Drum, 60 Strings as above.

1924

Respighi *The Fountains of Rome:*

Piccolo, 2 Flutes, 2 Oboes, English Horn,
2 Clarinets, Bass Clarinet, 2 Bassoons,
Contrabassoon, 4 Horns, 3 Trumpets,
3 Trombones, Tuba, 3 Timpani, Glockenspiel,
Harp, Celesta, Piano, Organ, 6 Shepherd Horns,
Record Player, 60 Strings as above.

This sampling of some outstanding scores shows how far we have
come since the time, just about 150 years ago, when Beethoven star-
tled the music world with the then extravagant orchestration of his
Ninth Symphony. Aside from the amassing of large forces of conventional instruments of the string, wind, and brass families, the expansion of the percussion section stands out prominently. After Richard
Strauss's wind-and-thunder machines in his *Alpine Symphony,* and
Respighi's use of a recording of the song of the nightingale in his
Pines of Rome, it seemed that musical instruments could do only so

much and no more. It was left to the twentieth-century phenomenon of electronic music to amplify traditional sound, combine electronic music with the sound emanating from traditional instruments, or present entirely new concepts of multiple sound.

It is quite clear that composers can perform miraculous feats of fantasy by using any or all of the orchestral tonal colors produced by the aggregate of old and modern musical instruments. They can invent new instruments, as Adolphe Sax did. They can revolutionize the tonal system, as Schoenberg and his disciples proved. They can revitalize the color scheme and the rhythmic structure of music, as Debussy, Ravel, Stravinsky, and Bartók did. Nevertheless, their orchestras remained basically the same in each instance, founded on orchestral concepts and ideas that had evolved during almost three centuries.

It is fascinating to conjecture what the future of the orchestra as we know it holds in store. Given adequate budgetary resources for further development, and given the grace, insight, and humility of musicians and audiences alike to recognize that true values are predicated neither on volume or quantity, nor on the achievements of any particular age, orchestral sound and dimensions will continue to evolve. Stagnancy has no place in its future.

CHAPTER FIVE

INTERPRETATION OR THE ART OF CONVEYING MUSIC'S MEANING

THE MOST IMPORTANT phase of musical enjoyment and intelligibility, second only to the act of creation itself, is the art of recreating the music and of conveying its meaning to the listener. A composer can spend untold hours committing to paper myriad notes of all descriptions that may add up to one of the all-time masterpieces of music. Such manuscripts may be doomed to join the thousands of pages that gather dust, waiting to be discovered someday, unless they are brought to life by knowledgeable minds, hands, or voices.

Through the inanimate symbols of his score the composer conveys his intentions, whether they follow a certain program or are strictly musical expressions of the moment. But it takes the interpretive artist to realize these intentions, first for himself and then, after painstaking study and contemplative consideration, for the listener. This is where music, theater, and dance – known collectively as the performing arts – differ completely from painting, sculpture, architecture, poetry, and literature. In the case of the latter subjects the encounter is direct: You can touch the canvas or sculpture; you can behold the work of architecture; and you can read the language of the book. You may wish for an interpreter, but at least you are familiar with the raw materials involved.

Not so with the performing arts. The playwright, the choreographer, and the composer can speak to you only through the interpreter. The latter becomes the vital link between the supplier and the consumer, the creator and the listener, reader, or viewer. Without the interpreter the creation remains mute.

Obviously this places a heavy responsibility on the shoulders of the performer. If the person has sufficient stature, his or her role is awesome and needs to be defined carefully. In the case of music, the first and foremost duty of the performer is to the creator, the composer. This demands a thorough knowledge of, and a complete identification with, the work the interpreter wishes to perform. It is by no means enough to learn the notes well and to possess the technical skills to be able to play, sing, or conduct them with ease. Being able to do so may be no more than craftsmanship. There are many who fall within that rubric, but craftsmanship and artistry are miles, often poles, apart.

The art of performance presupposes that any given composition be carefully thought out as to content and meaning; that it be studied in order to properly choose a technical approach to best serve that meaning; that the work be digested, rethought, and put aside at this point and be allowed to season and ferment like a good vintage wine. During this time one would be well advised to pursue an in-depth study of the composer as man and musician, the circumstances of his daily life, his surroundings, his motivation in writing the composition, his idiosyncracies of style, and the resources and capacities of the instrument(s) employed. After these conditions have been fulfilled, the artist may be assured of the likelihood of a satisfying performance.

While this procedure may consume far more time than many performers are willing to invest, truncating it would be tantamount to showing disrespect for the music and displaying a lack of sincerity to oneself, not to speak of the danger of shortchanging both the composer and the listener. Even an extraordinary facility to learn and grasp musical concepts, or a photographic memory that assures accuracy and instant recall, cannot replace an assiduous and healthy learning process. It is simply not honest to "learn" a piece of music today and perform it in a concert tomorrow.

INTERPRETIVE GUIDELINES OF COMPOSERS

How can the printed page of music assist the interpreter in so arduous a task? This depends upon the composer's communicativeness and the customs or modes of communication of his time. Guidelines and symbols of interpretation are practically nonexistent in the manuscripts of Bach and his contemporaries. Bach composed for his own performance purposes and for those of his close associates and members of his family. Hence, any musical directions were undoubtedly verbal, or perhaps the master himself may have been consulted.

It was not customary during Bach's time to provide on the printed page explicit indications for performance practice. Keyboard instruments, the mainstay for most vocal and instrumental execution, could not produce elaborate crescendos or diminuendos. The harpsichord could not respond to increasing or decreasing pressure of the fingers, and the organ did not have the capability to produce such gradual effects. This explains why seventeenth- or eighteenth-century manuscripts contain only an occasional forte or piano marking and practically no other markings of dynamics or even of phrasing. Much was simply left to the interpreter.

Even today there are marked differences of opinion among practicing musicians and teachers as to how to play or sing eighteenth-century ornaments and embellishments of notes, groups of notes, and phrases. In fact, an elaborate system of signs generally found above the notes has evolved, and equally intricate interpretations of these signs and symbols have been printed in various tongues, representing a musical language all its own. Accordingly, in the early eighteenth century great musicians of Italy, France, Germany, and other countries made known to the world their respective "translations" of this complicated sign language and its meaning to facilitate the recreation of masterworks. Most well-stocked music libraries can probably show you some of the leading volumes on the subject; for instance, Karl Philipp Emanuel Bach's *Versuch über die wahre Art das Klavier zu spielen,* François Couperin's *L'Art de toucher le Clavecin,* Giuseppe Tartini's *Traité des Agréments de la Musique* (originally known in Italian as *Trattato delle Appoggiature sia Ascendenti che Discendenti per il Violino*), all of which are available in English translation.

An interesting overview of the evolution of the sign language of musical interpretation can be gained by glancing at notations by representative composers of the last three centuries.

Haydn:	p *(piano),* f *(forte),* ff *(fortissimo)*
(1732–1809)	p – *crescendo il f* (soft, getting louder to *forte*)
Beethoven:	*mf e dolce* (moderately loud and gentle)
(1770–1827)	*sfp* (accented, then soft)
	sempre staccato e p (always detached and soft)
	crescendo – f – più f – ff (getting louder, loud, still louder, very loud)
	poco ritardando (getting a little slower)
	allegretto vivace e sempre scherzando (quite fast and always playful)
Schumann:	*markiert und kräftig* (marked and strong)
(1810–56)	*langsam – sehr zart* (slow, very gentle)
	so schnell als möglich (as fast as possible)
	ausdrucksvoll und sehr gehalten (expressive and very controlled)
Poulenc:	*ff mais sans dureté* (very loud but not coarse)
(1899–1963)	*décidé et en dehors* (decisive and to the fore)
	très doux et triste (very gentle and sad)
	strident et sans expression (strident and without expression)

EVALUATING DIFFERENT INTERPRETATIONS

It becomes readily apparent that composers increasingly provided directions, ranging from the general to the detailed, for the performance of their works. In addition, there are many scores that have been, and are being, edited, annotated, and extensively commented upon by musicians and scholars other than the composers themselves. Obviously this is most often the case with the works of early composers whose dearth of directive symbols invites the kind of printed interpretation and commentary synonymous with the process of editing. Thus, a skilled, erudite editor who may supply an elaboration on the composer's wishes and ideas will aid the interpreter in elucidating the true meaning of the "unadorned" notes of the score.

The word "aid" should be stressed here. While an edition based upon informed and scholarly research of a given master's work and style can be invaluable in deepening the interpreter's understanding, it can also reflect the subjective tastes of the editor, a fact the performer should not accept without questioning its validity. I have always found it advantageous to consult as many different editions of a masterwork as possible in order to determine those features I find to be most compatible with my way of interpreting the work. In the process one becomes aware of the many possibilities for the execution of a passage or phrase, thus stimulating one's own thinking.

I remember questioning the famed pianist Artur Schnabel regarding a fingering he had written in the score of a Beethoven sonata assigned by him for study that I found simply impossible to play. "Never mind it," he said. "I don't use it myself." He defended it as "a prompter to try different ways by yourself in order to find the one best suited to your own digital needs."

Whenever possible, I like to turn to the unedited facsimile of the first edition, the *Urtext* or original text, for the purpose of evaluating the validity of the interpretive details ultimately chosen, as compared with the stark reality of the composer's unedited notes. It is as though after much discussion I am accorded the privilege of communing with the creator of the music. The result is an enrichment of the mind and a cleansing of the spirit.

Such painstaking examination serves not only the performer in his effort to do his very best; it can also prove a boon for the composer, who may end up having his musical aims realized better than he himself might have imagined. Such identification with a work will also bring about further reevaluation and self-criticism, which will stand the artist in good stead for continual progress and self-improvement. Above all he will attain an awareness of his true role and a sense of humility, openmindedness, and fairness that will enable him to yield up his personal impulses and even his personal judgment and conviction for the sake of the composer's intentions, be they avowed or implied.

Ideally, then, the performing artist becomes a partner with the composer in the act of creation and recreation. Indeed, the performer can bring to a work his own convictions concerning approach, with the result that the composition can take on a different complexion with each individual interpretation without ever losing its intrinsic worth and beauty. In other words, the score can become the point of departure for a highly qualified, responsible interpreter to implement and enhance the innate qualities with which the composer has endowed his work. There are as many diverse and valid interpretations of the same score as there are artists to perform it. Therein lies the infinite beauty of music, and the never-ending challenge for those who wish to convey its message.

No composer can spell out exactly how he wants his creation to be performed. Hence, the interpreter's role takes on great importance and vitality. He must be able to read between the lines, as it were, and add his own convictions, based upon knowledge and experience, and his own interpretative ideas until the resultant mix seems to be just right for the work to appear in the best possible light. Great pianists, for example, have repeatedly recorded the thirty-two piano sonatas by Beethoven over the years, and each recording reflects a very different interpretation. Leonard Bernstein did the same with all of Beethoven's symphonies, and Herbert von Karajan restudied and reinterpreted many masterworks, as have many other responsible conductors. There is never, it seems, a definitive interpretation.

Finally, what does all this mean for the listener? How is the listener to judge between one interpretation and another? First of all, familiarity with a work through firsthand knowledge of the score and repeated listening create the personal criteria by which to evaluate a work. At times the circumstances that prevailed at first hearing can form the basis for future judgment. A personal empathy with a particular performer's treatment of a work may constitute a lasting, if not always unbiased, foundation for evaluation.

To reiterate what I have stated earlier: Have the courage of your convictions. Form your own judgment, provided that you have attained a level of listening experience to do so. Let it be tempered by openmindedness toward the opinions of others, in the knowledge that they, as well as you, can be right. Remember that for most of us an expert is a person who invariably agrees with our own views!

CHAPTER SIX

THE CONDUCTOR AND HIS ART

THE OLD ADAGE "Too many cooks spoil the broth" is appropriate to orchestral playing. Any major symphony orchestra has within its ranks many outstanding artists. Every one of them has formed a valid judgment as to how a given work should be performed. However, a musical performance must ultimately have a single leader to preside over it, for better or worse. Otherwise utter chaos could result, notwithstanding the validity of the individual orchestra members' views.

If a conductor is world-renowned, an orchestra's players will submit to his ideas quite willingly at the outset. A lesser maestro may have a harder time convincing members in the group to do things his way. After all, they have performed a given staple work more times than they have changed the hair on their bows or the reed in their mouthpiece. Why change yet another time? Here the strength of the conductor's personality is important. If the conductor is persuasive and has a fair degree of tolerance toward and respect for his fellow musicians – and, most importantly, if his musical reasoning is sound – he will win them over to his way of interpretation without too much difficulty or resentment.

The day of the "whip-cracking," tyrannical conductor is over. Today reason must prevail, or else the orchestra committee, whose members are elected in democratic fashion by their fellow artists, will try to have the conductor ousted. No more broken batons flying through the air; no more accusations of imbecility hurled at musicians; no more sarcastic remarks of which legends are made. The atmosphere is more gentlemanly, even businesslike, and generally saner. However, the need for authoritative leadership continues nonetheless, perhaps even more so in the absence of dictatorial approaches to conducting.

In tracing the history of the art of conducting, we find a proportionate relationship between the growing complexities of writing for orchestra and the growing demands on the all-embracing musicianship and interpretative powers of the conductor. If he is wise and able, the conductor will find ways of letting the orchestra know that he is one of them, while at the same time keeping just the right distance so that he will not succumb to becoming "one of the guys."

ORIGIN

In the annals of music as a performing art, the conductor as we know him today is a "Johnny-come-lately," relatively speaking. To be sure, someone always had to be in charge to see that the orchestra would start and end together, and that the beat would be observed by all musicians at the same time if possible. Even in the sixteenth century, when the Gabrielis created their special music to be performed both inside and outside Saint Mark's in Venice, there would have been one central figure – most likely the conductor himself – to coordinate the event, plus group leaders to assist with such a complex undertaking.

Time beating per se goes back even further, to the formation of musical groups. Whether it was a simple nod by the musician positioned most visibly for the others to see, some hand or head gesture by the leader seated at the harpsichord or organ, or the waving of the bow by the first violinist (known in England as leader, in Germany as *Konzertmeister,* and in the United States as concertmaster), direction was provided one way or another.

It was also customary for a musician to stand in front of the group, literally beating time with anything from a rolled up piece of paper to a stick hitting a desk or a staff striking the floor. Too much enthusiasm and vehemence in beating time could mean more than just an annoyance for the audience. In the case of the great Jean Baptiste Lully, it proved fatal. He used a long, heavy cane whose blow landed on his foot instead of the floor, inflicting a nasty wound, and the ensuing gangrene caused the composer's death.

In time composers began to endow their scores with a modicum of directions, since beating time was no longer quite sufficient. Tempo changes and gradations of tempo and volume, such as accelerando and ritardando, or crescendo and diminuendo, had to be indicated by one person whom the others could follow. Mozart did much of it from the keyboard, nodding his head when his hands were engaged, as many piano-playing conductors still do today. Haydn also directed from the keyboard instrument, although in the concerts that were organized by the violinist-conductor-impresario Johann Peter Salomon in London for Haydn's visits, the great master yielded guidance to Salomon, who was seated in the leader's chair. Thus the first violinist's visual direction evolved, which to this day can sometimes prove to be more comforting and precise to the rest of the orchestra than that of a conductor of doubtful gifts. A good concertmaster will always be alert to any emergencies, assuring his fellow musicians of firm and assertive leadership when needed.

THE CONCERTMASTER

Before discussing the concertmaster's position and his attendant duties, I would like to relate an amusing incident that illustrates some people's lack of knowledge on the subject. This story concerns one of the most famous concertmasters of all time, Mischa Mischakoff, who never served in any other capacity than that of concertmaster during his long, illustrious career, which took him from St. Petersburg in Russia to New York under Walter Damrosch, Philadelphia under Leopold Stokowski, Chicago under Frederick Stock, the NBC Symphony Orchestra under Arturo Toscanini, Detroit under Paul Paray and Sixten Ehrling. Mischa had just acquired a beautiful new home and was standing outside, waiting for his ride to the rehearsal, when a neighbor, a very prominent manufacturer, pulled out of his driveway and offered to take him where he was going. Noticing Mischa's violin case, which incidentally contained a world-renowned Stradivarius, he said, "Mr. Mischakoff, I didn't know you are a violinist!" Whereupon Mischa, somewhat perplexed, replied, "But you do know that I am the new concertmaster." "Oh, sure," said the neighbor, "I knew that all right, and I am proud to have you living next door to me. Please don't misunderstand me. But I always thought a concertmaster is the boss of the concerts, signing the paychecks, receiving leading citizens, representing the organization, and so forth."

For the average music lover the position of concertmaster has, indeed, always been somewhat nebulous. I have had a vice-president of a bank come backstage after a concert, in which I conducted one of our well-known symphony orchestras, and ask me, "Why does this violinist in the first chair get all the attention? He comes onstage after everyone else is seated and gets applause as though he were a soloist. Then you come out. Before you even acknowledge the applause of the audience, you shake this fellow's hand as though you hadn't seen him in years, but you just saw him backstage!" This man was obviously not aware of the etiquette according to which the conductor greets and thanks the entire orchestra through its leader, the concertmaster.

It is a historical fact that ever since the role of keyboard instruments began to wane as the basis of a performance, the stature of the first violinist increased. Not only did it become his responsibility to give appropriate visual direction with the bow or with body motions to coordinate the performance; that person truly became the leader of the orchestral forces. Even with the advent of a regular, full-time conductor, the concertmaster retained his role as the artistic representative of the orchestra. A concertmaster must have conductorial ability, for he may be called upon to actually lead the orchestra at a moment's notice in case of an emergency involving the conductor, or when the conductor wishes to listen, during a rehearsal, for ensemble and balance from the vantage point of the audience in the hall. In addition, the concertmaster is also expected to see that bowings and other directions are uniformly marked in all string parts. Next time you attend a concert, note how all the bows move in the same direction at the same time.

The concertmaster is responsible for directing sectional rehearsals in preparation for full-rehearsal sessions. Before such a session, as well as before the conductor emerges from the wings to begin the concert, the concertmaster rises from his chair to signal the oboe to play the tone A, by which all the musicians tune their instruments in order to achieve precision of pitch and intonation. He also auditions candidates for vacant string positions.

In short, the concertmaster is the conductor's right hand, having ready access to him at all times – the only orchestra member so privileged. He appears regularly as soloist with the orchestra, which enhances his stature as an artist as well as a leader. Thus, the conductor's handshake becomes symbolic, both for the concertmaster personally and, through him, for the entire assemblage of performers onstage.

THE EVOLUTION OF THE ART OF CONDUCTING

The powerful personality of Beethoven brought a marked influence to bear upon the art of conducting, as it also did for the course of music history in general. Beethoven was among the very first composers to give elaborate visual direction to the orchestra. At the same time he found it musically expedient to engage a conductor when he performed his Piano Concerto No. 4, for instance. In doing so Beethoven broke with the tradition whereby the soloist also took over the conducting duties.

As for Beethoven's elaborate conducting, we are told by contemporary observers that it was more elaborate than conducting. He would indicate every change of dynamics or volume with exaggerated body motions. A sudden piano effect would find him crouched down low, and he would then spring up from the podium like a giant cat for forte effects. Gradual increases or decreases in sound were directed by a corresponding raising or lowering of his entire body. It was also not unusual for him to shout directions above the orchestral playing, or to simply stand with his arms folded across his chest when things seemed to proceed at an even keel. Beethoven, incidentally, continued conducting in this manner even after he was completely deaf.

This necessitated the presence of a "ghost conductor," who took over behind the composer's back to prevent the performance from becoming chaotic. Tragic though Beethoven's conducting episodes may appear in view of his affliction, they do constitute a significant trend toward interpretative direction and away from mere policing of time and mechanics of unanimity of playing.

Another great milestone of nineteenth-century conducting was reached in 1820 when the renowned violinist and composer Ludwig Spohr (1784–1859) appeared in a London Philharmonic Society concert. Finding the orchestra ensemble to be ragged because of insufficient direction by the first violinist, Spohr decided to take things into his own hands. During rehearsals of his own orchestral works, he stationed himself at a separate music desk in front of the orchestra, produced a white baton, and proceeded to direct, stopping to make interpretative suggestions and drawing attention to details. This was the first time that any musician had placed himself in such a conspicuous position, and it was then and there that the modern conductor was born.

Only a few years later Felix Mendelssohn followed suit by conducting a London performance with a "white stick" especially made for him, although contemporary accounts seem to indicate that he used it while seated at the piano. He must have been a convincing leader, for some seven years later, in 1836 to be exact, Mendelssohn assumed the important post of conductor of the famed Gewandhaus Orchestra in Leipzig, Germany. There his superior musicianship and remarkable sense of style, coupled with his persuasive personality, created a musical organization that attained world renown. The position of the orchestral conductor was now firmly established. The degree of visual leadership became more and more a matter of temperament and individual personality. The larger the instrumental and interpretative demands of the score, the more important and necessary authoritative direction became. The orchestra increasingly looked to the conductor for help, for definite cues concerning entrances and cutoffs, and for the kind of musical inspiration that we take for granted today. But some intermediate steps still had to be taken.

Conducting in the opera pit, for example, became an ever-increasing challenge as opera composers created more and more intricate scores. Physical logistics often posed a formidable problem once the conductor assumed full charge of both the orchestra and of what transpired onstage. It had been customary for the opera conductor to be stationed immediately in front of and facing the stage in order to be in full view of singers and actors, who were comforted by this visual proximity. But the orchestra players were left behind, literally speaking, having to read the conductor's signals from the back as best they could, while the maestro ended up being stiff-necked in the process. It was not until Gustav Mahler was appointed conductor at the Vienna Court Opera in 1897 that sanity was restored. Mahler moved the conductor's podium to where it is located today, in front of the pit, where the director is visible to all the musicians and performers involved.

It is interesting to observe that so many of the early conductors were what you might call "do-it-yourselfers," composers who directed performances of their own works (e.g., Bach, Haydn, Mozart, Beethoven, Spohr, Mendelssohn, and later on Mahler). Berlioz, reputedly a very fine conductor and one of the greatest orchestrators of all time, had a thorough knowledge of the capabilities of all instruments, which qualified him eminently to practice the art of orchestral interpretation. Carl Maria von Weber was known to have conducted his own operas, although this was before the advent of the baton. Richard Wagner's experiences on the podium were varied, often as innovative as his creations. Johannes Brahms conducted his own orchestral works. Max Bruch was actively in charge of various musical organizations, among them the Liverpool Philharmonic Society, which he directed in 1880.

Giuseppe Verdi (1813–1901) took charge of his own works on special occasions. Pietro Mascagni (1863–1945) combined his composing career with that of a successful conductor, directing his operas in Europe, the United States, and South America. In fact, he succeeded Arturo Toscanini as music director at La Scala in Milan. Italo Montemezzi (1875–1952) conducted his opera *La Nave* at the Chicago Opera Company during the 1919–20 season and *L'Amore dei Tre Re* at New York's Metropolitan Opera. Igor Stravinsky (1882–1971) was a vigorous exponent of the "do-it-yourself" philosophy, directing most of his own works in live concerts and on records. Richard Strauss, Sergei Rachmaninoff, Paul Hindemith, Aaron Copland, Howard Hanson, and particularly Leonard Bernstein are prime examples of composers mounting the conductor's podium in recent times.

These masters form a link between a past that made it quasi-obligatory for a composer to face his own music, as it were, and a present that finds almost all great conductors selflessly devoting their lives to the pursuit of their profession. One of the terms of employment of Bach, Telemann, Handel, Haydn, Stamitz, and even Mozart (though the latter's term was of short duration) specified that they be in charge of all music at their respective court or church. That meant that they were expected to compose, direct, teach, and – in the case of Haydn – even see to it that the musicians' uniforms were properly pressed and their wigs cleaned and powdered. It would not have occurred to the aristocratic patrons of yesteryear to engage a separate conductor. Their music masters were multipurpose musicians. But, then, we must remember that the art of conducting per se had not yet emerged from the embryonic stage of mere time beating.

The growing complexities of scoring and instrumentation have made conducting a highly specialized, intricate activity that demands professionalism of the highest level. It would be quite difficult today to find a modern counterpart of a Gustav Mahler, someone who can compose ten major and very lengthy symphonies and, at the same time, perform all the functions of a musical director of a major orchestra, including planning a fifty-two-week season consisting of four concerts each week and conducting most of them, in addition to touring here and abroad, keeping a busy recording schedule, and planning special broadcasts and television appearances as well.

Conducting as a separate and highly skilled art form evolved gradually. It arose from an activity that composers considered secondary to their main occupation. Almost none of them, including Mahler and Richard Strauss, had any formal training to become conductors, other than that which is part of a thorough, general musical education.

The second half of the nineteenth century saw a new breed of conductor emerge: the virtuoso conductor, well equipped by way of training and early experience to devote his know-how, love, and energy to a burgeoning profession. Among the renowned names at this point in time were Hermann Levi and Hans Richter, both of Bayreuth fame; Sir Charles Hallé, affiliated first with the Manchester Orchestra in England and later famous for the ensemble that bore his name; Hans von Bülow, pianist and conductor of the Court Opera of Munich, son-in-law of Franz Liszt, whose daughter Cosima left Von Bülow for Richard Wagner; Arthur Nikisch and Felix Weingartner, both extraordinary masters of the baton, to mention only a few.

Since the turn of the century the establishment of symphony orchestras in many of the major cities, both here and abroad, has been on the upswing. Most of the musicians who took charge of these new organizations were recruited from the ranks of the opera houses. This is where a fledgling conductor in Europe gained his experience, starting as *répétiteur* ("singing coach"), an established French title for chorus master of an opera house. In Italian it is *repetitore,* in German *Repetitor,* all derived from *ripetizione* or *répétition,* meaning rehearsal. The duties of the répétiteur included the instruction of the singers in their parts, cueing them at rehearsals, at times even prompting them from the prompter's box during actual performances. This was a good way to become familiar with directing groups and ensembles while at the same time getting acquainted with full scores of operas. There were as many opera houses as symphony orchestras. Even some of the smallest towns in Italy and Germany, for instance, boasted their own opera company. Hence, early conductorial training was primarily opera-oriented. Some of Europe's great maestros – among them Arturo Toscanini, Bruno Walter, Victor de Sabata, Leo Blech, Erich Kleiber, Wilhelm

Furtwängler, Otto Klemperer, Arthur Nikisch, Georg Solti, Herbert von Karajan, and Sixten Ehrling – began their careers in the opera pit.

SOME TYPES AND TECHNIQUES OF CONDUCTING

A marked difference exists between operatic and symphonic conducting. The former is geared to the happenings onstage, with the orchestra having to accommodate every dramatic and vocal nuance of the singers, chorus, and dancers. The opera conductor must be a combination of drama and vocal coach, chorus and dance master, as well as leader of the orchestral forces. Concert conducting embodies all the multiple dramatic and musical demands of operatic conducting. By contrast, however, it is the orchestral and often the choral sound alone that pose the challenge. There is a sheer audible appeal as the instruments who take the place of singers become the stage characters, as it were. Their individual or group sound is no longer used in a supporting role, though in a musical sense that role is present in the case of the concerto for solo instrument and orchestra – a particularly challenging form for a conductor.

The shift of emphasis in conducting can be considerable. It is inherent in the nature of tone production that instrumental players require a conducting technique different from that used for individual or choral singing. For instance, in cueing a brass or woodwind instrument the conductor must anticipate the fraction of time needed for the embouchure to produce the sound, while a cue for a vocal group must be simultaneous with the emission of sound. Shaping instrumental sound interpretatively requires different arm and finger motions on the part of the conductor than those used in vocal conducting.

An orchestra needs to foster its musical as well as human relationship with its conductor every bit as much as he needs to establish a mutually beneficial *modus operandi*. Methods of conducting vary from one leader to another. Aside from the baton technique, and apart from a thorough and complete knowledge of the score, a conductor must develop ways and means by which to convey and even impose his conception of the music on the orchestra. Of course, verbal instructions and discussion help to bring about an understanding. However, conducting is not done with words but with gestures. These are executed with hand motions, particularly those of the left hand, since the right hand manipulates the baton to ensure rhythmic coherence. The left hand is used to shape dynamics and expression and should be withdrawn when there is no shading or nuance to convey. The more judiciously it is used, the more effective it is when it does come into play.

The eyes and facial expressions of the conductor are of greatest importance. An orchestra responds to such personal visual contact, perhaps even more than to elegant hand movements. Hence, the eyes of the conductor should be focused upon individual instrumentalists or groups of players, as needed, while the score on the stand should only serve for reference. To repeat an old admonition, a conductor should have the score in his head rather than his head in the score. All this always requires more rehearsal time than is generally available. Yet it is the carefully groomed relationship with the orchestra that in the end constitutes the most practical, useful, and vital part of the conductor's preparation and studies.

MUSICAL PREPARATION FOR CONDUCTORS

The opportunities for musical preparation for would-be conductors are within everyone's reach, limited only by the degree of ambition involved. However, even if you have subjected yourself to the rigorous study of all facets of music (including theory, harmony, composition, sight-reading, and a knowledge of instruments), and have the talent for such a complex career, you will find yourself completely stymied and frustrated unless you have at your disposal an instrument on which to practice – an orchestra. A hundred years ago a wealthy parent, wife, or father-in-law might buy an orchestra for you. This is how Serge Koussevitzky, the renowned maestro of the Boston Symphony Orchestra, got started back in his native Russia in the early 1900s. His father-in-law, a wealthy tea merchant, made his conducting career possible. With today's musicians' union regulations, even the wealthiest in-laws would think twice before investing such a sum for even the most promising career.

But what about the young students of conducting, whose only

asset is their determination to succeed in their chosen career? Books on conducting, such as *The Grammar of Conducting,* by Max Rudolf, with an introduction by George Szell, and *Conducting Guide to Selected Scores,* by Emil Kahn, are invaluable for study.

Conducting students may stand in front of a mirror and watch themselves conduct a performance of a recorded work. They may admire their elegant motions and inspiring facial expressions. However, while this can help an initial conception in certain instances, it can actually spoil any attempted approach of their own choosing, be it right or wrong.

Ultimately they must prove their mettle by standing in front of an orchestra, applying all the tricks of the trade they learned so diligently in a textbook, or from observing other conductors in actual performance. All things being equal, the orchestra members may even be kind enough to correct their mistakes, although that would require a most unusual compounding of just the right interpersonal chemistry.

Some answers do exist. Over the years there have been limited opportunities for young, gifted aspirants to be chosen as apprentices to well-established masters. Among the leaders in these farsighted, worthwhile efforts in modern times have been Herbert von Karajan and the Berlin Philharmonic; Leonard Bernstein, Pierre Boulez, Zubin Mehta, and the New York Philharmonic; George Szell, Lorin Maazel, and the Cleveland Orchestra, a stepping-stone to fame for James Levine; Sixten Ehrling, Antal Dorati, and the Detroit Symphony Orchestra; and Georg Solti and the Chicago Symphony Orchestra.

Encouraging and prestigious though such an appointment may be, it is of necessity limited in scope. Of course, the young would-be conductor has the enviable privilege of observing his master at close range in all rehearsals, concerts, broadcasts, and recording sessions, but his chances of actually conducting are few and far between. One notable exception was Leonard Bernstein, who substituted at the last moment for Bruno Walter and led the New York Philharmonic in a 1943 concert, resulting in sudden fame. Studying the maestro's score for all kinds of directions and interpretive details while watching him in action is invaluable, but it still amounts to planning the battle strategies rather than seeing frontline action.

Fortunately, some of the leaders in the field have spent a good deal of their time teaching and coaching, both privately and by giving master classes at some of our great schools of music here and abroad. Notable examples include: Eugene Ormandy, whose stewardship of the Philadelphia Orchestra far exceeded any other maestro's tenure, and who found the time to advise students at Philadelphia's Curtis Institute of Music; Sixten Ehrling's masterful leadership at New York's Juilliard School; England's leading conductors at London's Royal College of Music; and French masters at the Paris Conservatoire.

Some of the intensive conducting courses given by famous maestros have been very helpful. Many well-known masters have emerged from such conductorial "communes" as Pierre Monteux's Blue Hill in Maine; Serge Koussevitzky's Tanglewood in Lenox, Massachusetts, subsequently headed by successive conductors of the Boston Symphony Orchestra; and similar summer institutions in Europe.

Competitions for young conductors in various parts of Europe and America have also constituted a great boon for all participants. The obvious advantage in these competitions is the actual conducting experience with an orchestra, which is composed of peers of conducting students, under the watchful and critical eye of the maestro, who devotes the major part of the course's duration to precisely that type of supervision. Hopefully these opportunities will increase; ideally they will be organically linked to major orchestras as an integral "farm system," as it were.

At no time in the history of cultural pursuits has the world seen such a proliferation of orchestras as is now being experienced. Likewise, there are more outstanding conductors on the podium now than ever before. I am not sure whether the institution of the "permanent conductor and music director" is destined to survive. Easy jet travel beckons many maestros to serve more than one orchestra at a given time, and I fear that audiences, too, have grown a bit fickle in wanting to see different faces and observe different approaches to their favorite music. How much the orchestra itself can benefit from such "podium traffic" is a serious question. Some players may grow weary while working under the same conductor for many seasons. On the other hand, great permanent conductors such as Stokowski and Ormandy in Philadelphia, Szell in Cleveland, Solti in Chicago, or Karajan in Berlin have created great orchestras by their long-lived presence.

This is all the more reason for gifted young hopefuls to pursue every opportunity for training and experience with the utmost vigor and determination. The road is tough, and the obstacles and disappointments are often disheartening, but there is more room than ever for those with the strength of will and nobility of spirit to persevere.

CHAPTER SEVEN

ORCHESTRATION

WE HAVE EXAMINED the history of the instruments and how each produces its individual sound. We have also investigated the development of the orchestra and the evolution of aggregate sound. The second chapter showed us the ingredients that add up to a musical "meal." Now we have gained the status of a gourmet, having access to a huge spice box of instrumental flavors, as well as to the spacious orchestral kitchen equipped with many tools to combine them. We may now ask: What spices does the gourmet use in order to create the ultimate in musical epicurism?

This is not an inappropriate analogy for the art of instrumentation. Instrumentation denotes the ability to use instruments in a musical composition to their best advantage, for the utmost benefit of the work and its individual parts, and for the conveyance of its meaning or message.

Orchestration is, indeed, an art all its own. You may have the facility to invent beautiful melodies, to play them on an instrument, or to harmonize them on the piano. If you are a student of theory and form, you may even be successful in weaving your melodies into the kind of musical development and design that makes a composition out of an improvisation. But how do you translate your creation into orchestral terms? This is where the gourmet concepts apply.

Which instrument is best suited, in terms of range and color, to play a given part of your invention? To which combination do you entrust your harmonic foundation or your contrapuntal dialogue? All this requires a specialized talent and knowledge, and it is not uncommon for even a professional inventor of melodies to engage a highly skilled orchestrator or arranger to transcribe his melodies for orchestra.

Some composers allot themes to certain instruments while they work at the piano. Others commit their thoughts to paper in exact-scoring fashion, without the aid of the keyboard. Bach wrote in a steady stream. Mozart generated ideas faster than he could write them down, and even then his own piano part for some concertos was barely finished in time for the performance, since the instrumental parts for the orchestra had to be copied first. Beethoven, by contrast, often agonized over his creations at the piano. Even after he wrote or outlined a score on paper, additional corrections were numerous and mostly illegible. His manuscripts often show erased spots rubbed over, with corrections written above them. Rossini is said to have used a napkin in a restaurant to note down his sudden inspirations, whereas Hindemith was able to write full scoring on trains, planes, in cafés, or whenever the spirit moved him to do so.

It is impossible to offer here an intensive course in the art of orchestration. Suffice it to say that we are concerned with the ability to choose instruments for a composition according to their individual tonal idiosyncracies, and how they best fit into the scheme of sound for which the composer is striving. Obviously, anyone wishing to orchestrate has to be thoroughly acquainted with the capabilities and range of every instrument, the limitations of tone production, the dynamic and tonal characteristics of sound, and how all these factors best serve the composer's aim. Ultimately the choice is highly individual, thus adding yet another most vital ingredient.

On the following pages is a sample orchestration, namely, Beethoven's orchestral setting of Schiller's "Ode to Joy" in his Symphony No. 9.

It is not difficult to notice how the strings (first and second violins, violas, cellos, and basses) are used to encircle and embellish the sustained notes of the choir, much like Bach weaves a filigree of notes around a chorale in his chorale preludes, while all the wind instruments (see upper half of score) punctuate rhythmically the flow of Beethoven's invention. The result is an exhilarating, inexorable progression of music, which moves from strength to strength. No other choice of orchestration could have the same effect.

COMPARING AN ORCHESTRAL TRANSCRIPTION AND AN ORIGINAL COMPOSITION

A good way to appreciate the art of instrumentation is to listen to and examine the score of an orchestral transcription of a well-known piano composition. In this way one is able to hear how certain sounds, themes, and melodies that are familiar in the original version can be expressed in another framework with different types of "voices."

I should like to relate one of my own experiences while studying orchestration. It was my assignment to transcribe for orchestra the slow movement of the Piano Sonata No. 8 ("Pathétique") by Beethoven, the theme I play to open and close my radio program "Adventures in Good Music." This melody lies in the rich middle register of the piano:

Beethoven conceived it for the piano; hence any other choice appeared to me to be a sacrilege. Yet I wanted to meet the challenge, to choose an instrument with the richness of the middle register and the quality that would best match the piano line when played with a "singing" legato tone. The viola became my choice. I allotted the accompaniment, as played by the lower piano voices, to the lower strings, and saved the wind and brass instruments for the second and third parts of the movement (the B and C parts of the A-B-A-C-A form; see the final section on "Form" in Chapter Two). This melody, my daily companion, became even dearer to me.

To actually experience the sound of the transcription versus the original, it would be well worth your while to first listen to any of the piano pieces by Maurice Ravel and then turn to his own subsequent orchestral transcriptions – for instance, *Le Tombeau de Couperin* (two sections of which were omitted in the orchestral version), *Pavane pour une Infante Défunte, Sonatine, Alborada del Gracioso,* or *Valses Nobles et Sentimentales.* Listen to how every piano phrase is matched by instruments whose tonal affinity is closest to the original. This will not be easily discerned with just one hearing; patience is required to listen several times. The results are rewarding and extremely enlightening. Ravel was one of the greatest orchestrators of all time, and he loved choosing orchestral colors. In fact, he grew so fond of the orchestral version of these pieces that he no longer found sufficient satisfaction in playing the original piano version.

Among other masters of orchestration, I would recommend listening to works by Rimsky-Korsakov and Berlioz, both of whom wrote significant treatises on the subject. There is brilliance and inexorable rightness in their choice of instruments, making it virtually impossible for us to hear their compositions any other way. Other suggestions for listening are the orchestral suite from Rimsky-Korsakov's opera *Le Coq d'Or (The Golden Cockerel),* and the *Roman Carnival* Overture or the overture to the opera *Benvenuto Cellini* by Berlioz.

Ravel's orchestration of Mussorgsky's highly descriptive piano suite called *Pictures at an Exhibition* is also particularly noteworthy. Take the time to listen to the piano version while reading the description for each section as it unfolds, and then savor the flavor of Ravel's orchestral colors as he intensifies the meaning of each of the pictures, as well as the interconnecting "promenades" of the visitor who is moving from one picture to another.

After you have trained your ear to seek out the coloristic subtleties of these masters of orchestration, you will delight in the discoveries you will make in some of your favorite compositions for orchestra. The English horn solo in the largo movement of Dvořák's Symphony No. 9 ("New World") will have never sounded more right for the portrayal of deep-throated melancholy. The sensuous drive toward the end of the "Love-Death" section of Wagner's *Tristan und Isolde* becomes intoxicating, with its gradual ascent of interdependent themes and dynamic growth. Your thrill in hearing the approach to the finale of Beethoven's famous Fifth Symphony will no longer be just a general impression of elation; you will now hear how Beethoven achieves it by gradually increasing the sound of strings and timpani, from a triple-piano to the eight-bar growth of a crescendo, and ultimately to the jubilant unison playing of all first winds, brasses, and first and second violins, with the remaining instruments furnishing just enough basic harmonics for a solid, well-founded structural climax. Hearing now becomes knowing the source of your psychological sense of well-being while listening to music; the joys that await you are endless.

MIXING INSTRUMENTAL SOUNDS OR COLORS

Just as a painter's palette contains primary colors for mixing purposes, so a composer's traditional score depends upon the strings as its foundation. They are used throughout a work, with only short lapses of silence, for strings can sing in a most expressive way without possessing the highly individual timbre of an oboe or a flute. They also never have to stop for breath. You can generally look to the strings to enunciate some of the most melodic ideas of a work.

The composer produces various shades of tonal color by mixing the sound of different instruments. While each of the woodwinds has a very distinctive voice, their colors mix felicitously with those of the strings, although proportions must be judiciously based upon the characteristic timbre of each woodwind involved. Juxtaposing a low bassoon tone upon cellos and basses without the relief of higher tones would result in a somber tonal climate, like the combination of purples, blues, and blacks, if that is what the composer has in mind. On the other end of the spectrum, a high-register clarinet tone coupled with high flute and perhaps a shrill piccolo outcry should have some fairly frantic violin, viola, and cello activity in the lower register for support and tonal credibility. Without it the unsupported high tones might cause you to blink rapidly, just like a mixture of whites, yellows, light greens, and bright pinks might.

As for the use of brass instrumental sounds, the horns are undoubtedly the most adaptable. Unless the score calls for a blaring, very accented horn tone, its natural mellowness mixes easily with winds and strings. The heavy artillery of trumpets, trombones, and tubas is usually best reserved for either climaxes of great impact or for the support of a dynamic passage played by the rest of the orchestra. The approach to and the final section of the last movement of Beethoven's Fifth Symphony is a good example of the effect of the brass at precisely the right moment. Two horns, two trumpets, and three trombones produce the loudest brass clangor Beethoven ever mustered.

This does not imply that brass instruments are incapable of adding noble and soft colors to a score. Listen to the trumpet in the "Prelude" to Wagner's opera *Parsifal,* marked *piano, espressivo assai* ("soft, most expressive"), as it merges its distinctive sound in unison with three oboes and some of the first and second violins. This example embodies the trumpet's gentility.

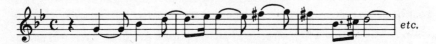

Or consider Berlioz's use of three trombones in his *Roman Carnival* Overture, marked *piano,* which surely belies the opinion of most music lovers that trombones are always strident:

The percussion group's contribution to the rhythmic vitality of a work is indispensable. From the standpoint of coloration and special effects, the use of various percussion instruments represents a great challenge. Think of the unforgettable opening of Beethoven's Violin Concerto, where four solitary timpani beats set the stage, joined on the fifth beat and at the new bar line by oboes, clarinets, and bassoons, only to reappear alone four bars later. I hope that this lofty example will whet your appetite for locating additional percussive and solo tonal colors. Their appearances are legion, and you will have the endless joy of discovering many similar examples.

DEVELOPMENT OF ORCHESTRATIONAL TECHNIQUES

The art of orchestration has grown increasingly elaborate and complex in direct proportion to the growth of the orchestra as a medium for musical expression. A number of composers abhorred the trend toward more and more massive sound and devised techniques reflecting a more subtle and refined utilization of traditional resources. Instead of heavily encrusted oils they preferred delicate watercolors. Claude Debussy was in the vanguard of these orchestrators, and his *Prélude à l'Après-midi d'un Faune (Prelude to the Afternoon of a Faun)* is a perfect example of that new direction. The realization that this was composed during the years 1892–94, the very years that brought forth Mahler's mammoth Second Symphony ("Resurrection") puts into sharp relief the vast differences of temperament and musical philosophy among great composers.

The constant changes in musical directions of the twentieth century demanded, and continue to demand, ever newer techniques of orchestration. Smaller orchestral dimensions were a natural reaction to the obesity of sound carried to the limits of the audience's tolerance. They now served composers in new and imaginative ways. Ironically, some of these same masters of composition were responsible for huge orchestral forces in the first place. Stravinsky's ingenious *L'Histoire du Soldat* is a good example. It is scored for only seven instruments, representing the full range of each instrumental group: violin and double bass, clarinet and bassoon, trumpet and trombone, and percussion. The piece also calls for three dancers and a narrator. This work of remarkable intimacy comes from the pen of a master who during the five previous years had given us music of huge proportions.

New sounds were being found everywhere, including such startling effects as: iron chains rattled onto the stage floor in Schoenberg's *Gurrelieder*, a scintillating assortment of sirens, typewriter, splashing water, pistol shots, roulette wheel, and rattle in Satie's *Parade;* and even airplane propellers in the American composer George Antheil's *Ballet Mécanique* of 1926. The next step was the evolution of orchestration without an orchestra, which is the essence of electronic music.

For almost three centuries orchestration has challenged the minds of music's greatest creators, while at the same time being an indispensable part of the serious studies of any true musician. Whether composing or performing, whether solo recitalist, chamber music artist, or conductor, the art of orchestration enlightens, enhances, illumines, and guides our every effort. A musician uses his command of orchestration like a writer chooses his words, a painter the infinite possibilities of color combinations, a choreographer various body movements, and an architect an infinite variety of materials, shapes, forms, and surroundings. Once aware of the art of orchestration, the enlightened listener's musical adventures are enriched immeasurably. The art's progress since the time of Monteverdi and Bach and the early classicists has been tremendous. I welcome you to a well-stocked musical kitchen and wish you "bon appétit" and good listening!

PART TWO

MUSIC IN THE FLOW OF HISTORY

CHAPTER EIGHT

THE CATEGORIES OF MUSIC: DEFINITION, HISTORY, AND EXAMPLES

MANY PEOPLE ENJOY a wide variety of types of music – from simple compositions to complex orchestral works – and may be totally unaware of how they evolved. Others prefer to learn about the backgrounds of composers and their works, including technical details of composition and other factors involved. Most people – composers, performers, and listeners – tend to think of music in terms of categories or classifications to which individual works can be assigned. For example, we may wish to listen to a concerto rather than to a sonata at any given time.

To mentally prepare ourselves to do so, it is necessary to become better acquainted with the chief classifications into which music is arranged. This chapter will serve as a source of ready reference in this regard; many of the categories are also discussed in Chapters Two and Nine.

For the sake of convenience, let us first identify the two basic kinds of music: *absolute music,* which we enjoy in and of itself; and *program music,* to whose underlying plot or story we respond at least as much as to the sound itself.

ABSOLUTE MUSIC

SONATA

The most basic definition of a sonata is a musical composition for any instrument, such as the piano, harpsichord, organ, violin, viola, cello, or any instrument of the woodwind or brass family. Each of these can appear unaccompanied, although most frequently the piano is involved. From the middle of the eighteenth century on, the piano part attained the same importance as the other featured instrument. For example, a sonata for flute and piano is vastly different from a flute piece with piano accompaniment. That difference lies in the implementation of certain principles of formal structure, which I have previously discussed in the section on "Form" in Chapter Two.

The sonata form is particularly evident in a sonata's first movement (usually marked allegro), where it consists of three sections – exposition, development, and recapitulation. There are generally at least two, at times three, additional movements; the second movement (marked adagio, andante, largo, etc.) is usually, but not always, slow and contemplative, in contrast to the active character of the first movement; the final movement (marked allegro or presto) is of a lively, often ebullient, nature. If an additional movement is included, it occurs as the third in a series of four movements and is either dancelike in character (minuet or gavotte) or a lighthearted, even humorous scherzo (literally "joke" or "jest") placed between the introspective second movement and the effervescent finale.

While the first movement must adhere to sonata form, the other movements can be written without regard for conventional principles of form, although composers often choose to employ them. Thus the second or slow movement as well as the last movement are also frequently composed in sonata form. The use of the form called Theme and Variations is a favorite among composers. Beethoven's Sonata No. 9 for Violin and Piano ("Kreutzer"), Op. 47, his Sonata No. 23, Op. 57 for Piano ("Appassionata"), and his Trio No. 6 for

Violin, Cello, and Piano ("Archduke"), Op. 97, all offer lofty examples of theme and variations for the slow movement. As there is no rigid order in musical composition, Beethoven places the slow movement in the third part of the "Archduke" Trio and the scherzo in the second part, thus reversing the usual order.

The Rondo form (see pp. 223–24) may be used in the sonata's last movement. The idea inherent in the rondo – the main theme returns at least three times – seems to lend that part of the work a natural air of finality.

The history of the sonata as a three-part concept dates back to the time of Bach (ca. 1650–1750) and originated with the allegro-adagio-allegro scheme of the Italian overture of Alessandro Scarlatti and his contemporaries. Bach used it amply. All but the first of his six Brandenburg concertos follow this plan, as do his *Italian Concerto* for harpsichord and his six organ concertos.

The eighteenth century also witnessed the flowering of the short, one-movement sonata, especially by Domenico Scarlatti, who wrote about 550 examples of this type. When first published in 1738, they bore the title *Essercizi per Gravicembalo*. It is assumed that some of these were to be assembled as parts of two- or three-movement sonatas.

The basic concepts of sonata form have remained essentially the same since the Mannheim School in the mid-eighteenth century and the Viennese classicists (viz. Haydn and Mozart), who shaped the sonata into the grand mold that served Beethoven as a model for his colossal use of the same design. The implementation of these concepts is as varied in content and personal style as the musical idiom and temperament of the composers using them. For example, Beethoven gave us a wondrous and poignantly developed "Marcia Funebre sulla Morte d'un Eroe" ("Funeral March on the Death of a Hero") in his Sonata No. 12 in A-flat Major, Op. 26, which was later equaled in intensity and bold design by Chopin's famous "Funeral March" in his Sonata No. 2 in B-flat Minor, Op. 35. Beethoven employed a fugue in the final movements of two of his last piano sonatas, Opp. 106 and 110, and in his Sonata No. 2 in G Minor for Cello and Piano, Op. 102, No. 2. César Franck composed the exquisitely lyrical last movement of his Sonata in A Major for Violin and Piano in canonic form. Twentieth-century American composer Samuel

Barber wrote a masterful fugue as the last movement of his Piano Sonata, Op. 26.

As I mentioned in the section on "Form" in Chapter Two, there are exceptions to the rule of the application of the sonata form to the first movement, notably the piano sonatas of Op. 27, Nos. 1 and 2, by Beethoven, the second of which is popularly known as the "Moonlight" Sonata. In both instances the composer disclaimed any adherence to the sonata model by calling the work *Sonata quasi una fantasia*.

Because of its remarkable longevity as a form of composition, its acceptance by composers of three centuries, and its capacity and flexibility for constant renewal of content, the sonata has emerged as the most vital and challenging category of instrumental music.

SYMPHONY

The word "symphony," of Greek derivation, means "sounding together." We associate the term today with a large-scale composition performed by an orchestra. The Italian word *sinfonia*, though synonymous today with symphony, was originally descriptive of an instrumental piece (e.g., a prelude to a suite or cantata, as used by Bach, or an operatic overture, as used by Alessandro Scarlatti).

As for its form, the symphony may be considered a sonata for orchestra. This implies the application of the sonata-form principle to the first movement, while the other movements may follow any other concept of form, as in the case of the sonata for solo instrument.

Most symphonies generally consist of four movements. There are also some notable single-movement and three-movement symphonies. In each instance the exigencies of variety, change of pace, and dramatic and emotional contrasts are brought to bear upon the symphony's subdivisions, as they are with the sonata.

The symphony as we know it today crystallized during the 1740s and 1750s under the influence of members of the Mannheim School, with the full potential of the form coming to fruition during the Viennese classical period, especially due to the prolificacy of Haydn and Mozart. At the time of the Mannheim School and the Viennese classics, the symphony was still looked upon as a form of musical entertainment, not unlike the suite and the divertimento. Only gradually did it acquire the depth of emotion and variety of mood and design that we associate with the later symphonies of Haydn ("Paris" and "London" symphonies) and Mozart (Nos. 31 through 41). It was Beethoven who catapulted the symphony to a level of prominence that inspired generations of subsequent symphonists. (The evolution of the symphony during the romantic and postromantic periods is discussed in Chapter Nine.)

Just as the solo sonata has proven its validity of form and its continuing vitality of concept in the solo literature throughout almost four centuries, so the symphony continues to remain the backbone of large-scale orchestral music. In every generation composers have been challenged to create works in symphonic form and style, thereby assuring the continual growth of music's grandest design.

CONCERTO

This popular form of composition implies a solo display of one or, at times, two or three instruments in collaboration with the orchestra. The degree of partnership among these forces has undergone an interesting evolution.

The word "concerto" originally meant a group of performers playing or singing together, as "in concert," or making a "concerted effort" of entertaining. The Gabrielis of sixteenth-century Venice called their motets, scored for choir and organ, *concerti ecclesiastici* (ecclesiastical concertos). Heinrich Schütz, a seventeenth-century German composer, titled his similar works *Kleine geistliche Konzerte* ("Little Spiritual Concertos"). Claudio Monteverdi (1567–1643) called one of his books of madrigals "concerto" because it contained instrumental accompaniments.

The late seventeenth and early eighteenth centuries witnessed a departure from the vocal implications of the word and a veering toward the exclusive use of instrumental solo groups, or *concertino*, in alternation with the full orchestra, *ripieno* or *grosso*. The type of composition that was created became known as Concerto Grosso. The masters of this phase of development were the Italian violinist-composers Arcangelo Corelli, Giuseppe Torelli, Giovanni Bononcini, and Tommaso Albinoni, to name a few.

The concerto grosso is highlighted in some of the masterworks of Vivaldi and Bach, who created various combinations of solo instruments for the concertino group, as exemplified by Bach's Brandenburg concertos, and in Vivaldi's brilliantly varied aggregations of strings, winds, and brass. Bach also produced the precursor of the modern piano concerto by writing the first such works for harpsichord and orchestra. Handel's organ concertos contributed significantly to the development of the keyboard concerto.

The crystallization of the sonata and symphony of the eighteenth century also signaled the emergence of the concerto for solo instrument, a turning away from the concept of multiple solo instruments of the baroque concerto grosso. The rise of the virtuoso concerto performer since the time of Mozart – the most eminent composer in this genre of his time, as well as one of the most brilliant performing artists of all time – can be followed in the progressive description of forms of composition in Chapter Nine.

The great instrumental performers, beginning with Mozart and throughout the eighteenth and nineteenth centuries, helped establish the concerto as a vital force in music. Mozart and his contemporaries knew well how to apply and adjust their playing technique to the burgeoning capacities of the emerging *Hammerklavier*. The concertos of Beethoven, written between 1795 and 1809, reflect not only the master's remarkable growth as performer and composer but also show how the instrument could not even remotely contain the massive sonorities Beethoven demanded of it. In the vanguard of those composers creating a concerto repertory at that time, although regrettably almost forgotten today, were Jan Ladislav Dussek (1760–1812), Johann Nepomuk Hummel (1778–1837), Friedrich Wilhelm Kalkbrenner (1785–1849), Carl Czerny (1791–1857), Ignaz Moscheles (1794–1870), and Sigismond Thalberg (1812–71).

For a discussion of concertos written during the romantic age, see pages 308–12; for special listening suggestions, see the Appendix, "Suggestions for Building a Record Library."

The form of the concerto can be compared to that of the sonata. In fact, we may loosely refer to the concerto as a sonata for solo instrument and orchestra – bearing in mind several modifications. For instance, the concerto, with very few exceptions, has only three movements. The most striking exception is the Piano Concerto No.

2 in B-flat Major by Brahms, which interposes a scherzo between the first and slow movements.

Another feature of the concerto that is not present in the sonata is the use of a Cadenza, which occurs most frequently toward the end of the first movement or, less frequently, in subsequent movements. A cadenza serves as a vehicle for a brief solo display of brilliance in the style of improvisation; it should be indigenous to the thematic material and musical mood of the movement of which it is a part.

The first movement of the concerto is generally in sonata form; the second movement is usually slow in tempo and lyrical in character. The concerto generally ends with a rondo, a form particularly conducive to a display of virtuosity because of its effervescent flavor.

Concertos or concertinos, smaller in scope and duration, have been written for every conceivable instrument – from pipe organ to mouth organ, piccolo to tuba, marimba to full percussion, and violin to double bass. The richest repertoire may be found in concertos for piano and for violin. There are also some notable concertos for multiple instruments, which are late eighteenth-, nineteenth-, and twentieth-century counterparts of the concerto grosso concept.

Because of its immense popularity, both visually as a focal point of virtuosic display and as a never-ending source of diversified sonorities, the concerto is a convincing mirror of the evolution of composition and performance.

CHAMBER MUSIC

This category includes music for an ensemble of instruments, with a separate and different part assigned to each player. This is the distinguishing feature between chamber and orchestral music, the latter requiring several identical parts for groups of players, such as violins, violas, cellos, and so on. However, as in orchestral music, it is the ensemble that is featured collectively in chamber music rather than the individual player.

Groupings in chamber music are based upon the number of players and the combinations of instruments involved, from duos for two instruments to pieces for nine instruments (nonets) and beyond. Performance by increasing numbers of musicians, and the complexities of the score, may require the assistance of a conductor.

The most frequently featured chamber music group is the string quartet. Most composers of note have found it challenging to try their hand at it, writing works for two violins, viola, and cello. The Viennese classicists first introduced this form, and the sheer number of their works is staggering. Two examples are:

Haydn   84 string quartets, 31 piano trios,
about 56 string trios,
divertimentos and nocturnes for various
    combinations.

Mozart   23 string quartets, 2 piano quartets,
7 piano trios, 37 sonatas for piano and violin,
2 flute quartets, 1 oboe quartet,
1 quintet for piano and winds,
1 clarinet quintet, 1 horn quintet,
1 trio for clarinet, viola, and piano.

Beginning with the quartets of Haydn and Mozart, every period has seen an enrichment of this musical form.

Beethoven advanced the cause of chamber music in general, and that of the string quartet in particular, in the most far-reaching manner – from the transparency of melodic and harmonic texture of his six early string quartets (Op. 18) to the almost symphonic language of the middle-period works – the three "Razumovsky" string quartets (Op. 59), the "Harp" Quartet (Op. 74), the "Serious" Quartet (Op. 95) – and ultimately to the uniquely profound late quartets, Opp. 127, 130–133, and 135. With these masterworks Beethoven established the string quartet as a medium of musical expression as viable and vibrant as the symphony. The combined sonorities, timbres, and tonal registers of the four stringed instruments, as employed by him and the other great Viennese masters, have fired the imagination and creative fantasy of practically every serious musician.

A further significant development was the doubling of viola or cello for purposes of added sonorities, thereby creating the string quintet. There are 12 quintets for two violins, two violas, and cello by Boccherini and 6 by Mozart; Boccherini also wrote no fewer than 113 string quintets for two violins, viola, and two cellos. Originating in the classical period, these concepts were brought to even greater heights with Beethoven's 3 quintets with two violas, and by Schubert's indescribably beautiful Quintet in C Major, Op. 163, with two cellos. Every music lover should experience the inner strength and serenity of this masterwork. Schubert also gave us the memorable "Trout" Quintet in A Major, Op. 114, for violin, viola, cello, double bass, and piano, published posthumously in 1829 and nicknamed after Schubert's song "Die Forelle" ("The Trout"), on which the composer wrote a set of charming variations as the quintet's fourth movement.

Beethoven's late quartets have proved to be far ahead of their time. In their linear treatment of the thematic structure and their innovative choice of tonalities they point the way to the six quartets of Béla Bartók. Between these two composers the quartets by Schubert, Schumann, Smetana, Brahms, Dvořák, and Tchaikovsky show us the form's accommodation of the most eloquent romantic thought and flavor, couched in the composers' individual speech and, as in the case of Smetana and Dvořák, national colors. Debussy's single quartet of 1893 represents yet another new phase of subtlety of tonal colors, this time in the finest impressionist tradition, paving the way for the highly characteristic creations of Ravel, Ives, Schoenberg, Berg, Webern, Hindemith, Barber, and other masters of the twentieth century.

Closely related to the string quartet and quintet, although of different textural consistency, are the string trio (violin, viola, cello), the string duo (two violins, violin and viola, or violin and cello), and the string sextet (two violins, two violas, and two cellos). In each case the true chamber music hallmark of having a different part assigned to each player prevails. Prime examples for the reader's listening pleasure are: four string trios by Beethoven; a string trio by Schubert; a duo for two violins by Spohr; a sonata for two violins by Prokofiev; duos for violin and viola by Mozart; duo sonatas for violin and cello by Ravel and Kodály; two string sextets by Brahms; and one string sextet by Schoenberg entitled *Verklärte Nacht (Transfigured Night)*.

We should next consider the many compositions that combine stringed instruments with piano or with wind instruments. As indicated in our discussion of the sonata form, there are a variety of sonatas for violin, viola, and cello, each with piano. Trios for violin, cello, and piano are equally numerous. Quartets for piano and strings are not as frequent but are very rewarding, and piano quintets – mostly string quartets with piano – contain some remarkable gems. Below are some examples you might consider.

Sonatas for violin and piano: any of the 37 (2 unfinished) by Mozart; 10 by Beethoven, including the well-known "Spring" Sonata No. 5 in F Major, Op. 24, and the "Kreutzer" Sonata No. 9 in A Major, Op. 47; 3 by Brahms; 2 each by Schumann, Fauré, and Bartók, all very rewarding; 1 superb example by César Franck; 1 each by Debussy and Ravel.

Sonatas for viola and piano: 2 by Brahms, originally scored for clarinet and piano; 1 by Hindemith; a Suite for Viola and Piano by Ernest Bloch.

Sonatas for cello and piano: 5 by Beethoven; 2 each by Brahms, Fauré, and Mendelssohn; 1 each by Debussy, Rachmaninoff, and Kodály.

Piano Trios: 31 by Haydn; 7 by Mozart; 6 by Beethoven, including the "Ghost" Trio in D Major, Op. 70, No. 1, and the "Archduke" Trio No. 6 in B-flat Major, Op. 97; 4 by Dvořák; 3 by Brahms; 2 by Mendelssohn; 1 each by Smetana, Saint-Saëns, Tchaikovsky, Ravel, and Shostakovich.

Piano Quartets: 3 by Brahms; 2 each by Mozart and Fauré; 1 each by Schumann, Chausson, d'Indy, Lekeu, and Martinů.

Piano Quintets: 1 each by Schumann, Franck, Brahms, Fauré, Dvořák, Bloch, and Schmitt.

Combinations with wind and brass instruments yield a rich harvest, both for participants and for listeners. Here are a few selected examples of lesser-known works to whet the appetite of the aficionado.

Sonatas for piano and winds: 2 by Brahms for clarinet and piano; 1 by Prokofiev for flute and piano; 1 by Beethoven for horn and piano.

Trios for winds or brass with or without piano: 1 by Mozart for viola, clarinet, and piano; 1 by Beethoven for clarinet, cello, and piano; 1 by Poulenc for oboe, bassoon, and piano; a sonata by Poulenc for horn, trumpet, and trombone; a sonata by Debussy for flute, viola, and harp.

Quartets, quintets, sextets, septets, octets, and nonets: quintet by Mozart for piano and winds; quintet by Beethoven for piano and winds; two quartets by Mozart for flute and strings and one for oboe and strings; quintet by Brahms for clarinet and strings; sextet by Poulenc for piano and winds; septet by Beethoven for strings and winds; octet by Schubert for strings and winds; nonet by Spohr for strings and winds.

Keep in mind that almost all chamber music may be classified as part of the sonata family. Thus, a duo, trio, or quartet is, in effect, usually a sonata for as many instruments since the first movement is generally built on the principles of sonata form.

Historically chamber music had a broader meaning before the advent of the public concert hall than it does today. In the sixteenth and seventeenth centuries any kind of music performed in large chambers or halls of aristocratic palaces and mansions – hence not accessible to the public at large – was referred to as chamber music, irrespective of the size or type of performing groups. Today the term connotes music for small ensembles, to be heard most advantageously in rooms of a size germane to the music's intended acoustical properties. Thus, a trio performing in a huge auditorium simply because it is composed of three "stars" who will easily attract a mass audience constitutes a breach of musical taste and can be a travesty of artistic purpose.

SUITE

This is an instrumental composition in which various sections or movements, most frequently of a dancelike character, are combined in free succession. The related French verb *suivre*, "to follow" – more closely reflected in the English word "pursuit" – may serve as a further link in the linguistic derivation of the word. The designation of "movement" for the various sections of the suite is reminiscent of the component parts of a sonata or symphony, for in each case the emphasis is on the contrasting content of each successive portion.

The suite is of baroque origin and connotes a series of dances, all written in the same key, with each dance representative of a different national style. For example, such a work often consists of an allemande of German derivation; a French courante; a Spanish sarabande; a French gavotte, minuet, or bourrée; and an English gigue. A rather elaborate prelude often heads this array of dances. Every language has its own version of this introductory section (*praeludium* in Latin, *prélude* in French, *preludio* in Italian and Spanish, and *Präludium* in German). They all denote an important, attention-getting opening that sets the pace for the entire work.

While the suite, although less elaborate in structure, existed before the time of Bach, it was Bach himself who utilized this form of composition freely and significantly, thus aiding and crystallizing its development. His six English Suites for Harpsichord and six French Suites for Harpsichord (the English suites headed by a *praeludium*), six Suites for Unaccompanied Cello, three Suites for Unaccompanied Violin, four Overtures or Suites for Orchestra, and six Partitas for Harpsichord are great milestones. The violin suites were originally called *partia* (the Italian *partita* denotes a "division into parts"). The famous "Chaconne" for unaccompanied violin constitutes the last part of the second Partita for Violin in D minor. This in itself is a masterpiece of unexcelled stature.

Listen to the third of Bach's four orchestral suites containing the well-known air, popularly referred to as "Air on the G String," an arrangement by the violinist August Wilhelmj of the original orchestral version.

Divertimento, cassation, and serenade are closely related to the concept of the suite; they are instrumental compositions consisting of various loosely connected movements. The cassations and divertimentos of Haydn and Mozart; the serenades of Mozart, Beethoven, Brahms, Dvořák, Tchaikovsky, and Elgar; and the Partita for orchestra by William Walton – all eloquently bespeak the close relationship and common denominator of their concept.

In addition, suites have been written by many composers of the last two centuries, such as Grieg's *Holberg Suite,* Milhaud's *Suite Provençale,* Sibelius' *Suite Champêtre,* and Hindemith's *Suite "1922,"* to mention a few. The term suite has also been applied to the assemblage of portions of ballet scores, such as Ravel's *Daphnis et Chloé,* Stravinsky's *The Firebird* and *Petrouchka,* and Tchaikovsky's *The Nutcracker.* The same is true of the use of orchestral sections of opera scores and of incidental music to plays or, more recently, to films. There are orchestral suites drawn from Kodály's *Háry János;* Bizet's *Carmen, La Jolie Fille de Perth,* and *L'Arlésienne;* Grieg's *Peer Gynt;* Prokofiev's film score *Lieutenant Kijé;* Sibelius' *The Tempest;* Korngold's *Much Ado About Nothing;* and Mendelssohn's *A Midsummer Night's Dream,* among many others. In each case the composer or an arranger has extracted parts of a complete score so as to create a logical succession of musical episodes effective for concert performance outside the context of the stage action in which the music originally appeared.

Theme and Variations

As the title of this section implies, a melody or a musical idea is repeated with various modifications of a rhythmic, melodic, or harmonic nature. The variation form endeavors to treat a theme in as many different ways as possible without abandoning its identity completely. The more inventive the composer, the more numerous the variations and the more daring the departure from the original theme, at times stretching to the limit our ability to recognize it.

Brahms's *Variations on a Theme by Haydn* is a classic example in this category. Its main theme is based on Haydn's quotation in his own divertimento of an ancient hymn known as "Chorale St. Antony." After introducing the hymn verbatim, Brahms proceeds to clothe it in eight different and most imaginative musical garments, from the romantic to the contrapuntal, from the ornamental to the light-textured, from broad, lyrical lines to rhythmic hunting calls, from a delicate siciliano (a Sicilian dance of pastoral character) for flute and viola to a version for muted strings. In the finale the original chorale is restated in all its majesty, thus completing the cycle. It should be noted that this restoration of the theme at the work's conclusion represents a technique favored by many composers.

Quite often a composer will borrow someone else's melody as a point of departure for his own musical adventures. Some notable examples are: Brahms's *Variations on a Theme by Handel,* taken from the latter's Suite for Harpsichord in B-flat Major; Beethoven's monumental set of variations on a waltz by music publisher Anton Diabelli; Mozart's charming variations on "Ah! Vous Dirai-je, Maman," also known as "Twinkle, Twinkle, Little Star"; and Max Reger's *Variations and Fugue on a Theme of Mozart,* taken from the first movement of Mozart's Piano Sonata No. 11 in A Major, K. 331.

At other times composers will borrow from themselves in selecting a theme. Among the outstanding examples in this category are: Beethoven's *Eroica Variations* for piano; Mendelssohn's *Variations Sérieuses* for piano; Elgar's *Enigma Variations* for orchestra; Schumann's *Études Symphoniques,* a wondrous set of variations for piano; Bach's *Goldberg Variations* for harpsichord; Richard Strauss's *Don Quixote* ("Fantastic Variations on a Theme of Knightly Character") for cello and orchestra.

Among the composer's variations on his own original theme we also find a host of examples in which the variation form is used in a movement of a large-scale work rather than as a single, independent piece. Here I would cite two famous examples by Schubert: his lovely treatment of his own song "Die Forelle" ("The Trout") as the fourth movement of his popular quintet for piano and strings, nicknamed the "Trout"; and Schubert's variations on the second theme of his song "Der Tod und das Mädchen" ("Death and the Maiden"), as the second movement of his String Quartet in D Minor; Haydn's "Emperor" Quartet, in which he uses his own Austrian "Emperor's Hymn" as the second movement of his String Quartet in C Major, Op. 76, No. 3; the first movement of Mozart's Piano Sonata No. 11 in A Major, K. 331, consisting of variations on his own theme; the second movement of Beethoven's "Appassionata" Sonata, Op. 57, the second movement of his "Kreutzer" Sonata, Op. 47, the second movement of his "Archduke" Trio, Op. 97, and the fourth movement of his "Harp" Quartet, Op. 74. One of the most popular of all examples of this genre is the second movement of Haydn's "Surprise" Symphony, No. 94.

Historically, various techniques may be applied to the writing of variations. Both the melody and harmony of the original theme can be maintained, with ornamentations of the melody or rhythmic changes assuring variety. This category generally includes a modal variation, a change from major to minor key, or vice versa. A good example is the second movement of Haydn's "Surprise" Symphony. The harmonic structure of the theme can remain essentially unchanged, while the variance of the melodic line is made to adjust to it. The chaconne, passacaglia, and ground fit this description, although in these instances the harmonic scheme is often shorter than a complete tune. At other times the bare division of measures and phrases is retained, reminding us of the original melody and harmonies; an example of this is Schumann's *Études Symphoniques*. Finally, there are variations in which there is no discernable reminder of the original theme except in name; for example, the second movement of Stravinsky's *Sonata for Two Pianos*.

RONDO

This popular form is frequently found as the last movement of sonatas, symphonies, and concertos. There are also many instances of rondos as completely independent compositions. An innate playfulness permeates this category of writing, which is due to the principal feature of the form itself, namely, the regular recurrence of the main section. It is much like singing a joyous refrain after many intermediary episodes.

Strictly speaking, it is the recurring section that is referred to as "rondo," while the other parts are known as "diversions." A concise description of the form is: A-B-A-C-A, with A representing the recurring rondo and B and C denoting the contrasting episodes. These contrasts are achieved by introducing completely different thematic material, as well as by changing tonalities away from the key of the main section. However, they always return to it.

The rondo is believed to have its origin in the rondeau, extant in medieval France both in poetry and in music. Its main feature is the recurring refrain, which developed from brief melodies into an increasingly elaborate structure. The rondeau is found abundantly in the literature of seventeenth- and eighteenth-century French clavecinists (composers for the harpsichord) such as Jean Philippe

Rameau, François Couperin, Jacques Champion de Chambonnières, and Louis Marchand.

Among the finest examples of the rondo's independent form are Mozart's Rondo in A Minor for Piano, K. 511; Beethoven's Rondo in C Major for Piano, Op. 51, No. 1; Mendelssohn's *Rondo Capriccioso* for Piano; Mozart's Rondo in D Major for Piano, K. 485; and Saint-Saëns's *Introduction and Rondo Capriccioso* for violin and orchestra. The rondo form in large-scale compositions is found in the final movements of most concertos of the Viennese classical period, as well as in corresponding movements of the Beethoven piano sonatas (for example, No. 8 in C Minor, Op. 13, the "Pathetique"). One of the most memorable examples among earlier works is the third movement of the Violin Concerto in E Major by Bach.

CONTRAPUNTAL MUSIC

Strictly speaking, counterpoint is not a category but rather a technique or musical language applied to compositions of a polyphonic nature, such as a round, a canon, a ricercar, or a fugue. Compositions that utilize this technique are called contrapuntal works, or music constructed by means of counterpoint. Counterpoint may also be applied to parts or movements of other musical forms discussed in this chapter, such as the third movement of the piano sonata by Samuel Barber. Presently, however, we will discuss compositions whose contrapuntal structure alone makes them possible.

Counterpoint is executed more easily than it can be described. The term is derived from the Latin *punctus contra punctum,* meaning "note against note" or, in a broader sense, "melody against melody." This suggests two or more melodies being played or sung simultaneously, each melody with an independent life of its own. Yet at any given moment when the intervals created by any of the component tones of the melodies are sounded at the same time, they form a consonance or a dissonance, depending upon how our ears perceive them (explained in the section on harmony in Chapter Two).

It is the texture of the work by which individual consonances and dissonances are weighed, much like a woven fabric whose horizontal weft may be made of perfect lines, while the vertical warp can create momentary blemishes, disturbances, or even optical illusions. A look at a simple and very familiar round may illustrate both point and counterpoint.

Every four measures an independent new voice enters, singing "Frère Jacques." There is harmony until at certain places (the syllables "les" and "dan") a clash occurs, individual tones forming a momentary dissonance. There we experience a fleeting "second" (two immediately adjacent tones).

In place of a single melody being supported by chords – the usual homophonic, one-voiced, way of harmonizing a tune – the horizontally passing melodies or voices of the round are identical in tones, phrase lengths, and words. The round is distinguished from unison singing in that each voice enters in succession rather than simultaneously. Hence, friction is created by superimposition. For instance, the question *"dormez-vous?"* ("are you sleeping?") asked by one voice occurs at the same moment that another voice commands *"Sonnez les matines!"* ("Ring the morning bells!").

The round is derived from the medieval "rota" ("wheel"), of which the best-known surviving example is the thirteenth-century English tune "Sumer is icumen in." This derivation implies a kind of perpetual continuation, each participant entering as often as desired, until it is agreed to stop the "round" motion, or the wheel, regardless of everyone's position in the melody at that moment.

The canon is also a polyphonic concept in which each voice enters successively and imitates the previous one. It is synonymous with the round if the melodies are identical in every way. In a free canon one voice can enter on a different tone or pitch than another voice yet still sing the same melody; hence the expression "canon at the fifth" or "canon at the fourth" (depending on the interval between the beginning tones of the different voices) rather than "canon at the unison" (when the beginning pitch of the different voices is the same). One voice may enter in contrary motion to the other, creating a "canon by inversion." One voice can be written in longer or shorter note values than the original melody, which produces "canon by augmentation" or "canon by diminution," respectively. A "crab canon" (or "retrograde canon") is one in which the imitating voice is written backward; if the imitating voice enters backward and upside down, the canon is known as "crab by inversion" (or "canon by retrograde inversion").

The ricercar (or ricercare), which originated in the sixteenth and seventeenth centuries, connotes various types of instrumental music. The Italian verb *ricercare* ("to seek out") comes closest to the meaning of such a composition, a "research" (a freer translation of the word) applied in finding ways of writing. Not every ricercar is contrapuntal, although this is the form that concerns us in this discussion.

The imitative or contrapuntal ricercar is the result of research of all types of canonic varieties and modifications of a theme. Bach, in his enlightening collection of contrapuntal compositions for instruments called *Ein Musikalisches Opfer (Musical Offering)*, wrote various pieces by the name of ricercar, using a theme given to him by King Frederick the Great during a visit to Potsdam.

The most elaborate treatment of counterpoint is found in the fugue, a composition of two or more parts all built on a theme that recurs in various voices, positions, and intervals throughout the work. The word fugue, meaning flight, applies to the procedure of each voice chasing or flying before the preceding one. The first part of the fugue, in which all participating voices make their initial appearance, is called the exposition or subject. This is followed by the episode, a new idea, or more often a treatment of part of a melody heard earlier. The episode generally leads to a different yet related key, and then a return to the original tonality at the end of the fugue.

Spaces that occur between entrances of the theme or subject, or between those of the episode, are taken up by intervening counterpoint, using parts of previously heard melodies.

The parts of melodies that fill the lapses can rival in importance even the main subjects and episodes. The result is a countersubject, a new melodic strain to which each voice adapts as soon as the original statement is completed and the next voice is about to enter.

Often the key of the subject in a choral fugue is not suitable for all voices. Soprano and tenor voices can sing easily in a higher key, while alto and bass voices have to be transposed into the dominant key (for instance, from C four steps lower to G). In such a case the melody in the dominant key is no longer called a subject but is known as an answer. The answer is "real" when it is an exact transposition of the subject; it is "tonal" when it has been modified by transposition.

The opening parts of a fugue for soprano, alto, tenor, and bass voices occur in the following order: subject-answer-subject-answer (also known as a sequence of *dux* and *comes* in Latin, or "leader" for subject and "companion" for answer in English. Another designation would be an antecedent and a consequent theme.

Just as is the case in the canon any of the component parts of the fugue can enter in various positions – reverse, upside down, inside out, abbreviated, or elongated. Thus, the overall structure of the fugue becomes a continual alternation of themes, expositions and episodes, subjects and answers, and subjects and countersubjects. While all have the contrapuntal treatment in common, the episodes are often of lighter musical complexion. As the structure unfolds, modulations into other keys take place; however, the exposition containing the main themes will return to the original main key for its last appearance.

If voices enter in close proximity, the term *stretto* is used, an Italian word meaning close, narrow, or squeezed together. The effect can be very exciting, showing the climactic cumulative impact of various entries, especially toward the end of a work.

Depending upon the number of subjects involved, we speak of double, triple, or quadruple fugues. Writing fugues is one of the most complex subjects in musical composition. While there are many independent, unattached fugues, some noteworthy ones are found as concluding parts of larger works, such as Bach's toccata and Fugue in D Minor, Prelude and Fugue in C Minor, the forty-eight preludes and fugues that constitute *The Well-Tempered Clavier,* and Beethoven's fugal treatments of his late piano sonatas and quartets, specifically No. 29 in B-flat Major ("Hammerklavier") and No. 31 in A-flat Major, and the Grosse Fugue in B-flat Major for string quartet.

Historically the procedure of imitation in contrapuntal fashion was first observed in the early thirteenth century. Not until some two hundred years later did masters of polyphonic style, such as Josquin des Prés, Heinrich Isaac, and Jacob Obrecht make use of the polyphonic structure in such works as canzone and ricercars. Johann Sebastian Bach represents the apex of the mastery of contrapuntal style in its most varied and sophisticated forms.

Other masters of the baroque period developed the form's potentialities, passing it on to the classicists, who in turn carried it into a new age beginning with Mozart and, particularly, Beethoven.

By and large, little was added during the romantic age, which laid greater stress on emotional content than on the refinement of a design as formal as the fugue. However, the twentieth century has seen a remarkable rebirth of the concept, kindled by such masters as Hindemith, Barber, and Dallapiccola. This is not to say that the fugue was without great proponents during the 1800s, as is shown by the rousing closing fugue of Verdi's *Falstaff.*

The categories of round, canon, ricercar, and fugue were brought to life through the inspirational and inventive power of generations of composers. Their creative efforts prove that counterpoint is far more than a cerebral exercise. Listen to Bach's organ fugues in a great church and you will experience a feeling of elevation that matches the grandeur of the edifice. Knowing the essentials of the fugue's structure will enrich that experience immeasurably.

PROGRAM MUSIC

ANTHEM

In its original meaning the anthem is a choral composition with English words drawn from the Bible or some other religious source. It is generally performed as part of the Protestant worship service, like the motet in the Roman Catholic service. The anthem can be sung without accompaniment, or it can be accompanied by an organ or an orchestra. It originated in the sixteenth century during the Reformation, and even though it was derived from the Latin motet, its development as part of the English liturgical order has proceeded on a completely independent course.

Generations of English composers, from the sixteenth century until the present, have contributed immensely to the repertory of the anthem. Among the leaders in the field are Thomas Tallis (c. 1505–85), Henry Purcell (c. 1659–95), G. F. Handel (1685–1759), S. S. Wesley (1810–76), Edward Elgar (1857–1934), Ralph Vaughan Williams (1872–1958), and Benjamin Britten (1913–76).

At the hands of Purcell and, particularly, Handel, the anthem became far more elaborate, replete with instrumental interludes and a great concluding chorus. Handel's anthems were written primarily for festive occasions, such as the *Dettingen Te Deum* of 1743, celebrating the English victory over the French at Dettingen during the War of the Austrian Succession.

In England the anthem became associated with various historical periods; for example, there are Elizabethan, Tudor, Restoration, and Victorian anthems. Some English composers are known today primarily for their anthems; for instance, Samuel Wesley's volume of anthems published in 1853 contain many standard works still heard today.

Anthems in our time are no longer exclusively in English, nor are they referred to exclusively in a religious sense. Their secular use is exemplified in the national anthems of various countries.

CANTATA

The cantata, which evolved during the baroque period, is a vocal composition based on a secular or religious narrative text and consisting of arias, recitatives, ensembles, and choruses. The word is derived from the Italian *cantare,* "to sing." Bach's many uses of this category – nearly two hundred church cantatas are still in use today – established it firmly, both chorally and for solo voice, as a form of composition whose validity has never waned.

Any choice from such an enormous wealth of masterpieces is bound to be a highly personal one. The following Bach cantatas are suggested for your listening pleasure:

No. 4 *Christ Lag in Todesbanden* ("Christ Lay in Bonds of Death"), a cantata for Easter Sunday with words by Martin Luther. This is the only cantata using the hymn melody exclusively, with each verse representing a variation of the chorale tune.

No. 147 *Herz und Mund und Tat und Leben* ("Heart and Mouth and Deed and Life") written for the fourth Sunday in Advent. This work contains the well-known and beautiful "Jesu bleibt meine Freude" ("Jesu, Joy of Man's Desiring"), a chorale melody that has been transcribed in various ways but is most familiar in the piano version by the great twentieth-century English pianist Dame Myra Hess.

No. 140 *Wachet auf!* ("Sleepers Awake!"), composed for the twenty-seventh Sunday after Trinity, based on the Gospels. Underlying the parable of the wise and foolish virgins is a famous hymn written by Philipp Nicolai in 1599, which carries the same title.

No. 208 *Was mir behagt* ("What Pleases Me") Bach's first secular cantata, written at the request of his employer in Weimar, a duke who was invited to help celebrate the birthday of a fellow nobleman. This cantata was actually performed during a banquet in a game-keeper's lodge; hence it became known as the "Hunting" Cantata. Its most familiar part is the lovely pastoral section "Schafe können sicher weiden" ("Sheep May Safely Graze"). This constitutes a perfect example of Bach's capacity to infuse a melody with spirituality within a very worldly context.

Just as Bach wrote cantatas for every Sunday of the church calendar, so masters of the classical, romantic, and modern periods wrote cantatas for special occasions. Among these are: Haydn's *Birthday Cantata for Prince Esterházy;* Mozart's *Die Maurerfreude (The Joy of the Masons),* one of Mozart's several contributions to the cause of Freemasonry; Beethoven's *Der glorreiche Augenblick (The Glorious Moment);* and other examples by Schubert, Schumann, Mendelssohn, Liszt, Brahms, Saint-Saëns, Vaughan Williams, Hindemith, Bartók, Debussy, Stravinsky, and Britten.

CHARACTER PIECE

The character piece, known in German as *Charakterstück,* is a form of piano music of the romantic period of a dramatic, epic, or lyrical nature, and of contrasting moods. It is generally written for piano in A-B-A form, which easily accommodates changes of content. Such pieces can either be designated by collective titles or by individual names suggesting the storytelling elements intended by the composer.

Mozart's *Fantasias,* Beethoven's *Bagatelles* (three sets, Opp. 33, 119, 126), Schubert's *Impromptus* and *Moments Musicaux,* and Mendelssohn's *Lieder ohne Worte (Songs Without Words)* are early examples of collective names.

An extremely satisfying example of a character piece is Schumann's *Arabesque,* Op. 18. Pieces under the heading of "cycles" include: *Fantasiestücke (Fantasy Pieces),* Op. 12; *Carnaval,* Op. 9; *Faschingsschwank aus Wien (Carnival Jest from Vienna),* Op. 26; *Papillons,* Op. 2; *Waldszenen (Forest Scenes),* Op. 82; *Davidsbündlertänze (Dances of the Members of the League of David),* Op. 6; *Kreisleriana* (derived from E. T. A. Hoffmann's pseudonym "Kapellmeister Johannes Kreisler"), Op. 16; *Kinderszenen (Scenes from Childhood),* Op. 15; and *Album für die Jugend (Album for the Young),* Op. 68. Some contain several basically independent pieces that are often performed separately such as "Aufschwung" ("Soaring") from Op. 12 and "Träumerei" ("Dreaming") from Op. 15.

Only musical considerations, such as the alternation of dramatic and introspective, fast and slow, or loud and subdued effects account for the order in which some of the cycles are organized. The *Forest Scenes* are arranged in a progressive order, suggesting the scenes upon which a wanderer might chance on his walk through the forest. Other sets of pieces are cyclic in the sense that component parts are completely interwoven with a central idea, and hence are difficult to perform separately. For example, *Carnaval* bears the subtitle *Scènes Mignonnes Composées sur Quatre Notes (Tiny Scenes Composed on Four Notes)*. The four notes spell out the name of the town of Asch, the home of a girl for whom Schumann had great affection.

In addition, there are three important and very rewarding sets of variations from the pen of Schumann, each forming a coherent entity built upon a central idea. The *A-B-E-G-G Variations,* Op. 1, are another Schumann tribute to an early infatuation. The young lady's name, A-Bb-E-G-G, is spelled out in actual notes and the variations are woven freely and imaginatively around the letters of the name. *Variations on a Theme by Clara Wieck,* Op. 14, Schumann's betrothed, are in effect a set of impromptus on Clara's melody. The most important of the variations are known as *Études Symphoniques,* Op. 13, consisting of twelve studies in the form of variations. The composer's great pianistic ability and idiomatic identification with his instrument pervades all of these rich contributions to the piano literature.

An interesting autobiographical trait can be found in most of these cyclic sets of piano pieces. Schumann related alternating musical moods to two aspects of his own dual personality, and symbolized them as Eusebius, the gentle and meditative persona, and Florestan, the active and impulsive individual. This dual identification is implemented by alternating meditative and active pieces. In *Carnaval* the names of Eusebius and Florestan are actually used to caption two such sections, a quasi-psychoanalytical device.

Equally worthwhile to peruse are Schumann's single-named sets, such as *Novelletten, Romances, Albumblätter,* and *Nachtstücke,* which are not unlike Schubert's *Impromptus* and *Moments Musicaux* in their expression of many moods and emotions.

Mendelssohn's collection of 48 *Lieder ohne Worte (Songs Without Words)* are also noteworthy. These are pieces written in songlike fashion, singable melodies with interestingly interwoven accompaniments. Some have been given descriptive titles by enterprising publishers, such as "Spring Song," "Hunting Song," or "May Breezes." A few titles were chosen by the composer himself, among them three called "Venetian Boat Song," and the "Duetto," a lyrical and spirited dialogue between a male and female voice.

A very special place must be reserved in this category of individual piano pieces for the highly personal art of keyboard writing by Frédéric Chopin. His harmonic treatment goes far beyond the practice of the time, and the technical demands of his works are, for the most part, formidable. He is often referred to as the poet of the piano because of his reputed sensitivity in his own playing and the lyricism inherent in many of his creations. Yet Chopin's music can also thunder with drama and a defiant spirit, so akin is it to the exile's strong patriotic feelings for his beloved Poland. Among the finest examples of his output are four ballades, twenty-seven etudes (each addressed to a specific technical skill, such as octaves, thirds, left-hand passages, arpeggios, etc.), three impromptus, nineteen nocturnes, twenty-five preludes, four scherzos, seventeen waltzes, a berceuse, and a barcarolle. Chopin's patriotism is manifested in his twelve stately polonaises and fifty-one mazurkas. These are great riches without which the piano repertory is unthinkable.

Johannes Brahms contributed to the genre of the individual piano piece with a series of rhapsodies, intermezzos, capriccios, and ballades. To know them is to gain a bit of insight into some facets of Brahms's complex personality.

Among Edvard Grieg's finest shorter piano works are the *Lyric Pieces,* sixty-six of them published in ten volumes. These most attractive miniatures – most are only two pages long – show Grieg's love of nature. "To Spring," "Butterfly," and "Evening in the Mountains" have rendered Grieg's work synonymous with the music of Norway. It is a joy for anyone to examine and reexamine this treasure chest of musical invention, the components of which run the gamut of human emotion. At the same time, the discerning performer and listener gains a valuable understanding of Grieg's unmistakably personal and distinctive harmonic language.

Franz Liszt, one of the most brilliant piano virtuosos of all time, enriched the literature of the piano with a wealth of highly romantic and exceedingly difficult compositions in the category called "character piece." There are twenty *Hungarian Rhapsodies,* twelve *Études d'Exécution Transcendante,* three Concert Etudes, two well-known Etudes subtitled "Forest Murmurs" and "Dance of the Gnomes," two *Legends* called "St. Francis of Assisi Preaching to the Birds" and "St. Francis Walking on the Waves." Liszt also composed a collection of impressions of his travels in Switzerland and Italy, issued under the collective title *Années de Pélérinage (Years of Pilgrimage).* These speak to us of Liszt the man and musician, and the state of his soul; they were written under the influence of his liaison with Countess Marie d'Agoult, his co-traveler on many journeys. Twenty-three compositions were published in three volumes. Poems by Byron, sonnets by Petrarch, a painting by Raphael, and a statue by Michelangelo are some of the sources from which Liszt, the romanticist par excellence, derived his inspiration.

Of a somewhat later vintage are two suites by Spanish masters: *Iberia* by Isaac Albéniz (1860–1909), and *Goyescas* by Enrique Granados (1867–1916). The first consists of four books, each containing three pieces, all of which paint penetrating tonal pictures of Spanish life and places. The second suite, composed of two books, each containing six pieces, evokes the spirit of Goya's paintings and tapestries chronicling life in eighteenth-century Madrid.

In France, nineteenth-century composer Emmanuel Chabrier wrote several very effective pieces for the piano, all typical of the romantic spirit. Among them are his *Dix Pièces Pittoresques (Ten Picturesque Pieces).* Gabriel Fauré, Chabrier's compatriot, composed an extensive list of impromptus, barcarolles, nocturnes, preludes, caprices, and variations – part of a rich legacy that helped shape the musical thinking of generations of subsequent French composers.

CHORALE

This category of church music had its origin as the hymn tune of the German Protestant Church, specifically the Lutheran Church, as early as 15 1. Martin Luther (1483–1546), a versatile musician, was responsible for the compilation of singable melodies and easily comprehensible texts suitable for congregational participation. He and his co-workers translated the words of the Roman Catholic hymns into German. For instance, "Te Deum Laudamus" became *Herr Gott, dich loben wir* ("Lord God, We Praise Thee"). Secular songs were then adapted to the texts. Another important contributor to this category of music was Luther's friend Johann Walther (1496–1570), who wrote *Geystliches Gesangk Buchleyn (Spiritual Songbook)*, a formidable collection of choral melodies containing some thirty-eight contrapuntal settings for multiple voices.

In the seventeenth and eighteenth centuries the chorale served as the heart of large-scale works, such as church cantatas and compositions for organ, including variations, preludes, and suites. All had the common goal of serving the congregation in singing, for the chorales used in all of these types of works were familiar to all the congregants.

Bach utilized such chorales in his cantatas, both for solo voices and in four-part harmonization. From among some two hundred of his church contatas, the following aptly illustrate the use of the chorale:

Cantata No. 4, *Christ Lag in Todesbanden* ("Christ Lay in Bonds of Death"), with words by Martin Luther.

Cantata No. 80, *"Ein feste Burg ist unser Gott"* ("A Mighty Fortress Is Our God"), based on Luther's own musical setting of Psalm 46. Bach used the melody as a point of departure, building a mighty aggregation of individual vocal passages, solos and duets, and remarkable embellishments for choir of the original melody.

Also in the category of the chorale is the chorale prelude, an elaborate organ composition woven around a hymn tune. It originated in Germany in the seventeenth century as an organ introduction to the hymn to be sung in the Lutheran Church. Contrapuntal techniques are frequently employed, as is the variation form, especially among the 143 chorale preludes by Bach. Bach's treatment of the chorale prelude tends to underscore as well as embellish the original tune, thereby strengthening and sustaining it.

INCIDENTAL MUSIC

This term refers to a collection of various orchestral pieces specially created to be interpolated between sections of a stage play or drama. Their function may be to preface the mood of an ensuing act or scene, to recall or elongate the atmosphere of, or musically comment upon, a scene just ended; or to generally entertain the audience between acts. In addition, parts of such music are composed especially for use as background for monologues or dialogues in order to render them more dramatic.

Incidental music can consist of dances, marches, mood pictures, occasional songs, preludes, overtures, or any other instrumental portions germane to any given part of the drama. Many sections of these scores are assembled into suites for concert performance.

Incidental music had its historical beginnings in the Greek theater and in medieval liturgical plays. Shakespeare often called for such music, as exemplified at the start of *Twelfth Night.*

Some notable examples of incidental music are: Purcell's dramatic music; Beethoven's music to Goethe's *Egmont;* Schubert's score to Wilhemine von Chézy's *Rosamunde;* Mendelssohn's *A Midsummer Night's Dream;* Bizet's music to Alphonse Daudet's *L'Arlésienne (The Woman of Arles);* Grieg's score to Henrik Ibsen's *Peer Gynt;* Delius' music to James Elroy Flecker's *Hassan;* and Virgil Thomson's film scores to *The Plough that Broke the Plains* and *Louisiana Story.* As is true of all compositions associated with stage action, the important musical question remains: Is the music of sufficient interest when performed in isolation, divorced from such stage action? A resounding "yes" is the answer in all of the cases stated above.

LIED

Literally meaning song, the Lied is a German poem, mostly of a romantic nature, set to music. The story of the poem is expressed by the combination of the singer's melody and the piano setting, which, instead of being a mere accompaniment, captures the mood of the poem as well as its human and philosophical implications. Hence piano and voice become indivisible partners of equal importance and responsibility.

Historically the Lied had its beginnings in the activities of the medieval minnesingers, German poets and musicians in the age of chivalry, of which the troubadours of France are a counterpart.

Throughout the polyphonic musical styles of the fifteenth and sixteenth centuries and the accompanied songs of the baroque period, the Lied was a popular form of expression in Germany, its content reflecting many activities of daily life.

The artistic interdependence of melody and piano setting emerged with the early lieder by Haydn, Mozart and Beethoven, who endowed the art form with a great lyricism and a newly found sense of drama. The German Lied reached its zenith during the romantic age. Composers of the time matched their music with the lyrical intentions of the German romantic poets. The greatest of all the lieder composers was Franz Schubert, who, with unfailing insight and feeling, created close to six hundred lieder, most of which have never been surpassed in beauty and coordination of their voice/piano relationship.

The realism of both poetic and musical thought is often pictorial in its concrete descriptive imagery. The whirring of the spinning wheel in Goethe's "Gretchen am Spinnrade" ("Gretchen at the Spinning Wheel") from *Faust;* the panic of father and son as they try to escape a phantom in "Der Erlkönig" ("The Erl King"); the restless urging of the adventurous "Der Musensohn" ("The Son of the Muses"); the noble simplicity of thanksgiving in Franz von Schober's "An die Musik" ("To Music"); the rippling of the brook and the impatience of the fisherman in Schubert's "Die Forelle" ("The Trout") – all create a realistic presence that enables us to follow each happening not only with our ears but with our mind's eye.

Also worthy of closer examination are Schubert's unforgettable song cycles, *Die schöne Müllerin (The Fair Miller's Daughter)* and *Die Winterreise (Winter's Journey),* both based on poems by Schubert's contemporary Wilhelm Müller. *Die schöne Müllerin* is a pastoral description of the rustic courtship of the miller's daughter and his apprentice, which is interrupted by the appearance of a hunter whose rivalry causes the apprentice to seek solace at the brook in whose gentle waters he finds final relief. *Die Winterreise,* more philosophical in content and almost autobiographical in nature, admittedly caused its composer extreme anguish and emotional excitement. The central idea presents a lonely wanderer on his journey in mid-winter, leaving behind the home of his beloved, who had deserted him. Passing scenes and recollections lead him to yearn for the end that eludes him.

Schubert perfected the technique of translating the poetry of words into a poetic symmetry of music. According to the spirit of the poem, he employed both a strophic arrangement and a through-composed style. Strophic refers to the fact that all stanzas of the poem are sung to the same melody. It is applied to simple lyrics, such as Schubert's "Das Heidenröslein" ("The Little Hedge Rose"). Through-composed connotes a new melody for each stanza. A dramatic text with constantly changing images and situations, such as Schubert's "Der Erlkönig", lends itself better to be "through-composed."

After Schubert, several other composers devoted themselves to this meaningful repertory of miniature dramas. Karl Loewe (1796–1869) is an undisputed master of the dramatic Lied known as the ballade, of which he wrote some 150 examples, often unjustly neglected by lieder singers. Loewe's fertile imagination and superb sense for the pictorial guided him in the creation of an art form all its own, the German ballade, derived from the English ballad, an extended poem for voice and piano. Among Loewe's masterpieces are such works as "Tom der Reimer" ("Thomas the Rhymer"); "Die Uhr" ("The Clock"); and "Prince Eugen, der edle Ritter" ("Prince Eugene, the Noble Knight"). It is a great joy to become acquainted or reacquainted with these jewels.

Following in the footsteps of Schubert, yet creating their own individual style of writing lieder, were Schumann, Brahms, Mendelssohn, Cornelius, Wolf, Mahler, and Richard Strauss. Several memorable examples of their work are listed here in the hope that they will induce the reader to widen his own research.

Schumann	"Die beiden Grenadiere" ("The Two Grenadiers")
	"Der Nussbaum" ("The Chestnut Tree")
	"Widmung" ("Dedication")
	the song cycles *Frauenliebe und -Leben (Women's Love and Life)*, based on poems by Adalbert von Chamisso, and *Dichterliebe (Poet's Love)*, with words by Heinrich Heine

Brahms	"Feldeinsamkeit" ("Nature's Solitude")
	"Wiegenlied" ("Lullaby")
	"Die Mainacht" ("May Night")
	"Ständchen" ("Serenade")
	the song cycles *Liebeslieder Walzer,* with verses by Georg Friedrich Daumer, and *Die schöne Magelone,* based on a folk legend told by Ludwig Tieck
	choral works: Rhapsody for alto solo, male chorus, and orchestra; "Schicksalslied" ("Song of Destiny"); "Triumphlied" ("Song of Triumph"); and "Gesang der Parzen" ("Song of the Fates")
Mendelssohn	"Auf Flügeln des Gesanges" ("On Wings of Song")
	"Gruss" ("Greeting")
	"An die Entfernte" ("To the Distant Beloved")
Wolf	"Verborgenheit" ("Secrecy")
	"Im Frühling" ("In Spring")
	"Das verlassene Mägdlein" ("The Lonely Maidservant")
	the great collections of lieder known as *Spanisches Liederbuch* and *Italienisches Liederbuch*
Mahler	lieder to texts by Rückert
R. Strauss	"Allerseelen" ("All Souls")
	"Heimliche Aufforderung" ("Secret Invitation")
	"Ständchen ("Serenade")
	"Zueignung" ("Dedication")

The word "Lied" has been used by composers of other nationalities to describe similar mergers of words and music in their respective tongues. Among these are Reynaldo Hahn, Claude Debussy, Guy Ropartz, and Francis Poulenc in France; Charles Ives, Aaron Copland, Samuel Barber, and Ned Rorem in the United States; Benjamin Britten, Hubert Parry, and Ralph Vaughan Williams in England; and Manuel de Falla in Spain.

MADRIGAL

The madrigal is one of the oldest vocal compositional categories. It dates back to the late thirteenth and early fourteenth centuries, when it first appeared in Italy as a designation for secular, unaccompanied songs for two or three voices. Free in character, the madrigal was unfettered by existing rules, such as *canto fermo* ("fixed song"), a melody forming the basis of polyphonic writing by which other melodies or voices are guided.

The text of the madrigal was generally short in duration, but it ran the gamut from pathos to humor, from the expression of intimate feelings to the description of daily happenings. The subject of the text was usually of a pastoral, idyllic, or love-song nature. The musical settings also were quite varied, employing a single lute or various instruments accompanying or conversing with the voices.

Among the composers who distinguished themselves in the art of madrigal writing were Carlo Gesualdo (1560–1613) and especially Claudio Monteverdi (1567–1643). In England the madrigal was made famous by such masters of the late sixteenth and early seventeenth centuries as Thomas Morley (1557–c. 1603), Thomas Weelkes (c. 1575–1623), John Wilbye (1574–1638), and Orlando Gibbons (1583–1625). No account of musical achievements of the time would be complete without the mention of one of England's greatest musicians, William Byrd (1543–1623), who contributed richly to all phases of music, and renowned English lutenist-composer John Dowland (1563–1626), whose services were sought by various courts.

The madrigal became very popular in England beginning in the late sixteenth century. As a vehicle of free expression it has served multiple purposes, from the religious to the patriotic, from simple songs of nature and love to elaborate manifestations of social life. As a vocal form the madrigal found its counterpart in other countries as well. In the sixteenth century Dutch and Flemish visitors to Venice, Florence, and Rome transplanted it to their native countries. In France many of the *chansons* ("songs") were actually madrigals. In Spain the *villancico* (from *villano*, "rustic"), which consists of poems set to music, took on the madrigal style, while in Germany

Hans Leo Hassler (1564–1612) established the form as a souvenir from his student days with Gabrieli in Venice.

The madrigal has undergone a remarkable rebirth in modern times, especially the interest in its freedom of character displayed by twentieth-century English and Italian composers.

MASS

The mass represents the most solemn form of worship in the Roman Catholic Church. Musical settings of the High Mass – as opposed to the Low Mass, which is celebrated without singing – present an enormously rich kaleidoscope of some of the finest and musically stirring choral compositions down through the ages. The term "mass" has an interesting linguistic origin; it is taken from the last sentence of the service: "Ite, *missa* est (congregatio)," literally, "Depart, the congregation is dis*miss*ed."

When we speak of the music of the mass, we refer to the invariable parts known collectively as the Ordinary, namely Kyrie, Gloria, Credo, Sanctus with Benedictus, and Agnus Dei. However, in its earliest settings (i.e., from the time of the Gregorian chant to c. 1250) the music of the mass known as the Proper, consisting of the parts that change seasonally and daily, was of greater musical interest. The portions of the Proper include: Introit, Gradual, Alleluia or Tract, Offertory, and Communion. The chants for the Proper, which are derived from the Psalms, are considerably older than the settings of the Ordinary. Since about 1300 only the parts of the Ordinary were composed, at first polyphonically and then in accordance with the general musical practices of each successive age.

Another form of the mass is the requiem, the *Missa pro defunctis (Mass for the Departed)*, so named because the opening Introit begins with the words "Requiem aeternam dona eis Domine" ("Give them eternal rest, O Lord"). Musically this mass is regularly structured, except for the omission of the joyous parts of the Ordinary (viz. the Gloria and Credo); the replacement of the Alleluia (of the Proper) with a Tractus or Tract consisting of psalm verses; and the addition of a sequence entitled "Dies Irae" ("Day of Judgment").

The composition of the mass as we know it today, namely, settings of the Ordinary in the order mentioned above, emerged as a major musical force in the age of polyphonic writing (c. 1400–1600). Dufay, Palestrina, Isaac, Obrecht, and des Prés contributed significantly to the establishment of the portions of the mass as a unified cycle. Quite often we find a short secular theme, by which the entire work came to be known, forming the connecting link among the parts; for instance, *L'Homme Armé* ("The Armed Man") is a tune used by some thirty composers during the course of two centuries. An interesting custom of the period was the addition of choral lines to an existing theme or tune, known in Italian as *canto fermo* ("fixed song") or *cantus firmus* in Latin.

In the absence of such a tune the designation *Missa sine Nomine (Mass Without Name)* is encountered quite frequently. In contrast to mass settings of considerable length, the *Missa Brevis (Short Mass)* is a form that has proven to be very popular through the centuries.

Many outstanding examples of music composed for the mass are included in the next chapter. The following are merely highlights among settings of the mass by composers of successive generations:

Bach	Mass in B Minor
Haydn	Mass in Time of War, Nelson Mass, Theresien-Messe
Mozart	Missa Brevis in C Major ("Sparrow Mass"), Coronation Mass,
	Mass in C Minor ("The Great Mass"), Requiem
Beethoven	Missa Solemnis in D Major, Mass in C Major
Cherubini	Mass in C Minor
Schubert	6 masses
Gounod	9 masses

Verdi, Berlioz, Dvořák, Bruckner, Saint-Saëns, Fauré, Brahms, and Britten all wrote elevating examples of the requiem mass.

Additional proof of the vitality of the music for the mass is found in the many ways in which it has been adapted to contemporary musical trends, such as jazz, folk, ethnic, rock, and nationally oriented examples, many of which deserve to have history bestow longevity upon them. Among national examples are the *Slavonic Mass* by the Czech composer Leos Janáček, the Missa Brevis by the Hungarian master Zoltán Kodály, and portions of the liturgy by the Armenian composer Komitas Vartabed should be singled out. No other form of music, not even the sonata and symphony, reaches back through so many centuries, only to emerge as a challenge for each generation to mirror its own time.

MOTET

Among vocal polyphonic categories, the motet is the most important and one of the oldest forms. Ever since the Middle Ages and the Renaissance, and during the course of more than seven centuries of its existence, the motet has traversed many stages in its evolution. Hence, it would be misleading to offer a comprehensive, general meaning.

In its original form the motet is defined as a composition for unaccompanied choir with a sacred text, sung in Latin for performance in the service of the Roman Catholic Church. The origin of the word dates back to the thirteenth century, when words (*mots* in French) were added to vocalized or wordless fragments of a Gregorian chant, known as "clausula."

Not long afterward the motet took on a secular complexion as well, according to practices prevalent in different countries. The motet was generally written in three-part contrapuntal form. The lowest part was derived from Gregorian chant, while the upper two parts, called *duplum* and *triplum,* were sung to different words, either sacred or secular. The varied meanings of the texts added a new and interesting dimension to the already multiple tonal nature of the contrapuntal setting.

The motet flourished in the fourteenth and fifteenth centuries at the hands of its great masters, Guillaume de Machaut of France, Guillaume Dufay of Belgium, and John Dunstable of England, whose polyphonic technique of imitative entries of voices paralleled and influenced the development of the instrumental fugue.

As time went on, the motet mirrored the compositional style of each successive historical period, retaining its main feature of a setting of a sacred Latin text for solo or choral voices, with or without instrumental accompaniment, with continuing contrapuntal texture. In the seventeenth and eighteenth centuries Latin gave way to languages indigenous to the country of origin. Bach's five unaccompanied motets constitute the zenith in this category. *Jesu, meine Freude,* for five-part a cappella chorus, is one of the loftiest and technically finest motets of all time. Its eleven sections represent a unique symmetry of text and musical treatment. Verses of the chorale alternate with passages from the Epistles, with two scriptural portions for three-part chorus or solo voices situated at equal distances from the beginning and the end of the work.

Schubert, Mendelssohn, and Brahms also composed motets, both unaccompanied and with instruments.

OPERA

This category of composition is one of the most popular and artistically comprehensive. It denotes a large dramatic work in which the greater part, if not the whole, is sung by soloists and ensembles, with instrumental accompaniment ranging from chamber-music proportions to a full-sized orchestra. The word "opera" is common to all major languages. Originally it was a contraction of the Italian *opera in musica* (a "musical work"). With this remarkable oversimplification the opera is distinguished from the stage drama or play.

The association of drama and music dates back to the early stages of civilization. Opera's forerunners before 1600 were the aristocratic masques, miracle plays, moralities, and mysteries, religiously or morally oriented entertainment for the public at large. Opera as we know it today had its beginnings in the late sixteenth century.

The earliest example of the period was a work entitled *Dafne,* based on a poem by the Florentine writer Ottavio Rinuccini (1562–1621), set to music by the Florentine composer and singer Jacopo Peri (1561–1633). *Dafne* was first performed for a private audience in the palace of Jacopo Corsi in Florence during the carnival season of 1597. Unfortunately the music has not survived. The story has its roots in Greek mythology. Dafne, the Italian name for Daphne, daughter of the Thessalian river god Peneus, is saved from the pursuits of Apollo when her mother, Gaea, conveniently changes her into a laurel tree. In its day the plot must have had attractive theatrical possibilities.

Another early Florentine example is *Euridice,* again based on a Rinuccini poem, with music by Peri and his Florentine colleague Giulio Caccini. This earliest surviving opera was first heard and seen in Florence in 1600 as a wedding entertainment for Henry IV of France and Maria de' Medici. The story, an early version of the well-known mythological tale of Orpheus and Eurydice, is labeled *dramma* ("tragedy"); *Dafne* was a *favola per musica* ("fable set to music"). In *Euridice* the singing was mostly of a recitative style. Supporting harmonies were sparse and rather colorless, with a small contingent of instruments furnishing the figured bass.

In 1607 a significant milestone in early baroque opera was reached, when Claudio Monteverdi's *L'Orfeo* was performed in Mantua, where the great Cremonese-born master was employed as a violist by the Duke of Mantua. The libretto by "Alessandrino" Striggio is based on the legend of Orpheus and Eurydice. From every point of view this is a work superior to anything that preceded it; the harmonic structure is far richer and the instrumental participation is more interesting. There is even a prelude in the form of a toccata, which constitutes the earliest known precursor of the operatic overture. Above all, the dramatic action appears to be far more varied and convincing. Monteverdi was the first to succeed in breathing life and passion into opera.

Not long after this memorable high point in the history of opera, the first public opera house, the Teatro di San Cassiano, opened its doors in Venice in 1637. It was preceded only by the beautiful but very private Barberini family theater in Rome, which first opened in 1632. Other opera houses followed in comparatively close succession. As a result, opera was no longer the exclusive domain of the nobility and its invited guests but rather a vital art form available to a growing and enthusiastic public.

As with the advent of the public concert hall, this development placed more challenging demands on librettists and composers, and the opera's subject matter and plot became ever wider in its appeal. Instead of employing mythological themes, composers began to turn to historical subjects for their plots. Here again, Monteverdi was a pace-setting composer. His last operatic masterwork, *L'Incoronazione di Poppea (The Coronation of Poppea),* originally staged in Venice in 1642, was the first example of an opera based upon a historical event. The librettist Francesco Busenello drew upon the story of Nero, the tyrannical emperor of Rome, for the opera's central character. The listener will be impressed with its lyric beauty and varied character types, which includes comic figures to offset the generally serious impact of this opera, one of the greatest works of its genre of the entire century.

The juxtaposition of comic elements and serious scenes, a feature quite common to early Italian opera, heralded the arrival of comic opera, or *opera buffa*, the Italian designation by which it became known and admired. Its principal features – a farcical story, a happy ending, recitatives expressed with great rapidity, tunes of a popular nature, and patter songs – lead, a century later to *The Beggar's Opera* (1728) by John Gay and John Christopher Pepusch, Offenbach's satirical masterpieces in the 1850s and 1860s, and Gilbert and Sullivan's immortal operettas of the 1870s through the 1890s.

As the seventeenth century progressed, Italian opera served as a model for the composers of the courts of Vienna, Brussels, Warsaw, and Paris. The French, in particular, developed their own operatic concepts, which were steeped in their heritage of classical drama and the tradition of French ballet.

French opera undoubtedly owes its existence and growing success during the baroque era to the Florentine Giovanni Battista Lulli, who at the age of fourteen changed his name to Jean Baptiste Lully, and became a violinist with Louis XIV's royal orchestra, a ballet dancer, and at the age of twenty, assumed the leadership of the court orchestra. After writing music for a successful series of comic ballets based on Molière's plays, in which he participated in adjunct roles as a dancer and actor, Lully became the founder of *tragédie lyrique*, the French counterpart of Italian opera of the time. His *Cadmus et Hermione* (1673), *Alceste* (1674), *Thésée* (1675), and *Atys* (1676) are far more spectacular than anything that baroque operagoers had ever seen. There were elaborate ballet scenes with heavily involved choral forces, a significant role for the orchestra, popular tunes, and stories of greater dramatic interest.

A look at English opera of the time reveals a noticeable indebtedness to the masque, which had its beginnings in Italy and France, but which flourished in England during the sixteenth and seventeenth centuries. The masque was an elaborate form of entertainment intended for the delight of the court, a combination of poetry and a variety of vocal and instrumental music, dancing, acting, scenery, and costumes. Subjects were generally of a mythological, allegorical, or imitative nature, with mimicry being an important feature. The close resemblance of masque and early opera is obvious. A representative example of the masque is a work entitled *The Triumph of Peace* (1633), with music by William Lawes; his brother, Henry, composed the score for John Milton's *Comus,* a masque conceived for performance at Ludlow Castle in 1634.

The development of opera in England during the seventeenth century was retarded by the refusal on the part of the Commonwealth and Restoration Society (1649–60) to accept stage entertainment in general. However, it would be difficult to surpass the utter beauty and dramatic impact of the 1689 opera *Dido and Aeneas* by Henry Purcell, England's greatest master of the time. Anyone who has ever heard an outstanding rendition of Dido's lament ("When I am laid in earth") will agree that here is an all-time high in the entire history of opera. It also shows that flamboyance, so readily associated with baroque music and art, here finds its counterpart in introspection of a noble sort.

Further highlights of baroque opera were created by the Italian composer, violinist, and singer Alessandro Stradella, whose own romantic entanglement with the mistress of a Venetian nobleman became the subject of an opera by the German operatic master Friedrich von Flotow about 180 years later. Stradella distinguished himself through his contributions to the evolution of vocal forms and the early concerto, both proof that his reputation has been much underrated and his creative abilities largely unrecognized.

Sicilian-born Alessandro Scarlatti was the most industrious and significant master of Italian opera in its formative baroque stage. He held prestigious positions in Rome, Naples, and Florence, imparting his knowledge and power of inspiration to a new generation of European composers who sought him out for study and guidance. Among his 115 operas, 150 oratorios, and approximately 600 cantatas, masses, and motets are found some superb, fully developed arias.

In the history of early opera in Germany, Heinrich Schütz and Reinhard Keiser are prominent figures. Keiser alone wrote 120 operas, the great majority of which are lost to us today.

In keeping with the artistic trends of every age, opera grew steadily into the complex, multifaceted form to which masters of every period have brought their highly specialized, multiple talents, and for which audiences have shown their deeply felt and faithful devotion – and, at times, even addiction. For the teaming of composer and librettist – sometimes the same person – or the bringing together of the greatest musicians and literary figures, the challenge remains a formidable one. The component arts of operatic performance present demands of incomparable proportions in order to achieve a truly memorable fusion. Vocal and instrumental music, poetry, drama, dance, acting, stage design, costuming, lighting and engineering, directing, and conducting each require the highest degree of professionalism.

Achievements in opera are often considered in the light of national efforts. Thus, in each period we speak of an Italian, French, Russian, or German school of opera. This is a good way to judge indigenous merits and national customs, as well regional, cultural, and social roots and influences. Obviously, the union of linguistic idiosyncracies and national tonal coloring is a potent force.

Opera, perhaps more than any other category of music, has the capacity to describe, respond to, and capture many significant moments in history. Only a chronicler who is equally at home with each component art can accomplish this feat. Thus, the opera becomes far more than entertainment; it becomes a panoramic unfolding of life.

As for some of the subdivisions of opera and their definitions, the following provides a brief summary:

Opera Seria   Italian opera of the eighteenth century, based upon a serious story, usually divided into three acts.
   Example: *Idomeneo* by Mozart

Grand Opera   Opera of large dimensions, in which the entire libretto is set to music, with almost no spoken dialogue. The basic arbitrariness of this definition becomes evident from the realization that a work such as Beethoven's *Fidelio* would not fit this description, while many a less important one would. The emphasis on the word "grand" applies to the elevated quality of the music and the seriousness of the composer's aim.
   Example: *Aida* by Verdi

Opera Buffa　"Comic opera"; also known as *opéra bouffe* or *opéra comique* in French and *Komische Oper* in German. These are designations of an opera of a light character, both musically and dramatically, with a generous helping of comic elements and an obligatory happy ending.

> Examples: *Orpheus in the Underworld* by Offenbach (opéra bouffe)
>
> *The Abduction from the Seraglio* by Mozart (singspiel influenced by Italian buffo style)
>
> *The Barber of Seville* by Rossini (opera buffa)

Operetta　A light and sentimental counterpart of comic opera, with spoken dialogue, music often of a dancelike character, and ballets.

> Example: *The Merry Widow* by Lehár

Chamber Opera　An opera of reduced dimensions, employing a small or chamber orchestra, with very few participants; based on a story of an intimate nature.

> Example: *The Old Maid and the Thief* by Menotti

For additional discussion and suggestions of operas for your listening pleasure, see Chapter Nine and the Appendix.

ORATORIO

This is a work based upon a substantial story of a religious or spiritual character, written for solo voices, chorus, and orchestra. The oratorio is often performed in church or, more often, in a concert hall. In scope it resembles an opera, but costumes, acting, and scenery are absent. However, the earliest examples of the oratorio form (such as Emilio del' Cavalieri's "Representation of Soul and Body," written in 1600), were staged with costumes and scenery. The plot is less dramatically described, and the emphasis is more on the chorus than on solo voices. Today's oratorio performance resembles opera in concert form. The difference between the cantata and the oratorio is that the latter is longer and has a more narrative format.

Historically the word "oratorio" is derived from its original place of performance, the oratory or oratorio of the Church of Santa Maria in Vallicella in Rome, where in the sixteenth century Filippo Neri inaugurated services of a popular nature, including sacred plays, reading from the Scriptures, and the performance of *laudi*, or hymns of praise and devotion. St. Filippo Neri founded the order of priests called Congregation of the Oratory, or Oratorians.

Significant baroque contributions to the literature of the oratorio were made in Italy by Giacomo Carissimi (1605–74) with his compositions *Jephtha, Judicium Salomonis, Jonas*, and *Balthazar;* by Alessandro Stradella (1642–82), with his major work *San Giovanni Battista;* and by Alessandro Scarlatti, who composed 150 oratorios, although he is better known today for his early operas. In France Marc-Antoine Charpentier (c. 1636–1704), a student of Carissimi, wrote some 20 oratorios that he termed "Histoires Sacrées" ("sacred stories") and "tragédies spirituelles" ("spiritual tragedies"). Charpentier was equally famous as an operatic composer at the court of Louis XIV.

In Germany Heinrich Schütz (1585–1672) was the outstanding composer of the seventeenth century. Specifically, his *Historia der . . . Auferstehung . . . Jesu Christi (Story of the . . . Resurrection . . . of Jesus Christ)* and *Historia von der Geburt Jesu Christi (Story of the Nativity* or *Christmas Oratorio)* are among the finest of the age. His passions predate Bach's oratorios and passions by almost one hundred years and remain singular in their dramatic appeal. Johann Sebastian Bach endowed his settings of the mass, as well as his passions and cantatas, with some of the characteristics of the oratorio. For example, his *Christmas Oratorio* consists of a number of separate cantatas, as does his *Easter Oratorio.* Yet Bach's intent and the tremendous impact of all of his contributions of a spiritual nature transcend our attempt to categorize them.

The consummate master of the late baroque period was Handel, whose dramatic treatment of the oratorio's content and subject matter has never been surpassed. Although Handel was German by birth, his oratorios may all be considered English creations in their use of the English language and their unfailing appeal to British audiences. The list of oratorios by Handel is truly impressive: *Esther* (1720), *Deborah* (1733), *Saul* (1739), *Israel in Egypt* (1739), *Messiah* (1742), *Samson* (1743), *Semele* (1743), *Joseph and His Brethren* (1743),

Belshazzar (1744), *Judas Maccabaeus* (1746), *Joshua* (1747), *Solomon* (1748), *Theodora* (1749), and *Jephtha* (1751), to mention only the best known. All of these were first heard in London, with the exception of *Messiah,* which had its world premiere in Dublin.

Dublin officials invited Handel to preside over the performance of his creation for the benefit of one of the city's charity organizations. This could not have come at a more propitious time in Handel's personal life. Handel was then in his late fifties, and his supremacy as an opera composer in England had been seriously challenged. Londoners were growing increasingly disenchanted with the prevailing form of Italian opera with which Handel's works had been identified. At this juncture the oratorio offered a welcome change in Handel's creative outlook, providing an outlet for his enormous sense of the dramatic and the theatrical. *Saul* and *Israel in Egypt* constituted peaks in the field of oratorio writing. With the Dublin commission Handel's career reached its zenith. *Messiah* had generated in Handel a feverish religious fervor. With singular devotion to the text, prepared for him from the Scriptures by Charles Jennens, who had collaborated with Handel three years earlier in producing the oratorio *Saul,* Handel completed the monumental score of *Messiah* in the incredibly short span of twenty-five days, foregoing food and sleep at times and hardly ever leaving his rooms. We are told that upon completion of the famous "Hallelujah Chorus," he told an assistant, "I did think I did see all Heaven before me – and the great God himself!"

The City of Dublin and its churches placed the finest instrumental and vocal forces at Handel's disposal. The first performance of *Messiah* on April 13, 1742 at the Music Hall on Fishamble Street was a spectacular success. At first the London premiere on March 23, 1743, seemed disappointing by comparison. But the immense emotional power unleashed by the "Hallelujah Chorus" assured the work's eventual immortality and Handel's lasting popularity. Recitatives, solo sections, and choruses are on such consistently exalted levels and the orchestral underpinning is of such unfailing quality that *Messiah* has become synonymous with the most inspiring and most inspired example of oratorio writing. Here the glory of baroque music has reached a pinnacle shared only by Bach's great Mass in B Minor.

The list of oratorios, stretching from Cavalieri to Britten and spanning a period of nearly four hundred years, is rich, varied, and representative of composers of many countries and national styles. A partial listing of exceptional post-Handelian oratorios follows:

Haydn	The Creation (1798), The Seasons (1801)
Beethoven	Christ on the Mount of Olives (1803)
Spohr	The Last Judgment (1825)
Mendelssohn	St. Paul (1836), Hymn of Praise (1840), Elijah (1846)
Berlioz	The Childhood of Christ (1854)
Franck	The Beatitudes (1879)
Elgar	The Dream of Gerontius (1900)
Honegger	King David (1921)
Walton	Belshazzar's Feast (1931)
Britten	A War Requiem (1962), often referred to as an oratorio

OVERTURE

Today the overture is known both as an introduction to an opera, operetta, oratorio, incidental score, or ballet and as an independent concert work. It is always exclusively an instrumental work. However, the introductory function long predates that of a separate composition. Both have in common a quality of arresting the attention of the listener, often in a rhetorical manner. The listener is aware of a sort of disclosure about to be made, irrespective of whether the overture serves as a foretaste of the mood of the ensuing large work or whether the subsequent drama is contained within the confines of the overture itself.

In the late seventeenth century Jean Baptiste Lully established the operatic overture; for instance, it served as introduction to his opera *Thésée* (1675). His invention, known as the French overture, was composed of two sections: one slow and generally containing a majestic dotted rhythm; the other fast and imitating a songlike subject. Sometimes there would be a return to the slow character of the first part. Examples are found in Handel's *Messiah* and Purcell's *Dido and Aeneas*. Bach and Telemann wrote independent French overtures that are known as suites because of various ensuing dances.

In Italy in the 1600s Alessandro Scarlatti shaped the opera overture, known as *sinfonia avanti l'opera* ("symphony before the opera"). It was in three parts, namely, Allegro-Adagio-Allegro. This scheme became the model for the modern symphony and its sequence of movements. In the classical period that followed, the three parts merged into a single movement, which often adapted the then-emerging sonata form. Christoph Willibald Gluck (1714–87) introduced the concept of the overture as a preparation for the audience of the general character of the proceedings to follow.

Many overtures convey the mood of the stage action, evoke the atmosphere of the drama, and even afford a hint of the ending of the plot. All this can be accomplished with appropriate tonal and harmonic colors. At times composers become more specific by quoting in the overture actual tunes that are later associated with certain actions or scenes in the opera – or in the drama, in the case of an incidental score.

Many examples bear witness to the effectiveness of this device, among them the overture to Mozart's *Don Giovanni;* Beethoven's *Leonore* overtures, nos. 2 and 3; Weber's *Der Freischütz;* Verdi's *La Forza del Destino;* Rossini's *William Tell;* Wagner's *Tannhäuser* and *Die Meistersinger;* Mendelssohn's *A Midsummer Night's Dream;* and Beethoven's *Egmont.* The latter two examples represent well-known overtures that are used as part of incidental music to stage dramas. All are overtures to large-scale scores of such stature and musical interest that they rank high as staples of symphonic orchestral literature.

The concert overture as an independent composition is of early romantic vintage. It often turns out to be a miniature symphonic poem or tone poem. Among many fine examples are such works as Mendelssohn's *The Hebrides* (or *Fingal's Cave*) Overture; Rimsky-Korsakov's *Russian Easter* Overture; Tchaikovsky's *1812 Overture,* the overture-fantasies *Romeo and Juliet* and *Hamlet;* Dvořák's three concert overtures: *In Nature's Realm, Carnival,* and *Othello;* Walton's *Portsmouth Point;* Elgar's *Cockaigne* concert overture; and Barber's *Overture to "The School for Scandal."*

In addition, there are some outstanding concert overtures composed for special occasions rather than for programmatic purposes. Brahms assembled German student songs in his *Academic Festival Overture*, written in 1881 and prompted by his receiving an honorary doctorate in 1879 from the University of Breslau. Copland's *An Outdoor Overture* was composed in 1938 to appeal to the youth of America. William Schuman wrote his *American Festival Overture* in 1939 for a "festival of American music."

The essence and spirit of the overture is best exemplified by the fact that many symphony concerts begin with such a work. For musical reasons alone, the overture emerges as the ideal curtain raiser, both literally and figuratively.

SYMPHONIC/TONE POEM

Conceived in the romantic period, the music in this category evokes extramusical ideas. It can describe the content or capture the spirit of poems, historical incidents, geographic scenes, or natural phenomena. Thus, the symphonic poem embodies the very essence of program music. It is composed in one continuous movement, with appropriate subdivisions affording a musical panorama of the composer's vision.

Franz Liszt first used the concept as a fully developed, separate orchestral entity, although earlier, shorter works may already be called tone poems by virtue of their melodramatic or descriptive nature. Among these are the following compositions: Beethoven's *Coriolan* Overture, based on a play by Heinrich Josef von Collin treating the same subject as Shakespeare's *Coriolanus;* Mendelssohn's *Ruy Blas* concert overture, suggested by a play by Victor Hugo; or Schumann's *Manfred* Overture, prompted by Byron's dramatic poem. This would indicate that many overtures can fit into the category of descriptive tone poems.

Specific examples of such works by Liszt include *Ce Qu'on Entend sur la Montagne (What One Hears on the Mountain)*, based on a poem by Victor Hugo; *Tasso* (Byron); *Les Préludes* (Lamartine). Additional tone poems that may be of interest are Smetana's *Má Vlast (My Fatherland)*, a cycle of six tone poems, including the famous *Moldau (Vltava)*. Other tone poems of national orientation include

Borodin's *In the Steppes of Central Asia,* Sibelius' *Finlandia,* and Saint-Saëns's *Africa.* Respighi based his trilogy – *The Fountains of Rome, The Pines of Rome,* and *Roman Festivals* – on specific scenes and moods encountered in the Eternal City.

Tchaikovsky, Saint-Saëns, Franck, Debussy, Sibelius, and Dukas all used sources from literature, legend, and mythology in their music: Tchaikovsky's *Romeo and Juliet* and *Hamlet;* Saint-Saëns's *Le Rouet d'Omphale* and *Phaëton;* Franck's *Les Éolides, Le Chasseur Maudit, Les Djinns,* and *Psyché.* Richard Strauss's array of symphonic poems include *Don Juan* (Lenau), *Death and Transfiguration* (Ritter), *Till Eulenspiegel's Merry Pranks* (based on an old German legend), and *Thus Spake Zarathustra* (Nietzsche). Debussy's *Afternoon of a Faun* (Mallarmé), Sibelius' *En Saga, The Swan of Tuonela, Lemminkäinen's Return, Pohjola's Daughter* (all after the Finnish epic *Kalevala*), and Dukas' *The Sorcerer's Apprentice* (Goethe) follow the example of the highly programmatic and romantic tone poem.

CHAPTER NINE

THE PERIODS OF MUSIC
IN RELATION TO
HISTORY AND
THE OTHER ARTS

WE TEND TO categorize all works of art according to their time of origin. Somehow our power of perception seems to function better if we are able to think in terms of chronological order. It is as if viewing an art object, reading a work of literature, or listening to a musical composition triggers a subconscious reaction, revealing all the sensory experiences that we associate with any given stretch of history. If any new creative encounters elude our imaginary cardfile of classifications, we have difficulty assimilating them.

Music, like the other arts, has undergone and continues to be subject to constant change, which we may refer to as schools, movements, or simply periods. We speak of Renaissance music, works of the baroque and classical periods; we refer to romanticism, impressionism, expressionism; we describe music as being neoclassical or atonal; and if we find that it is not readily accessible, we are likely to classify it in that pool of indefinables known as abstraction.

We even go so far as to attach opening and closing dates to each of the classified periods. For instance, baroque music was in existence from approximately 1660 (the time of Henry Purcell) to 1750 (the year of Bach's death); it may even be subdivided into early, high, and late baroque. Classicism in music generally covers the period from 1750 to about 1809, the year of Haydn's death. That delineation would place Beethoven (1770–1827) midway between the classical and romantic periods; his works may be characteristic of either period, depending on whether a specific work favors form over content, or whether it is very passionate (i.e., romantic) in mood.

While all this makes for convenient recall, we should understand that art can no more be relied upon to take on a new look beginning with a definite date than spring can be counted on to arrive on March 21 just because the calendar says so. All works of art reflect aspects of human nature and daily life, no matter how nebulous the association. Hence, change occasionally occurs as a sudden or violent phenomenon; more often it happens as an imperceptible merging and overlapping of artistic styles.

It is fascinating to observe how the arts mirror the course of human events and the forces that bring them about; from this point of view we can examine artistic – and specifically musical – practices through the ages. In a sense, we musicians and music lovers are at a disadvantage from the very beginning. The history of the visual arts and literature affords us a glimpse of centuries of creative activity. "Venus de Milo" speaks to us eloquently of the state of the art of sculpture c. 125–100 B.C. The works of the early philosophers, such as Socrates, Pythagoras, Plato, Aristotle, and the dramas of Euripides, Aeschylus, Aristophanes, and Sophocles all testify to the lofty thoughts of their creators. The writings of Catullus, Vergil, Horace, Ovid, Plutarch, Tacitus, as well as the teachings of St. Basil, St. John Chrysostom, and other liturgists of the Eastern Orthodox Church give proof even today of the vitality of their artistic, philosophical, or religious thought.

Tangible evidence of early musical practices, on the other hand, is only available in far more recent times, although musical expression of some kind, no matter how primitive, is surely as old as man. We see musical instruments of the earliest flute, lyre, and harp variety depicted in Egyptian tomb paintings executed almost a millennium and a half before Christ. However, the difference lies in the fact that we can study the earliest trends of art and literature from available sources of ancient vintage, while the earliest recorded musical examples come to us about fourteen centuries later than the tomb paintings. Even at that, these musical specimens reveal no trend or practice, nor do they point to any early musical notation. Such a development had to wait another thousand years or so.

Generally speaking, historical recollections of so-called early music begin in the Renaissance. Works of that time have been reconstructed successfully and can be heard both in concert and on records. History books allot two centuries to the Renaissance – from the fourteenth to the sixteenth centuries – with the artistic focus on Italy, specifically Florence and Rome. What about music in earlier times? Surely the music of the Renaissance must have existed earlier, if in different form, for its masterworks could not have sprung onto the scene from nowhere. Even a brief examination is rewarding.

ANCIENT CIVILIZATIONS

William Fleming, the distinguished art scholar and musician, reminds us in his excellent book *Art, Music, and Ideas* that in ancient Greece the word "music" connoted any endeavor that was associated with the muses, the daughters of Zeus and Mnemosyne. Music thus encompassed practically all human intellectual and emotional pursuits: the arts, science, poetry, drama, history, as well as dance and song.

Little is known about the independent use of musical instruments, individually or in groups, such as we find them depicted on ancient Greek vases and in reliefs of the Hellenic period (c. 776–323 B.C.). Based on historical evidence, it is safe to assume that music was linked to poetry, drama, and dance. Rhythms and melodies were used to create a variety of moods that would parallel and underscore changes in the literary text or poem with which they were combined. This function gave rise to the striking variety of Greek scales, known as modes, some of which are still in use today. They are of singular importance, for they give us an idea not only of the complexion of the earliest type of music but also of their use to evoke various moods. Thus, we gain an impression of how an early civilization coped with differences between intellectual and emotional responses.

Each of the Greek modes or scales was named after a different region of the country. Of these, the mode and rhythms of Phrygia, located in the north of Asia Minor, seemed to have the popularity of today's hit tunes. By all accounts they induced wild excitement, and the emotional reaction was frowned upon by those who favored the Dorian mode, which signified a more dignified style of music.

Each musical faction had its own choice of instruments to represent it. Dorian music favored the stringed instruments of the time, such as the lyre and the kithara – the symbol of Apollo, in whose hands it represented the Greek ideal of harmonious moderation. They were used for the accompaniment of songs and choruses. The Phrygian mode's excitement was caused by the sensuous sound of the aulos, a double-reed pipe adopted for the orgiastic music symbolized by Dionysus.

The muses seem to have endowed the great Greek dramatists with many talents: They conceived both text and music and then produced and enacted their creations as well. Even Richard Wagner, who came close to combining most of these functions to achieve his *Gesamtkunstwerk,* or totally integrated work of art, fell short of the Greek dramatists' accomplishments, since he could not act out or sing any of the roles that he created. During the Hellenic period the chorus played a most vital role both musically and dramatically in shaping the theatrical productions.

Little or no documentation has come down to us regarding music of the Roman period, roughly from the seventh century B.C. to the second century A.D. Both visual references and literary sources seem to indicate that the sound of music was overwhelming, emanating from oversized instruments, and quite obviously serving mass events. In addition to choruses, music's function in Roman times involved so-called "incidental effects to the drama." None of these seem to have been noted down in any fashion; most likely they were improvised and disappeared with their creators. However, it is possible to imagine Roman parades, sporting events, and ceremonial occasions staged in huge amphitheaters and interspersed with the powerful sound of massed choruses and instruments of the time.

The transition from late Roman civilization to the early Christian Era shows a change of emphasis in the role of music. Its dramatic and ceremonial use gradually gave way to music in the service of divine worship. A predecessor of this important development was the Hebrew chant of the ancient synagogue, which established a tradition, both musically and ideologically, that continues to this day. The diversity brought about by the Greek and Latin musical heritages, plus the Hebrew influence, formed a base broad enough to serve both Western and Eastern religious persuasions. Objectively speaking, it is difficult to take sides vis-à-vis the music of their respective liturgies. At the risk of oversimplification, a basic difference may well be found between the two types. Music of the early Western Church displays a more energetic and forceful approach in its functions of enhancing worship, while music of the Byzantine, Slavic, and Greek churches has a more contemplative quality about it.

THE MEDIEVAL AGE

From the standpoint of its impact on its own period and on the future development of musical styles, the most important milestone of the early Christian Era is that vast body of music known as Gregorian chant. It originated at the end of the sixth century, although it actually represented the culmination of years of development, which, in fact, continues into modern times.

A very special thrill can be derived from listening to an unadulterated version of Gregorian chant rendered by a well-trained monastic choir. The original Latin lends a special flow of prose to Gregorian chant that enables it to transcend the centuries. Translation serves no purpose other than to lend intelligibility to the text for today's audience.

If you have the opportunity, do listen to the nobility of the liquid lines of Gregorian chant. The absence of conventional bar lines frees the melodies to adjust naturally to the inflections of the text, rather than the words having to bend to the rhythmic scheme of conventional music. To put it another way, Gregorian chant may well be likened to musical prose, while the setting of Handel's *Messiah*, for instance, can be considered musical poetry. In Gregorian chant the music fits the rise and fall of the words, while in the Handel masterwork phrases and words are made to fit the symmetry of the music.

It was in the tenth century that a system of notation to preserve and convey music was finally formulated. In the Abbey of Cluny, located near Mâcon in the Burgundy region of France, the Abbot of Cluny, Odo, devised the earliest order of musical notation by using letters of the alphabet for the successive steps of the scale, from A to G. This enabled the singers of the choir to learn to read notes that they had hitherto memorized by rote.

About one hundred years later, Guido d'Arezzo, a Benedictine monk and French-born theorist, crystallized a system of notation that survived all sorts of musical development to become the universally accepted way of recording notes. Using his predecessor's concepts as a base, d'Arezzo evolved the musical staff, assigning successive notes to lines and spaces.

D'Arezzo also arrived at an order of syllables, known as solmization. Each step of the scale was given a syllable that when read in context spelled out the beginning of a sentence of a hymn to St. John the Baptist. The first syllable of each line was sung to a note in rising succession:

The first letters of the Latin name of St. John, Sancte Ioannes, were used as the seventh step of the solmization (namely "Si"); and "Ut" was replaced everywhere but in French-speaking countries with "Do," which proved to be easier to sing. Thus, our Do-Re-Mi dates back some nine centuries. The system of solmization is still used, as it was in medieval theory, as a means of reference and of ear training.

Guido d'Arezzo, thought to have been born near Paris (c. 997), is today considered the father of musical notation and the Abbey of Cluny its birthplace. Unfortunately, the abbey's magnificence and its inspirational influence were comparatively short-lived. After barely nine centuries the imposing complex of buildings fell victim to revolutionary vandalism in 1798. However, restored examples of sculpture survive in another French abbey church at Vézelay suggest a synthesis of the arts (i.e., a visual interrelationship of music, literature, sculpture, and architecture) that is truly remarkable for its time. The crowning tops of two of the abbey's pillars depict in exquisite detail the eight tones used in ancient psalmody, each represented by an instrument of biblical vintage, replete with illuminating inscriptions. By examining these precious relics we can gain a revealing glimpse of what musical life at the medieval Abbey of Cluny must have been like.

In similar fashion the *Chanson de Roland (Song of Roland)* opens a vista for us into another phase of medieval music, namely, the art of the minstrels, as practiced by the *jongleurs* (street singers and magicians) at the end of the first millennium. Historically the *Song of Roland* is an epic blow-by-blow account of the battles of Charlemagne and his forces against the pagan hordes, with the avenging of his nephew Roland's heroic death. Musically it heralds a folk art that leads us to the ballads and narrative songs of the nineteenth and twentieth centuries, as well as to the descriptive settings by Franz Schubert, including such favorites as "Der Erlkönig" ("The Erl King"), or the Scottish tale of "Thomas the Rhymer" by Karl Loewe. Following in the tradition of minstrels are such popular balladeers of our time as Burl Ives and the Weavers. Their ancestors date back as far as the year 1000, when the chanting of poetic verses became a favorite way to convey legends as well as everyday tales, often emphasized by groups of listeners and bystanders joining in the refrain.

Much like our modern camp meetings and songfests, the medieval jongleurs would aggregate in retreatlike fashion to explore each other's latest achievements. Accompaniment was usually furnished by instruments of the lyre or viol variety. Eventually the jongleurs dropped their sleight-of-hand tricks or juggling and concentrated on making music. Thus their art merged with that of the minnesingers of Germany and the troubadours and trouvères in France. The songfests culminated in the professional competitions glorified by Richard Wagner in the "Sängerkrieg" ("Singers' Contest") in his opera *Tannhäuser,* and in the popular contest adjudicated by the elders of the trade guilds in the finale of *Die Meistersinger von Nürnberg.*

The art of storytelling through song in its many forms emerged

from the *Song of Roland,* and its pictorial counterpart, the Bayeux
Tapestry of the eleventh century. This monumental artwork –
consisting of seventy-nine panels composed of wool embroidery on
linen and centering around William the Conqueror's historic deeds
– is as fine a visual equivalent of epic balladry and narration as can
be found anywhere. It may be seen in the little town of Bayeux in
Normandy, France, as well as in various reproductions. Our knowledge of medieval art and music and their further evolution would
indeed be poorer were it not for the availability of these great docu-
ments.

THE GOTHIC AGE

No greater and more thrilling historical example of a synthesis of
the arts can be found than the towering cathedrals of the Gothic
period, of the late twelfth and thirteenth centuries. Anyone who has
seen the cathedrals of Chartres, Rheims, Amiens, Rouen, or Beau-
vais can never forget their utter grandeur. Solo and choral chanting,
prayers recited by the entire congregation, and readings from the
pulpit all were amplified manyfold as they reverberated from the
lofty heights of pillars and ricocheted off the massive walls, echoing
from countless crevices and recesses of various sculptors' and architects' boundless fantasies.

Such expansiveness challenged church musicians to seek far more
elaborate and diversified means of composing liturgical creations
than had previously been known. The sweeping, melodious prose of
Gregorian chant, though further enhanced by the boundless interior
space of such cathedrals, needed a more vertically structured enclo-
sure. The superimposition of voices upon one another, or the simultaneous sounding of various melodic lines, emerged as the answer to
this requirement. Now the great cathedrals began to resound with
music that was truly a match for their noble grandeur. As part of
this new and expanded utilization of sound, the chants of the liturgy
were entrusted to groups of solo voices, alternating with larger vocal
bodies. These alternating groups would often be stationed at opposite sections of the cathedral; the acoustical effects of this antiphonal
style of chanting must have been breathtaking.

Gradually an ever greater independence of vocal parts emerged.

Divergent melodies were not only arranged in juxtaposition but often expressed different words and thoughts, at times in different languages, such as French and Latin. Scholars have even found examples of a prayer chanted in Latin, upon which the singing of a French love song was superimposed. The result must have been perplexing, to say the least. Different melodies, incoherent texts, dissonant sounds, and clashing rhythmic patterns all combined to create an excitement that had never been experienced before. Layer upon layer of strands of melodies achieved a verticality of sound that aspired upward toward the pointed arches of the lofty vaults.

This diversity of sound and word seemed to be a reflection of the concurrent religious and secular functions of the Gothic cathedral itself in many parts of Europe. It had always been centered in a populated area, whose townspeople found in its manifold activities the nerve center of their daily lives. The Gothic cathedral was the ubiquitous edifice for worship, as well as a place for town meetings, a theater for religious plays and dramas, a concert hall for the performances of chants and polyphonic compositions, and a regional museum in which art objects were housed, from indigenous iconography to sculpted, painted, and carved artworks.

The beauty of all this lay in the fact that order could be discerned in the seeming chaos. In the music that was performed, as each melody moved along its own course, a sweeping alternation of consonance and dissonance occurred, of rhythmical clashes and resolutions. When heard in the context of an entire work, they gave the impression of harmonic unity. Counterpoint (from the Latin *punctus contra punctum*) flourished during this period.

A remarkable union of music and the expansive dimensions of Gothic architecture was achieved. Its cradle may be found in the great cathedrals of the Île-de-France, specifically in the School of Notre Dame in Paris. Such composers as Léonin and Pérotin (the latter was born c. 1155) served the Cathedral of Notre Dame in the late twelfth and early thirteenth centuries. Their lasting achievements consisted of collections of music written in various parts, illustrating in theory and practice how to fit them into a contrapuntal order of musical rather than cerebral appeal. They helped bridge the gap inherent in the very essence of Gothic art, namely, between the finite and the infinite.

THE RENAISSANCE

Artistic and literary accomplishments of staggering proportions occurred during the fourteenth and fifteenth centuries, primarily in Italy. During a one-hundred-year period there emerged a host of great thinkers and artists: the philosopher Thomas Aquinas; the Florentine painter Giovanni Cimabue and Giotto di Bondone, his successor as leader of the Florentine school, famous for his frescoes in Assisi, Padua, and Florence; the father-and-son team of sculptors, Niccolò and Giovanni Pisano of Pisa; Dante Alighieri, who produced a masterpiece, *The Divine Comedy;* followed in close succession by the poetry of Francesco Petrarca and the romantic prose of Giovanni Boccaccio. Even more awesome is the fact that within a mere forty-five-year span there emerged countless masterpieces by Sandro Botticelli, Leonardo da Vinci, Michelangelo Buonarroti, Lorenzo de' Medici, Niccolò Machiavelli, Baldassare Castiglione, Raffaello Santi (Raphael), and Tiziano Vecelli (Titian).

All these names come to mind when we think of the Renaissance, a period in history that evokes a feeling of great respect and admiration for the flights of imagination and lofty accomplishments of these masters. However, just exactly what was *reborn,* as the term "renaissance" implies, is not readily definable. Surely the creations of these great artists in their respective fields represented far more than a mere return to values of antiquity, which they so eloquently surpassed. Even the proverbial Dark Ages served as stepping-stones of great significance, as we have seen in the section on the Gothic age. Hence, the word "rebirth" should be understood to connote a new phase of a continuing evolution rather than a reawakening after a culturally stagnant period, as its literal meaning implies.

From a humanistic point of view, this new phase of creative evolution reflected an awareness of man's ability to reason and rationalize rather than to blindly believe, his ability to temper unconditioned faith with gradually acquired scientific knowledge and judgment. Access to facts was enhanced immeasurably by the advent of the printing press, and the quest for scientific truths was aided by an

ever-increasing facility and expansion of travel. Man became imbued with his innate potential for knowledge. All of these new virtues found their way into the artist's approach to his work. Painting
and sculpture now began to mirror life and the world as they actually were rather than depicting them in an idealized, impersonal
manner. Literature and philosophy became much more realistic and
daring; the closing years of the Renaissance witnessed the challenging thinking of Desiderius Erasmus and Martin Luther, as well as
the crowning achievements of Albrecht Dürer and Michelangelo.

While the term "renaissance" is applicable in the fields of literature, painting, sculpture, and architecture, it is without any real
foundation in music. As a creative art, music was far too young to
be "reborn," and its beginnings were far too nebulous to have benefited from a renaissance. Actually, its strength had been demonstrated in the demanding practice of Gothic contrapuntal writing,
and in the melodious glories of Gregorian chant. In a sense, the songs
of praise known as *laudi spirituali*, of the early Renaissance, ascribed to the followers of St. Francis of Assisi, do constitute a return
to the spirit of the medieval jongleurs and minstrels. In fact, the
practitioners of these songs called themselves "jongleurs de Dieu,"
"minstrels of God".

Musicians of the Renaissance were among the first to acquire fame
as composers; their names stand out today as recognizable musical
personalities. For instance, Josquin des Prés of Belgium (c. 1440–
1521) – a singer in Milan's cathedral, a member of the papal chapel,
in the service of Louis XII of France and Emperor Maximilian I, and
later in the ducal chapel of Ferrara – was one of the most celebrated
and prolific masters of his day. His works are distinguished by their
breadth of expression. They include more than thirty settings of the
mass, over fifty motets, and many secular songs.

Giovanni Pierluigi da Palestrina (c. 1525–94) – born in and named
after the little town near Rome – served various Roman churches.
His compositions distinguish him as one of the main exponents of
counterpoint. His complete works comprise some thirty-four
volumes. Palestrina occupied a unique place in the history of his
time, for he was charged with the realignment of church music
according to the guidelines of the Counter-Reformation, determined
by the Council of Trent. In his position as organist and choirmaster

of the Julian Chapel at St. Peter's in Rome, where he spent the last twenty-three years of his life, Palestrina established a trend toward greater clarity of musical and verbal expression, resulting from a penetration of secular elements brought about by the Counter-Reformation. He was also known as an undisputed master of contrapuntal writing for unaccompanied voices, both in liturgical compositions and in the secular madrigal style. His work points forward to the orchestrally supported masterpieces of the late baroque.

Palestrina's most famous contemporary was Roland de Lassus, known as Orlando di Lasso (1532–94). He is considered the greatest representative of the Flemish school, a consummate master of expressive choral singing. Di Lasso traveled widely and was acclaimed everywhere he went. None of his contemporaries was more prolific than he; his output includes psalms, magnificats, motets, masses, songs, and madrigals in Italian, German, and French. Di Lasso devoted the last thirty-four years of his life to his musical duties at the court of Munich.

Another renowned composer from Flanders was Guillaume Dufay (1400–74), chorister and later canon of Cambrai Cathedral. Dufay functioned as composer and singer in the papal chapel during his stay in Italy. His peasant background brought an important dimension to his work. He made earthy folksongs respectable by lending their peculiar charm to the lofty purpose of the mass. Thus, we find a popular song of the day, "If my face is pallid, know the cause is love," serving as the basis of a Dufay mass. This reflects one of the features of the true spirit of the Renaissance, namely, that faith in all its manifestations should mirror all aspects of daily living. (See also the section on the mass, pp. 241–43.) Dufay has come to be admired today for the remarkable lyricism of his writing, both of a spiritual and a mundane persuasion.

Jacob Obrecht (c. 1450–1505), one of the Netherlands' leading composers moved about successfully among Dutch, Belgian, and Italian posts. His numerous settings of the mass and his motets and multilingual songs were often ahead of their time in terms of compositional treatment.

Heinrich Isaac (c. 1450–1517), a Netherlander who traveled widely, excelled in elaborate polyphonic settings of parts of the mass. Of lasting importance, however, was Isaac's association with Lorenzo de' Medici, one of the greatest personalities of the Florentine Renaissance. He was the personification of what we call today a true Renaissance man: humanist; philosopher; patron of the arts and sciences; and active supporter of painters, musicians, sculptors, and writers. It was Lorenzo, known as "il Magnifico," who succeeded in transplanting Heinrich Isaac from his native Brabant to Florence in order to occupy the post of music director at the cathedral as well as the Medici Palace. Isaac set to music some of Lorenzo's verses, which were at times humorous, often folksy and pastoral, and whose spontaneity ensured their immortality. Of particular interest in our own time are the lines contained in one of Lorenzo's carnival songs:

> *Quanto è bella giovinezza,*
> *Che si fugge tuttavia!*
> *Chi vuol esser lieto, sia:*
> *Di doman non c'è certezza.*
> Fair is youth and free of sorrow,
> Yet how soon its joys we bury!
> Let who would be, now be merry:
> Sure is no one of tomorrow.*

The fruits of the collaboration between Lorenzo and Isaac resulted in the rise of the madrigal, which was to become one of the most popular song forms, first in Italy and subsequently in England. Although it had already appeared before Lorenzo's time, the madrigal emerged as one of the lasting secular contributions of Renaissance music. It represents a marriage of poetry and music that presaged the romantic Lied of nineteenth-century Germany (see pp. 236–39).

As we consider Renaissance music, a rather remarkable fact becomes apparent. The most significant enrichment in the arts of painting, sculpture, and architecture was accomplished by Italian artists; hence we look upon the Renaissance as a primarily Italian phenomenon. While the evolution of music in Italy was equally formidable in many respects, it was brought about mainly by musicians who had come to Florence and Rome from Belgium and the Netherlands. Their polyphonic style may well be considered the

*Cited in William Fleming, *Art, Music, and Ideas*, p. 173.

crowning glory of Renaissance music. Isaac's musical supremacy in Florence was matched by Des Prés's superb artistry in the service of Rome's Sistine Chapel. Their work now became Italian by definition. But their disciples carried the spirit of Italy's adopted music back to other European countries, thus bringing it full circle.

Quite apart from these cultural riches, yet still well within the time span under consideration here, was the artistic life of Venice. Void of the climate of patronage that Rome and Florence enjoyed, Venice created its own highly distinctive ambience. The magnificent Byzantine architectural masterpiece, the Basilica of San Marco, which was begun some six centuries earlier, was primarily responsible for the designation of the city as the meeting place of the Orient and the Occident. Of course, it was also the unique geographic location of Venice that engendered a lively interchange of goods and ideas indigenous to both worlds. This unforgettable city – which inspired such painters as Giorgione, Tintoretto, Titian, the brothers Gentile and Giovanni Bellini, and even the young Albrecht Dürer – developed a musical life all its own.

Cradled by the basilica, music took a new direction in Venice. St. Mark's both demanded and accommodated innovations to which the edifice and the spaciousness of the surrounding Piazza San Marco were predisposed. The two separate choir galleries located on opposite sides of the basilica, each provided with its own organ, challenged composers to write choral and instrumental music that could be performed separately as well as jointly, with one choir often answering the other in an antiphonal manner. Members of the congregation might unknowingly have gotten a foretaste of what we today call stereophonic sound. On special occasions additional choirs and instrumental groups would render music especially composed for their processional across the vast square. Their sound was designed to merge with and be supported by the organs within the basilica as the procession drew near, thus adding yet another new dimension, namely, multiplicity of emanation.

A Flemish musician, Adrian Willaert (c. 1490–1562), from Bruges, was called upon to become "maestro di cappella" ("master of the chapel") at St. Mark's, where he served for the last thirty-five years of his highly productive life. Willaert was the first composer to write music for two antiphonal choirs, supported by two organs. This genre of choral music, known as *cori spezzati* ("divided choirs") became a chief characteristic of the Venetian style.

Willaert's pupil, Venetian-born Andrea Gabrieli (c. 1510–86) became one of the renowned practitioners of the art of organ playing, which in turn attracted foreign pupils to Venice. Among them was the Dutch organist, composer, and teacher Jan Pieterszoon Sweelinck (1562–1621), whose toccatas and "echo" compositions transplanted the Venetian tradition to Holland and subsequently to the next generation of organists, such as Samuel Scheidt (1587–1654) and Heinrich Scheidemann (c. 1596–1663) of northern Germany. Sweelinck became the pivotal force of inspiration that led from Venice, via Johann Pachelbel and Dietrich Buxtehude, to the grandeur of the organ writing of Bach and Handel.

The most illustrious pupil of Andrea Gabrieli was his nephew Giovanni Gabrieli (c. 1554–1612), also a native of Venice, whose work left the greatest imprint upon Venetian culture. As a result of the tenure of Willaert and the Gabrielis, Venice became the music capital of the Renaissance world. Their bold innovations in choral writing, the brilliance of their instrumental conception, exemplified in the confrontation of brass and wind ensembles, and their emphasis on the virtuosity of organ playing as enunciated in the toccata and the ricercare – both elaborately conceived and demanding keyboard compositions of the time – pointed the way to the creative spirit of the baroque period. Of equal importance for the evolution of the major forms of music was the Venetian style of pitting groups of singers and instrumentalists against one another, a "concertato" or "concertante" style which culminated in the concerto grosso and early concerto of the baroque.

Giovanni Gabrieli and his pupil Heinrich Schütz, who was to become Germany's greatest master of the early baroque, developed the combination of vocal and instrumental forces of the *Symphoniae Sacrae (Sacred Symphonies)*, another forerunner of elaborate baroque concepts. These, along with the madrigals, the first operas, vespers, magnificats, and motets by Gabrieli's successor at St. Mark's, the incomparably gifted Claudio Monteverdi, formed an immense reservoir of inspiration and a solid foundation for a new age.

It was the rebirth of the human spirit and genius that made the Renaissance an era of discovery, adventure, and dedication, the scope of which has never been surpassed. The Renaissance may be seen as the kindling force that shaped modern man. It provided the same generating power to music as to the rest of the humanities.

THE REFORMATION AND COUNTER-REFORMATION

The quest for new avenues of thought, new directions of artistic expression, and a preoccupation with man's place in a universe perceived differently than it had been by previous generations together formed the heritage of a great age. Increasingly, they also served as a challenge to master an uncertain future. The next century and a half, from approximately 1500 to 1650, represented a seething epoch in the history of mankind. Its discoveries, and its political, scientific, and philosophical achievements altered the course of human existence. Horizons were expanded, both physically and spiritually, by the opening up of a new world, while empires vied with one another for the domination of the old world. New and exciting paths were charted in astronomy and physics by Nicolaus Copernicus, Galileo Galilei, and John Kepler. The philosophical theory of Baruch Spinoza, the advances in mathematics by Blaise Pascal and René Descartes, Dr. William Harvey's realization of the circulation of the blood as a basic fact of medicine – all these breakthroughs stirred the imagination, just as John Locke's scientific research into the functions of the human mind enlarged the scope of its thought processes.

The march of progress was bound to disturb the equilibrium of the Renaissance, based as it was upon the secure order of a finite world. The religious upheaval of the Reformation brought about a quasi-militant Counter-Reformation that reversed many of the artistic gains of free expression. Yet, this countermovement in turn prompted a reappraisal of the positive values of the past. They now appeared in an even brighter light in the face of ever-widening advances in scientific and material gains and a growing awareness of the passage of time.

Some of the older, established masters weathered the storms of action and reaction. In 1547, thirteen years after the beginning of the Counter-Reformation, Michelangelo was called upon to accept the post of architect of St. Peter's Basilica in Rome. Despite the censorship of the printed page, Copernicus' world-shaking theories of the revolution of celestial bodies in space prevailed, as did Andrea Palladio's remarkable *Four Books on Architecture.*

At the same time, many new artistic directions were undertaken. El Greco, Spain's greatest painter and adherent of the Counter-Reformation, was eminently successful in combining his spiritual convictions with an emotional expressiveness that heralded the artistic conceptions of an age to come. Diego Velázquez, on the other hand, became a great exponent of genre scenes, achieving a unique mastery of the use of light and space.

Peter Paul Rubens (1577–1640) worked in Italy for eight years and then returned to the Low Countries and to France, bringing with him techniques learned in Venice. Charles I of England would later ask Rubens to paint the ceiling of London's Banqueting House, which still plays a role in the city's musical life today. Van Dyck, Rubens' pupil, would receive the monarch's call for what turned out to be a remarkable series of portraits of Charles's children.

One of the true geniuses of the time, deserving of a place alongside Michelangelo, was the multitalented Gianlorenzo Bernini (1598–1680), sculptor, architect, and painter. Bernini designed the Eternal City's most familiar site, St. Peter's Square, with the infinite spaciousness of its pillared colonnades, as well as the altar within St. Peter's Basilica, containing the papal chair. Bernini's "Fountain of the Rivers" in Rome's Piazza Navona is a splendid example of the nobility of artistic concepts, as we recall Bernini's other distinguished activities in behalf of the Louvre in Paris and the influence of his fountain designs upon Versailles.

In music, too, the sixteenth and early seventeenth centuries were both a time of tradition and of innovation. Spain's foremost musician of the period, Tomás Luis de Victoria (c. 1549–1611), devoted himself exclusively to writing music for the church, a phase of composition for which his contemporaries in the Low Countries and Italy were so well known. Together they paved the way for the masses, motets, passions, and cantatas of later masters, whose large-scale conceptions of these forms necessitated their move from the church setting to the concert hall.

Other sixteenth-century styles in music also gained even greater scope. The toccatas and fantasias for keyboard were ennobled by such masters of the late seventeenth century as Pachelbel and Buxtehude. As stated earlier, the principle of contrast inherent in the divided-choir style found its way instrumentally into the concerto grosso, a forerunner of the modern concerto.

BAROQUE

The baroque period, spanning the seventeenth and early eighteenth centuries, made many great contributions to the arts. The variety and quality of the accomplishments of the baroque age are as difficult to classify as the age itself is to succinctly define.

The Dutch school of painting, headed by Rembrandt van Rijn, Frans Hals, and Jan Vermeer; the French artists Nicolas Poussin and Charles Lebrun; the architects Louis Le Vau, Jules Hardouin-Mansart, and Christopher Wren; the writers Pierre Corneille, Jean Baptiste Molière, Jean Racine, John Milton, John Dryden, William Shakespeare, and Francis Bacon – all were responsible for a new, increasing sense of artistic creativity. Versailles in France, El Escorial in Spain, and St. Paul's Cathedral in London parallel, in their magnificent construction, the manifold dimensions of Henry Purcell's *Dido and Aeneas*, Handel's *Messiah*, Bach's Mass in B Minor, St. Matthew Passion, St. John Passion, and his great organ toccatas, fantasias, and fugues.

Similarly, the promise of the early operas of Jean Baptiste Lully and Jean Philippe Rameau, as well as the daring keyboard music of François Couperin, Johann Sebastian Bach, and Domenico Scarlatti all pointed toward a virtuosity of performance. This lavishness of thought and grandeur of design became the fiber of the baroque period.

Concerning the term "baroque," it is important to realize that most of the words used to designate artistic periods or styles were first utilized in a derogatory sense. Thus, we find "baroque" referred to as "a degenerate bastard of the Renaissance" in the book by Germain Bazin entitled *The Baroque*. In France in the late sixteenth century "baroque" was used to connote something bizarre or badly made. Until the nineteenth century it remained a synonym for "absurd" and "grotesque." Even today we still think of "baroque" as something irregular in shape, possibly due to the assumption that the word is derived from the Portuguese word *barrôco,* an irregularly shaped pearl. This association often turns up in a vernacular way. If you wish to acquire an empty wine bottle in France, you most likely will be asked, *"Normale ou baroque?"* ("baroque" meaning "uneven" or "odd in shape").

"Unusual" and "irregular" are just two qualities found in baroque art. The latter combines extraordinary fantasy and simple truth, a singular approach and a multiplicity of purpose, the noble and the modest. In this respect the baroque age has quite a bit in common with the romantic period and should be considered its mighty harbinger and older relative.

In music the baroque period spanned the lifetimes of many great composers and marked the evolution of numerous fundamental concepts of composition and principles of performance. It was a period of growing expressiveness, both creatively and interpretatively, an age whose restraint we have come to appreciate all the more, having experienced the excesses and penchant for overindulgence that followed in the wake of the romantic age.

In music, as in the other arts, the sciences, and the conception of the universe itself, baroque implies fundamental transformations. The distances from the simplicity and directness of music by Henry Purcell to the triumphant affirmation of faith expressed in the "Hallelujah Chorus" of Handel's *Messiah,* or from a courante in a harpsichord suite by Jacques Champion de Chambonnières, who was harpsichordist to Louis XIV, to Bach's mighty Toccata and Fugue in D Minor for Organ are tantamount to man's idea of the earth before and after Copernicus' book entitled *On the Revolutions of the Celestial Spheres* or the shift from a blind belief in miracles and superstitions to the scientific rationalization of the universe. Yet all of these are classified glibly under the rubric "baroque." While this was an age of seemingly irreconcilable differences, there is the all-embracing element of continuity inherent in the evolution of embryonic forms and ideas to their present state. Surely in music, as in all human endeavors during this fertile period, there have never been greater and more varied achievements. Although it took almost two centuries, the music world was finally given a measure of, and with it a healthy appetite for, the immense riches of sound and musical expression.

COMPOSITIONAL FORMS AND STYLES

Most of the forms and categories of the large-scale compositions that exist today had their genesis in the baroque age.

For instance, the sonata – a concept with one of the widest ranges of application – was first used to connote a variety of instrumental music. Its original meaning was simply a "sound piece," suggesting the equivalent of a certain type of *canzona* ("song"), sometimes referred to as a *canzon da sonar* ("song for playing"). Gabrieli's *Sonata pian'e forte* predates the word's present meaning and illustrates the implicit dynamic contrasts. The opposites inherent in the varying tempos and moods of the different movements of today's sonata are an outgrowth of such instrumental works of the later sixteenth century, while the contrasts posed by the components of the sonata form (see page 210) are the result of a late baroque evolution. The same is true of those forms based upon sonata principles: the sinfonia, later the symphony, the concerto, and most categories of chamber music, such as the duo-sonata, trio, quartet, quintet, sextet, and others.

Conversely, the history of the theme-and-variations form can be traced back to the sixteenth century, when Spanish and French masters used them in the accompaniment of lute songs, in contrapuntal settings, in alternations of melodies, and as a distinctive aid for contrasts of interpretation, particularly by the English keyboard composers. The popularity of this form was further enhanced by the Viennese classicists of the eighteenth and early nineteenth centuries and continues to be of interest to modern-day composers.

An outstanding example of this form, written during the baroque period, is a series of thirty variations by Johann Sebastian Bach, commissioned by Count Kaiserling, a former Russian ambassador to the Court of Saxony. The count is said to have suffered from insomnia, a condition he hoped to ameliorate by asking his court harpsichordist, Johann Gottlieb Goldberg, to entertain him with musical performances. Goldberg happened to be a pupil of Bach, who named the commissioned work *Goldberg Variations* after his able student. Bach endowed the work with a masterful plan – consisting of alternation between virtuosic, freestyle variations and those of a contrapuntal, canonic nature – unsurpassed in the entire literature of keyboard music of this genre.

One of the most important forms of baroque music is the suite, consisting of a series of fairly short movements of a dancelike character and all written in the same key. Again Bach may serve as an excellent example, for he wrote numerous suites, both for solo instruments and for orchestra (see pp. 219–21).

Also of baroque origin is the rondeau, used by the French harpsichordists or clavecinists in the seventeenth century. The rondeau later became the rondo, which exists both as a separate composition and as the final movement of some symphonies, sonatas, and concertos.

Likewise, the fugue, the most highly developed contrapuntal form, represents a distinctive contribution of the baroque period. It evolved during the seventeenth century and reached its greatest heights at the hands of Johann Sebastian Bach, the supreme master of counterpoint. (For a more detailed discussion of the fugue, see pp. 226–28.)

As was previously mentioned, the concerto, one of the most popular musical forms of our time, had its early roots and development in the baroque period. Yet another form of composition of the era is the oratorio, which was brought to full maturity by Georg Friedrich Handel as the baroque drew to a close.

Historically the baroque period offers a link between oratorio and opera, with religious subject matter often being the common denominator. The birth of opera as we know it today – the complex interrelationship of music, drama, acting, dance, costumes, lighting, and stage design – occurred during the baroque era. (For a more detailed look at opera and oratorio, see pp. 244–52.)

Another vocal contribution of the baroque period is the cantata. Like its instrumental counterpart the suite, it consists of various vocal sections recounting a coherent, continuous story that can either be spiritual or worldly. The word "cantata" is derived from the Italian verb *cantare* ("to sing, intone, or chant"), while "sonata" is based on the verb *sonare* ("to sound") and "toccata" on the verb *toccare* ("to touch"). Many masters of the period were attracted to the cantata as a form of composition, but no one was more prolific or universally acclaimed in his utilization of the cantata than Johann Sebastian Bach, who wrote one for every Sunday of the church year (see p. 230).

The profusion of forms whose origin falls within the baroque era is truly remarkable. Equally noteworthy are the means of expression that helped to perpetuate these forms, thereby stirring the imagination and exciting the fantasies of future generations of composers.

First and foremost, the baroque period witnessed the evolution of most of the instruments to the stature of orchestral and solo use for which they are known today. This is the period of the great Italian violin makers, such as Stradivari and Amati. By the end of the baroque era most wind instruments had taken on their present shape as well as their tonal and technical capacities. The chief instrument of the time, however, was the harpsichord. The harpsichord's ability to blend with the other instruments and its tonal self-sufficiency for solo purposes made it indispensable. The great composers of the age confided to it their innermost musical thoughts, and entrusted it with the brilliance of their interpretive abilities. The harpsichord was used to furnish the all-important harmonic structure known as *basso continuo* ("figured bass") or "thorough bass," which served as the harmonic foundation for most compositions.

To experience the versatility of the harpsichord, listen to the sonatas of Domenico Scarlatti and Antonio Soler, the *ordres* or suites by François Couperin, the *Biblical Sonatas* by Johann Kuhnau, and such incomparable masterpieces by Bach as the English and French suites, the partitas, the *Italian Concerto* in F Major, the concertos for one, two, and three harpsichords, as well as the *Brandenburg Concerto No. 5,* in which the harpsichord is joined by the flute and the violin as solo instruments. This is only a partial sampling of a veritable treasure trove of baroque repertory for you to enjoy.

The figured bass, is in itself an achievement, a kind of musical shorthand whose realization was imperative for the performances of most compositions of the time. The bass notes of a keyboard instrument (harpsichord or organ) were provided with figures indicative of the harmonies to be played. Therefore

would call for the following harmonies:

This system originated in the early seventeenth century and was in use up until the time of Haydn or the middle of the eighteenth century.

A related use of the bass line, known as *basso ostinato* ("obstinate bass"), occurs when a bass motif is repeated throughout a work, with the upper part(s) built upon it in theme-and-variations fashion. It is also referred to as ground bass, which consists of a phrase persistently repeated in the same low register of a composition. In Bach's Passacaglia in C Minor, the ground bass upon which the variations of this ingenious work are constructed can be clearly heard.

During the baroque period there was an increased emphasis on the importance and variety of tonal color for the purpose of expression and interpretation. Aided by the growing refinement of instruments, composers now began to provide for greater nuances and subtleties that would reflect the increasing emotional sensitivities of the romantic age. The late baroque period witnessed the manufacture of ever larger harpsichords and the transition to the Hammerklavier, as well as the improved tonal resources of organs.

The contrasting style of the concertato, stressing the tonal "rivalries" between solo instruments and accompanying sonorities, paved the way for the brilliant concerto writing that baroque masters initiated in such an impressive fashion. The art of ornamentation, which was first practiced at the performer's discretion as an improvisational device, provided for the embellishment of a melodic line. Eventually baroque composers created a shorthand that incorporated certain symbols to indicate the proper execution of ornaments (e.g., *tr.* to indicate a trill) and to allow instrumentalists to perform in an expressive manner, based upon their natural inclination, yet still remain faithful to the composer's wishes. This language of ornamental signs became so extensive that a special literature consisting of treatises on its proper execution arose toward the end of the baroque period.

An equally valuable practice that we owe to the baroque era is the art of improvisation, although its beginnings may be assumed to reach back several centuries to a time when notation was either nonexistent or in its infancy. To this day improvisation implies an original, spontaneous creation not relying upon predetermined notation. It was considered a must for a gifted musician to be able to extemporize on the spur of the moment, in keeping with practices of the time, or utilizing compositional practices of other periods.

Before leaving this great era, I should like to name some of my favorite baroque composers, chosen from among so many who should be mentioned. My suggestions of representative works for listening are limited to a bare minimum. Obviously, Bach and Handel cannot possibly be given their due with only a few representative listening suggestions; a more complete listing of their works may be found in relevant sections of Chapters Eight and Nine, as well as in the Appendix.

| Henry Purcell | Stage works: *Dido and Aeneas; The Fairy Queen* |
| | Four Odes for St. Cecilia's Day |

Arcangelo Corelli	Concerti grossi, Op. 6
François Couperin	*Pièces de Clavecin (Harpsichord Pieces)*
Antonio Vivaldi	*Concerti for Diverse Instruments*
	The Four Seasons, Op. 8
	Gloria in D
	Musique de Table (Suites)
	Suite in A Minor for Flute and Strings
Jean Philippe Rameau	*Pièces de Clavecin en Concert*
Domenico Scarlatti	Sonatas for Harpsichord (or Piano)
Giovanni Battista Pergolesi	Opera buffa: *La Serva Padrona (The Maid as Mistress)*
Johann Pachelbel	Kanon
	Suite in B-Flat for Orchestra
Tommaso Albinoni	Various concerti for winds and strings
Johann Kuhnau	*Biblical Sonatas for Harpsichord*
Heinrich Schütz	*Symphoniae Sacrae* (small sacred concertos)
Claudio Monteverdi	*Scherzi Musicali;* madrigals
Giovanni Gabrieli	*Canzoni for Brass Choirs*

THE LATE EIGHTEENTH CENTURY

The principles established during the baroque period would continue well into the future. Their application would be subject to changing social climates and new crosscurrents of philosophical thought and artistic practice. The second half of the eighteenth century produced some of the most profound changes yet to affect man's daily pursuits. The years 1776 and 1789, marking the American and French revolutions, respectively, signaled a new era on both sides of the Atlantic, with far-reaching political, social, economic, and cultural changes that would alter the course of history and open up bold new vistas of artistic and creative freedom.

Only a few years before the outbreak of the American Revolution a monumental multivolume work was published in Paris that mirrored the spirit of the time better than any single literary or musical masterwork. In collaboration with leading French historians, writers, scientists, and musicians – including such figures as Jean d'Alembert, philosopher and mathematician; François-Marie Arouet Voltaire, poet, historian, and philosopher; and Jean-Jacques Rousseau, musician and philosopher – Denis Diderot began to compile his *Encyclopedia, or a Classified Dictionary of the Sciences, Arts, and Trades,* known in the original French as *Encyclopédie ou Dictionnaire Raisonné des Sciences, des Arts, et des Métiers.* The Age of Reason had found its most detailed literary document: a collective work whose scope shook the foundations of unquestioned traditions and reflected man's restless search for truths and definitions. It embodied all those qualities that became the watchwords of the impending revolutions: equality and dignity, hope and optimism, and a share in a better life for everyone, both materially and intellectually.

Rococo

In art and music a noticeable transition occurred, bridging the gap between the opulent tastes of the aristocracy and the elegant manners of the bourgeoisie. In the visual and decorative arts, such as sculpture, painting, and architecture, a late eighteenth-century style developed that came to be known as rococo. This term refers to the eighteenth-century French taste, embellishments in the shape of rocks and shells, called *rocailles* or *coquilles.* While it often bordered on the frivolous, the rococo style represented a trend toward the domesticated, a harbinger of great democratic changes to come.

In music rococo is far more difficult to define. It is often equated with the "style galant," as the French first called it. Here, too, it could be interpreted as a shift from the elaborate sweep of the baroque to music of a lighter and more elegant kind; for example, from the grand contrapuntal structure of a Bach organ fugue to a singable melody with accompaniment, as in the duet "Là ci darem la mano"

("Give me your hand") from Mozart's *Don Giovanni*. A comparable analogy in painting would be the multi-bodied splendor of Rubens' "Garden of Love" (1632–34), a full-blown, fantastic revelry, replete with floating cherubs, presided over by the figure of Venus, with the painter seen urging his wife to join the festivities; and Fragonard's satirically elegant painting "The Swing" (1766–69), which depicts the sensuous pleasure of a young nobleman secretly observing his lady friend's display of skirts.

In literature, too, comparisons are quite easy to come by. One may contrast Shakespeare's tragedies at the turn of the seventeenth century with Beaumarchais' bitingly satirical criticism of contemporary society in *The Barber of Seville* (1775) and *The Marriage of Figaro* (1784). Actually, this type of "style galant" was not new. In 1731 Bach specified his partitas, the first part of his *Clavierübung,* as ". . . Sarabands, Gigues, Minuets and other *galanteries."* Moreover, the highly ornamented style of the French and Italian harpsichordists, headed by Couperin and Scarlatti, may be considered as counterparts of the florid style of such rococo painters as Watteau, Boucher, and Fragonard. This is why rococo is often considered an extension of the baroque.

Yet music once again defies such explicit classifications. The second half of the eighteenth century is dominated by such names in music as Christoph Willibald Gluck, Carl Philipp Emanuel Bach, Johann Christian Bach, Franz Joseph Haydn, Wolfgang Amadeus Mozart, Luigi Boccherini, and, of course, Ludwig van Beethoven, who had already experienced great triumphs by the time the century drew to a close.

During the mid- and late eighteenth century the Mannheim School in Germany initiated a significantly new and expressive style of orchestral playing that would become the very foundation of the Viennese classical school of Haydn, Mozart, Beethoven, and Schubert. The Mannheim School functioned at the same time that the greatest masterpieces of Bach and Handel were being written (viz. during the late baroque period), proving the transitional character of the period.

CLASSICISM

In order to simplify matters, let us consider rococo in music as a style of compositional technique and interpretation. The movement that was germane to music at this time, rather than to the visual arts, is known as classicism. This term is used in various contexts. Here it applies primarily to the Viennese classical school and, more generally, as the antithesis to the era of romanticism that followed but whose spirit hovers over many of the creations of a "classical" nature.

The overlapping tendencies are seen more vividly when we consider contemporaries in the fields of literature and philosophy: Emmanuel Kant (*Critique of Pure Reason*), Gotthold Ephraim Lessing (*Emilia Galotti, Nathan the Wise, Minna von Barnhelm*), Johann Gottfried von Herder (*Letters for the Furtherance of Humanity*), Johann Wolfgang von Goethe (*Götz von Berlichingen, Egmont, The Sorrows of Young Werther, Faust, Iphigenia in Tauris, Torquato Tasso, Hermann and Dorothea*), Friedrich von Schiller (*The Robbers, Don Carlos, Wallenstein, Mary Stuart, The Maid of Orleans, William Tell*), Lorenzo da Ponte (librettos for *The Marriage of Figaro, Don Giovanni, Così Fan Tutte*), Jane Austen (*Sense and Sensibility, Pride and Prejudice, Northanger Abbey, Persuasion*). All are as classical in their choice of subject matter as they are romantic in the implications of their "messages."

We think of music during this period as being based upon accepted conventions of form and expressing ideas of aesthetic value and restraint. It is music for its own sake, music of formal unity, music mostly without a program. Perfect examples are the last three symphonies of Mozart, Nos. 39, 40, and 41, written in 1788; the Haydn Symphony No. 88, composed in 1787; the first two Beethoven symphonies, composed in 1800 and 1802, respectively; and most of the trios, quartets, quintets, and other works of the time for small ensembles. In fact, chamber music per se may be considered the finest genre of classical music of the period, for it is generally devoid of subtitles, which supply a programmatic "crutch" for listeners.

Yet it would be ludicrous to assume that classical music as described here is cerebral music to which only the intellect of the trained musician and the highly experienced listener can respond. The axiom that "classical" connotes a stress upon form over content is a misleading oversimplification.

Listen undisturbedly to the slow movement of the Mozart Symphony in G Minor, No. 40, or to Beethoven's Second Symphony or his String Quartet, Op. 18, No. 2, and you will find honest, warmly expressed feelings. Fortunately for all of us, here music speaks for itself, and words or descriptive titles can neither aid nor alter our emotional responses. The fact that we can react emotionally to music for its own sake, without the aid of image-inducing words or directions, is a meaningful sign of the music's innate validity or worth.

Why, then, am I devoting so much time to the classification of periods? I am guided by the firm belief that a music lover cannot live by emotional reactions alone; that the realization of the continual process of bold experimentation supplies the forward thrust that enables us to fathom the eternal state of flux, the very lifeblood of creativity.

CLASSICAL OPERA

What about vocal music in the context of this discussion? If a program evokes an emotional involvement more readily – hence becomes romantic by its very nature – can we think of vocal music as being classical in the true sense of the word? The answer is decidedly yes. While it is true that any vocal composition must be considered "program music" by virtue of the words recounting a story, we recognize the noble restraint of Orfeo's aria "Che farò senza Euridice?" (freely translated as "Now my love has gone forever?") from Gluck's *Orfeo ed Euridice* as being classical despite its intense emotional appeal. Compare it with Violetta's farewell to the world ("Addio! del passato") in Verdi's *La Traviata* and you will easily realize that vocal expression of deeply felt emotions can be classified as classical or romantic.

Opera, in fact, experienced a profuse flowering during the classical era. It also proved to be a highly popular form of musical entertainment, with the plot being overshadowed by the music. A parallel may be drawn between the satirical element inherent in rococo painting and literature (e.g., Fragonard and Beaumarchais) and the avid acceptance of the same features found in opera buffa, Italy's version of comic opera.

A classical example in the truest sense is Pergolesi's operetta *La Serva Padrona (The Maid as Mistress)*. Although it was first performed in 1733 as the intermezzo ("between the acts") of a serious opera by the same composer, it did not gain prominence until 1752 – long after the composer's death at the age of twenty-six – when it became the focal issue of a heated controversy in Paris about the respective merits of Italian and French music, known as "La Guerre des Bouffons" ("The War of the Comedians").

The classical opera buffa found its culmination in *Le Nozze di Figaro (The Marriage of Figaro)* by Mozart, the greatest musical genius of the age – and likely of all time. It was first performed in 1786. Two contemporary literary masters, both true "rococoans," provided the story: Beaumarchais with his comedy *La Folle Journée ou Le Mariage de Figaro (The Crazy Day or The Marriage of Figaro)* and Lorenzo da Ponte with his libretto. Mozart here proves his supreme mastery as a musical dramatist, with an unmatched comprehension of psychological truths vis-à-vis the human foibles of all the characters, irrespective of their social standing or their behavioral eccentricities. His music endows the delightful comedy with a gamut of human emotions, turning an opera into a mirror in which the society of the time and of the future could view itself with rare candor.

This great work was succeeded the following year by an opera that is unique in its emotional insight and dramatic characterization. *Don Giovanni* or *Il Dissoluto Punito (Don Juan* or *The Rake Punished)*, with a libretto by Lorenzo da Ponte based on a story by Giuseppe Bertati, is in effect both a tragedy and a comedy, as suggested by Mozart's own subtitle: *dramma giocoso.* As the story and the descriptive exploits of the world's best-known lover unfold, Mozart's ingenious music leads us with true-to-life tonal images from one episode to the next, from one psychological portrayal to another, touching upon all the human qualities of the characters involved and exposing their every emotion.

Don Giovanni is a work that is classical in its musical logic and in its central idea of the pursuit of ideal beauty. At the same time, the adventure of love, both for the lover and the beloved, disgust at the realization of the unattainable, tragic deaths at the opening and close of the opera, haunting scenes of the pursuit of the culprit – all these are in the greatest romantic tradition. Once again we are confronted with the impossible, namely, to attempt to label or classify the fruits of genius. Neither the French "style galant," nor its German offshoot, "empfindsamer Stil" ("style of sensitivity," an expression of true and natural feelings allowing for a continual change of affection), proves adequate in the search for categorization of such a masterpiece.

Mozart was also the consummate master of the genre of opera known as "singspiel," a German comic opera with spoken dialogue, the counterpart of the English "ballad opera" and the French "opéra comique." Although they are a phenomenon of opera in the classical period, many of the underlying stories and the casting of characters in the work are of a highly romantic nature, making the singspiel a perfect bridge to German romantic opera. Mozart's *Die Entführung aus dem Serail (The Abduction from the Seraglio)*, premiered in 1782, is the example par excellence, a delightful score filled with memorable melodies and ensemble singing. With it Mozart transformed a fashionable medium of the day into one of the finest examples of its kind, a magnificent work of art by any standard.

In his last operatic creation, *Die Zauberflöte (The Magic Flute)*, Mozart again created an opera where superb musical inventiveness, fantasy, and searching allegory, which treats of freemasonry and Austria's political circumstances, transcend the singspiel definition. One cannot cease to be moved by its basic human truths, presented with childlike purity and striking dramatic insight. This masterwork was composed in Mozart's final year, 1791, and was first performed just two months before his death. *Die Zauberflöte* was commissioned by Emanuel Schikaneder, an actor, singer, and impresario at the Theater an der Wien, known for its presentation of the singspiel. Schikaneder also furnished the libretto of the opera, consisting of a series of plots filled with many contrasts and opposing forces, an oriental, exotic setting, and the triumph, amid countless obstacles, of love over evil. Every lover of music should experience the thrill of seeing and hearing this incredibly beautiful and wondrous work. To recommend excerpts for the purpose of sampling the opera would be easy enough, for the entire work is a sheer delight; but one must hear these excerpts in the proper context to fully understand Mozart's triumph. Such an experience enriches and ennobles the listener immeasurably.

In the history of opera of the classical period, Christoph Willibald Gluck (1714–87) deserves special mention. Gluck distinguished himself for his leadership in the establishment of musical drama. He sought basic simplicity and truth in his compositions, as opposed to the artificial mannerisms and alienation from the realities of life that he found in the Italian operatic tradition of the time. His masterwork, *Orfeo ed Euridice,* eloquently embodies his concern for the expression of honest feeling and noble sentiment. During his stay in Paris Gluck incurred the displeasure of the followers of the Italian trends in opera, who, if not for the intervention of Marie Antoinette, were determined to prevent the production in Paris of Gluck's opera *Iphigénie en Aulide,* based on a drama by Racine, which in turn was derived from the writings of Euripides. Those favoring Italian opera did succeed, however, in importing to Paris one of Italy's most acclaimed composers, Niccolò Piccinni (1728–1800), resulting in a historic rivalry. Both Piccinni and Gluck were asked by the directors of the Paris Opéra to compose a work based, once again, on Euripides, namely, *Iphigénie en Tauride.* Gluck clearly emerged as the superior composer. With his singularity of artistic purpose and the realism of his dramatic approach, he paved the way for Mozart as well as for some of the masters of the romantic period.

CHURCH MUSIC

We must not overlook that phase of classical vocal music in which both Haydn and Mozart excelled, namely, music for the church. Until the advent of the concert hall in the late eighteenth century, musical performances in general could be heard in the homes of the aristocracy, in the theater, or, more accessibly, in the church. We have seen how earlier composers lavished much of their creative ability on writing music for worship. It was during the classical period that church music was elevated to a new level at the hands of the two great Viennese masters.

Not since Bach had there been music of such beauty and spirituality as to vie with the loftiness of purpose it was meant to serve. From the twelve masses and settings of the Te Deum, Salve Regina, and Stabat Mater by Haydn, to the eighteen masses, the vespers and litanies, and the incomparable Requiem by Mozart (his last work, left unfinished), church music gained a stature that was never surpassed, either in the sincerity of its aim (viz. to dignify the divine service) or in its determination to avoid theatricality.

Do listen to the Requiem by Mozart, completed by his pupil Franz Xaver Süssmayr upon the master's explicit instructions. With tones of his Requiem on his lips, Mozart bade members of his family a final farewell as he was dying.

An interesting sidelight should be mentioned here. It was in 1782 that Constanze Weber, Wolfgang's betrothed, became ill. Mozart vowed that if she recovered, so they could be married, he would compose an elaborate mass as a token of his gratitude. His wishes were granted. Constanze recovered and the wedding took place on August 4, 1782. A year later, at which time Mozart presented his wife to his father, who was displeased with the union, Mozart had completed most of the promised mass. The Credo section's "Et incarnatus est," in particular, is hauntingly beautiful. Much has been conjectured as to why the entire work was never finished, second thoughts about Mozart's marriage not being the least of the assumed reasons.

MUSICAL FORMS AND COMPOSITIONS

The classical period is distinguished instrumentally for the further development of the orchestra (see Chapter Four). The form of composition whose growth paralleled that of the orchestral ensemble was the symphony. Its repertory was greatly enriched by the many works of Haydn and Mozart.

The underlying form of the symphony, the sonata, was also enhanced by Haydn, Mozart, and above all by Beethoven. The growth of the solo sonata for keyboard was aided immeasurably by the concurrent evolution of the pianoforte. Thus the piano may be considered the "instrument of the hour" of the classical era.

Ever since the time of the classicists, principles of the sonata form have been applied to all types of chamber music, from the duo sonata to the trio, quartet, quintet, and on to larger ensembles. While the sound capacity of all other forms of music grew proportionally with the steady burgeoning of the orchestra – in terms of its tonal capabilities and virtuosic demands – chamber music in all its forms remained essentially unaltered. The expansion of ideas and possibilities of sound had to take place within the limits of the same basic ensemble. A Prokofiev string quartet may differ acoustically, structurally, and harmonically from a Haydn quartet, but the four instruments employed have not changed much during the intervening two hundred years, even though the accessories of violins, violas, and cellos (e.g., the height of the bridge, the raw material of the strings, the curvature of the bow, the position of the sound posts inside the instruments) have modified the sound that Haydn might have heard.

The development of the concerto for solo instrument and orchestra, also founded upon the sonata form, was advanced from its early baroque beginnings by the great classicists. The piano concerto in particular owes its spectacular development to the twenty-seven concertos written by Mozart. As the piano and the orchestra grew, so did the demands upon the performer's virtuosic ability. Even in this direction Mozart set the pace, performing many of his own piano concertos in public. His great artistic imagination and knowledge of instrumental capacities also made it possible for other instruments to attain concerto stature. It was Mozart who wrote five violin concertos, two for flute, four for horn, one for bassoon, one for clarinet, one for flute and harp, one for violin and viola known as *Sinfonia Concertante,* and one by the same name for strings plus oboe, clarinet, horn, and bassoon as solo group. There are some seventeen sonatas for organ and strings by Mozart, in addition to the multiple piano concertos, one for two pianos and one for three pianos.

Haydn, too, left us many examples of classical concerto writing. Among them are some thirteen keyboard concertos – in addition to three for violin, one for cello, two for horn, one for trumpet – and a particularly rewarding *Sinfonia Concertante* for violin, cello, oboe, and bassoon; all, of course, are with orchestral collaboration.

Just as Bach and Handel embodied the high baroque – some of their music being analogous to the lavish architectural style of the seventeenth and early eighteenth century, such as Christopher

Wren's St. Paul's Cathedral in London, Claude Perrault's Louvre in Paris, and Louis Le Vau and Jules Hardouin-Mansart's Versailles – so the masters of the Viennese classical school, Haydn and Mozart, represented the structural logic of the time. Here reason – the watchword of the Enlightenment – found its most elaborate application in music. This is not to imply that reason in this context became synonymous with a cold intellectual process. It is the creative genius of Haydn and Mozart that accomplished the seemingly impossible, namely, to endow the principles of reason and logic with the expressive fiber and warmth of human emotion that assured their universal acceptance. These same qualities may easily be discerned in their shorter works, and in the absence of the discipline of formal design of large-scale compositions.

During the final decades of the eighteenth century some of the great literary masterworks, such as Goethe's *Faust, The Sorrows of Young Werther, Egmont,* and Schiller's *Die Räuber (The Robbers)* were imbued with the kind of romantic fervor that became known in Germany as "Sturm und Drang" ("Storm and Stress") – after a similarly titled play by Friedrich Maximilian von Klinger published in 1776. This designation came to denote an entire literary movement marked by the love of freedom and nature as seen through the eyes of the young, impetuous creator. While this phenomenon was short-lived in the literary field, its application to music lasted throughout the romantic era and became synonymous with the growing pains of the young composer searching for identification and self-expression. Incidentally, many of the literary works of the Sturm und Drang period inspired musical settings by various composers.

ROMANTICISM

If preceding artistic epochs were difficult to place within temporal limits because of constantly shifting changes, it becomes nearly impossible to do so in the case of the romantic movement. To merely contrast it with classicism, which is traditionally considered its opposite, is as arbitrary and artificial as is the attempt to bring all the confluent ideas and trends of romanticism itself under one convenient "roof."

To be a "romantic" is a permanent state of mind and heart that can never be confined to any segment of time. Its characteristics include: a yearning for the infinite, for the unattainable; identification with nature, and with the joys and sorrows of life; and a desire to fathom the purpose of existence and to gain a fuller understanding of man's destiny, both here on earth and in the afterworld. Above all, romanticism is filled with opposite extremes: a love of solitude and a love of another; a search for the exotic and a nostalgia for the familiar; a wish for fame and notoriety and a need for the simplicity of isolation; a penchant for growth and self-improvement and a longing for the "good old days." Sometimes romanticism is a reaffirmation of the realization that the unattainable is, after all, just that – unattainable, which does not keep the romanticist from striving for it.

The French writer Théophile Gautier described the 1820s in his *History of Romanticism* as follows: "What a marvelous time. Walter Scott was then in the flower of his success; one was initiated into the mysteries of Goethe's *Faust,* which as Madame de Staël said, contained everything. One discovered Shakespeare, and the poems of Lord Byron: the Corsair; Lara; the Gaiour; Manfred, Beppo; and Don Juan took us to the Orient, which was not banal then as now. All was young, new, exotically colored, intoxicating, and strongly flavored. It turned our heads; it was as if we had entered into a strange new world."*

Indeed, romanticism became virtually an upheaval of mind and emotions, and both were continually nurtured, aroused, and challenged. The sheer force of its irrepressible march under the banner of the French Revolution – with its watchwords "Liberté, Égalité, Fraternité" – propelled it across Europe's borders and into the New World. The political changes of the 1840s brought many Central European and German musicians to America, who carried with them the romantic traditions of Vienna and Bohemia.

In England William Turner antedated the impressionist painters by eighty years, and John Constable depicted nature with the kind of mellow coloring reminiscent of the tonal palette of Beethoven's "Pastoral" Symphony in its more bucolic moods. Lord Byron, Walter

*Cited in William Fleming, *Art, Music, and Ideas,* p. 293.

Scott, Percy Bysshe Shelley, John Keats, Charles Dickens, Robert Burns, and William Wordsworth became the standard-bearers of British romantic literature, while their German colleagues Johann Wolfgang von Goethe, Joseph von Eichendorff, Heinrich Heine, Eduard Mörike, Ludwig Uhland, and Friedrich von Schiller helped shape the uniquely romantic age of their country. It was due to the blossoming of German poetry of the time that the Lied was born, that indivisible union of words and music to which some of the greatest German romantic composers contributed their finest efforts.

France produced its own distinctive brand of romanticism. French painters such as Eugène Delacroix used a highly characteristic color palette to convey the emotional content of their compositions. Within a few decades their work would inspire that uniquely French, innovative group of artists known as the impressionists. Romanticism also witnessed the exceptional talents of Jean Auguste Dominique Ingres, Théodore Géricault, Honoré Daumier, and François Millet. In literature, too, French masters such as Honoré de Balzac, Alexandre Dumas, Victor Hugo, and George Sand showed a remarkable gift for characterization and psychological insight.

The creative diversity of these artists, writers, painters, and poets matched their differing personalities and temperaments. While this is generally true of any artistic age, that very diversity became the common denominator of romantic art in particular; for, in the broadest terms, the emphasis of romantic art is centered upon the free expression of individual, subjective reactions and shows a greater concern for man's emotions and instincts than his intellect.

Clearly, romanticism is a multicolored vision, common to music, poetry, and art, as well as to philosophy and the sciences, transcending the boundaries of a specific time period. The courage and self-sacrifice inherent in the scientific discoveries of the Renaissance are matched in our own time by the daring of walking on the moon. The ingenuity of a Bach fugue awes us as much as the enormity of a Beethoven symphony. Shakespeare's tragedies move us as deeply as the dramas of Victor Hugo, and Rembrandt's "The Night Watch" speaks as eloquently of the type of military groups employed by the Netherlands to rid themselves of the Spanish yoke in the sixteenth century as Delacroix's "Liberty Leading the People" brings back with irresistible force the glories and the pains of the July Revolution of 1830 in France. It is the reader's, the listener's, the viewer's own sensitivity of reaction that determines the validity of romanticism in time and space. Limiting it chronologically to the nineteenth century would mean the denial of romantic qualities in Mozart's *Don Giovanni* or in Shakespeare's *Romeo and Juliet* simply because of their respective dates of origin.

Thus, it is not merely a question of the technique of composition, the organization of the words of a poem, or the brushstrokes of the painting; rather, it is the intensity of human feeling conveyed by these creations that give credence to the creator as a romantic artist. To put it yet another way: It is less a question of *how* than *why* a work is executed, what its message is.

Returning to music itself, any attempt to identify romanticism ought to begin with Ludwig van Beethoven. Here is a most typical case of romanticism's omnipresence.

LUDWIG VAN BEETHOVEN

Beethoven (1770–1827) was born during the height of music's classical period. Both Haydn and Mozart, by virtue of their prolificacy in the creation of examples of the classical forms of music, had emerged as the era's consummate masters. Young Ludwig showed his independent and even obstreperous leanings early, both in his personal behavior and in his individual approach to music.

At age eleven and a half he was obliged to contribute to the support of his family by becoming assistant organist in the court chapel in Bonn, Germany, and shortly afterward harpsichordist in the court orchestra. A visit to Vienna when he was seventeen convinced him of the need to live in this musical capital of the world. In 1792 at age twenty-two he left his Rhenish home to take up permanent residence in Vienna. There Beethoven came under the influence of Haydn, whose classical ideas he absorbed, as evidenced by Beethoven's early sonatas for the piano, the first three of them dedicated to the elder master, and by his first symphony. But in each instance the danger of derivativeness was easily overcome by the young artist's independent ideas and inspiration.

Beethoven's fame as composer and pianist was not long in coming, and his acceptance by Vienna's music-conscious aristocracy was proof of his professional stature and the strength of his personality.

In 1802 Beethoven experienced a personal crisis. He had become painfully aware of a steadily increasing deafness, a condition he at first could neither face nor tolerate. At the age of thirty-two he was convinced that his world and his usefulness in it had come to an end. While spending the summer of that year in the little town of Heiligenstadt, near Vienna, he penned what he intended to be his last will and testament. This heartrending document, the Heiligenstadt Testament of 1802, proved to be a catharsis for Beethoven, purging him of the demons that had beset his spirit, so that he was able to come to terms with his state of health. The sheer power of his will and his romantic ideals conquered the depths of his despair. The time could not have been more right for him to become the champion of freedom and personal triumph in a world that had just begun to fathom the emotional, social, and intellectual repercussions of the French Revolution.

The master's newborn strength now enabled him to pour forth a steady stream of masterworks, showing him at the peak of his creative powers. For the next twenty-five years his inspiration did not fail him. Only two years after he had informed the world that his end was at hand, Beethoven conceived one of the most powerful scores in the entire history of artistic creation. Around the turn of the century Napoleon Bonaparte was successfully altering the map of Europe. Like Consul Bonaparte, Beethoven espoused the causes of freedom and personal liberty, which represented the very fiber of romantic thought; and the musician was moved to pay homage to the statesman by dedicating to him a mighty symphony that Beethoven called "Eroica." Beethoven's completion of this third symphony coincided with Napoleon's proclaiming himself emperor; the musician's disappointment was so complete that his wrath knew no bounds. He saw in Napoleon's deed the betrayal of all the goals so dear to his heart. In a rage Beethoven tore up the title page bearing the dedication to Napoleon, hurled it to the ground, and stamped on it, proclaiming, "He will now trample on the rights of man as I trample on this paper." The dedication was changed to read: "Sinfonia Eroica composta per festeggiare il sovvenire d'un grand uomo" ("Heroic Symphony composed to celebrate the memory of a great man"). Napoleon, a traitor in Beethoven's mind, had unknowingly occasioned a monumental tribute to heroism itself, now anonymous in nature but all the more powerful in its implications. To this day, many a solemn occasion, such as the passing of a great leader, will prompt a performance of the "Eroica" in tribute – heard in concert or on special broadcasts.

From a musical standpoint Beethoven's "Eroica" constitutes a definite departure from any previous symphonic work. Its duration is much longer than that of any preceding symphony (some fifty minutes on the average, depending upon the conductor's conception). No previous composer had ever included a funeral march in a symphony, which Beethoven selected as the noble second movement of his work. While the nobility and majesty of the first movement is truly uplifting, the fourth movement is unsurpassed in the grandeur of its design – in effect, two sets of variations, each based on a theme of towering strength, and including an imposing fugue. The third movement, a scherzo, offers a respite from the relentless impact of the other movements without, however, affording a break in the flow of memorable ideas, building each restless thought to an inexorable climax. No one can begin to understand Beethoven without becoming thoroughly acquainted with the "Eroica."

Familiarity with Beethoven's works is an enriching and enduring experience. Beethoven has remained the greatest architect of large-scale compositions, a design that is impressively displayed in an imposing large number of masterworks: nine symphonies, seven concertos (five for piano, one for violin, one for piano-violin-cello), sixteen string quartets, four string trios, six piano trios, one trio for clarinet-cello-piano, one septet for strings and winds, one quintet for piano and winds, one string quintet, ten sonatas for violin and piano, five sonatas for cello and piano, one sonata for horn and piano, twenty-one sets of piano variations and, above all, thirty-two monumental piano sonatas.

Beethoven was first and foremost a pianist, an active performer on that instrument for many years. The piano remained the prime vehicle for the expression of his ideas. On his walks through the Viennese countryside he conceived many of his musical thoughts, enacting them with wild gestures, humming and singing them as he went along. Often he would hurry home to try out at the piano what his inner ear had heard. The scope of his inventiveness and the strength of his retention are all the more awe-inspiring when we recall that total deafness prevented him from actually hearing the magical sounds of his imagination. Although he never ceased yearning for the fulfillment of a normal personal life, the goal eluded him.

His only opera, *Fidelio, oder die eheliche Liebe (Fidelio, or Conjugal Love),* attests to his unshaken belief in the strength of marital union, a state that he was never to enjoy. His personal letters and the dedications of many of his compositions reveal his compassion for shared love and betray the identity of some of the recipients of his declared feelings. His song cycle *An die ferne Geliebte (To the Distant Beloved)* speaks eloquently of his emotional capacity for love. But the most painstaking research has failed to reveal the identity of this beloved who prompted such rapturous discourse.

Of equal importance in his life was a broad love of humanity and an all-embracing religious philosophy. What greater proof of both is there than his strong attraction to Schiller's "An die Freude" ("Ode to Joy"), which became the rousing finale of his Ninth Symphony. Beethoven's preoccupation with the concept of the brotherhood of all men under the fatherhood of one God forms a recurring theme in his writings and conversations. In his final symphony Beethoven presents this peak of humanitarian thought and feeling with a force both sublime and explosive. The three preceding, purely orchestral movements scale heights of unprecedented exaltation as well, and the entire monumental score bestows grandeur and spiritual strength upon any listener who will give it his undivided attention.

Although Beethoven's religiousness was not proven by church attendance, his belief in God was uncontested throughout his life. The great Missa Solemnis in D Major, the Mass in C Major, and the oratorio *Christus am Ölberg (Christ on the Mount of Olives)* are abiding testimonials to the power of his faith.

Interest in the music of Beethoven has never diminished; neither has the impact of his style of writing. Consider, for example, the broad sweep of his majestic melodies (e.g., the slow movement of the "Emperor" Concerto or the first movement of the Violin Concerto), the titanic thunder of his dramatic temperament (e.g., the first movements of the Fifth Symphony and the Third Piano Concerto; the piano sonatas, Op. 31, No. 2 ["Tempest"] and Op. 57 ["Appassionata"]), the jubilation of his psychological conquests (e.g., the final movements of the Fifth Symphony, the "Emperor" Concerto, and the Ninth Symphony), the contagious optimism of his positive moods (e.g., the third movements of the first and fourth piano concertos, the Violin Concerto, the String Quartet Op. 59, No. 2), the lovable, special brand of clumsy romping (e.g., the fourth movement of the Eighth Symphony), and the exalted philosophy and wisely intimate introspection of his late works (e.g., the last four quartets and the last three piano sonatas). Here is a legacy of which subsequent composers stood in awe.

The towering figure of Beethoven dominated that period generally considered transitional from classicism to romanticism. He was the personification of both. Romanticism's flowering in the 1820s was due, in great measure, to his prophetic conceptions of musical forms and sound. He propelled them far into the future as standards by which generations of creative masters were to measure their ideas.

Romantic Composers and Compositional Forms

In music, as in the other arts, romanticism exhibits a world of contradictions. In writing his *Waldszenen (Forest Scenes),* a set of lovely pieces for the piano, Robert Schumann moves as far away from society, both literally and figuratively, as anyone can. By contrast, consider the Requiem by Hector Berlioz, a work for mammoth forces, which was intended to honor those who died during the Revolution of 1830. Listening to it, you will realize an alternately delicate remoteness and vociferous exposition of intimate feelings.

When Frédéric Chopin wrote his mazurkas, he felt alone in his private world, while Franz Liszt espoused the jubilation of his countrymen when he wrote and performed his Hungarian rhapsodies – although the urge to express nationalistic fervor was the motivating force in both instances. Felix Mendelssohn's treatment of supernatural forces in his incidental music to Shakespeare's *A Midsummer Night's Dream,* a delightful example of musical "featherstitching," is far removed in style from Richard Wagner's summoning up of gods and demons in his *Ring des Nibelungen.*

All six composers mentioned here – Schumann, Berlioz, Mendelssohn, Chopin, Liszt, and Wagner – were born within the same decade

(1803–13). Of these, the first four composers may be considered early romanticists within the context of this discussion. They were preceded by Carl Maria von Weber and Franz Schubert. The most important works of this period were written between 1820 and 1850.

The middle period of romanticism (c. 1850–90) encompasses the most prominent works of Liszt and Wagner, along with César Franck of Belgium, Anton Bruckner of Austria; Bedrich Smetana and Antonin Dvořák of Bohemia; Giuseppe Verdi of Italy; Stanisław Moniuszko of Poland; Charles Gounod, Camille Saint-Saëns, Georges Bizet, Emmanuel Chabrier, Gabriel Fauré, and Jules Massenet of France; Johannes Brahms of Germany; Peter Ilyich Tchaikovsky, Modest Mussorgsky, Alexander Borodin, and Nicolas Rimsky-Korsakov of Russia; and Edvard Grieg of Norway.

The years 1890 to 1910 produced late or neoromantic works by Edward Elgar of England; Gustav Mahler of Bohemia and Vienna; Giacomo Puccini of Italy; Richard Strauss and Max Reger of Germany; Jan Sibelius of Finland; Carl Nielsen of Denmark; and Isaac Albéniz and Enrique Granados of Spain, to mention only a few familiar names. From this imposing list we may gain an intimation of the endless variety of personal expression of the time.

By examining the types of compositions for which these masters are justly famous, one can understand other aspects of the diversity inherent in romanticism. Earlier (see pp. 236–8) I discussed the Lied and its supreme mastery by Franz Schubert (1797–1828). He, like Beethoven, was a pivotal force in the transition from classicism to romanticism. A singing quality pervades the great majority of his entire musical output. The nine symphonies, the various works of chamber music, piano sonatas, the impromptus and *moments musicaux* for piano, the waltzes and ländler (a type of peasant dance) – all show a special brand of lyricism that had never quite been experienced before.

Robert Schumann (1810–56) is an equally prominent composer of lieder cycles. His *Frauenliebe und -Leben (Women's Love and Life)* depicts in ideally cyclic form the German poet Adalbert von Chamisso's vision of life's stages, from the realization of first love to marriage, motherhood, and the disappointment of a first indiscretion. What could be more illustrative of the romantic artistic ideal than the most human of all experiences retold by way of a marvelous merger of words and music? *Dichterliebe (Poet's Love)* is another masterful cycle, utilizing poetry by Heinrich Heine, describing the joys and pains of love.

Schumann's individual lieder attest to the composer's great gift for musical storytelling. Inspired by the long-awaited marriage to his beloved Clara, Schumann composed many of his lieder in 1840, the year they were married; most of them were love songs.

Of particular pictorial interest among Schumann's lieder is a dramatic ballad for which Heinrich Heine's poetry was the source of inspiration – "Die beiden Grenadiere" ("The Two Grenadiers"). This is the story of two French soldiers returning home from Napoleon's doomed Russian campaign. When they hear of their emperor's capture, they prefer a soldier's death, buried fully armed so that they may rise to protect their monarch as he crosses their graves. The climax is created by Schumann when he quotes a few noble strains from "La Marseillaise" to signify the grenadiers' devotion unto death to their emperor. Again, romanticism reaps a rich harvest, replete with a touch of musical nationalism to match the poem's patriotic fervor. (Additional suggestions for lieder listening, especially by such superb masters as Brahms, Hugo Wolf, and Richard Strauss, may be found on page 239.)

An extremely rewarding and favorite form of romantic composition is the character piece for piano. Possessing unusual dramatic and lyric capacities, this genre is designed to convey moods, emotions, and programmatic thoughts. (A section about these instrumental songs without words by such masters as Mendelssohn, Schubert, Schumann, Chopin, Brahms, and Grieg appears on pp. 231–34.)

Romanticism's most characteristic creation is the symphonic poem or tone poem, which appears in many powerful scores for full symphony orchestra and is usually in one continuous movement. Musically such a work either recounts actual scenes and happenings of an underlying literary source or evokes the overall spirit of a poem. The basic idea was soon expanded by other composers to include episodes of national life or indigenous national scenery. (For specific examples of this type of composition, see pp. 254–55.)

THE ROMANTIC SYMPHONY

The symphony, which grew to maturity under Haydn's and Mozart's loving care and was molded by Beethoven, was now ready to respond to romanticism's whims and demands.

Here we must come to terms with definitions. The symphony, a sonata for orchestra, is generally regarded as the prototype of absolute music, music for its own sake, independent of any programmatic idea or plot. Yet we have experienced symphonies by Mozart and Beethoven whose pathos and dramatic content stir our emotions. Even though the symphony as a compositional concept stresses form over matter, we cannot deny its power to involve us in a way that is thoroughly subjective. The symphonic masters – Beethoven, Mozart, and Haydn – show us over and over again the truth of this fact. Indeed, Beethoven forges far deeper into "romantic" territory with his third, fifth, sixth, and ninth symphonies than the early romantics – Schubert, Weber, Spohr, and Mendelssohn – do in their respective symphonies.

Nonetheless, the following masterworks should be considered required listening:

Schubert's Symphony No. 8 ("Unfinished") and his magnificent Symphony No. 9 ("The Great").

Mendelssohn's Symphony No. 3, inspired by his visit to Scotland; his Symphony No. 4, composed during his travels to Italy; and his Symphony No. 5 ("Reformation"), composed for the three hundredth anniversary of the Augsburg Confession and utilizing the Lutheran chorale "Ein feste Burg ist unser Gott" ("A Mighty Fortress Is Our God") at the heart of the final movement.

Schumann's four symphonies are filled with the same romantic melodic ardor that lends so much distinctiveness to his earlier piano works and his lieder. His first is called the "Spring" Symphony, a reflection of his psychological state of elation at the arrival of his long-awaited wedding day. Schumann's third symphony, named "Rhenish," conveys the composer's impressions of a visit to the majestic cathedral in Cologne, and of the mirth of a Rhenish folk festival.

If I were to choose the prototypical romantic symphony, I would nominate the *Symphonie Fantastique* by Hector Berlioz. De Musset's translation of De Quincy's *Confessions of an English Opium Eater* had originally inspired the composer to call this work "An Episode in the Life of an Artist." The symphony was prompted by the heat of Berlioz's love for the Shakespearean actress Harriet Smithson, who paid no heed to the composer's declarations. Yet he provided a detailed program for the five movements of the symphony, which shows the progressive heightening of the composer's fantasies: He becomes impassioned at the sight of Harriet as a Shakespearean actress; he meets Harriet at a dance; she occupies his thoughts while he walks in the countryside; a nightmare reveals to him that he killed his beloved and is condemned to death at the gallows; the finale pictures him as the central figure of a witches' sabbath. Berlioz uses a recurring theme, known as *idée fixe*, which he assigns to the solo clarinet to signify the appearance of his beloved in each of the five movements, altering the clarinet's tune to fit the changing spirit of the music as it progresses from one episode to the next. The symphony lives up to its name and our romantic expectation in a most detailed autobiographical fashion.

Other composers who contributed significantly to the symphonic repertory in a nationally coloristic way include Franz Liszt, with his *Dante* and *Faust* symphonies. It is also a pleasure to become reacquainted with the Bohemian splendor of Anton Dvořák's distinctively personal approach to symphonic writing. The Symphony No. 9 in E Minor ("From the New World"), composed in 1892–95 during Dvořák's stay in America, where he served as director of the National Conservatory in New York, is justly famous for a wealth of memorable melodies. The influence of folksong and dance, joined to his own mercurial temperament and coupled with a mastery of form and orchestration, combine to rank Dvořák's nine symphonies among the finest of the romantic age. His pace-setting use of popular Bohemian dances in the confines of the symphony was just as innovative in its way as was Beethoven's inclusion of a funeral march in his Symphony No. 3.

At about the time Dvořák was "nationalizing" the symphony, there appeared Tchaikovsky's six symphonies, all brilliant examples of his mastery of the form. The utter abandon of the last movement of his Symphony No. 4, compared with the nostalgic wistfulness of the second movement; the majesty of the Symphony No. 5, from the brooding "Fate" theme at its beginning, the noble horn solo of the second movement, and the *con grazia* waltz of the third movement to the exultant climaxes of the finale; the exuberance of the third movement of his Symphony No. 6, contrasted with the lugubrious melancholia of the first movement, the relief of the dancelike scherzo, and the despair and passion of the finale – all combine wondrously to personify the many facets of the greatest of Russian romantics. The emotions that are manifested in his music describe the essence of the nature of romanticism far better than any scholarly analysis. Of additional interest are Borodin's three symphonies, Rimsky-Korsakov's three symphonies, Balakirev's two symphonies, and Glazunov's eight symphonies.

All four symphonies of Johannes Brahms (1833–97) are excellent examples of an ideal union of classical form and the noblest of romantic content. In his Fourth Symphony, Brahms endows the finale with a passacaglia – a type of composition found primarily in baroque music – with the ardor of his own brand of romanticism.

Brahms did not complete his first symphony until he was forty-three years old, although he had begun preliminary sketches fourteen years earlier. He was intimidated by the thought of treading the stage that Beethoven had commanded with such prominence and majesty. Although Brahms's Symphony No. 1 is often called a successor to Beethoven's nine symphonies, there is no more basis for comparison between these two composers than there is between two great writers or painters, each strong and completely individualistic in his own right.

Brahms's Symphony No. 1 represents a new level of craftsmanship and highly intense dramatic content. The first movement is of heroic proportions. The emotional warmth of the second movement, with its alternation of idyllic and sensuous themes, the gracefulness of the scherzo, and the epic magnitude of the finale make this one of the most outstanding symphonic creations ever conceived.

Also within this period are noteworthy works by French and Belgian composers. César Franck's Symphony in D Minor is part of the staple repertoire of every major orchestra. Paul Dukas, composer of the tone poem *The Sorcerer's Apprentice,* wrote a single symphony, as did Ernest Chausson, an extremely gifted French musician. There are two exhilarating symphonic examples by the youthful Georges

Bizet. The first is an effervescent masterpiece written when he was seventeen – his Symphony in C, discovered as late as 1933. The later symphony, *Roma* (1880), is in effect a suite consisting of four delightful sections, each named after and inspired by a great Italian city and introducing quasi-Italian tunes. The *Symphony on a French Mountain Air* for orchestra with piano solo, one of Vincent d'Indy's three symphonies, zestfully incorporates folk material from the Auvergne region in the heart of France.

French lucidity and detailed craftsmanship pervade the three symphonies of Camille Saint-Saëns. The last of these is known as the "Organ" Symphony, a mighty cascade of sound calling for organ and piano for four hands to supplement the rich orchestration.

Postromantic Composers and Their Works

Approaching the turn of the twentieth century, those masters whose romantic style of writing prevailed – as if oblivious to the newer trends around them – are referred to as postromanticists. Among the most notable composers of the era are Anton Bruckner (1824–96) of Austria and Gustav Mahler (1860–1911), the Bohemian-born musician. Each has nine complete symphonies to his credit, almost all of them of gigantic proportions. Both attained recognition and appreciation late in their careers. However, temperamentally and ideologically the two were complete opposites.

Anton Bruckner was of peasant stock, provincial in outlook, and untraveled. He taught organ and music theory and held the post of organist at the Cathedral of Linz in Austria. His compositions reflect a mysticism derived from his religious convictions as a staunch Catholic. They never quite enjoyed the esteem abroad that they had in his native Austria, although the faith and devotion with which an increasing number of conductors in recent years have persisted in presenting them is shedding belated light on their lofty values. Of great importance are the Symphony No. 4, which bears the revealing subtitle "Romantic"; the Symphony No. 7 (the most successful symphony during Bruckner's lifetime), a work closely interwoven with the composer's great devotion to Richard Wagner; and the Symphony No. 8, which, despite its formidable length, has been received with considerable success whenever the work's vitality and the listener's interest can be maintained by a strong performance.

Gustav Mahler, on the other hand, was a cosmopolitan who combined the duties of a very successful orchestral and operatic conductor with immensely taxing activities as composer of a large number of grand-scale works. While Bruckner's music displays religious tendencies of an earth-centered kind, Mahler's works explore the mysteries of life after death. His symphonies reveal his existentialist preoccupations.

Mahler's Symphony No. 1, which the composer subtitled "The Titan" (after the novel of the same name by Jean Paul Richter), initiates the informed listener into the composer's metaphysical world. Dividing the work into two large parts, he called the first "Days of Youth. Youth, Flowers, and Thorns," and the second "Human Comedy." Individual movements (two are ascribed to each of these large parts) are headed: "Spring Without End"; "Full Sail!"; "Stranded: Funeral March à la Callot"; and "From Inferno to Paradise." These subtitles were later dropped by the composer. Written when Mahler was twenty-eight, this first symphonic score shows the composer at his most exuberant and vigorous. Quotations from a spring song used in his own song cycle *Lieder eines fahrenden Gesellen (Songs of a Wayfarer)* in the first movement, a robust Austrian ländler and trio section in the second movement, the grotesquely funereal atmosphere of the third movement, and the climactic finale incorporating earlier material in an ingenious development – all combine to present the listener with a positive clue to Mahler's world.

As for his Symphony No. 2, known as "Resurrection," Mahler lets us share his existentialist searching with his own remarks: "I have called the first movement 'Celebration of the Dead'; and if you wish to know, it is the Hero of my first symphony whom I bear to the grave. Immediately arise the great questions: Why have you lived? Why have you suffered? Has it all been only a huge, frightful joke? We must all somehow answer these questions, if we are to continue living, yes, even if we are only to continue dying. Whoever hears this call must give a reply. And this reply I give in my last movement."

Bruno Walter, the legendary conductor who was also Gustav Mahler's closest disciple and friend, found "moods, emotions and thoughts . . . dissolved within the music" of the first three movements. In the fourth movement "man sings of his trust that the dear Lord may vouchsafe him a little light to show the way into the life beyond." The finale uses soprano and alto solo, chorus, and orchestra with organ to "reply for the first time to the sorrows, the doubts, and the questions of his soul," according to Bruno Walter. This gigantic movement is subtitled "The Great Summons," and it was inspired by Friedrich Klopstock's poem "The Resurrection."

Mahler's philosophical and metaphysical concerns as expressed in his music were not readily accepted by audiences of his time. In fact, it took many decades – he died in 1911 at the age of fifty – before the missionary persistence of his disciples (headed by Bruno Walter) to keep Mahler's music before the concertgoing public met with some success. Mahler's Fourth Symphony served as the bridge to today's overwhelming acceptance of his work by an ever-increasing audience.

The Symphony No. 4 is Mahler's shortest and most lyrical symphony. Its highlight is the inclusion, in the last movement, of a beautifully naive vocal description of heavenly bliss, using words from medieval German folk songs. The fantasy of this work, the easy accessibility of the music, and the most direct use of compositional devices typical of Mahler (which are far more elaborately employed in his other symphonies) enable the Fourth Symphony to serve as another excellent introduction to Mahler's world.

On the opposite side of Mahler's symphonic spectrum is his Symphony No. 8, known as the "Symphony of a Thousand" because of the immense number of performers it requires: eight solo vocalists, two mixed choruses and a boys' choir, a much enlarged orchestra, and an organ. Again the composer provides two parts: "Veni Creator Spiritus," based upon the ninth-century church hymn, for two choruses; and "Concluding Scene from *Faust*," a symphonic poem with chorus, set to the second part of Goethe's text.

Mahler's symphonic output is mostly spiritual, expressing highly subjective and sometimes painfully wrought philosophies. Another important trait of Mahler's scores is their detailed directions for the performance of even such small components as phrases, motifs, and notes. It is as if the composer wanted nothing left to chance – or to the conductor's discretion. In addition to their interpretative implications, these directions also afford us an invaluable glimpse of Mahler's greatness as a conductor.

Mahler's lieder and song cycles, although basically belonging to a different category, are symphonic in scope. Listen to the cycle *Das Lied von der Erde (The Song of the Earth),* which Mahler himself considered a symphony and which was only performed after his death; the above-mentioned *Lieder eines fahrenden Gesellen;* and *Kindertotenlieder (Children's Death Songs). Das Lied von der Erde* calls for mezzo-soprano, tenor, and orchestra; it is set to a German translation of old Chinese poems. The *Lieder eines fahrenden Gesellen* calls for contralto and orchestra; it is set to Mahler's own poems, inspired by his youthful love for Johanna Richter. *Kindertotenlieder* requires the smallest instrumental ensemble; it consists of a cycle of songs set to poems by Friedrich Rückert, in memory of the death of Rückert's own children.

Another superior individualist among symphonists who composed well into the twentieth century was Jean Sibelius (1865–1957) of Finland. Sibelius was a romanticist who dared to pursue his self-charted course at a time when Arnold Schoenberg and Igor Stravinsky were revolutionizing our tonal system of composing. In his seven symphonies (1899–1924) Sibelius showed a distinctive approach to orchestral conception, coupled with a personal sense of instrumental color. As in the case of Grieg's identification with the music of Norway, Sibelius has often been called the "Voice of Finland," his music being descriptive of his country's rugged and wintry scenery. For the sheer power of symphonic invention, listen to the first, second, and fifth symphonies, with their compelling climaxes and logically, beautifully developed thematic material.

Sergei Rachmaninoff (1873–1943) composed three symphonies of a highly personal idiom, both thematically and in terms of harmonization and orchestration, which should be of interest.

Unjustly neglected until 1965, the hundredth anniversary of his birth, were the six symphonies by Carl Nielsen, Denmark's greatest composer. Written between 1894 and 1925, they represent the romantic tradition in yet another individualistic fashion. Nielsen at times displays a naiveté not unlike that of his esteemed countryman Hans Christian Andersen. His Symphony No. 6 is the only one that may be termed modern. Interestingly, in the "Humoresk" movement the trombone slides produce a simulated yawning effect, by which Nielsen appears to express his boredom with the new schools of music all around him. Listen to Nielsen's Symphony No. 1 for a taste of good symphonic Danish fare!

Completely twentieth century in origin but romantic in musical content are the nine symphonies by the prolific English master Ralph Vaughan Williams (1872–1958), written between the years 1910 and 1957. Most of these reveal a pronounced kinship with English lore and folk elements: *A Sea Symphony,* with a choir intoning words by Walt Whitman; the *"Pastoral"* Symphony; *A London Symphony;* and the *Sinfonia Antartica.*

Vaughan Williams' compatriot Edward Elgar (1857–1934) created two highly romantic symphonies of large-scale proportions, written between 1908 and 1911. Other composers from the United Kingdom who can be considered romantic symphonists are Charles V. Stanford (1852–1924) of Ireland (the third of his seven symphonies is known as the "Irish"); Arnold Bax (1883–1953) of England, who composed seven symphonies; and William Walton (1902–83) of England, whose modernistic harmonies do not obscure his romantic allegiance.

The Romantic Concerto

During the romantic age, the improved tonal capabilities of instruments, their greater adaptability to the detailed markings in scores, the advent of larger halls and audiences, as well as the increased virtuosity of performing artists combined to bring forth the "virtuoso concerto" to serve as an excellent musical vehicle of the time.

A brief look at the romantic concerto will provide the dual joy of familiar encounters and of rare discovery. Once again we reach back into the classical period in order to single out those examples that qualify as "romantic" because of their intrinsic dramatic content. Mozart's piano concertos K. 466 in D Minor and K. 491 in C Minor are both exceptionally dramatic works, far ahead of their actual date of origin – both were written in March 1786. Other movingly romantic piano concertos of Mozart are K. 488 in A Major and K. 467 in C Major.

Among the high points of the entire concerto literature are Beethoven's piano concertos nos. 3, 4, and 5, his incomparable violin concerto, as well as the triple concerto for violin, cello and piano, a work of remarkable inventiveness. In these are contained drama, majesty, pathos, nobility, playfulness alternating with tension, and beauty of melody of the most memorable kind. Every music lover should afford himself the chance of knowing them well.

Carl Maria von Weber composed two sparkling piano concertos in 1810 and 1812 that presaged the idiomatic melodies of his famous stage creations, *Der Freischütz, Euryanthe,* and *Oberon.* Weber was active as a piano virtuoso during the early years of his brief career, and his concertos attest to his mastery of pianistic writing. Of equal interest during this early romantic period are his *Konzertstück* (not a concerto in the formal sense) for piano and orchestra, replete with a romantic plot; two clarinet concertos, a bassoon concerto, and two miniature concertos (or concertinos), one for clarinet and one for horn.

Among the outstanding concerto composers of the time is Felix Mendelssohn, with two splendid examples for piano (1831 and 1837), and a violin concerto (1844) to his credit, in addition to other very youthful works in both categories. In each instance Mendelssohn's extraordinary gift for lyricism is expressed with consummate craftsmanship. The violin concerto, in particular, has gained a secure place among the finest and most popular works in the violin repertoire.

Frédéric Chopin wrote two piano concertos (both in 1830) of great romantic beauty, as one might expect of this composer who was a pianist first and foremost. In either concerto it is possible to envision each of the three movements as individual pieces for solo piano. In the first concerto in E Minor the slow movement, a larghetto with the subtitle "romance," is in the finest of Chopin's introspective "character" pieces. In the second concerto in F Minor Chopin provides a hauntingly beautiful nocturne as a second movement, which was admittedly inspired by the nineteen-year-old composer's frustrated love for a fellow pupil at the Warsaw Conservatory.

The single piano concerto by Robert Schumann, composed between 1841 and 1845, is of unsurpassed beauty. While the piano remains the chief protagonist, or focus, throughout the concerto, the orchestra is used effectively in the manner of complete cooperation. In the highly poetic intermezzo of the second movement, the interweaving of piano and orchestra is of particular delight, a true interplay of musical ideas. The brilliant yet nostalgic first movement eventually finds a comfortable link with the rhythmically fetching finale.

Franz Liszt's two piano concertos (1849 and 1857) show a supreme mastery of pianistic ability and reveal the virtuosity that so distinguished one of the first of the great piano recitalists. Also among the all-time favorites of the entire piano concerto literature are the first concerto by Tchaikovsky and three concertos by Rachmaninoff. A rare combination of majesty, nostalgia, exuberance, and brilliance marks the Tchaikovsky work, while Rachmaninoff's contributions represent a special admixture of the same ingredients, tempered with this Russian master's own wistful yearning.

Johannes Brahms's contributions to this category include two works for piano (1854 and 1878–81), one for violin (1878), and the Double Concerto for Violin, Cello, and Orchestra (1887), his last major orchestral work. The close linkage of solo instrument and orchestra, which Beethoven had established in his last two piano concertos, found its highest application at the hands of Brahms.

In the case of the virtuoso violinist-composer of the romantic age, it was nearly impossible to find another Mozart who was equally at home with keyboard and violin. Most of the great masters of the age composed at the piano and sought out renowned violinists for counsel when composing a violin concerto. Ferdinand David, famed violinist, teacher, and pupil of Ludwig Spohr, advised his friend Mendelssohn. Leopold Auer, mentor of such renowned violinists as Mischa Elman, Jascha Heifetz, Nathan Milstein, and Efrem Zimbalist, was called upon by Tchaikovsky for advice but meted out unheeded discouragement instead. Joseph Joachim, distinguished violinist, teacher, and quartet leader, collaborated with Brahms at the latter's request.

Most of the other creators of the romantic violin concerto either knew the instrument intimately or were themselves acclaimed master violinists. The legendary Niccolò Paganini comes to mind immediately. We may recall pictures of the lanky, emaciated figure with long bony arms drawing the bow across the strings as if aided by diabolical forces, as rumor would have it. He was quite likely the greatest string virtuoso of all time. The legend of Paganini was deepened by the fact that he refused to allow almost any of his works to be printed during his lifetime. Today five violin concertos are extant, all filled with tricky fireworks yet also displaying creative genius, so that even the fanciest of finger acrobatics are of artistic worth. Feast your ears on any of them, but listen especially to the Concerto No. 2 in B Minor, whose last movement, "Rondo à la Clochette," imitates an eerie little bell that has become known as "La Campanella" by virtue of Liszt's piano transcription of the original tune.

Another remarkable master of the violin was Giovanni Battista Viotti (1755–1824), who exerted a lasting influence as performer, teacher, and composer. His twenty-nine violin concertos and illustrious pupils – such as Rodolphe Kreutzer, to whom Beethoven dedicated his famous Sonata in A Major, Op. 47, for violin and piano; Jacques Rode, who played Beethoven's last violin sonata, Op. 96, for the master; and Charles Auguste de Bériot, the brilliant Belgian violinist and composer – surely entitle Viotti to more lasting fame than has been his.

Ludwig Spohr (1784–1859) is another virtuoso violinist who composed a significant number of works for his own performances and enriched the repertoire of the romantic concerto. In addition to writing fifteen concertos, Spohr enjoyed great fame as a concert violinist throughout Europe, as a teacher, and as one of the first orchestral conductors.

The Polish master Henryk Wieniawski (1835–80) was one of the outstanding violinists of his day, serving as violinist to the czar of Russia and holding the post of professor at the Brussels Conservatoire. He composed two highly acclaimed violin concertos.

Special mention should also be made of the Belgian school of violinist-composers, which included Charles Auguste de Bériot (1802–70), a professor at the Brussels Conservatoire who published concertos, studies, and instruction books, this despite the fact that he was blind for the last twelve years of his life; Henri Vieuxtemps (1820–81), De Bériot's most famous pupil, who wrote six violin concertos; and Eugène Ysaye (1858–1931), who served for a while as director of the Cincinnati Symphony Orchestra and composed beautifully romantic works for the violin.

Concertos by the following masters further enriched the list of romantic works in this category: Saint-Saëns, who composed three brilliant violin concertos and five important piano concertos; Max Bruch, the German conductor and composer, whose Violin Concerto in G Minor remains a perennial favorite.

The impressive Violin Concerto by Sibelius stands out among many early twentieth-century romantic creations. Its taxing virtuosity and great originality lend it a special status among musicians and audiences alike. There is nobility and majesty in the first movement, sonorous low-register beauty and passion in the second-movement romanza, and an irresistible rhythmic drive in the finale.

The English composer Edward Elgar is distinguished for his violin concerto and Frederick Delius for a cello concerto. Russian composer Alexander Glazunov is remembered for his two concertos for violin and one concerto for cello.

Among great cello concertos of the period, surely those by Schumann, Dvořák, Saint-Saëns, and Lalo must be singled out for their memorable beauty, ideally suited to bring out the cello's rich sonorities.

CONCERTED WORKS IN THE ROMANTIC AGE

The nineteenth century brought to life another genre of composition that has found much favor with performers and music lovers: the concerted piece for solo instrument and orchestra. This category has the appeal of a concerto yet is generally much shorter in length and does not follow the sonata form, which is required of at least the first movement of a regular concerto.

Excellent examples include:

- two very beautiful romances for violin and orchestra by Beethoven
- various sets of variations for violin by Paganini
- *Introduction and Allegro Appassionato* for piano and orchestra by Schumann
- *Konzert-Allegro* for piano and orchestra by Schumann
- *Konzertstück* for four horns and orchestra by Schumann

- *Introduction and Rondo Capriccioso* for violin and orchestra by Saint-Saëns
- *Variations on a Rococo Theme* for cello and orchestra by Tchaikovsky
- *Andante Spianato and Grande Polonaise Brillante* for piano and orchestra by Chopin
- *Grand Fantasy on Polish Airs* for piano and orchestra by Chopin
- *Rondo à la Krakowiak* for piano and orchestra by Chopin
- *Variations on Mozart's "Là ci darem la mano"* for piano and orchestra by Chopin
- *Kol Nidrei* (fantasy on the ancient Hebrew chant) for cello and orchestra by Bruch
- *Burleske* for piano and orchestra by Richard Strauss
- *Ballade* for piano and orchestra by Fauré
- several brilliant pieces for violin and orchestra by Wieniawski
- *Hungarian Fantasia* for piano and orchestra by Liszt

A special place in the repertoire is occupied by two works that, though not strictly in the concerto category, are full-length works running the gamut of emotions and displaying great technical diversity. One is the *Symphonie Espagnole* for violin and orchestra by Édouard Lalo; the other is a Hebrew rhapsody for cello and orchestra entitled *Schelomo,* by the Swiss-American composer Ernest Bloch. The latter is a remarkable portrayal of the complex personality of the biblical King Solomon, with the cello nobly and searchingly representing the voice of the king.

OPERA IN THE ROMANTIC ERA

Romanticism could not have found a more perfect vehicle with which to unite all its varied aspects than opera. Creating larger-than-life situations with overwhelming candor, the composer, librettist, and director combined talents to harness the forces of instrumental and vocal music, including chorus, soloists, and ensembles, acting and dance, poetry and prose, lighting, stage scenery, and costumes.

Let's consider Beethoven's only opera, *Fidelio*. Its moving story concerns the unswerving love of a wife who frees her husband from incarceration and death. Joy and sorrow, love and hatred, and jealousy and trust were now captured for the first time with all the intensity of their meanings. The fusion of so many of the component arts was aided by fantasy – the play of unfettered emotions – which distinguished the creative artist of the romantic age. On a broader plane, *Fidelio* mirrors man's eternal struggle for freedom as felt so nobly and profoundly by Beethoven, the champion of the cause of human liberty. The story of Florestan and Lenore thus becomes the vehicle with which to project a truly romantic work of exceptional eloquence.

The association of music and drama dates back to the dawn of civilization – ranging from the choral songs and dances of ancient Greek drama, the religious dramas and mystery plays of the Middle Ages, to the recreation of Greek drama, with declamatory song supported by a keyboard instrument or lute, in the Renaissance. Opera advanced steadily during the baroque and classical periods to become a highly complex amalgam of the arts. But it was the nineteenth century that became the most propitious period for operatic creativity.

Composers with a theatrical bent were easily inspired by the visions of the great dramatists of the time. Goethe was responsible for Gounod's *Faust*, Thomas' *Mignon*, Massenet's *Werther*; Schiller for Verdi's *Luisa Miller, I Masnadieri (The Robbers), Don Carlos*, and Rossini's *William Tell*; Victor Hugo for Verdi's *Ernani, Rigoletto*, and Ponchielli's *La Gioconda*, based on Hugo's *Angelo, Tyran de Padoue*; Dumas' tragedy *La Dame aux Camélias* formed the basis for *La Traviata* one of Verdi's most popular operas. Donizetti's *Lucia di Lammermoor* was based on Sir Walter Scott's *The Bride of Lammermoor*; Pushkin's short story "The Queen of Spades" was expanded by Tchaikovsky, and the same poet's historical drama *Boris Godunov* furnished part of Mussorgsky's colorful opera of the same name. The writings of William Shakespeare are recreated in Berlioz's *Béatrice et Bénédict* (based on *Much Ado About Nothing*); Verdi's versions of *Otello, Falstaff* (based on *The Merry Wives of Windsor*), and *Macbeth;* Thomas' *Hamlet;* and Gounod's *Roméo et Juliette.*

Famous writers and playwrights were often employed to write the libretto (lit. "little book"), the name given to the accompanying text of an opera. Among the renowned librettists of the romantic age were Lorenzo da Ponte (1749–1838), who provided Mozart with librettos for *Le Nozze di Figaro, Così fan Tutte,* and *Don Giovanni.* Eugène Scribe (1791–1861), was so productive – his complete works comprise seventy-six volumes – that he employed many collaborators, who became known as the "Scribe factory." Composers turned to him more often than to any other librettist, attesting to his unerring theatrical sense. Among them were Daniel Auber for thirty-eight operas, including *La Muette de Portici, Fra Diavolo,* and *Le Cheval de Bronze;* Vincenzo Bellini for *La Sonnambula;* Gaetano Donizetti for five operas, including *L'Elisir d'Amore* and *La Favorita;* Giacomo Meyerbeer for five operas, among them *L'Africaine, Les Huguenots,* and *Le Prophète;* and Giuseppe Verdi for *I Vespri Siciliani* and *Un Ballo in Maschera.*

The Italian librettist and composer Arrigo Boïto (1842–1918) served Verdi in creating *Otello* and *Falstaff;* and the Austrian poet and dramatist Hugo von Hofmannsthal (1874–1929) collaborated with Richard Strauss on *Elektra, Der Rosenkavalier, Ariadne auf Naxos, Die Frau ohne Schatten, Die ägyptische Helena,* and *Arabella.*

The most readily remembered partnership in the creation of delightful light opera is that of W. S. Gilbert and the English composer and conductor Arthur Sullivan. The fruits of their collaboration – including *Trial by Jury* (1875), *H.M.S. Pinafore* (1878), *The Pirates of Penzance* (1879), *Iolanthe* (1882), *The Mikado* (1885), *Ruddigore* (1887), *The Yeomen of the Guard* (1888), and *The Gondoliers* (1889) – are perennial favorites. Their tunefulness, craftsmanship, and, above all, their brilliantly satiric criticism of existing social conditions have secured for them a lasting place among musical and literary parodists.

It should be noted here that there are some illustrious examples of romantic composers who wrote their own texts, particularly Richard Wagner, Peter Cornelius, and, in our time, Gian Carlo Menotti.

In true romantic fashion, sources such as history, legend, biblical stories, and mythology inspired composers in their search for operatic subject matter. For instance, the story of the Swiss patriot Wilhelm Tell was used by Schiller and Rossini; the fairytale of Hansel and Gretel, as told by the Grimm Brothers, was made into a highly successful opera by Engelbert Humperdinck. A Russian folktale was utilized in Rimsky-Korsakov's opera *The Snow Maiden*. Biblical stories prompted a number of operatic masterpieces by means of adopted texts, among them Saint-Saëns's *Samson et Dalila*, Verdi's *Nabucco*, and Rossini's *Mosè in Egitto*.

Wagner drew heavily on the Teutonic *Nibelungenlied* for his operatic tetralogy *Der Ring des Nibelungen*, consisting of *Das Rheingold*, *Die Walküre*, *Siegfried*, and *Die Götterdämmerung*.

Romanticism was the age of "grand opera," which meant serious works of an epic or, at times, historical nature, with a "blood-and-thunder" plot, and a large cast in which one or more of the main protagonists meet a violent end. We sympathize and suffer with them in their vicissitudes and we identify with their lot, so real is our involvement in this art form. There is no spoken dialogue in grand opera. The recitative (see page 26) comes as close to simulated speech as this genre of opera allows. The story and its message is conveyed with all the forces at the composer's command: arias, ensembles, choral and balletic scenes, and, of course, effective staging, acting, pertinent changes of scenery and decor, lighting, and the collaboration and support of the orchestra. Everything that transpires in the orchestra pit and onstage becomes the responsibility of the conductor, who must coordinate all these forces according to painstakingly prepared signals for orchestral entrances, balancing, shaping, shading, and split-second precision for the ensemble.

While this has always been true of opera, it is of even greater importance in grand opera as practiced since the nineteenth century because of the numerous forces involved in the performance. Chaos could result from even the slightest oversight by the conductor; think of the multitude onstage during the triumphant return of Radames in the second act of *Aida*, where even the horses must be carefully trained to perform on cue.

One example vividly demonstrates the close involvement of the opera and its composer in the cross-currents of the political climate of the day. In 1842 Verdi's opera *Nabucco* was presented at the Teatro alla Scala in Milan. The work tells of the Babylonian captivity of the Hebrews, and of King Nebuchadnezzar's fate and fortunes. At the time of the performance Italy was struggling to shake off the

Hapsburg yoke and yearned to establish itself as a united nation under the rule of the House of Savoy and King Victor Emmanuel.

The highlight of *Nabucco* occurs when the chorus of captive Hebrews, longing for a return to their beloved homeland, intone the haunting lines "Va, pensiero, sull'ali dorate" ("Go, my thoughts, on gilded wings"). The audience, hearing the poignant and solemnly infectious music that Verdi's genius provided for these words, identified its own political lot with that of the Hebrews in the opera. It joined in, and from then on the chorus became a sacred second national anthem.

As the revolution of 1848 drew nearer, this chorus and the name of the composer were heard all over Italy, despite the attempts of the Austrians to suppress such agitation. "Viva Verdi" became not only a cry of tribute but an identification with the political cause, for to the masses VERDI spelled *V*-ittorio *E*-mmanuele *R*-e *d'I*-talia (Victor Emmanuel King of Italy).

When speaking of nineteenth-century grand opera, many prototypes come to mind. In each case it is the story, as well as its musical treatment, that makes it "grand." Also, in each instance the length of the opera needed for the plot to unfold is considerable, so that at times its very length may be one of the factors that keeps a fine work from being a regular part of the repertory. Cases in point are *Guillaume Tell* by Rossini, *Les Troyens à Carthage* by Berlioz, *Les Huguenots* and *Le Prophète* by Meyerbeer, and some of the Wagnerian masterpieces, such as *Rienzi*, one of his early works.

In a broader sense, grand opera applies to any work conceived in the grand manner: heroic or epic stories, larger-than-life scenes, massive ensembles, dramatic singing interspersed with lyric sections (depending upon the character depicted), elaborate ballets, and significant participation by a large orchestra. *Aida* fits this description in every respect. But ultimately it is Verdi's memorable score, containing some of opera's most beautiful passages, that assures it a lasting place in the hearts of music lovers.

Romantic opera of nineteenth-century Italy was highlighted by several masters whose works live on as part of the repertory of the world's leading opera houses. In addition to Rossini, Bellini and Donizetti will be remembered for the lyrical charm of their creations, as well as for the unerring dramatic instinct of their theatrical inventiveness, as exemplified by Bellini's *La Sonnambula, Norma,* and *I Puritani,* and Donizetti's *Lucia di Lammermoor, L'Elisir d'Amore,* and *Don Pasquale,* among others.

The zenith of Italian opera was reached by Guiseppe Verdi, romantic opera's undisputed Italian master. No one wrote more popular or more memorable melodies, which we identify with the characterizations in any given work. The voice was his primary concern, and he wrote for it with an informed knowledge of its capabilities and with a superb theatrical sense. Of his twenty-six operas, among his best loved are *Rigoletto* (1851), *Il Trovatore* (1853), *La Traviata* (1853), *Un Ballo in Maschera* (1859), *La Forza del Destino* (1862), *Don Carlos* (1867), and *Aida* (1871).

Verdi's first operatic effort was *Oberto, Conte di San Bonifacio* (1839), first produced and acclaimed at La Scala in Milan. This success prompted the famous opera house to commission three new works by the young composer, of which the first, *Un Giorno di Regno* (1840) was a disquieting failure. But the success of his next opera, *Nabucco* (1842), made him an idol; his name appeared on all items usually associated with twentieth-century ideas of publicity advertising, from dishes to shirts and dresses. The political climate was propitious enough to assure Verdi's popularity both among his countrymen and the music world at large. *I Lombardi* (1843) became Verdi's first opera to be heard in the United States.

Ernani (1844) furnishes additional proof of the interrelationship between artistic creation and the political and social climate of the time. Its career was a stormy one for political reasons. As with *Nabucco,* the Austrian domination of Italy made itself felt in terms of actual censorship imposed by the occupying regime. *Ernani*'s libretto was felt to be too inflammatory and a thorough revision was ordered. While this had little effect on the vigor of Verdi's music, it did arouse the opposition of Victor Hugo, upon whose drama *Hernani* the libretto was based. Yet all these surrounding circumstances remain subservient to the intrinsic musical and dramatic values of the score.

Macbeth (1847) and *Luisa Miller* (1849) became the crowning final works of Verdi's rich and creative first period, to be followed by the masterpieces previously mentioned. The innovations are striking with which this great master endowed his last two operatic creations

– *Otello,* written in 1887 when he was seventy-three, and *Falstaff,* composed in 1893 when he was almost eighty. With these works Verdi arrived at a new stage of compositional technique, consisting of rhythmical and harmonic changes and a greater equality of vocal and instrumental forces without abandoning his careful attention to the expressive qualities of solo voices.

In France the nineteenth century witnessed the growth of opéra comique and its subsequent development into lyric opera. Gounod's *Faust* and Ambroise Thomas' *Mignon* are notable examples, as are such later works as Bizet's *Carmen,* Delibes' *Lakmé,* Massenet's *Manon,* Saint-Saëns's *Samson et Dalila,* and Halévy's *La Juive.* Grand opera was represented by Meyerbeer's notable creations, including *Les Huguenots, Le Prophète,* and *L'Africaine,* and by Hector Berlioz's massive opera *Les Troyens,* which requires two successive evenings for a complete performance.

Russia heralded the romantic era with a national school of opera, initiated by Mikhail Glinka's *A Life for the Tsar* (originally called *Ivan Susanin*) (1836) and *Russlan and Ludmila* (1842). Grand opera Russian style is exemplified by the enormous dramatic power of Modest Mussorgsky's *Boris Godunov* (2nd version, 1874), a work whose national colors are apparent both in subject matter and musical treatment. Alexander Borodin's opera *Prince Igor* (1890) shares the same flavor; the music of its colorful "Polovtzian Dances" sequence is a popular favorite. Highly romantic, both in content and musical expression, although not in the same nationalist sense, are Tchaikovsky's operas *Eugene Onegin* (1879), *The Queen of Spades* (1890), and the rarely performed *Maid of Orleans* (1881).

National opera was further enriched by such colorful folk creations as Smetana's *The Bartered Bride* (1866), Dvořák's *Rusalka* (1901), the Pole Stanisław Moniuszko's *Halka* (1858), and the Czech Jaromír Weinberger's *Schwanda the Bagpiper* (1927). Also of romantic character are the Hungarian Zoltán Kodály's *Háry János* (1926), a delightful operatic treatment of the popular Hungarian tale of a prodigious liar; and the Spaniard Enrique Granados' *Goyescas* (1916), inspired by Goya's paintings and tapestries.

The great American contribution to the genre is George Gershwin's *Porgy and Bess* (1935), a profoundly human portrayal of the lives of South Carolina's blacks in the 1930s. It is a remarkable work, filled with deep insight and compassion.

German romantic opera is dominated by two masters whose works are separated by less than fifty years: Carl Maria von Weber (1786–1826) and Richard Wagner (1813–83). With *Der Freischütz* (1821) Weber created the prototypical romantic opera, replete with a haunted forest, supernatural forces, superstition steeped in legend, and simplistic rustic sentimentality. Of his ten operas, it was with *Der Freischütz* and, to a lesser degree, *Euryanthe* (1823) and *Oberon* (1826), that Weber created milestones of German romantic opera, which found its apotheosis in the music dramas of Wagner.

Richard Wagner's early brand of romanticism is founded upon elements of literature and legend, which merged with the composer's own formidable capacity for fantasy. *Der fliegende Holländer (The Flying Dutchman),* composed in 1843, and *Lohengrin,* composed in 1850, are early examples of Weber's influence. Wagner's unique accomplishment was the successful creation of a new type of opera that aspired to a union of all the arts *(Gesamtkunstwerk).* The emphasis was no longer on solo arias and separate vocal ensembles; rather, the voices and orchestral forces merged with the stage action to create an indivisible drama in which the individual identity of the constituent forces was sacrificed to the philosophical impact of the whole.

Orchestral and vocal writing now took on symphonic dimensions, which lent intensified expressiveness to the stage action. A helpful guide for the listener and viewer is Wagner's use of the *Leitmotiv* ("leading motif"), called *idée fixe* in French. Berlioz used it in his *Symphonie Fantastique,* as did Liszt and Richard Strauss in their symphonic poems. In Wagner's case it was a means by which to identify characters, ideas, and objects as they recurred in different situations and at different times in the drama, much as one might catalogue or list certain thoughts under pertinent headings.

For instance, in each of the four component dramas of *Der Ring des Nibelungen* the same motif is heard every time the "ring," the "sword," "gold," or "Valhalla" (the abode of the gods) is in evidence, or merely hinted at. Other identifying melodies are used for the appearance of leading characters in certain situations. These leit-motifs vary in rhythm and structure of intervals to accommodate the changing events and locales, and to adapt to the characters' involvement in different surroundings and within different contexts.

The evolution of Wagner's concept of a fully integrated artistic creation is first revealed in *Tannhäuser* (1845), and particularly in *Lohengrin* (1850). Wagner's later creations – *The Ring, Tristan und Isolde* (1865), and *Parsifal* (1882) – bring his artistic philosophy to full fruition. Here is romanticism exhibiting a total freedom and intensity of expression within the framework of an amazing inter-pretative flexibility, based upon masterful orchestration and adapt-able under the baton of Wagnerian conductors of note. The fascina-tion of it all lies in the fact that the lasting impact of these operas is derived from their gripping musical and dramatic content rather than a technical understanding of the myriad complexities of assem-bling the score.

Wagner's expansive designs could hardly be realized in the con-ventional theater of his time. Traditional opera stages were inade-quate to serve his scenic demands, and the average opera house could not contain the multiplicity of his acoustic requirements. He found a personal champion and an ardent partner in the fulfillment of his dreams in King Ludwig II of Bavaria. With the monarch's help – and later on the basis of public subscription – a special theater was built for the sole purpose of performing Wagner's operas in the little Bavarian town of Bayreuth, in the south of Germany. Even though performances of Wagner's operas are limited to the annual Bay-reuth Festival season, the festival's organizers have remained true to the original premise of its existence.

One of the main physical features of this theater is a very large and completely submerged and enclosed orchestra pit. Wagner's intention was to have his orchestral sound merge with the stage action in a manner so as not to distract the viewer with the sight of that sound's source. This arrangement places an even heavier responsibility on the conductor, for both the auditory and visual contact with the stage rests entirely with him; the orchestra is not only out of sight but at times also out of distinct hearing range from the stage. However, the audience gains immeasurably from this unique combination of an unobstructed view and an undisclosed source of sound, which affords the viewer the full impact of Wagner's fantasy.

The question is often raised: How do I get closer to Wagner? His works seem so fantastic and complex. Obviously, a working knowledge of the various plots and an understanding of Wagner's intentions in conceiving the music is an indispensable prerequisite. An acquaintance with musical excerpts of any of the Wagnerian creations prior to experiencing an entire work will also prove helpful. These excerpts will then be greeted as old and valued friends when they reappear within the larger context. *Die Meistersinger von Nürnberg,* Wagner's folksiest and only comic opera, is recommended as an introduction to his work.

The central figure of *Die Meistersinger* (1868) is Hans Sachs, the patriarchal town cobbler of Nürnberg, as well as poet, composer, self-taught philosopher, and the most beloved and respected among the sixteenth-century mastersingers. In casting him in the role of the trusted elder, Wagner endowed his opera with the truth of history – Sachs was real, not invented – and with the radiant warmth of the events surrounding him, even down to the detail of Sachs's philosophical relinquishing of an elder bachelor's love for a much younger belle of the town. It is as though Sachs's humanity reached the heart of a master whose place in history is secure not so much for the portrayal of human beings but for the depiction of gods and legendary heroes, articulated in dramatic musical gestures. Wagner remains one of the greatest revolutionary dramatists the world of music has ever known.

NATIONALISM

The composer, like other creative artists – indeed, like all of us – is a child of his time and his surroundings. He is influenced by social customs and conventions, political circumstances, and his environment. Every cultural age has left a significant imprint upon the conscious or unconscious behavior of those who shared it. Just as the needle of a sensitive graph reacts to the slightest change, so an artist's sensitivity responds to the happenings of his day.

We have seen how music can mirror the climate of the time, how some composers can even be prophetic in their intuitive vision of things to come. One of the most powerful influences can be found in those elements that help to shape national history. Obviously the time has to be right for such sources of inspiration to leave their mark. The romantic period in particular – with its hard-won freedom of expression, its love of liberty, and its glorification of love of country – provided the perfect setting.

In the aftermath of the French and American revolutions, with their disavowal of class distinctions and all the inequities for which they stood, man's yearning for social equality and political independence found its most fervent expression. The Napoleonic wars, the multiple revolutions in Austria, Germany, and Italy, and, finally, the Franco-Prussian War of 1870 resulted in a new national awareness even without the charting of new national boundaries.

It was left to the creative artist – the poet, the painter, the architect, the sculptor, and the musician – to participate in these events, often in a most significant way. They began to explore their national heritage for any hidden traces of indigenous and meaningful manifestations in word, tone, or visual symbol, often lifting them out of their original context in order to weave them into a colorful fabric of their own creation.

Sometimes they would render these in a detailed musical account of national happenings or geographically characterize their native land. We find such nationalistic trends in Weber's opera *Der Freischütz*, which depicts the spirit of German romanticism. The inspiration for many of Schumann's instrumental and vocal compositions

323

was derived from his close association with the literary works of the German romantic poets of the time. Chopin glorified Polish dance elements in his mazurkas and polonaises. Liszt's Hungarian heritage is evident in his Hungarian rhapsodies.

Among the leading creators of instrumental national color were the Bohemians Bedřich Smetana and Antonin Dvořák, whose Czechoslovak homeland was under Austrian domination. Among the finest examples of Smetana's work are his six tone poems, collectively known as *Má Vlast (My Fatherland)*. Each of these bespeaks Bohemian history, legend, scenery, landmarks, and patriotic backgrounds. The best known is the second, *Vltava (The Moldau)*, a musical depiction of the great river, from its two life-giving springs in the Bohemian forest to its majestic passage toward the great city of Prague and its eventual merging into the far horizon. With uncanny tonal fidelity the composer describes the river's colorful course and the events that take place along its shores: a hunt, a peasant wedding, and the revels of wood nymphs and naiads in the evening. The other five poems of the cycle are *Vyšehrad*, named after an ancient citadel in Prague; *Sarka*, a rock valley that was the site of an old Bohemian legend; *From Bohemia's Fields and Groves*, the composer's detailed description of a summer's day in the country; *Tabor*, an expression of faith of the old Hussite warriors; and *Blanik*, which evokes an old Hussite hymn to serve as a call for the liberation of the Bohemian people.

Smetana's compatriot Antonin Dvořák was equally successful in evoking Bohemian lore, setting to music such little-known folk ballads as *The Water Sprite, The Midday Witch*, and *The Wild Dove*. More importantly, he created the prototypical flavor of Bohemian national music, a wondrous mixture of nostalgia and longing (the French aptly call it "mal de pays") interlaced with jubilant joy and wistful introspection, as if smiling through tears.

I suggest that you listen to any of Dvořák's *Slavonic Dances*, which combine all of these traits, often in the incredibly short space of about three minutes. Even his large-scale works, such as his symphonies, concertos, and chamber music, reveal the Bohemian spirit at its best.

Dvořák's penchant for expressing longing and nostalgia is perhaps most easily discernible in the works he wrote in America while he was director of the National Conservatory in New York (1892–95). His "New World" Symphony, the "American" String Quartet, and the Cello Concerto were all written during his tenure in the United States. You will detect in them unmistakable traces of his nostalgia for his homeland.

Both Smetana and Dvořák carried their national identity into the field of opera in works based upon Bohemian tales and endowed with Bohemian tunes (see page 319). We must not forget the proclivity of these masters for songwriting, both for single voices and for vocal and choral ensembles. The best known example is Dvořák's "Songs My Mother Taught Me," taken from his set of lovely *Gypsy Songs.*

Johann Strauss II (1825–99), a contemporary of the Bohemian masters, may well be considered under the heading of nationalism in music. Vienna-born and domiciled, he created the finest Viennese waltzes, such as "The Blue Danube," "Tales from the Vienna Woods," "Emperor Waltz," "Voices of Spring," "Wine, Women, and Song," and "Vienna Blood." He also wrote such immortal operettas as *Die Fledermaus (The Bat)* in 1874 and *Der Zigeunerbaron (The Gypsy Baron)* in 1885. Nationalism here becomes localized, for Strauss wrote music primarily about the city of Vienna of his time. That time was politically charged with intrigue and subversion. Strauss's compatriots looked to his music and to the national dance that it so eloquently enhances as a welcome escape from daily reality. Strauss waltzes have long outlived their time because of their intrinsic musical value.

The first truly national opera comes to us from the pen of the Russian composer Mikhail Glinka. Here is a typical case of a gifted creator turning expressly to national colors and national history, sharing his aspirations with kindred artists and writers, such as Alexander Pushkin and Nikolai Gogol. The result is an opera in five acts entitled *A Life for the Tsar* (1836), with a libretto by Baron Georgy Fyodorovich Rozen and an epilogue by Glinka. It is based upon the Russo-Polish conflict of 1633, after the boy Michael Feodorovich became the first of the Romanovs to ascend the Russian throne.

Glinka was followed by a group of self-professed Russian nationalists, known as "The Five" – Mily Balakirev, César Cui, Alexander Borodin, Modest Mussorgsky, and Nicolas Rimsky-Korsakov –

all of whom contributed greatly to the enrichment of an unmistakably Russian musical idiom. Listen to Cui's *Orientale,* excerpts from Mussorgsky's *Khovanschina,* Rimsky-Korsakov's *Russian Easter* Overture, Borodin's "Polovtsian Dances" from *Prince Igor,* and Balakirev's *Overture on Russian Themes.*

The Russian national musical tradition was brought to even greater heights by that country's most famous composer, Peter Ilyich Tchaikovsky. Although not always consciously nationalistic in his intentions, he could not hide his national identity in his music. Therein lies perhaps the most impressive proof of the validity and strength of the premise of nationalism: a latent reservoir from which to draw inspiration and creative power without consciously identifying the source. Listening to Tchaikovsky's eloquent symphonic output – the majesty of the outer movements and the brooding melodies of the slow sections will substantiate this claim, while the patriotic implications of such works as *Marche Slave* and the *1812 Overture* bear witness to the composer's national identification. The latter two are perfect examples of history literally turned into music.

Of all the national tonal colorations, those inherent in Spanish music are particularly distinctive. Unlike most European national music, that of Spain reflects a mixture of influences, the most prominent being the Moorish presence in the southern portions of the country. Eight centuries of North African occupation brought into play complex and colorful Arabic rhythms, scales, and instruments, as well as an abundance of oriental ornamentations of melodies.

Through the ages Spain has always been the meeting place of many cultures, due to its geographic position between the Mediterranean Sea and the Atlantic Ocean, between Africa and Europe. Add to this the "cante hondo" and "cante flamenco" characteristics of the songs of Andalusia, Gypsy and a variety of European influences, as well as those of the Western Hemisphere, and you arrive at a potent musical mixture, difficult to define but easy to savor. Try listening to some of the works of Isaac Albéniz, Enrique Granados, Joaquín Turina, or, more recently, Manuel de Falla and you will be impressed by the irresistible aura of their music.

An equally potent instrumental national color is found in the music of Hungary. Some distinctive traits are embedded within the rhythmical as well as the melodic structure of Hungarian music. An accented short first beat, followed by an offbeat longer note creates a typical Hungarian "snap," which finds its counterpart in the Hungarian language where the accent on the first syllable of a word is a common occurrence. The tonal characteristics of Hungarian music often involve a sweeping, upward movement, at times spurred on and interlaced by the percussive sound of the cimbalom, Hungary's national instrument.

It should be mentioned here that Hungarian and Gypsy music are in no way synonymous. Gypsy music exists by virtue of its chameleonlike adaptation of melodic and rhythmic features of the adopted country into its own freestyle existence. Hungarian music, on the other hand, is indigenous and firmly rooted. It has been strongly defined by the *Hungarian Rhapsodies* of Franz Liszt and the compositions of Béla Bartók and Zoltán Kodály.

Not all national music is as easy to recognize as the examples thus far provided. Quotations of actual folk tunes and dances obviously simplify matters. Even if not readily known to the listener, they do constitute a kind of label by which to classify the compositions using them. Some fine examples are: *English Folk Song Suite* by Ralph Vaughan Williams; *Rákóczi March* by Berlioz; *Dances of Marosszék* by Zoltán Kodály; *Gayne* ballet suites, filled with spirited Armenian dances, by Aram Khachaturian; *Midsommarvaka (Midsummer Vigil)*, a Swedish rhapsody by Hugo Alfvén; *Suite Provençale* and *Suite Française* by French composer Darius Milhaud; *Roumanian Rhapsodies* by the Roumanian Georges Enesco; and the Concert Rondo *Krakowiak* or the *Grand Fantasy on Polish Airs* by Poland's native son, Frédéric Chopin, to mention only a few. They all make for genuine listening pleasure.

Nationalism in music has been further enriched by the many "travel souvenirs" that imaginative composers have collected during their sojourns in foreign countries. Spain and Italy seem to top the list of those lands whose influences upon such travelers have been especially important. Try listening to Emmanuel Chabrier's *España*, Claude Debussy's "Soirée dans Grenade" and *Ibéria*, Maurice Ravel's *Rapsodie Espagnole* and *Alborada del Gracioso*, Édouard Lalo's *Symphonie Espagnole* for violin and orchestra, Rimsky-Korsakov's *Capriccio Espagnol*, and Glinka's *Jota Aragonesa*. These, among others, are as Spanish-sounding as the creations of any native

Spaniard. As for some "adopted" Italian pieces, I suggest Gustave Charpentier's *Impressions d'Italie,* Tchaikovsky's *Capriccio Italien,* Hugo Wolf's *Italienische Serenade,* the last movement of Felix Mendelssohn's "Italian" Symphony, and the Italian set of Franz Liszt's piano works entitled *Années de Pélérinage (Years of Pilgrimage).* The spirit of Italian song and dance is evident in each one of these.

There are also those composers whose musical expression is so completely embedded within the tonal fiber of their country, and whose love of their native musical language is so persuasive, that they in effect *created* a national musical idiom. Their music has become synonymous with the national musical speech of their country. For example, there is Edvard Grieg, who is wholly identified with Norwegian music; Jean Sibelius, the outstanding Finnish composer; and, in a more esoteric sense, Carl Nielsen, who is closely associated with the music of Denmark.

The omission of any country in this section is, of course, unintentional. Just about every nation has its own musical heroes among its composers, and the examples cited here should serve only to prove this point, as well as to provide an incentive for further research.

In a discussion of American music, it is necessary to keep in mind that it should be considered quite apart from "Music in America" (the subject of the next chapter). While this is true of any country, in this particular case we must ask ourselves: Is there such a thing as American music? The answer is decidedly *yes.* However, it is not arrived at as easily as for most other countries. Our country is a proverbial melting pot; an unparalleled confluence of many national sources and folk elements comprise our cultural heritage.

How do you forge an indigenously American sound from all this? The answer is that there is no single sound indigenous to America, simply because the constituent elements are too numerous and too widely divergent. But therein lies the great challenge for the creative musician.

Charles Ives (1874–1954) is a case in point. Not only did he use American tunes in his own inimitable, dissonant, and even irreverent way – listen to his second symphony or his *Variations on "America"* – he also injected into the American musical fabric a new concept: a tonal celebration of such major American holidays as Washington's Birthday, Decoration Day, the Fourth of July, Thanksgiving Day, all assembled under the title *Symphony: Holidays*. He marked the score "Recollections of a boy's holidays in a Connecticut country town." Ives also tackled some descriptive reminiscences of American scenes in his *Three Places in New England*, subtitled "The 'St. Gaudens' in Boston Common," "Putnam's Camp, Redding, Connecticut," "The Housatonic at Stockbridge." One may be puzzled by his harsh harmonic treatment, the absence of convenient tonalities, the interweaving of bits of familiar melodies. But an unmistakably American atmosphere pervades these works, whether it is characteristic of New England or the country general.

Other Easterners before Ives, such as the so-called Boston group (see p. 363) were successful in forging new musical paths, but they were more beholden to the European tonal tradition.

Of more recent vintage are: William Schuman's *New England Triptych*, consisting of "Be Glad, Then, America," "When Jesus Wept," and "Chester"; Morton Gould's *Spirituals for Orchestra;* Roy Harris' "Abraham Lincoln" Symphony (Symphony No. 10); Walter Piston's *Three New England Sketches*, consisting of "Seaside," "Summer Evening," and "Mountains"; Aaron Copland's *Lincoln Portrait;* and Virgil Thomson's film score *Louisiana Story*.

An interesting fact emerges from all this discussion. The utopian one-world concept – perhaps never to be achieved – has found prophetic fulfillment in music. The dream of the brotherhood of all men under the fatherhood of one God, as Beethoven and Schiller expressed it so eloquently and powerfully in the former's Ninth Symphony, may well remain confined to the world of the arts; but the mere fact that human beings can seriously and spontaneously aspire to it affords an inestimable hope for all mankind.

Nationalism forms a vital link in that aspiration. It grants us the opportunity to know ourselves and others better, enabling us to confront each other without abandoning our own individuality. However, nationalism also presents a potential built-in danger if it is misused. History is not devoid of examples of how nationalism in music can be made to misguide entire nations under the musically enunciated claim of "God is on our side." Sadly, such associations with certain kinds of music cannot easily be blotted out from human memory.

There is only one yardstick. Namely, whether the music, national or otherwise, can stand up to the highest standards of composition when nationalism as a programmatic issue becomes a secondary consideration. *The Moldau* will be cherished not only as a milestone in the history of Bohemian music but as a great and colorful composition. That is the ultimate criterion. Even though national music may sometimes be relegated to the limited glories of regionalism, there will always be composers who cannot hide their national birthright. Why should they, especially when they show their colors with forthright honesty and with the conviction of their artistic standards. In the words of Emerson, "The most original genius is the most indebted man."

THE TWENTIETH CENTURY: REALISM

With the approach of the twentieth century, we find many forces emerging simultaneously in an attempt to come to terms with a radically changing contemporary world. Postromanticists and neo-classicists reaffirmed the legacies of the past, while impressionists and realists were determined to break away in order to espouse new opportunities and envision the new horizons opened up by industrial progress and increased scientific knowledge. It became increasingly difficult to remain unaffected by the rapid construction of buildings made of new materials such as cast iron. Synthetic products made their appearance in various places, including on the painter's palette, where man-made substances began to replace natural earth pigments and minerals.

Similarly, a standardization of the production of wind and brass instruments made it easier for composers to satisfy their fantasies for modern, more voluminous, or cryptically detailed instrumentation. Writers, painters, and composers alike could now have their creations disseminated more quickly and widely thanks to the rapid advances of mechanical printing and reproduction processes, yielding lithographs, sheet music, and books in large numbers at reasonable prices.

Many of these artists were ahead of their time creatively and did not live to witness the actual turn of the century. Henrik Ibsen of Norway and Charles Dickens of England were preoccupied with sociological issues, while the realism of Émile Zola and Gustave Flaubert projected their contemporary observations into a new age. Joseph Mallord William Turner's preimpressionist canvases are as far removed from – though contemporary with – those of Jean Louis Géricault and John Constable as Wagner's *Ring* is from Bizet's *Carmen*.

In the operatic field, Wagner's most important successor in Germany was Richard Strauss (1864–1949), who in 1905, at the age of forty-one, emerged on the operatic scene with one of opera's most controversial scores, *Salome*, based on a biblical story made into a play by Oscar Wilde. Though shocking in its portrayal of perversion, it also represented a powerful fusion of drama and music.

For his next operatic milestone, *Elektra* (1909), Strauss sought the collaboration of the Austrian poet and librettist Hugo von Hofmannsthal, who reverted to the theater of ancient Greece and a tragedy by Sophocles for inspiration. But here the parallel with Wagner's evocations of an ancient past ends. Strauss's music, though unmistakably reflecting his own speech and idiomatic expression, complements the psychoanalytical frenzy of the story with a suitably harsh score. Realistically Strauss matches the emotional crises of the plot with pronounced musical dissonances and lustfulness of the characters with sensuous harmonies.

Just as *Die Meistersinger* constitutes a complete change in Wagner's dramatic creations, so *Der Rosenkavalier* (1910) represents Strauss at his most human and compassionate. The artistic union of Strauss and Hofmannsthal here created one of the finest comic operas of all time, filled with infectious good humor and a deeply moving philosophy of life. The closing trio, in which the middle-aged "Marschallin," Princess von Werdenberg, relinquishes her young lover Octavian to Sophie – a philosophical counterpart of Hans

Sachs giving up Eva to Walter – is one of the most inspired pages of vocal writing in music. Both the scores of *Die Meistersinger* and *Der Rosenkavalier* also yield some memorable orchestral sections that have become staples of symphony concerts, such as the "Prelude" to *Die Meistersinger* and the *Rosenkavalier Waltzes* of Richard Strauss.

Other Strauss-Hofmannsthal operas followed, such as *Ariadne auf Naxos (Ariadne on the Isle of Naxos)* in 1912; *Die Frau ohne Schatten (The Woman Without a Shadow)* in 1917; *Die ägyptische Helena (The Egyptian Helen)* in 1924–27; *Arabella,* in 1930–32; and *Die schweigsame Frau (The Silent Woman)* in 1935; but none could surpass or even equal the earlier ones.

The opulent-sounding music of Mahler, Wagner, Bruckner, and Richard Strauss dominated the scene from the last decades of the nineteenth century well into the twentieth. Their overpowering presence overshadowed but did not obliterate concurrent trends that were also flourishing. These new directions were spawned by the excesses of romantic expression, now grown to overblown dimensions.

Composers, painters, sculptors, and writers, weary of this excess romantic "baggage," sought refuge in naturalism and realism. It was in the field of opera that basic differences were readily apparent. Italy took the lead, where the term *verismo* ("realism") became the watchword. No more superhuman gods and heroes, no more massive scenes populated by armies, crowds, horses, gilded carriages, and ballets that overflowed the stage. *Verismo* emphasized everyday situations involving ordinary characters on a one-to-one basis, often taking people from the working classes, pictured in believable circumstances, as their subjects.

The first such opera was *Cavalleria Rusticana* (1890) by Pietro Mascagni, a poignant story of jealousy and broken hearts, set in a Sicilian village. No more than five characters are involved, and the music is accordingly small in scale, lyrically beautiful, and completely attuned to everyday emotions. The same credible realism is found in Ruggiero Leoncavallo's *I Pagliacci (The Clowns),* an 1892 opera recounting the terrible consequences of jealousy. It is usually presented with *Cavalleria* on the same bill. Umberto Giordano (1867–1948) contributed to *verismo* with his most important opera,

Andrea Chénier (1896), a work based on the life of the poet Chénier, a historical figure. France's *verismo* contribution was Gustave Charpentier's *Louise* (1900), the charming story of the love affair of an artist and a seamstress, imbued with the spell of Paris' bohemian quarter of Montmartre.

The greatest realist of Italian opera and the most outstanding late-romantic opera composer is Giacomo Puccini (1858–1924). His lifetime saw many fundamental changes in music. His compositions are deeply imbedded in the sounds and techniques of the romantic era, even though they can be evenly divided into pre- and post-1900.

Puccini himself once said, "The only music that I know how to make is of small things." He was not temperamentally inclined to create grand opera as Wagner and Verdi had done. But in the world of workaday happenings, the world of love and emotional conflicts, the world of simplicity of purpose Puccini is the undisputed master. His highly personal brand of lyricism is filled with tenderness and couched in an unsurpassed sense of drama, with an uncanny inclination for artistic theatricality. His orchestral scores are endowed with a unique sense of harmonic colors and melodic sensuality. The continuing popularity of *Manon Lescaut* (1893), *La Bohème* (1896), *Tosca* (1900), *Madama Butterfly* (1904), and *La Fanciulla del West (The Girl of the Golden West)* – commissioned by the New York Metropolitan Opera Company during the composer's visit in 1907, and first performed there in 1910 – attest to Puccini's supreme position as the musical spokesman of everyday life.

Less frequently heard, but no less exquisite, are *La Rondine* (1917), and *Il Trittico* (1918), which consists of *Il Tabarro (The Cloak)*, *Suor Angelica (Sister Angelica)*, and *Gianni Schicchi*, the most popular of the three. The only opera in which Puccini succumbed to a story derived from legend and utilized mass scenes is *Turandot* (1926), based on a play by the Venetian dramatist Carlo Gozzi, with its locale that of ancient Peking. This turned out to be his last opera, one he did not live to complete. His colleague, Franco Alfano, was entrusted with the task of its completion.

With *Turandot* Puccini proved his capacity for such new technical devices as exotic timbres, the use of dissonances, and unconventional scales. The year was 1926, and a musical newness made itself felt in many different ways.

IMPRESSIONISM

In painting, younger artists turned their backs on romantic sensuality and fantasy, as well as on the resurrection of a legendary past. They, too, embraced the reality of the day by portraying what the eye perceived at the moment rather than what the mind directed the eye to envision.

In 1874 Claude Monet exhibited a canvas in Paris entitled "Impression – Sunrise." A critic latched onto the word "Impression" and attached a derogatory connotation to it. Little did he realize that his criticism was turned into a positive identification of a new movement in art called impressionism. This term describes a new approach to visual art, as well as new techniques with which to achieve it. Impressionist painters were concerned with recording that which they saw at a moment's glance, an instant's vision, with the kind of vague, incomplete contours that only a fleeting impression can offer. Light and color now received preference over definite outlines, and the implication of shifting illumination, achieved through new techniques, won out over the limitations of premixed colors. This was accomplished by daubing splashes and strokes of component colors onto the canvas, leaving it to the eye of the beholder to mix them, a task that required the viewer to stand at a certain distance from the object.

Try to view a reproduction of any of the impressionist masterpieces – for example, Monet's "St. Lazare Station" – from a fair distance. There are no definite contours of the train, platform, or hangar; rather, there is a merging of steam, smoke, and indefinite atmosphere with the vaguely outlined objects – quite different from Honoré Daumier's painting, "The Third-Class Carriage," for instance, painted only fifteen years earlier.

Similar analyses can be made of other great masterpieces of the period, such as Paul Cézanne's "Mont Sainte Victoire"; Camille Pissarro's "Avénue de l'Opéra"; Monet's differing impressions of Rouen Cathedral at various times of day; Édouard Manet's "Bar at the Folies-Bergère," with its trompe-l'oeil mirror reflection; Auguste Re-

334

noir's "Le Moulin de la Galette"; and Alfred Sisley's "Bridge at Villeneuve."

Poetry during this period was characterized by indefinite sounds and a flow of words for the sake of euphony. The words, when considered separately, may seem unrelated or even without tangible meaning, thereby beckoning the reader's mind and imagination to assimilate and identify their meaning. The word "symbolism" was used to describe this technique of writing, and poets such as Stéphane Mallarmé, Paul Verlaine, Arthur Rimbaud, and Charles Baudelaire became known as symbolists.

In music the chief exponent of impressionism was Claude Debussy (1862–1918), one of the greatest masters in the use of tonal color. The revolution he achieved almost singlehandedly amounted to a complete and irrevocable break with the romantic tradition of composing, without, however, denying the romantic spirit. It is not only what you do but how you do it that gives the romantic premise a literally moving musical description. This is what Debussy accomplished in the first of his second set of piano compositions, known as *Images.* Listen to the piece entitled "Cloches à Travers les Feuilles" ("Bells Across the Leaves") and imagine yourself standing at the edge of a range of trees and bushes, with the sound of ringing bells from afar wafting across gently vibrating leaves. Debussy, sensitive to the impressions of the moment, leads us to fuse these images with the sounds of the music we hear.

Impressionism became a major force in the evolution of visual, verbal, and tonal art, constituting a giant step in our modern age, with Claude Debussy's contributions being of enormous importance. Strangely, the merger of the visual and aural may not have been his aim at all. In writing *Ibéria,* the second of a set of three *Images* for orchestra, he insisted that he did not intend to portray Spanish scenes by composing Spanish-sounding music. Instead, he made it quite clear that he wished to register impressions made upon his consciousness by certain aspects of Spanish life. The names of *Ibéria's* three sections underline his intention of recording impressions rather than actual descriptions: "In the Streets and Byways," "The Fragrance of the Night," and "The Morning of a Festival Day."

The same is true of Debussy's famous symphonic sketches entitled *La Mer (The Sea).* Here the individual titles (see p. 10) describe the tone poet's impressions of the magic of the sea at various times of day and under changing climatic conditions. The masterly orchestration, undulating string patterns, haunting melodies by muted trumpet and English horn, interchanging fragments of rhythmic changes, and the sustained and swelling passages of strings and chorale-like brass provide a collage of sound that enables us to participate in the artist's fantasy.

Debussy's most significant contribution to piano literature is his two books consisting of twelve preludes each. The word "prelude" is used in the freest possible sense, allowing each piece to be a completely independent impressionistic entity. Debussy seems to want the performer to conjure up his or her own ideas about the purpose of the music, thus becoming a true partner of the composer in a free play of fantasy. Debussy states the title of each prelude only at the conclusion of the score – in small letters and in parentheses – as if asking, "What is your impression of the piece?", and then, in that small print, responding, "This is what I had in mind."

The titles add up to a most revealing miniature encyclopedia of various aspects and concepts of the age of impressionism, appropriate for use by poets, designers of tapestries or embroidery, painters, novelists, as well as composers. Here are some examples of Debussy's intentions, as manifested in the captions taken from his two books of preludes:

"Voiles" ("Sails"), a fine example of the use of the whole-tone scale

"Le Vent dans la Plaine" ("The Wind in the Plain")

"Les Sons et les Parfums Tournent dans l'Air du Soir" ("Sounds and Odors Blend in the Evening Air"), based on a poem by Baudelaire

"Ce Qu'a Vu le Vent d'Ouest" ("What the West Wind Saw")

"Brouillards" ("Fog"), expressing vague tonalities

"Feuilles Mortes" ("Dead Leaves"), melancholy chords descriptive of the subject matter

"Bruyères" ("Heaths"), an evocation of the sun's rays through the woodland.

Among the best known of Debussy's preludes are "La Cathédrale Engloutie" ("The Sunken Cathedral"), "Minstrels," "La Fille aux

Cheveux de Lin" ("The Girl with the Flaxen Hair"), and "Feux d'Artifice" ("Fireworks").

It is in these miniatures for the piano, as well as in the *Estampes (Prints)* – consisting of "Pagodes," "Soirée dans Grenade," and "Jardins sous la Pluie" ("Gardens in the Rain") – that Debussy's interpretative techniques revolutionized the art of piano playing. He employed a deft use of pedaling, including a careful knowledge of how to use the sustaining, or middle, pedal. His tonal palette contains the whole-tone scale, plus clusters of chordal harmonies as are found in "The Sunken Cathedral," oriental scales and ancient church modes, and changing meters and rhythmic patterns. They are among the building blocks of a new direction in music, which replaced romantic, programmatic, well-defined, and convoluted plots with subtle references to fleeting impressions and sensations. The impasto of romantic painting was replaced with sensitive pastel shades and watercolor effects.

In writing for orchestra, Debussy typically avoided the formal symphony, composing instead orchestral scores of a free nature, which utilized his marked sense of tonal color and instrumental capabilities. Here the impressionist period is well exemplified by his three nocturnes for orchestra: "Nuages" ("Clouds"), "Fêtes" ("Festivals"), and "Sirènes" ("Sirens"), in addition to *La Mer (The Sea)* and *Ibéria*. His popular *Prélude à l'Après-Midi d'un Faune (Prelude to the Afternoon of a Faun)*, inspired by a symbolist poem of the same name by Stéphane Mallarmé, composed in 1892–94, is early proof of Debussy's new language, an exquisite expression drawn in soft hues, with a solo flute evoking a wondrous world of bucolic fantasy.

There is ample evidence of Debussy's mastery of traditional forms, which he imbued with his new tonal idiom. Listen to his String Quartet in G Minor, Op. 10 (1893). It is a unique work, solidly based on established elements of form but far different in content and treatment of instrumental color from any other preceding chamber work. There are three sonatas for various instruments, part of a projected group of six, dating from the composer's last years (one for cello and piano; one for flute, viola, and harp; and one for violin and piano). All are remarkable in their successful recreation of baroque forms. Lovers of vocal music should not overlook Debussy's songs, many of them based upon symbolist poems, including such gems as

"Beau Soir," "Il Pleure dans mon Coeur," and "Mandoline." Or listen to "Fêtes Galantes," which consists of settings of Verlaine poems, among them "En Sourdine," "Claire de Lune," and "Fantoches." The second is unrelated to the well-known piano piece "Claire de Lune," which is part of a suite known as *Suite Bergamasque.*

Also worth hearing is a lyric poem for women's chorus, solo soprano, and orchestra, called *La Damoiselle Élue (The Blessed Damozel),* an unusual work by a daring young composer. (Debussy was only twenty-five at the time.)

In 1902 Debussy's only completed opera, *Pelléas et Mélisande,* was first performed at the Opéra-Comique in Paris. Fashioned after the drama of the same name by the Belgian symbolist playwright Maurice Maeterlinck, who won the Nobel Prize for literature in 1911, Debussy created a new kind of opera. A span of ten years was needed to write it. For the first time the essence of impressionism had found its way into the field of opera. Instead of the usual set scenes and climaxes, there are only subtle impressions. The play is set in a never-never land, the action is filled with symbols, and the characters remain indistinct. Debussy infused the score with speechlike declamation rather than straightforward arias and ensembles. The orchestral part is as understated as the vocal line.

Needless to say, the work was beset by insurmountable difficulties during its entire production period. The reception by bewildered audiences and musicians was mixed. Even to this day, opera lovers steeped in the Gounod-Massenet-Verdi-Puccini tradition find it difficult to assimilate this revolutionary opera into the standard repertory. Approach this opera after you have a good working knowledge of Debussy's multifaceted style of expression and coloration.

Impressionism found disciples in other countries, although none quite matched Claude Debussy in both the breadth of his imaginative ideas and their successful realization. The period was comparatively short-lived, but it left an indelible imprint on future generations.

In Spain Manuel de Falla (1876–1946), after meeting Debussy in Paris, showed an inclination toward impressionism, particularly in his 1916 work for piano and orchestra, *Noches en los Jardines de España (Nights in the Gardens of Spain).* It is significantly subtitled

"Symphonic Impressions." In England Frederick Delius (1862–1934), who settled permanently in France when he was twenty-six, wrote in an impressionist vein, as exemplified in his tone poem *On Hearing the First Cuckoo in Spring* (1912). In America Charles Tomlinson Griffes (1884–1920), whose short lifespan of thirty-five years did not allow him to fully develop his obvious talent, wrote a tone poem for orchestra entitled *The White Peacock* (1919), which first appeared in 1917 in a piano version. Inspired by lines from a poem by William Sharp (pseud. of Fiona Macleod) as well as by Griffes' own fascination with peacocks, it shows the delicacy of treatment and the undulation of movement reminiscent of *Prelude to the Afternoon of a Faun.*

To these and other composers of the period, impressionism was one of several means of expression. For instance, De Falla created his own brand of Spanish music. It consists of far more than infectious rhythms, castanets, and guitars; far more than a mere utilization of Spanish tunes and dances. He probed deeply into the soul of his people and evoked it in terms of a personal mixture of vibrant pulsation, *cante hondo* (Andalusian "deep song"), and an infusion of oriental chant. Listen to some excerpts from his ballet-pantomime *El Amor Brujo (Love, the Sorcerer),* and you will gain a taste of this greatly talented master's musical idiom.

New Musical Directions in the Twentieth Century

The examples of impressionism in this section are contemporary with an age of brazen contrasts and extroverted attitudes, reflecting the approaching age of social, scientific, and industrial growth, with its resulting upheavals. Yet impressionism itself was too introverted and delicate by nature to survive such radical changes. But it did cast its spell over those who would allow themselves to see, hear, and savor it.

Meanwhile, romanticism's influence had by no means come to an end. The reproductive and regenerative powers of romanticism are firmly rooted in life itself. So large a "family" as romanticism will always have rebellious offshoots, and impressionism was not to be the only sibling. Some composers maintained their ties with traditional forms and imbued them with new vitality, thereby strengthening their own roots even as they asserted the newness of their conceptions. Others became true renegades, tearing tradition asunder in order to promulgate new ideas and values. It is this great diversity that dominates most of the modern period, from the early twentieth century on.

One of the most controversial turn-of-the-century musicians was the Frenchman Erik Satie (1866–1925), who is often derided because of his many eccentricities. He rebelled, to be sure, not so much against existing musical orders but against musicians who took themselves too seriously – including his teachers at the Paris Conservatoire. Satie used to make his living as a pianist and writer of popular tunes in a Montmartre cabaret, which accounts for the whimsical and popular elements in his serious music. He developed a style all his own, deriving his inspiration easily from his own observations, from his study of Gothic art (*Danses Gothiques* for piano, 1893), decorations on a Greek vase (*Trois Gymnopédies*, 1888), American ragtime (the ballet *Parade*, 1917), and a translation of texts from Plato's Dialogues (*Socrate*, a symphonic drama for voices and chamber orchestra, 1919).

The outlandish names that Satie attached to his compositions heightened the controversy over his true worth. What was one to think of a musician who called his works *Three Pieces in the Shape of a Pear, Flabby Preludes, Provocations of a Big Wooden Simpleton, Next to Last Thoughts,* and so on? Yet it was precisely his sense of satire and wit that constitutes the newness of his outlook. Some of France's best-known composers acknowledged their debt to Satie's innovative spirit and writing technique, among them Debussy, Ravel, and Milhaud.

Maurice Ravel (1875–1937) is a supreme master of this century. His achievements defy any classification into a particular period or school. He was accused by some of imitating Debussy, who, along with Satie, Ravel's teacher Fauré, and Chabrier, exerted an unquestionable influence on his creative processes. The truth is, however, that Ravel's approach to composition is highly individual. His loyalty to past periods is exemplified in his String Quartet; his *Sonatine* for piano; his *Introduction and Allegro* for harp, flute, clarinet, and string quartet; his *Trio* for violin, cello, and piano; his two piano concertos, and, most prominently, his piano suite *Le Tombeau de Couperin (The Tomb of Couperin),* in which he invokes the age of François Couperin with a series of early eighteenth-century dances.

Ravel endowed these traditional forms of composition with his own distinctive harmonies and melodies, at times based upon ancient modes, yet always refreshingly lucid and constructed with directness and logic. Listen to the *Sonatine* and the piano suite, and you will realize how precisely and naturally every note falls into place. It is because of these clear-cut and well-sculpted lines that it is difficult to see any justification for calling Ravel an impressionist.

Never was there a greater master of instrumentation and orchestration. Ravel's tonal colors, carefully chosen and skillfully mixed, sparkle with brilliance and effervescent energy. Who can resist the subtle hues, the sudden flashes of luminescence, the gradually built excitement of pulsating rhythms, and the sensuous syncopations of his choreographic poem *La Valse?* This is truly intoxicating music, as are the two suites extracted from the ballet score *Daphnis et Chloé.*

If any specific influence can be earmarked in Ravel's music, it is his recurring penchant for Spanish colors and subjects. The fact that he was born near the Spanish border, in the Basque region of France, of a Basque mother may have been one of those subliminal influences that eventually surface. For example, there is the *Rapsodie Espagnole,* one of his major works for orchestra, filled with the undulating warmth of Spanish nights ("Prélude à la Nuit") ("Prelude to the Night"), the throbbing rhythms of the "Malagueña" and "Habanera," and the irresistible excitement of the exploding "Feria" ("Festival"). There is the comic one-act opera *L'Heure Espagnole (The Spanish Hour)* and the vivacious *Alborada del Gracioso* (often translated as *Morning Song of a Jester*). The latter forms part of a then-daring new work for piano, a suite called *Miroirs (Mirrors),* consisting of five pieces displaying a most imaginative harmonic treatment and enormous technical difficulty.

Ravel, a very fine pianist who often performed his own compositions in public, used the instrument as a vehicle for enlarging the piano's capabilities. His *Gaspard de la Nuit* (three poems for piano inspired by the French writer Aloysius Bertrand), his *"Valses Nobles et Sentimentales* (suggested by Schubert's waltzes of the same name), and, above all, the highly descriptive, scintillating *Jeux d'Eau (Play of Water)* are memorable examples. If you give free reign to your imagination, listening to the *Jeux d'Eau* will permit you to envision the spraying cascades of water, prompted by a line of poetry by Henri de Régnier: "A river god laughing at the waters as they caress him."

One of the finest examples of Ravel's vocal writing is a set of three poems for voice and orchestra called *Shéhérazade,* with texts from a series of poems by Tristan Klingsor (pseud. of Léon Leclère) – haunting proof of Ravel's fascination with the exotic. An exploratory listening to many of Ravel's vocal masterworks is highly recommended. In some instances his exemplary capacity to adapt existing melodies to individual treatment can be every bit as striking as his original writing for voice. Listen to his exceptionally beautiful arrangement of the ancient Kaddish of the Jewish liturgy, in which he clothes the venerable chant in an instrumental setting eminently worthy of the prayer's age-old dignity.

I suppose I shall never be able to hide my unbounded enthusiasm for Ravel's genius in choosing tonal colors. It may be revealing to relate a statement made to me by one of the master's personal friends: "Ravel loved to write at the piano, but he did so with instrumental timbres in mind. Once he orchestrated an original piano piece (which he did on various occasions) he no longer wanted to play it on the piano." No true account of music in the twentieth century would be possible without paying homage to this supreme master of tonal coloration.

The aesthetic ideals of Erik Satie found ready acceptance by a group of young Frenchmen who became known as "Les Six" ("The Six"). With the intellectual encouragement and support of the playwright Jean Cocteau, this group formed an association in 1916 based upon bonds of friendship and mutual respect rather than upon any common compositional goals that might enable us to recognize them as a school or a movement. The group consisted of Louis Durey, Arthur Honegger, Darius Milhaud, Germaine Tailleferre, Georges

Auric, and Francis Poulenc. Each became known in his or her own right, particularly Honegger, Milhaud, and Poulenc, who made lasting contributions to French music during the early part of the twentieth century. If any common direction can be detected at all, it is a neoclassical one, though their individual styles and ways of achieving it are completely distinctive. Directness of purpose and refreshing simplicity and transparency stand in opposition to the teachings of impressionism, which were prevalent in their youth. It was Milhaud who related to me their joy in getting together on Saturday evenings, usually in his home, where they would play their newest opuses for each other, to be followed by an evening on the town, or vice versa.

Particularly rewarding are the symphonic works of Honegger; Milhaud's *Saudades do Brasil (Nostalgic Souvenirs of Brazil)* for piano, *Scaramouche Suite* for two pianos, and *Le Bal Martiniquais* for orchestra; Poulenc's delightful concertos, piano pieces, chamber music, songs, as well as his sobering spiritual works. The compositions of these masters display an urbane, Parisian style and show the influence of travel. Milhaud wrote some of his works during his stay in Rio de Janeiro, where in 1917–18 he served as secretary to then French minister Paul Claudel. Les Six were loyalists to tradition but remained delightfully spirited in their presentations.

In Poland Karol Szymanowski (1882–1937) ushered in a new era of music of and about his country, a direction that had been charted by Stanisław Moniuszko some seventy years earlier. His musical language remained romantic, and he enunciated it in works of a strong patriotic flavor, such as his ballet-pantomime *Harnasie* and his Stabat Mater. His junior compatriots – Witold Lutosławski (b. 1913), Kazimierz Serocki (b. 1922), Tadeusz Baird (b. 1928), and Krzysztof Penderecki (b. 1933) – represent a break with romantic tradition, pursuing abstract and atonal tendencies, at times tinged with a Polish national flavor.

Armenia's Aram Khachaturian (1903–77) never lost his proud and colorful national idiom, despite the fact that his entire musical education unfolded in Moscow after the Russian Revolution. A traditionalist at heart, he colored all his works with unmistakable Armenian nationalism.

Bohuslav Martinů (1890–1959) of Bohemia (presently Czecho-slovakia) is a classic example of a composer whose personal language utilizes bold harmonic innovations to express traditional classical forms, such as the symphony and concerto. I recommend that you listen to the concertos and chamber music of this original and gifted composer.

Hungary's outstanding composers of the twentieth century are Béla Bartók (1881–1945) and Zoltán Kodály (1882–1967). They have in common an unquenchable thirst for authentic folk elements of their native land. This is where the similarities end, however. Kodály utilized collected folk material in his compositions, quoting from it in many instances. Bartók, on the other hand, treated it as an inspi-rational starting point for his own original musical idiom, one of the most invigorating in the early decades of this century. Listen to his *Dance Suite* for orchestra, his three piano concertos, his two violin concertos, his Concerto for Two Pianos, Percussion, and Orchestra, and, above all, his *Concerto for Orchestra,* one of the most inspiring creations of our age. Also of special interest are Kodály's *Psalmus Hungaricus* for tenor solo, mixed chorus, children's chorus, and or-chestra, in addition to the aforementioned orchestral suite extracted from the stage music to *Háry János.* For local color of a more modern hue, *Dances of Marosszék* and *Dances of Galanta,* both for orchestra, are particularly appealing.

Among the Swedish composers of this period whose music offers an amalgam of national/romantic material clothed in a relatively modern style are Hugo Alfvén (1872–1960), Kurt Atterberg (1887–1974), Lars-Erik Larsson (b. 1908), Hilding Rosenberg (b. 1892), and Dag Wirén (b. 1905). A younger generation of Swedish composers, including Karl-Birger Blomdahl (1916–68), Sven-Erik Bäck (b. 1919), and Ingvar Lidholm (b. 1921) represent a new linear and at times expressionistic direction. Blomdahl is the composer of an opera, called *Aniara,* which takes place in space – a science-fiction achieve-ment. Alfvén's *Midsommarvaka* (Swedish Rhapsody No. 1), is a pe-rennial favorite. Larsson accomplished the rare feat – although Hin-demith did it before him – of writing a concerto or concertino for every conceivable instrument.

England occupies a leading position among composers of our time. With Benjamin Britten as undisputed master, Malcolm Arnold, Arthur Bliss, Frank Bridge, George Butterfield, Edward Elgar, Gustav Holst, John Ireland, Michael Tippett, Ralph Vaughan Williams, and William Walton restored England's worldwide reputation after a relative decline during the baroque and rococo eras.

A great many works were influenced by jazz in the early part of the century. Composers of many nations came under its magic spell, headed, of course, by America's own George Gershwin. Alexandre Tansman of Poland; Ravel and Milhaud of France; Weill of Germany and the United States; Copland, Gould, Barber, and Schuller of the United States – all bear the unmistakable imprint of the new art form in some of their compositions. (See also the next chapter on "Music in America.")

What of the renegades, the true pathfinders who defied tradition, fame, and popularity, incurring instead the mistrust and even the wrath of a bewildered, uninitiated, and often hostile public? And who is to say whether their efforts warrant support now or in the future, or whether they should be relegated to oblivion? Could critics be relied upon to guide an unprepared public in either direction?

These questions are not new ones. They have been posed in every period, because audiences and frequently even musicians themselves have been loathe to embrace the new. It does not happen very often that complete newness is judged as greatness at its first appearance, though there are some rare instances of resounding successes at first hearing, among them Stravinsky's *L'Oiseau de Feu (The Firebird)*, first performed at the Paris Opéra in 1910, and Bartók's *Concerto for Orchestra*, premiered in Boston in 1944.

Consider counterparts in the other arts, such as the complete breakthroughs in architecture: the varying functional and philosophical designs of Frank Lloyd Wright ("Falling Water" at Bear Run, Pennsylvania; Guggenheim Museum, New York), Walter Gropius (Bauhaus structures, Dessau, Germany), Le Corbusier (Savoye House, Poissy, France), Ludwig Mies van der Rohe (Seagram Building, New York, in collaboration with Philip Johnson); and Eero Saarinen (the Gateway Arch, St. Louis, Missouri). Then consider the many showpieces of sculpture in public places, such as the works by Henry Moore in Antwerp or at Lincoln Center in New York, or those by Alexander Calder in Chicago or in Grand Rapids, Michigan. What of the new, sleek lines in the sculptures by Constantin Brancusi

("Bird in Space," Philadelphia Museum of Art), Amedeo Modigliani ("Head," Tate Gallery, London), Jean Arp ("Two Heads," Museum of Modern Art, New York), and Alberto Giacometti ("Palace at 4 A.M.," Museum of Modern Art, New York).

By the same token, many art lovers have yet to come to terms with abstraction in painting. Here the profusion of twentieth-century masters rivals in number anything that art history had ever known. Sensational breaks with tradition were effected by such leaders as Wassily Kandinsky, Henri Matisse, Piet Mondrian, Georges Braque, Oskar Kokoschka, Marc Chagall, Pablo Picasso, Joan Miró, Willem de Kooning, Jackson Pollock, Robert Rauschenberg, and many others.

The traditional question "What does it mean? What is it supposed to represent?" has no place in abstract art. Cubism, with its linear play of cylinders, cones, and flat surfaces as seen in Picasso's famous "Three Musicians," or Braque's "Oval Still Life," though first perceived as distorted figures and lines, did furnish a stepping-stone of sorts from the concrete to the abstract.

Even expressionism in painting (such as "Dancing around the Golden Calf" by Emil Nolde of Germany or "The Blue Rider" by Kandinsky), despite the initial shock it caused in the art world, is now considered another logical step in the direction of abstract art. If we view these and other examples repeatedly we find ourselves gradually becoming more receptive as we discover new and fascinating color combinations and psychological values, so that even the tormented lines and bodies in the paintings that relate to a world of harshness and misery become comprehensible.

Just as abstraction in art did not burst upon the scene overnight, so music broke with the romantic and postromantic past in a gradual manner. It is within this context that we should consider new trends, schools, directions, and accomplishments in music of our time and accord them the same degree of openness and patience we reserve for earlier styles.

EXPRESSIONISM

Expressionism is an aptly chosen term descriptive of both the visual arts and music during this period. It links the essentially German school of painting – of which Kokoschka, Nolde, and Ernst were the chief exponents – with the composers often designated by the label expressionist, namely, Schoenberg, Berg, Webern, and occasionally Hindemith and Krenek. They shared a style of introspection prompted by an emotional and psychological insight of a highly subjective kind. These states of mind, the complete opposite of the "impressions of the moment" of the immediately preceding period, constituted a return to romantic ideals – with obvious modern and even distorted overtones.

Arnold Schoenberg (1874–1951), who conceived the most revolutionary changes in music, was born in Vienna and spent his early years in the traditional pursuit of a general and musical education. His first major composition, *Verklärte Nacht (Transfigured Night),* was originally scored for string sextet (1899), and was later revised for string orchestra (1917). Inspired by a sensuous poem by the German writer Richard Dehmel, Schoenberg created a highly romantic, emotional, and atmospheric score that bears no hint whatever of the Schoenbergian upheaval only a few years away. The same is true of his cantata for narrator, solo voices, chorus, and an enormous orchestra, entitled *"Gurrelieder" (Songs of Gurre),* which was begun in 1901 and finished a year later. This work is based on a setting of poems by the Danish poet Jens Peter Jacobsen, recounting a love story of the Middle Ages, with the castle of Gurre as the setting. Except for the use of a *Sprechstimme* ("song speech") – a type of narration using a mixture of song and speech (also used by Alban Berg in his operas *Wozzeck* and *Lulu*) – this major work is in the finest postromantic tradition.

In 1909, after some transitional and ill-received compositions, Schoenberg – now thirty-five and in full command of his creative powers – turned to atonal writing, or non-tonality, as he preferred to call it. The word "atonal" implies the complete absence of a tonal center, with its conventional comfort and sense of well-being derived from a chord of resolution after the tension of dissonances (see the section on "Harmony" in Chapter Two). Non-tonality presumes a state of constant dissonance as a way of musical life.

Yet, Schoenberg infused a new order into this seeming chaos by employing a twelve-tone system. Since this order dominates much of the early twentieth century, a brief discussion of it is in order. This system is based on the twelve tones of the chromatic scale (see p. 29), a scale that employs only half steps. This twelve-tone row can be utilized as written; rearranged to any of the eleven other positions; reversed or inverted; played simultaneously in parts or as a unit as chords or clusters of chords; or portions can be used "serially" in melodic fashion. The possibilities are endless and afford complete freedom within a cerebral rather than a strictly musical order. No tone can be repeated until all others are used.

Repeated hearings will most likely be needed for Schoenberg's *Five Pieces for Orchestra* (1909). It may be difficult at first to appreciate, but there should finally emerge some logical elements to "hold on to," such as a consistent bass motive in the first section, entitled "Presentiments"; the lyrical theme and countertheme of the second section, called "The Past"; the changing sounds of the same chord in different positions in the third section, "Colors, or the Changing Chord"; the lively passages for woodwinds and brass in the fourth section, "Peripeteia"; and the contrapuntal effects derived from the juxtaposition of parts of a principal melody and changing accompaniment in the fifth and final section, "The Obbligato Recitative."

These listening aids are signposts by which you may become accustomed to listening to a new musical phenomenon: serial music. Enlightenment comes with increased familiarity.

An appreciation of this modern period must include a working acquaintance with certain compositions by Alban Berg (1885–1935), Schoenberg's countryman and most illustrious pupil. In addition to the Violin Concerto and the operas already mentioned, Berg's *Lyric Suite* for string quartet (1926), a concert aria in three parts for soprano and orchestra called *Wine* (based on poems from Baudelaire's *Le Vin*), and *Three Pieces for Orchestra* deserve special mention. These works reveal Berg's gift for combining traditional and modern ways to achieve a distinctive new entity.

Anton von Webern (1883–1945), another famous Schoenberg disciple, departed completely from the premise of tone representing a certain pitch; he used the twelve-tone row to express rhythm and color. The dodecaphonic or twelve-tone system now became the point of departure for a technique for its own sake, namely, the serial technique, which attracted a new generation of musicians, the vanguard of the avant-garde period, spearheaded by such well-known names as Karlheinz Stockhausen and Pierre Boulez. Music was now thought of as an experimentation with bare essentials, without any structural or thematic identification. Webern's *Symphony for Chamber Orchestra* (1928) is a good example of conciseness and fragmented, bare necessities, abandoning any thematic concerns. Abstraction had seemingly reached its peak.

In any discussion of periods in music Igor Stravinsky (1882–1971) should be allotted a special place, for he created a musical creed all his own. He was imbued with a new sense of space in music, as was his visual counterpart Pablo Picasso. For Stravinsky this meant foregoing traditional tonality and the associated gravity of the "key center," just as for Picasso it meant the breaking up of traditional contours, perspectives, and concrete likenesses. For both artists this new sense of space meant a new artistic awareness of the principles of order. Chaos for its own sake was ruled out from the start. Both artists spent their entire lives in search of new dimensions, new resources, new means of expression, and new media through which to channel their changing and growing ideas.

Focusing on Stravinsky, we find that with explosive force he established himself as the harbinger of the new, the different, and the original, with three masterworks, all of which were written and received their world premieres before his thirty-first birthday: *L'Oiseau de Feu (The Firebird)* in 1910, *Petrouchka* in 1911, and *Le Sacre du Printemps (The Rite of Spring)* in 1913 all hewed a new path. In each case the story is inspired by Russian lore and legend, which other composers of the time might have approached in a more orthodox way, applying freely the exotic colors of ancient Russian origin.

Stravinsky elected instead to assert himself with dissonances, the simultaneous use of various keys and tonalities, known as polytonality, and, above all, through the vibrant use of constantly changing rhythms based on shifting meters, displaced accents, and syncopated patterns. Melodies, though fragmentary at times, were by no means absent. Their richly varied dynamic and rhythmic treatment lent them an air of primitive force. This is particularly true of *The Rite of Spring,* whose score, in keeping with the pagan story, creates a powerful impact of primal proportions. What gives this work its uniqueness are Stravinsky's deployment of savagely pounded rhythms and themes, made all the more obtrusive through constant repetition; and his orgies of primitive orchestral sound, achieved through painstaking attention to the details of tone production, especially among percussion instruments. While the composer's intention was to portray an ancient Russian ritual of pagan times, the music hypnotizes us so that we become frenzied participants. The newness of the music is achieved through the ingenious utilization of existing means and modes of expression (melody, harmony, rhythm, and tonal color) rather than by means of a new system of tonal rows such as Schoenberg was soon to conceive.

The Firebird and *Petrouchka* are equally fascinating in their bold new approach to orchestration and their means of musical portrayal. To be sure, Stravinsky had the advantage of the continual hand-in-glove collaboration of the choreographer Michel Fokine and the visionary guidance of Serge Diaghilev, for whose Ballets Russes the scores were commissioned. But it was the composer's genius for unprecedented scoring and instrumental coloration that was responsible for the creation of some of the most spectacular masterworks of this century. *The Rite of Spring* caused outrage and dissension when it was first performed in Paris in 1913, with supporters and dissenters scuffling and even spitting at one another. But a bright new star had risen on the horizon, one that would determine the future course of music for many generations.

A new Stravinsky period can be detected some five years after *Le Sacre du Printemps.* This was a period of simplicity after the complexities of the great early ballets, one also marked by more economical writing, as exemplified by *L'Histoire du Soldat (A Soldier's Story),* written in 1918, which was scored for only a narrator, three dancers, and seven instruments (see also p. 205). Other works Stravinsky created during this period are the ballet *Pulcinella* (1919), with music based on Pergolesi, and the *Octet for Winds* (1923). These show the composer's neoclassical tendencies of the time, which extended over a period of thirty years. Another highlight of this period is the *Symphony of Psalms* (1930), written "to the glory of God" to commemorate the fiftieth anniversary of the Boston Symphony Orchestra.

At the age of seventy Stravinsky once more embraced a new direction – the twelve-tone system – which had first been established by Schoenberg as a modern musical language. The *Septet* for strings, winds, and keyboard (1953) is a significant example. The next step was the adoption of a complete serial technique, as in the *Variations for Orchestra* (1965). No other composer so dominated our time as did Igor Stravinsky. Through his works the various stages of musical composition of an entire century may be studied.

Another great influence for new generations of composers is Paul Hindemith of Germany (1895–1963). Not beholden to any system or "ism" of the modern period, he created his own completely personal musical style and language, based on a fascinating use of polyphony, multi-rhythms and tonality. He may be termed neoclassical in his utilization of traditional forms – chamber music, concertos, symphonies – which he used as molds for his distinctive ideas. Dissonances were employed as natural devices to facilitate the flow of his linear writing. Harmonic relationships were formed as accidental, multitonal steps in a continual tonal motion. Hindemith's music is distinguished by its inexorable logic, vigorous individuality, and earnestness of purpose.

One of the finest examples of Hindemith's art is his opera *Mathis der Maler (Matthias the Painter)*, composed in 1934, with the composer's own libretto, based upon the life of the sixteenth-century painter Matthias Grünewald, whose visions are captured in his magnificent panels of the Isenheim Altarpiece in Colmar, Alsace. Hindemith extracted a three-movement symphony from this operatic score. The titles of each movement match the visual contents of the altar panels: "Concert of the Angels," "The Entombment," "The Temptation of St. Anthony."

For additional Hindemith listening, the following works are

recommended: *Der Schwanendreher (The Organ-Grinder),* a "Concerto on Old Folk Melodies for Viola and Small Orchestra" (1935); *Nobilissima Visione,* a ballet in five scenes (1938); *The Four Temperaments:* Theme with Four Variations for strings and piano (1940); *Symphonic Metamorphosis on Themes by Weber* (1943); Concerto for Woodwinds, Harp, and Orchestra (1949).

NEOCLASSICISM

Neoclassicism is easier to discern among individual composers than it is to describe as a unified period or movement. That it occurs in the twentieth century shows its motivating function, namely, to recreate seventeenth- and eighteenth-century concepts of form in the contemporary style of our own time.

It is in this sense that we should look at the symphonists of our era. Leading the list in a most commanding way are the Russian masters Sergei Prokofiev (1891–1953) and Dmitri Shostakovich (1906–75). Significantly, it was Prokofiev who called his first symphony, written in 1917, the year of the Russian Revolution, "Classical." Admittedly, the composer wished to adapt the classical example of Haydn and Mozart to the techniques and idiosyncracies of his time and personality. The outcome is a highly successful merger of two worlds, filled with harmonic dissonances, characteristic leaps of melody, and sudden rhythmic surprises.

Prokofiev went on to justify handsomely his reputation as a neoclassicist and symphonist in the broadest sense by composing six more symphonies, a sinfonietta, five piano concertos, two violin concertos, a cello concerto, two quintets (one for wind and strings and another for strings alone), two string quartets, nine piano sonatas, and sonatinas and suites for piano.

There are many compositions to prove that Prokofiev was also a modernist. His ballet suites *Chout (Buffoon), Le Pas d'Acier (The Age of Steel),* and his *Scythian Suite* are as abrasive in sound as are his operas *The Love for Three Oranges, The Flaming Angel, War and Peace,* or his symphonic suite *Lieutenant Kijé.* His ballets *Romeo and Juliet* and *Cinderella,* and his cantata *Alexander Nevsky* offer both melodic beauty and Prokofiev's wit and harshness.

No one should forego the privilege of choosing from the long list of Prokofiev's works for memorable listening experiences. I suggest the "Classical" Symphony, as well as the Symphony No. 5 (a powerful masterwork), the concertos, the piano sonatas (No. 7 has great vitality), and excerpts from *The Love for Three Oranges* and *Romeo and Juliet*. Prokofiev thrills us with a consummate mastery of forms, a musical language of exhilarating strength, a marvelous wit when appropriate, and beauty and breadth of melody.

Another towering contemporary figure is Prokofiev's compatriot Dmitri Shostakovich, who, because of his genius and his productivity, is considered the leading composer of twentieth-century Russia. Personally I would suggest a twin leadership, but if sheer numbers of works is the criterion, Shostakovich has no equal in our time. Fifteen symphonies, fifteen string quartets, two sets of twenty-four preludes each for piano (the second with fugues), concertos, chamber music, ballet scores (*The Age of Gold* is the best known), operas (*Lady Macbeth of Mtzensk* is politically controversial) are formidable proof of his fecundity.

At their best, Shostakovich's works reveal a majesty, an original voice, a great sense of satire and rhythmic diversity, and at times even unabashed melodies.

Fifteen years Prokofiev's junior, Shostakovich was only eleven when the Russian Revolution of 1917 began. He, more than Prokofiev, knew no other order than that of the twentieth-century Russian regime. It was all the more difficult for him to have been in and out of favor ideologically. Yet his music survives on its own merits, although he could not have escaped outside influences.

His Symphony No. 1, written at age nineteen, is a remarkable work of virtuosic proportions and of infectious drive. His Symphony No. 5 is a maturely triumphant one, and his Symphony No. 7 ("Leningrad") is descriptive of the soul of a people at war. It was begun one month after the Nazi invasion of Russia and during the siege of Leningrad.

Symphony No. 9 has a melodic charm all its own, while *The Age of Gold*, Shostakovich's ballet score of 1930, is spiced with typical wit. His concertos for piano, violin, and cello offer many virtuosic thrills.

Also among the most noteworthy of contemporary Russian masters are Aram Khachaturian (1903–78), Dmitri Kabalevsky (b. 1904), and Nikolai Miaskovsky (1881–1950).

We have come full circle in our exploration of the spans of time during which the creation of musical composition underwent important changes. Since we can readily discern these changes in retrospect, it is justifiable to call the divisions of time during which they occurred "periods," all the more so because the parallel developments in art and literature are often striking enough to add credence to such temporal delineation. I should like to underscore the fact that hindsight makes it all possible. Each generation has always been a partner in the eternal process of creation. Since that process mirrors, parallels, and even presages the currents of life and human events, it often proceeds quite imperceptibly unless these changes come upon us with cataclysmic force. Day follows day, and we are too busily engaged in routine pursuits to take notice. Like life itself, artistic creation is and remains in a constant state of flux.

There have been too many incidents where the intuition of the perceptive artist has pointed him unwittingly toward future artistic developments for us to call them mere accidents of history. As if endowed with prophetic vision, such an artist strides ahead of his age, unfortunately often leaving behind his public. Thus it was that some composers retired to electronics studios of broadcast centers and universities across Europe and America to evolve new methods of composition; the music they created is made up of sounds not produced by musical instruments but sometimes exclusively the result of electronic devices.

Traditional instrumental or vocal sounds had already been replaced by such recorded sounds as percussion, speaking voices, or various noises, which were then subjected to various tempo and pitch changes, played backward, and made into a kind of montage on tape. In 1948 the Frenchman Pierre Schaeffer, based in Paris, called the result *musique concrète*. In other words, the final sound was premixed and available on tape. Electronic music as we know it today, on the other hand, has the assemblage of sound in common with traditional music, only it is assembled by electro-acoustical means. No premixing here; but the music is synthetic rather than naturally produced. The resulting variations are immense, including creating specific and unconventional scales for each work, devising highly detailed timbres far beyond the capabilities of conventional instruments, and producing intensities and duration of dynamic properties of which no human performer is capable.

In addition to this vast diversification of sound, extramusical varieties can be made available by combining electronic sound with that of one or more traditional musical instruments or voices. The field is a fascinating one. Eventually music lovers will begin to understand the principles involved. Then the basic choice will have to be made intelligently and not just emotionally.

This newest period differs from all the others in that the sound emanating from the musical instruments we have come to love has been replaced by extramusical devices. In past periods we may have struggled with, or even despaired of, new idioms and a new musical language. But we did have at least a cursory knowledge and understanding of the raw material involved and how the musical language was produced. Electronic music poses far weightier questions, which time, greater familiarity, and, above all, more tolerance will answer.

CHAPTER TEN

MUSIC IN AMERICA

AMERICA OCCUPIES a very special place among the countries that have developed their own indigenous music over the years. It has taken the United States a little over two hundred years – the length of its existence as a nation – to assume the leading position that it commands today in the world of music. This accomplishment is even more impressive when one considers the predominance of the Viennese classical masters at the turn of the eighteenth century and the increased productivity of romantic composers during the nineteenth century throughout Europe. All this was happening at a time when America was only slowly finding its musical way, from a mere social grace to a significant professional activity.

COLONIAL ORIGINS

From the beginning, native American musicians were joined by colleagues from other lands – at first almost exclusively from Europe – who brought with them the fruits of their various backgrounds and experiences. These Americans greatly benefited from this exchange; because of the lack of equivalent teaching facilities, they were largely self-taught. These influences existed long before 1776. Among the most important ones were those of the German religious group, the Moravians, who came to America in 1735 along with the brothers

357

John and Charles Wesley, who composed a great number of hymns as Methodist preachers.

The Moravian Church of Bethlehem, Pennsylvania, and of Winston-Salem, North Carolina, assembled a treasure trove of hymns and of ensemble music, which played an important role in the annals of early American music. It was in Bethlehem, too, that the works of significant European contemporaries were first heard in concert – among them compositions by Johann Christian Bach, Haydn, and Mozart – having been brought over from Europe by early settlers. In fact, some Haydn quartets and early symphonies received their first American hearing in Bethlehem, Pennsylvania.

In turn, Moravian immigrant composers contributed their own creations to the musical life of their new home. The foremost among them was John Frederick Peter (1746–1813), a native of Holland and a composer of outstanding church music. His six string quintets, written in Winston-Salem in 1789, constitute the first important chamber music written in America.

Musicians from England and Scotland were equally effective in imparting knowledge and experience to those living in the New World. William Tuckey of the British Cathedral in England conducted the first American performance of Handel's *Messiah* in 1770, two years prior to its first German hearing. Philadelphia was the goal of many British musicians, among them James Bremner of Scotland, who was to become the teacher of America's first native composer, Francis Hopkinson (1737–91), co-signer of the Declaration of Independence and a close associate of Washington, Franklin, and Jefferson. Among Hopkinson's various works are *Seven Songs for the Harpsichord or Forte Piano*, reputedly the first secular songs written in America. They were dedicated to George Washington one year before his election to the presidency.

Other important composers of the time were James Lyon (1735–94) of Newark, New Jersey, known for his odes and psalm tunes, and William Billings (1746–1800) of Boston, composer of "fuguing tunes" (early rounds), and of some of the most popular anthems of the day, such as "The Rose of Sharon" and "Chester." Billings, a tanner by trade, was primarily self-taught. He gathered a basic knowledge of composition from American reprints of English theory books, although he insisted on his own "intuitive" rules. Impoverished father of a large family, ridiculed because of a very unattractive appearance, but of iron will and determination, Billings succeeded in becoming one of the first American musicians who was widely accepted.

While popular tunes and ballads were in vogue during the actual revolutionary years, with "Yankee Doodle" and "Hail Columbia" among the most popular, native composers continued to aspire to more elevated musical horizons. The French Revolution, with its aftermath of political and social unrest in many parts of Europe, brought about the decline of aristocratic patronage. As a result, many European musicians tried to seek their fortunes in the New World.

England's contingent became prominent as teachers, organists, and members of theater orchestras in such eastern cities as Philadelphia and Baltimore. Alexander Reinagle of London, friend of Carl Philipp Emanuel Bach, arrived in 1786. He was known not only for his stature as a pianist and violinist but also for his winsome personality and attractive bearing. Among his pupils was Nelly Custis, adopted daughter of General Washington. Reinagle became one of early America's most prolific composers. His piano sonatas, reminiscent of Haydn's style, are of lasting interest.

The spirit of Haydn's symphonies also found expression in the works of another outstanding immigrant-musician, James Hewitt, who arrived in New York in 1792. In London he was conductor of George III's court orchestra; he was also a member of the orchestra that Haydn conducted during his London visit in 1791. First as the organist of New York's Trinity Church and then as the leader of concert orchestras and bands, Hewitt brought with him a musical tradition that greatly enriched his new surroundings. Of historical significance is his piano sonata of 1797 entitled *The Battle of Trenton*, a highly descriptive work. It contains the popular tune "Yankee Doodle," in the tradition of Johann Kuhnau's programmatic *Biblical Sonatas* of a century earlier.

Other immigrants from England who contributed to the early musical scene in America were Raynor Taylor of Baltimore and Philadelphia and William Selby and Gottlieb Graupner of Boston. The Dutchman Peter Albrecht Van Hagen and his family made a name for themselves by establishing one of the first music stores and publishing houses in Boston. All these newcomers helped raise the level of musical sophistication in early America.

NINETEENTH-CENTURY MUSICAL ACCOMPLISHMENTS

The nineteenth century saw the rise of the first American music educator, Lowell Mason (1792–1872), whose lasting fame rests upon his pioneering efforts in behalf of the American public school music system. He served as the first music superintendent of public schools in Boston. Mindful of the fact that ongoing music education in schools was dependent upon the training of new generations of teachers, Mason instituted intensive periods of instruction in his "musical conventions" (meetings for teachers) and established the New York Musical Normal Institute, the first professional training school for public school music teachers. He also became famous as the composer of such hymns as "Nearer, My God, to Thee." His sons continued the family tradition by way of a publishing house in New York and the manufacture of the still-famous Mason & Hamlin pianos. Daniel Gregory Mason, Lowell's grandson, carried the family name into the twentieth century as the distinguished composer of symphonic and chamber music.

Another important composer of the nineteenth century is Stephen Collins Foster (1826–64). His birth in Lawrenceville, Pennsylvania, on July 4 coincided with the fiftieth birthday of the United States. With very little musical education Foster was able to write some of the most endearing and memorable melodies. Over two hundred songs attest to his inventiveness. Among them are "Old Folks at Home," "Oh! Susanna," "Camptown Races," "My Old Kentucky Home," and "Jeanie with the Light Brown Hair." Foster became the American counterpart of the German romantic songwriters of his time, expressing the sentiments, love, humor, and humanity of a wondrous new country trying to establish its artistic identity.

Another first among American musical achievements was in the field of keyboard virtuosity. Louis Moreau Gottschalk (1829–69), born in New Orleans of an English father and a Creole mother, became known as "the king of pianists." Young Gottschalk studied in Paris with various French masters, culminating with instruction by Hector Berlioz. At the same time, he became acquainted with Franz Liszt and Frédéric Chopin, both of whom predicted a great future for him. Gottschalk's career blossomed during the 1850s, when his travels as concert pianist took him to Cuba and South America. Acclaimed in Buenos Aires, and particularly in Rio de Janeiro, he died shortly after conducting a huge musical festival in Rio in 1869.

As a composer Gottschalk wrote brilliant piano pieces that evoke the spirit of his travel adventures, such as "Midnight in Seville," "Souvenir de Cuba," "Le Bananier," and "La Savane." To this day his most popular work is "The Banjo," a pianistic description of the sound of that plucked instrument. Gottschalk was the first American-born musician to gain international acclaim.

The mid-nineteenth century also witnessed the beginnings of organized educational and concert activities in a country torn by the tragedies of the Civil War. Oberlin College in Oberlin, Ohio, offered music courses as early as 1835. The Peabody Institute in Baltimore opened in 1868. The Oberlin Conservatory became a separate entity in 1865; the New England Conservatory of Music in Boston followed in 1867, as did the Chicago Musical College and the Cincinnati Conservatory of Music. Symphony orchestras came to prominence in such auditoriums as Philadelphia's Academy of Music, dating back to 1857, and Cincinnati's Musical Hall, dating back to 1878.

New York's orchestral history started back in 1842 when the Philharmonic Society of New York presented its first concert at the Apollo Rooms on Broadway. The conductor was Ureli Corelli Hill (1802–75) of Connecticut, a student of Ludwig Spohr in Germany. Today's Philharmonic-Symphony Society of New York is the result of a merger in 1928 of the New York Symphony and the Philharmonic.

Theodore Thomas organized his own orchestra in New York in 1862 and in Chicago in 1891. His rival Leopold Damrosch founded the Symphony Society of New York in 1878, an organization that was later to merge with the Philharmonic. Other major American cities followed suit during the last decades of the century.

October 22, 1883, was the day on which the Metropolitan Opera House opened its doors in New York with a gala performance of

Gounod's *Faust,* sung in Italian because most of the cast was Italian. This was not, however, the beginning of opera in that city. Thirty years earlier the Academy of Music at Fourteenth Street and Irving Place had been the home of opera, produced by James Henry Mapleson of London's Drury Lane. The new "Met" was catapulted to fame by the conducting artistry of Leopold Damrosch, who had come from Germany in 1871.

His son, Walter, assumed his father's mantle as leader of operas and oratorios, and then as conductor of the New York Symphony Society. Generations of music lovers appreciated his imaginative concerts, which featured many first performances of composers' works; his educational concerts were later broadcast coast-to-coast.

The 1870s and 1880s were noteworthy for a number of significant musical developments. Harvard University, America's first college, was also the first institution of higher learning to establish a full professorship of music. The first musician to hold this newly created post was John Knowles Paine (1839–1906) of Portland, Maine, a gifted composer and inspiring teacher. The curriculum of musical form, harmony, and counterpoint that he set up at Harvard became the basis for music courses at other American colleges and universities. As a composer Paine became known as the first American to create large-scale works, including symphonies, symphonic poems, cantatas, chamber music, piano and organ compositions, and incidental scores for plays. Above all, he was the teacher of an entire generation of American composers, among them Arthur Foote, Daniel Gregory Mason, Frederick Converse, and John Alden Carpenter.

One of the earliest American music festivals, the Ann Arbor Festival of the University of Michigan, began in 1879 and is still extremely popular. The Boston Symphony Orchestra gave its first concert in October 1881, thanks to the devoted and untiring efforts of a musician-turned-banker Henry Lee Higginson. He was the first of many individuals of private means to become patrons of music, thus creating a new and all-important phase in the history of patronage of the arts in America.

As a showcase for the New York Symphony Orchestra, New York's Music Hall opened its doors in 1891, with festivities that lasted five days. Tchaikovsky came from Russia, as an honored guest, expressly for the purpose of conducting the New York Symphony

Orchestra and Oratorio Society in some of his works. The generosity of Andrew Carnegie made the building of the Music Hall possible. Seven years later, in 1898, its name was changed to Carnegie Hall in his honor.

Since that time, Carnegie Hall has become synonymous with the aspirations and successes of the world's greatest artists. Down through the decades and in our own time they still look upon their Carnegie Hall appearance as the stamp of authenticity and the highest artistic achievement. Located at the corner of Fifty-seventh Street and Seventh Avenue, Carnegie Hall is now a historic landmark, saved by the persevering efforts of the great violinist Isaac Stern and his associates.

The American musical scene of the late nineteenth century was also enriched by the first government-chartered school of music, the National Conservatory of Music of America, founded by Mrs. Jeanette M. Thurber (1851–1946), a New York music patron. It was she who engaged Antonin Dvořák as its director from 1892 to 1895.

The Boston Group and Their Contemporaries

A group of American-born composers was destined to make significant contributions to musical life in the United States during the waning years of the 1800s. They became known as the Boston Group or the New Englanders. Among its members were George Whitefield Chadwick (1854–1931) of Lowell, Massachusetts; Arthur Foote (1853–1937) of Salem, Massachusetts; Horatio William Parker (1863–1919) of Auburndale, Massachusetts; and Mrs. H. H. A. ("Amy") Beach (1867–1944) of Henniker, New Hampshire. While definitely influenced by German masters – both Chadwick and Parker studied with Rheinberger in Munich – the Boston Group may well be considered American classicists with respect to form of composition, although their chief works are romantic in content. Amy Beach, too, who became best known for her songs and for her piano concerto and chamber music, spent a good deal of time in Germany concertizing. Chadwick's teachers, besides Rheinberger, included Salomon Jadassohn, the famed Leipzig musician. Under his tutelage Chadwick wrote one of his best-known compositions, the *Rip van Winkle* Overture, one of the earliest and finest pieces of orchestral Americana. His orchestral suite *Symphonic Sketches* ("Jubilee," "Noël," "Hobgoblin," and "A Vagrom Ballad") are still heard occasionally in concert.

Chadwick, in turn, became an educational force in America. He served as director of the New England Conservatory from 1897 to 1931. Horatio Parker, Edward Burlingame Hill, Daniel Gregory Mason, and William Grant Still were among his most respected students. Parker, today remembered primarily for his choral music, also wrote works for orchestra, chamber music, piano, and organ. His opera *Mona* was premiered at the Metropolitan Opera in 1912. From 1894 to 1919 Parker served as director of the music department at Yale University.

Foote, a Harvard graduate, was the only member of the group trained entirely in America. For some sixty years he was active as a much sought after piano teacher in Boston, organist of that city's First Unitarian Church, and co-founder of the American Guild of Organists. His *Serenade in E* for strings remains in the orchestral repertoire, testifying to Foote's remarkable craftsmanship and compositional scope. His chamber music, church compositions, numerous songs, and piano and organ pieces should be explored by the serious music lover.

Undoubtedly, one of the best known native composers of the period was Edward MacDowell (1860–1908), who was born in New York. Though a contemporary of the New England group, his work was more far-reaching and his sense of individualism more pronounced. His parents, of Quaker background, were determined to provide the kind of training commensurate with his extraordinary talent. At fifteen MacDowell traveled with his mother to Paris, where he won a scholarship to study at the famed Conservatoire and became a fellow student of Claude Debussy. At age seventeen he went to Germany to continue his studies with Joachim Raff, director of the Frankfurt Conservatory. He soon enjoyed the friendship and respect of Franz Liszt, who arranged for MacDowell's works to be published.

MacDowell's formative years (from age seventeen to thirty-five) were spent in Germany, a background that his compositions reflect. Upon his return to America, MacDowell settled first in Boston as composer and teacher, then in New York as head of the newly formed music department of Columbia University. Upon his death in 1908 MacDowell's wife saw to it that his summer retreat in Peterborough, New Hampshire, was turned into a colony for composers, artists, and poets, who are selected to work there still today in idyllic surroundings – a living monument to one of America's most notable composers.

MacDowell's compositions include sonatas and a considerable number of smaller pieces for piano, among them the well-known *Woodland Sketches,* of which "To a Wild Rose" and "To a Water Lily" are the most famous selections, some major works for orchestra, two piano concertos, and the *Suite No. 2* ("Indian Suite"), which uses melodies of the North American Indians.

THE BAND

A musical ensemble of particularly American character is the band, composed of varying numbers of wind instruments, from the brass band to the marching band to the concert band. Given the nature of its component instruments, band musicians can also perform while walking or marching, in contrast to the members of a symphony orchestra, who must remain in place. This widens the use of the band for activities of various kinds.

John Philip Sousa (1854–1932), "The March King," was extremely successful in popularizing the band. His career started in 1880 as director of the United States Marine Band. Twelve years later he organized his own ensemble, which soon emerged as one of the first "concert bands." Sousa's own marches are exemplary for the inventiveness of their melodic material, their harmonic treatment, and the way in which he embellished the innate rhythmic appeal of the march.

Some of Sousa's finest compositions, such as "The Stars and Stripes Forever," "The Washington Post," and "The Gladiators," have become world-famous examples of the march form; they have also been played in symphony concerts under such conductors as Toscanini. In addition to almost one hundred marches, Sousa also wrote operettas, such as *The Bride Elect, El Capitan,* and *The Free Lance.*

Edwin Franko Goldman (1878–1956) and subsequently his son,

Richard (b. 1910), developed the band into an organization of symphonic scope. This, in turn, inspired many composers to write specifically for the concert band, such as Samuel Barber, Darius Milhaud, Vincent Persichetti, Roy Harris, Virgil Thomson, and William Schuman. Increasingly, original compositions have been added to the large number of arrangements for band of symphonic works, creating an imposing literature for this medium.

TWENTIETH-CENTURY COMPOSERS
AND THEIR WORKS

Musical America strode confidently into the twentieth century. Native composers were obviously still in the minority, and musical organizations were mostly led by foreign-born musicians. But the stage was set for an era that was to see the New World emerge as a vital force on the international music scene.

The early decades of the century saw the establishment of symphony orchestras in cities such as Baltimore, Cleveland, and Los Angeles, with new auditoriums erected to serve as their homes.

A few examples are Boston's Music Hall, which dates back to 1900; Chicago's Orchestra Hall, erected in 1904; and Cleveland's Severance Hall, which was completed in 1931. As the century progressed, the old vied with the new for acoustical excellence, from the refurbishing of grand old movie houses in Miami and Pittsburgh to magnificent edifices in New York, Los Angeles, San Francisco, St. Louis, Denver, and many other cities.

Early in the twentieth century the world's greatest performing musicians began to grace America's shores. The singers Emmy Destinn, Feodor Chaliapin, Maria Jeritza, and Giovanni Martinelli sang at the Metropolitan Opera House. Mary Garden made history in Chicago; Lillian Nordica and Louise Homer in Boston. Enrico Caruso's American debut had taken place as early as 1903 at the Met. Seven years later he sang Don José in *Carmen* in San Francisco. Early the next morning he had to save his life by fleeing town with many others while the city burned as a result of a devastating earthquake.

Virtuoso instrumentalists – violinists Fritz Kreisler, Mischa Elman, and Efrem Zimbalist; the trio with pianist Alfred Cortot, violinist Jacques Thibaud, and cellist Pablo Casals; pianists Josef Hofmann, Leopold Godowsky, Ignace Paderewski, Artur Schnabel, and Sergei Rachmaninoff – thrilled American audiences for the first time from around 1910 through the 1920s.

Many conductors, most of whom were brought over from Europe, soon made a name for themselves as outstanding musical leaders. They built their young orchestras with great enthusiasm, for they themselves were young. Frederick Stock in Chicago, Leopold Stokowski in Cincinnati and then in Philadelphia, Ossip Gabrilowitsch in Detroit, Nikolai Sokoloff in Cleveland, Pierre Monteux in Boston, followed by Serge Koussevitzky in Boston were all under fifty years of age when they assumed their respective posts. Their talent and charisma made it possible to assemble orchestral players of superior quality, assuring world renown for their organizations. Many of the world's renowned masters of the baton began to appear as regular guest conductors of American orchestras. Heading the list were Bruno Walter, Victor de Sabata, Arturo Toscanini, Felix Weingartner, and Arthur Nikisch.

In 1937 a second great orchestra was formed in New York specifically for Arturo Toscanini, the NBC Symphony Orchestra. It was so completely identified with the personality of Toscanini that it was disbanded upon the conductor's retirement in 1954, although it lived on for a while as the Symphony of the Air. More recently it became the American Symphony Orchestra.

Opera, too, made great strides as the new century progressed. In 1908 the Metropolitan Opera of New York obtained the services of its great new manager, Giulio Gatti-Casazza from Italy, along with Arturo Toscanini as conductor. Chicago, Boston, San Francisco, and Philadelphia were soon on the way to operatic fame.

Meanwhile, the advent of phonograph records, which began with the invention of disk recording by Emile Berliner in 1887, and the beginning of wireless transmission of music in 1906, was to bring music ever closer to the consciousness of those who could not as yet attend musical events in person. Radio became a powerful reality in the 1920s, and the recording industry eventually grew into a major vehicle for the dissemination of music. Also during this time music schools opened their doors to those who could benefit from special-ized instruction, among them the Institute of Musical Art (1904) in New York, which was to merge in 1926 with the Juilliard School of Music, the Curtis Institute in Philadelphia (1924), the Eastman School of Music in Rochester, New York (1921), and the Cleveland Institute of Music (1920).

Another milestone in the field of education was the founding of the Music Educators' National Conference in 1907, an organization de-voted to the furtherance of music teaching in the public schools.

COMPOSERS – EARLY DECADES OF THE NEW CENTURY

As we move further into the twentieth century, we find American composers becoming increasingly aware of native themes upon which to build their works.

Arthur Farwell (1872–1952) of St. Paul, Minnesota, founded the Wa-Wan publishing press, championing works utilizing the folk music of America. He wrote such compositions as "Dawn," "The Domain of Hurakan," "American Indian Melodies," all based on Indian themes; songs of the prairie and spirituals attracted his at-tention in equal measure.

Edgar Stillman Kelley (1857–1944) of Sparta, Wisconsin, showed the influence of Puritan tunes and Indian songs in his second sym-phony, which he called *New England Symphony* (1913), and his pen-chant for historical subject matter in his oratorio *The Pilgrim's Progress* (1918). Of particular interest, too, are his Chinese orchestral suite *Aladdin* (1915), based upon native music which Kelley heard in San Francisco's Chinatown, and his symphonic suite *Alice in Wonderland* (1919).

Henry F. B. Gilbert (1868–1928) of Somerville, Massachusetts, a student of MacDowell, was successful in creating meaningful utiliza-tions of Negro tunes. His *Comedy Overture on Negro Themes* (1911), *Negro Rhapsody* (1913), and the *Dance in the Place Congo* (1908) are cases in point. The latter work was first written as an orchestral piece, and was later transcribed as a ballet, produced in 1918 in New York's Metropolitan Opera House. It is interesting to note that the Russian nationalist school and French-oriented opera inspired Gilbert to consider his own national roots. As a young man he went to Europe on a cattle boat to hear the premiere of the opera *Louise* by Charpentier in Paris, having been told of its use of quasi-popular themes.

Henry Kimball Hadley (1871–1937), also of Somerville, Massachusetts, was a pupil of Chadwick. Among the most prolific of the American composers of his time, he wrote five symphonies, five operas, tone poems, overtures, choral works, and a number of chamber music compositions. Hadley's influence was also felt in the field of conducting. He served as conductor of the San Francisco Orchestra and the Seattle Symphony, and as associate conductor of the New York Philharmonic (1920). In 1934 he conducted the first concert at the Tanglewood music festival in Lenox, Massachusetts. In addition, Hadley founded the National Association for American Composers and Conductors, which was dedicated to the cause of American music.

Daniel Gregory Mason (1873–1953) of Brookline, Massachusetts, was a student of John Knowles Paine at Harvard, Chadwick in Boston, and Vincent d'Indy in Paris. He wrote chamber music and symphonies, among them *A Lincoln Symphony*, his third, all in the tradition of the German romantic era. A significant writer and lecturer on music, Mason served as MacDowell Professor of Music at Columbia University.

Edward Burlingame Hill (1872–1960) of Cambridge, Massachusetts, also studied with Paine and Chadwick, as well as with the famous organist Charles Widor in Paris. As professor and later as chairman of Harvard's music department, Hill followed an academic family tradition. His grandfather was president of Harvard, and his father was a professor of chemistry. He was the first American composer who championed the cause of French music, lecturing on the subject both here and at French universities. Some of his musical output shows French impressionist traits. His three symphonies, a violin concerto, a piano concertino, and chamber music deserve to be heard.

Other noteworthy composers at the beginning of the twentieth century include Rubin Goldmark (1872–1936), the New York-born pupil of Dvořák during the latter's tenure at the National Conservatory in New York. His uncle was Karl Goldmark, the Hungarian composer of the opera *The Queen of Sheba* and the "Rustic Wedding" Symphony. Rubin's own compositions show a definite American bent. They include a Requiem prompted by Lincoln's Gettysburg Address, a *Hiawatha* Overture, a *Negro Rhapsody*, and *The Call of the Plains*. Rubin Goldmark headed the composition department at Juilliard for twelve years (1924-36), during which time he was able to inspire future leaders in American music, such as Aaron Copland, George Gershwin, and Vittorio Giannini.

Increasingly composers, both native and foreign-born, leaned toward a utilization of folk sources in their music.

Charles Ives (1874-1954), a turn-of-the-century American individualist, had an experimental style of composing that preceded the revolutionary departure from tonal tradition brought about by Schoenberg, Berg, Stravinsky, and Webern. It took musicians and audiences a long time to appreciate his dissonant treatment of American tunes and subjects in such works as Sonata No. 2 ("Concord Sonata"), *Three Places in New England, Variations on "America,"* "Holidays" Symphony, as well as in his string quartets and symphonies. Ives's four symphonies (all written before 1917) are entirely unconventional in their fragmentary use of American tunes, their dissonant clashes, and avant-garde textures. Yet they drew their inspiration entirely from American life and experiences. Ives emerged as one of America's most original creative musicians.

Charles Wakefield Cadman (1881-1946) of Johnstown, Pennsylvania, infused his works with Indian themes. John Powell (1882-1963) of Richmond, Virginia, showed Afro-American influences in his *Rapsodie Nègre* for piano and orchestra, and used American folk tunes in his other orchestral works, including his Symphony in A ("Virginia Symphony"), which was commissioned by the National Federation of Music Clubs in 1932. John Alden Carpenter (1876-1951) of Chicago became interested in American themes while a student of John Knowles Paine at Harvard, although his studies with Edward Elgar in Rome and his acquaintance with Debussy's work in Europe changed the course of his compositional orientation.

A strong interest in American tonal and historical elements was evidenced by the Swiss-born composer Ernest Bloch (1880-1959), who came to America in 1916. His *America, an Epic Rhapsody* in three parts, written in 1926, constitutes an enthusiastic tribute to his adopted land. This work is, in effect, a musical history covering the period from 1620 and the landing of the Pilgrims to 1926 and a promise for the future, with the audience participating in the singing of an impressive finale, "The Fulfillment Through Love." Bloch is especially notable in the field of Jewish music, in which he excels in the depiction of tonal and historical elements of a Jewish nature, as exemplified in his splendid rhapsody for cello and orchestra entitled *Schelomo,* his *Sacred Service* ("Avodath Hakodesh"), and his suite for violin and piano entitled *Baal Shem.*

As a teacher and later as director of some of America's great schools, first at the David Mannes School in New York (1917), then at the Cleveland Institute of Music (1920) and the San Francisco Conservatory (1926), Bloch inspired a large number of future musicians, thus adding another dimension to his American contributions.

Charles Tomlinson Griffes (1884–1920), born in Elmira, New York, may well be considered the impressionist among American composers. His orchestral works, including *The Pleasure-Dome of Kubla Khan* (based on a Coleridge poem), his *Poem* for flute and orchestra, and his piano pieces known as *Four Roman Sketches* (based on William Sharpe's poetry and including the lovely work entitled *The White Peacock*) are proof of this young musician's creative capacity. His untimely death at the age of thirty-six cut short a promising life.

RAGTIME

This musical phenomenon would become synonymous with the American musical scene because it was born, raised, and nurtured on American soil without the help of foreign tutelage. It was during the last years of the nineteenth century, the so-called Gay Nineties, that ragtime was born. Its infectious rhythmic sparks burst into flames that were to kindle the love of Americans as well as Europeans.

This was music, simple and unsophisticated at first, whose syncopated beat was spread by traveling musicians, both black and white, first in the towns and villages along the Missouri and Mississippi, and soon throughout the land. Spawned by the plantation songs of the minstrel shows, ragtime was and remained primarily a form that exercised the improvisational skill of pianists, but also of singers.

Ragtime – based chiefly on the conventional triads of tonic, dominant, and subdominant (see Chapter Two) – was easily accessible to both performers and audiences. Yet it took a special gift to combine the steady flow of rhythm of the left-hand accompaniment with the syncopation of the right-hand melody. The emotional and noticeably physical effect of this constant "offbeat" drive was compelling and difficult to resist. Syncopation as a rhythmic device was not new, but its continuous use seemed to evoke a frenzied response in its listeners.

The greatest single personality among ragtime composers was Scott Joplin (1868–1917), famous for his innumerable "rags." "The Maple Leaf Rag" (1899) is one of the best known. His music's popularity was due not only to Joplin's inventiveness but also to the faith of the publishing firm of John Stark & Son of Sedalia, Missouri. Their partnership was the force that bestowed permanence upon ragtime. Joplin carried his passion into the field of opera with *A Guest in the House* (unpublished) and *Treemonisha,* published in 1911 but not performed with scenery or orchestra until 1972 in Atlanta.

Other ragtime pianists of the time were Tom Turpin (c. 1873–1922), known for his "Harlem Rag"; James Sylvester Scott (1886–1938) and his "Climax Rag" (1914); and Louis Chauvin and his "Heliotrope Bouquet" (1907). St. Louis and New Orleans became the centers of the ragtime movement, and the music there was exported enthusiastically throughout America and Europe.

BLUES

By the second decade of the twentieth century ragtime's popularity had declined. It was the talent of a black musician, W. C. Handy (1873–1958), whose song "The Memphis Blues" (published in 1912) signaled the dawn of a new form of popular expression, the blues. The roots of this style seem to go back to Civil War days. The blues would serve as the cornerstone of America's most important contribution to twentieth-century music, namely, jazz.

The blues may be described as a kind of lament, a slow song generally sung by one person, bemoaning loneliness, lost love, or, more philosophically, the painful lot of the black people. The most famous example is Handy's composition "The St. Louis Blues" (1914).

Musically the accompaniment is composed of basic chords, with a predominance of the dominant seventh symbolically underlining the yearning for a resolution, which eludes the content of the text. The chief characteristic of the melody, however, is the inimitable "blue note," a temporary wavering of intonation between the true tone and its flattened pitch.

Another important feature of the blues song is known as the break, which consists of a pause in the text at the end of a line, leaving room for the voice or the accompanying instruments to improvise briefly. The rhythmic pattern of the bass, as conceived by Handy, was akin to that of the tango, habanera, or other Latin-American dances.

Among the great blues singers of the time were Gertrude "Ma" Rainey (1886–1939), Bessie Smith (c. 1894–1937), and Bertha "Chippie" Hill (1905–50). However, the pivotal figure in the transitional stage of ragtime and blues to jazz was Ferdinand "Jelly Roll" Morton (1885–1941), whose recordings of all these musical phases as he knew them – made at the request of the Library of Congress in 1938 – have become a true American musical treasure. Fortuitously, by 1910 every well-known singer and quite a few instrumentalists were able to record their music. If this had not been possible, many of the vital links of early American music in their formative stage would be lost to the world.

Jazz

Whether jazz was a natural outgrowth of blues and ragtime, was conceived simultaneously, or predated them is uncertain. We do know that it first began to develop in New Orleans just before 1900, which brought it to the attention of an increasing number of Americans and Europeans about the same time the work of Scott Joplin was still in vogue.

Jazz had its noticeable origins with the music of the New Orleans parades and processions, as can be heard during the Mardi Gras festival. This music was played by brass bands, and when the dancing began and mirth and frolic abounded, the band musicians were inspired to improvise with syncopated rhythms, blue-note trumpets, and trombone slides off the beat. In short, the music got "hot" and was jazzed up.

It seems that the process of "jazzing" existed before the term "jazz" itself became a household word. Without Joplin and the blues singers jazz would be unthinkable. What Joplin did at the piano larger groups would soon imitate – perhaps an ensemble of plucked instruments, such as the mandolin, guitar, and banjo, later joined by the clarinet, trombone, string bass, and drums. The latter replaced primitive percussive effects on a washboard.

After a while the sung blues was imitated by those instruments which, when played accordingly, approximated the sound of the human voice, such as the saxophone, the clarinet, or even the trombone, with the piano joining the other instruments in the role of accompanist. The chief prerequisites were a fine ear, a keen sense of rhythm, and a natural gift for improvisation. The ability to read music was not necessary; in fact, it became a liability rather than an asset. Once a tune or song was agreed upon, a few rhythmic snaps of the fingers by the leader was all that was required to get things going. One instrument started, and the melody was then surrounded with embellishments by other instruments, alternating with it and adding to it in an exhilarating free-for-all, with the percussion alone policing the order established by the beat.

One thing is certain: Jazz was originally the province of black musicians. They alone endowed it with the authentic qualities of unfailing rhythm, authentic blue notes, and a very special brand of improvisation. The feeling for jazz had to be inborn, an expression of centuries of suffering and resignation. In time other musicians generally assimilated it, partly by osmosis, partly through a conscious effort to create new aspects of jazz. However, they all discovered that jazz is not music that can be studied from a score.

By 1920 most Louisiana jazz men went to live in Chicago, and it was there that jazz developed as a separate musical art. One of its exponents was the trumpeter Joseph "King" Oliver (1885–1938) and his band, with Louis Armstrong as second trumpet. Their performances of "High Society," "Canal Street Blues," and "Mabel's Dream" shaped a jazz style that was to have the greatest influence; their characteristic sound spread around the world thanks to their records. It was still the New Orleans style – trumpets carrying the lead, right on the beat, with the clarinet improvising a counterpoint, usually in the high register, and the trombone furnishing a brass counterpoint, with an emphasis on the offbeat.

Louis Armstrong soon left "King" Oliver's band to become, in time, the king of jazz. His impeccable technique and extraordinary creative gifts enabled him to develop a singing tone and a brilliant improvisational capacity that was to serve as a model of jazz performance.

New York was not far behind in promoting jazz. It became the city of the big band, with Fletcher Henderson, Fats Waller, and the incomparable Duke Ellington heading the list of jazz musicians and bandleaders.

The 1930s brought the swing era, a phase of jazz in which a simple harmonic base was unvarying, even rigid, so as to allow the melody to continue along its improvisational rubato path, assured of harmonizing with the accompaniment whenever the latter reentered. The foremost representative of this style was William "Count" Basie; other outstanding jazz musicians especially popular in the 1930s and 1940s include Lionel Hampton, Cab Calloway, Earl "Fatha" Hines, Coleman Hawkins, Lester Young, Art Tatum, and Erroll Garner.

It is impossible to list here all the great bandleaders and their illustrious colleagues, nor can one outline all the various subsequent phases of jazz. Suffice it to say that jazz left an indelible imprint upon the course of music history. Jazz remains a phenomenon that must be felt and experienced to be fully appreciated. Louis Armstrong said this most succinctly when he was once asked by a woman reporter, on behalf of her newspaper readers, "Just what is jazz?" His answer was: "Honey, you tell 'em if they gotta ask, they ain't ever gonna know."

Jazz, a uniquely American art, has virtually conquered the world as a most effective and lasting musical emissary. Its basic concepts have been subject to, and continue to undergo, many variations. Some of these have been hailed as "new jazz," notwithstanding the fact that like jazz its life-giving force is the pulsating regularity of rhythm, which provides the foundation for ever-changing, ever-challenging improvisations.

It is only natural that such a potent force as jazz should eventually make itself felt in concert music. Debussy and Satie had given it an occasional nod. Jazz was responsible for such compositions as *Ragtime* for Eleven Instruments (1918) and *L'Histoire du Soldat* (1918) by Igor Stravinsky; *Kammermusik No. 1* (1921) and *Klaviersuite "1922"* (1922) by Paul Hindemith; and *La Création du Monde* (1923) by Darius Milhaud. However, it was George Gershwin (1898–1937) who gave the impetus to composers in America, as well as abroad, to emulate his example of incorporating jazz elements into concert music. His influence surely played a role in the creation of such scores as *Jonny spielt auf* (1927) by Ernst Krenek; *Music for the Theater* (1925) by Aaron Copland; *The Threepenny Opera* (1928) and *Rise and Fall of the City of Mahagonny* (1930) by Kurt Weill; and *Concerto for Jazz Band and Symphony Orchestra* (1954) by Rolf Liebermann, to name a few.

It was in 1924 that the popular bandleader Paul Whiteman asked George Gershwin to collaborate with him in a gala concert at New York's Aeolian Hall, designed to merge modern jazz with "serious" music. Gershwin came through by writing his *Rhapsody in Blue* in ten days. He performed it on the piano at the concert on the twelfth of February, with Whiteman conducting Ferde Grofé's orchestration of the score. It was an immediate success and has remained a lasting example of the interrelation of jazz and classical music.

A year later Gershwin received the recognition few jazz composers had enjoyed up until that time. Walter Damrosch, the renowned conductor of the New York Symphony Orchestra, commissioned Gershwin to compose a piano concerto for performance with the orchestra. Gershwin the jazz musician was now to be reckoned with as a serious composer. In December 1925 he was the proud soloist in his own *Concerto in F*. He then wrote a symphonic work, *An American in Paris*, which was premiered in 1928 by the New York Symphony Orchestra. Here the composer utilized the mood of blues to great effect in depicting the homesickness of an American in Europe.

Many memorable tunes, conceived in the manner of jazz, had established Gershwin's fame as a popular composer before the events described above. In fact, his musical comedies were filled with true hit tunes, such as "Fascinating Rhythm" and " 'S Wonderful," which represent the spirit of the Roaring Twenties in their verve and sense of constant motion. A high point in Gershwin's career as a composer came in 1935, when he completed his opera *Porgy and Bess*. A recreation of Negro life in Catfish Row on Charleston's waterfront, its arias and songs are in the greatest American jazz tradition.

The name of George Gershwin has become the symbol of American music all over the world. No other composer has left a more lasting imprint on the musical life of America.

AN OVERVIEW OF
THE AMERICAN MUSICAL SCENE

As we have seen, America marveled at the virtuosity of the world's great musical performers when they visited this country in the early decades of the twentieth century. The educational dependence of American musicians upon European training continued for some time. One had to earn one's laurels in European opera houses and concert halls before becoming accepted at home. Given the comparative youth of our educational facilities as compared with the long-established fame of their European counterparts, this was not surprising.

American composers at the turn of the century journeyed to Germany for inspiration during their formative years. That trend continued, a hiatus during World War I notwithstanding. Such organizations as the Berlin Opera and the same city's recital halls were still important for the debut of budding American performers.

France became equally important. For years to come, the American Conservatory in Fontainebleau was chosen for study by young

American musicians. Specifically, the pedagogical genius of the *grande dame* of French music, Nadia Boulanger, attracted a great number of these aspiring musicians. Aaron Copland (Boulanger's first full-time American student), Walter Piston, Roy Harris, Virgil Thomson, Douglas Moore, Herbert Elwell, Bernard Rogers, David Diamond, and Arthur Berger were among the many who were highly stimulated and motivated by the musical logic and impeccable craftsmanship of Mlle. Boulanger.

The advent of the forces that precipitated World War II and that event's aftermath brought about a wave of immigration of some of Europe's finest musicians, among them Paul Hindemith, Béla Bartók, and Arnold Schoenberg. The resultant collective American and European forces created a large reservoir of musical knowledge, experience, and artistic and pedagogical talent, enough to satisfy both native and foreign-born hopefuls. Young Americans in quest of musical knowledge and experience no longer needed to travel to Europe.

Gifted students found compassionate, highly devoted mentors of more than local repute. Howard Hanson (1896–1981), former director of the famed Eastman School of Music in Rochester, New York, and a renowned conductor and composer, was an early champion of American music. He furthered and encouraged the careers of young American composers by bringing new music to the attention of the general public nationwide as well as to professional groups, such as the Music Teachers' National Association. Under his leadership an entire school of Eastman graduate composers emerged, among them Gardner Read, Burrill Phillips, Robert Palmer, William Bergsma, and Ulysses Kay. Hanson espoused the position that American music is music by Americans, whether composed by musicians born here or by first-generation immigrants.

Many of Howard Hanson's own compositions are noteworthy. His seven symphonies, five symphonic poems, and such miscellaneous works as *Serenade for Flute, Strings, and Harp* (1946) and *Pastorale for Oboe, Strings, and Harp* (1949) are eclectic in nature. *Merry Mount,* Hanson's only opera, has a libretto based on Nathaniel Hawthorne's *The Maypole Lovers of Merry Mount,* which recounts the story of Thomas Morton, his maypole, and the entanglement of a Puritan pastor with one of the Cavaliers' girls. *Three Songs from*

"Drum Taps" (1935, based on texts by Walt Whitman) is impressive in its setting for chorus and orchestra.

It is hardly possible to supply here a complete list of American composers in our time. Their numbers are great, and their contributions are considerable. I should, however, like to draw the reader's attention to the names of some of those individuals whose creative efforts have become synonymous with the evolution of American music.

WALTER PISTON (1894–1976) is widely recognized as one of America's leading composers. For many years he was a professor of music at Harvard University. His eight symphonies, a ballet suite called *The Incredible Flutist,* and his *Three New England Sketches* for orchestra are in the classical tradition and form part of the standard repertoire of many orchestras.

WILLIAM GRANT STILL (1895–1978), a gifted black composer, successfully utilized idioms and subjects associated with his people in such works as *Africa, Afro-American Symphony, Lenox Avenue* (a tonal impression of Harlem), and his opera *Troubled Island,* with a story set in Haiti by Langston Hughes, a renowned black poet.

ROGER SESSIONS (1896–1985), eclectic in his musical tendencies, daring in his devotion to American music, and unperturbed by critical judgment of his work, is a fastidious creator and an inspiring teacher. His operas *The Trial of Lucullus* and *Montezuma* as well as his symphonies and string quartets are especially noteworthy.

VIRGIL THOMSON (1896–1989) is a gifted composer as well as a writer about music, whose works have been the source of considerable controversy over the years. *Symphony on a Hymn Tune,* the operas *Four Saints in Three Acts* and *The Mother of Us All* (both with texts by Gertrude Stein), and orchestral suites extracted from the film scores *The Plough That Broke The Plains* and *Louisiana Story* are among his lasting achievements.

QUINCY PORTER (1897–1966), master of traditional musical forms, left a remarkable legacy as a teacher at such renowned institutions as Vassar College, the New England Conservatory, and Yale University. His string quartets, symphonies, and concertos have become part of the standard orchestral repertoire.

Roy Harris (1898–1979) greatly influenced a new generation of young American composers through his leadership in promoting new music and as a teacher at various universities and colleges. He was a prolific, though often controversial composer of music that is typically American in character. His symphonies are considered to be neoclassical, and their names indicate the composer's avowed intentions: Symphony No. 4 ("Folk Song"), Symphony No. 6 ("Gettysburg Address"), Symphony No. 8 ("San Francisco"), Symphony No. 10 ("Abraham Lincoln"). I consider Roy Harris' Symphony No. 3 one of the great compositions of our time.

Elliott Carter (b. 1908) enjoys special significance as a composer of traditional musical forms imbued with intellectual logic. String quartets, variations for orchestra, and concertos are special cases in point, as are such earlier works as ballet legend in one act entitled *Pocahontas* (1939); *The Defense of Corinth* (1941), scored for speaker, male chorus, and piano, four hands; and the Double Concerto for Harpsichord, Piano and Two Chamber Orchestras (1961).

Samuel Barber (1910–81) is one of America's major composers whose works are performed worldwide. They are especially memorable for their power of invention and superb craftsmanship. His popular *Adagio for Strings; Overture to "The School for Scandal";* two symphonies; three *Essays for Orchestra;* concertos for violin, cello, and piano; the operas *Vanessa* and *Antony and Cleopatra;* the ballet score *Medea;* works for voice and orchestra entitled *Knoxville: Summer of 1915* and *Prayers of Kierkegaard;* and his piano sonata will long remain in the forefront of American music.

William Schuman (b. 1910) has helped shape various facets of the American musical scene, from teaching to publishing, as director of publications of the music house G. Schirmer, to the presidency of the Juilliard School of Music, and ultimately that of the entire complex of Lincoln Center for the Performing Arts in New York. Schuman is one of our major symphonists, having written ten symphonies to date. A violin concerto, a fantasy entitled *A Song of Orpheus* for cello and orchestra, *New England Triptych, American Festival Overture, Judith: Choreographic Poem for Orchestra,* and various works for chamber music attest to the diverse creativity of this unique master.

MORTON GOULD (b. 1913) is best known for his use of popular subjects in concert form. These include: *Spirituals for Orchestra; Latin-American Symphonette, Interplay* for piano and orchestra; *Philharmonic Waltzes;* and the ballet score *Fall River Legend.*

PETER MENNIN (1923–83) is another of America's distinguished educator-composers, who was president of New York's Juilliard School. Mennin has nine symphonies to his credit. A great number of vocal and instrumental chamber music compositions bespeak his exceptionally inventive power and superior craftsmanship.

WALLINGFORD RIEGGER (1885–1961), HENRY COWELL (1897–1965), PAUL CRESTON (b. 1906), ELIE SIEGMEISTER (1909–91), ALAN HOVHANESS (b. 1911), and DAVID DIAMOND (b. 1915) are all leaders in the burgeoning field of American music.

At this time we should turn our attention to several individuals who deserve special mention, Aaron Copland and Leonard Bernstein, both prolific contributors to the twentieth-century music scene in America.

Many of Aaron Copland's compositions are of a distinctively American complexion. From the film scores *Of Mice and Men, Our Town,* and *The Red Pony* to the ballet music *Billy the Kid, Rodeo,* and *Appalachian Spring;* from such works associated with American literature as *Lincoln Portrait, Twelve Poems of Emily Dickinson,* and *Old American Songs* to the opera *The Tender Land,* Copland's inspiration, drawn from American sources, is self-evident. All these compositions belong to one special period in the composer's life – the 1940s and 1950s.

Copland's musical output attests to his wide range of interests. He is as much at home in traditional forms of music as he is in atonal or serial music. His film and ballet scores belong to the former category, as do his works for students – an operetta for high school use entitled *The Second Hurricane* (1937) and *An Outdoor Overture* (1938). Representative of his serial music are his *Quartet for Piano and Strings* (1950), *Piano Fantasy* (1955–57), and *Connotations for Orchestra* (1962), to mention a few. *El Salón México* (1936) and *Danzón Cubano* (1942) attest to his interest in Latin-American tonal colors.

Of equal importance is Aaron Copland's lifelong concern with music's educational aspects. He was a teacher and lecturer for many years at the Berkshire Music Center at Tanglewood, Massachusetts; a visiting professor at many universities and institutions of musical learning; a guest conductor and pianist in his own and other composers' works, performing with the world's leading orchestras; and the author of such books as *What to Listen for in Music* (1939), *Our New Music* (1941), and *Music and Imagination* (1952). Few have so enriched the American scene by precept and example as has Aaron Copland.

In his capacities of conductor, pianist, and educator, Leonard Bernstein brought music, both as an art and as an educative process, to millions, young and old, via television, radio, live concerts, and university lectures. His multifaceted talents, coupled with an unmatched capacity for communication, enabled him to imbue the masses with his love of music. As a composer his three symphonies *(Jeremiah, The Age of Anxiety, Kaddish); Serenade for Violin, Strings, and Percussion;* ballet score *Fancy Free;* musicals *On the Town, Candide* (now an opera) and, above all, *West Side Story* are of major importance in their respective fields.

Leonard Bernstein was born in 1918 in Lawrence, Massachusetts. He first studied piano with Helen Coates, who became his lifelong executive secretary and personal assistant. As a student at Harvard University he studied composition with Walter Piston and Edward Burlingame Hill. His teachers at the Curtis Institute of Music in Philadelphia included Fritz Reiner in conducting, Isabelle Vengerova in piano, and Randall Thompson in orchestration. After 1941 Bernstein became closely associated with Serge Koussevitzky. In

1943 he was engaged as assistant conductor of the New York Philharmonic.

In November 1943 Leonard Bernstein attained sudden world notoriety when he was called upon unexpectedly to conduct a coast-to-coast broadcast concert of the Philharmonic, substituting on short notice for the ailing guest conductor Bruno Walter. His illustrious career launched, Bernstein now guest-conducted the major orchestras of the world. From 1959 until 1969 he was music director of the New York Philharmonic, and since then he has held the title of laureate conductor.

As director of the Berkshire Music Center at Tanglewood, Massachusetts, and professor at Brandeis and Harvard universities, Leonard Bernstein exerted a formidable influence upon a new generation of musicians. He wrote several books, including *The Joy of Music* (1959) and *The Infinite Variety of Music* (1966). His Norton Lectures at Harvard (1973) are available on records. The world mourned his death in October 1990, and the city of Vienna lowered its flags to half-mast.

MUSICAL COMEDIES

Let us now take a brief backward glance at a special genre – musicals. We think of this musical form as being associated specifically with New York's Broadway, where most of the musical comedies gained their fame. While many were first performed there, some were originally tried out in other cities before reaching New York.

Historically the American musical comedy follows the tradition set by Offenbach in Paris; Johann Strauss, Lehár, and Von Suppé in Vienna; and Gilbert and Sullivan in London. Like the operetta, it sets to music love stories that are sentimental, nostalgic, and often exotic in character. Many memorable melodies have long outlived the now-forgotten complete works in which they first appeared.

Among the distinguished contributors to this genre are:

VICTOR HERBERT (1859–1924), Irish-American conductor and composer of such operettas as *Babes in Toyland, Naughty Marietta,* and *Sweethearts.*

GEORGE M. COHAN (1878–1942), actor, playwright, and producer, with such memorable show tunes to his credit as "Give My Regards to Broadway" and "I'm a Yankee Doodle Dandy."

RUDOLF FRIML (1879–1972), Bohemian pianist and composer, best known for such operettas as *High Jinks, Rose Marie,* and *Vagabond King.*

SIGMUND ROMBERG (1887–1951), Hungarian-American composer, creator of music for the operettas *Blossom Time, The Student Prince,* and *The Desert Song.*

JEROME KERN (1885–1945), prolific composer of scores for musicals; perhaps best remembered for his music to *Show Boat,* which includes the song "Ol' Man River."

COLE PORTER (1893–1964), creator of such popular musical comedies as *Red Hot and Blue, Dubarry Was a Lady, Something for the Boys,* and, above all, *Kiss Me Kate.*

IRVING BERLIN (1888–1989) who combined his remarkable talents as a prolific song writer, theatrical producer, and music publisher; he wrote music for such notable shows as *This Is the Army* and *Annie Get Your Gun.*

RICHARD RODGERS (1902–79) first teamed up with lyricist LORENZ HART and then with OSCAR HAMMERSTEIN II; produced a series of scores that have never been surpassed in popularity in the history of American musicals. *A Connecticut Yankee, Babes in Arms* (co-authored by George Kaufman and Moss Hart), *Pal Joey,* and *I Married an Angel* were joint efforts by Rodgers and Hart. *Oklahoma!, Carousel, South Pacific, The King and I,* and *The Sound of Music* are among the Rodgers and Hammerstein productions which became all-time hits.

FREDERICK LOEWE (1901–88), as composer and ALAN JAY LERNER (1918–1986) as lyricist collaborated on such popular musicals as *Brigadoon, Paint Your Wagon,* and *My Fair Lady.*

FRANK LOESSER (1910–69), with *Guys and Dolls* and *The Most Happy Fella;* VINCENT YOUMANS (1898–1946), with *No, No, Nanette;* and KURT WEILL (1900–50), with *Knickerbocker Holiday, Lady in the*

Dark, and *One Touch of Venus,* also deserve special mention here as distinguished composers.

Among successful composers of a later generation I should like to single out Stephen Sondheim (b. 1930). In addition to his contribution of lyrics to Leonard Bernstein's *West Side Story* and Jule Styne's *Gypsy,* he wrote the words and music for his own shows, such as *A Funny Thing Happened on the Way to the Forum* and *Sweeney Todd, the Demon Barber of Fleet Street.*

Making no claim to completeness, this impressive list may serve to remind us of a unique phase of our American musical heritage which continues to delight audiences in this country and abroad.

Music Education: Incentives and Challenges

Most composers derive a goodly part of their income from teaching, unless their ability to secure commissions and their prolificacy in executing them can assure their financial independence – not a common occurrence these days. Their teaching responsibilities, however, can be of greatest value to members of a new generation of composers. America, especially, has been blessed with a profusion of excellent music departments on many college and university campuses, which are staffed with outstanding professionals.

A fledgling European musician has always veered toward a professional school of music, an academy, or a conservatory. But only in America can one find the counterpart of a renowned conservatory within the framework of a great institution of higher learning. From Indiana University, one of the prime examples, to the University of Southern California, from the University of Michigan to Sarah Lawrence College, from the University of Washington to the University of Illinois – to mention only a cross-section – serious students of music have an exceptional opportunity for growth under the tutelage of well-known composer- and performer-teachers.

Arthur Shepherd at Cleveland's Western Reserve University; Walter Piston at Harvard; William Schuman at Sarah Lawrence, prior to his assuming the post of president of the Juilliard School of Music; Norman Dello Joio at Sarah Lawrence; Roger Sessions at

Princeton; Ernest Bloch at the University of Southern California; Paul Hindemith at Yale; Otto Luening at the University of Arizona, Bennington College, and Columbia University; Arthur Berger at Brandeis – these are only a few cases in point to illustrate the remarkable institution of composer-in-residence.

There is an even greater number of performing artists whose inspirational teaching by precept and example has guided young and talented pupils along the path to professional careers. Historically our national treasures in this phase of musical education date back to the early 1920s, when the Juilliard Graduate School in New York and the Curtis Institute in Philadelphia secured the services of some of the finest international artists for their faculties.

The singer Marcella Sembrich, cellist Felix Salmond, pianists Ernest Hutcheson, Josef and Rosina Lhévinne, Carl Friedberg, Alexander Siloti, Olga Samaroff Stokowski, and James Friskin taught at Juilliard. Violinist Leopold Auer – teacher of Jascha Heifetz, Mischa Elman, Nathan Milstein, and other great artists – agreed to accept students both at Juilliard and Curtis. In addition, the Curtis faculty listed among its roster the violinists Efrem Zimbalist (later its president), Carl Flesch; the singers Elisabeth Schumann and Emilio de Gogorza; and the pianists Moriz Rosenthal and Isabelle Vengerova. Fritz Reiner was available for special conducting students and Carlos Salzedo for students of the harp. Even those interested in becoming music critics were guided at the Curtis Institute by Samuel Chotzinoff.

The violinists Ivan Galamian and Dorothy Delay succeeded in shaping new generations of concert artists at Juilliard. The influence upon pianists of Rudolf Serkin, at the Curtis Institute, was as profound in the field of humanism as it was all-encompassing in an artistic way.

Some outstanding artists have chosen to combine teaching with an active performing career, thereby providing a dual source of inspiration for their students: violinist Josef Gingold, cellist Janos Starker, and pianist Menahem Pressler at Indiana University; the Cleveland Quartet at the Eastman School of Music; violinist Jascha Heifetz and cellist Gregor Piatigorsky at the University of Southern California; and pianist Theodore Lettvin at the University of Michigan.

Such artists who serve on the music faculties of our universities and colleges ensure the continued existence of superior schools of music within large academic institutions.

Private teaching has reached high levels of excellence thanks to increasing standards of pedagogy and the determination of many individual teachers to maintain a remarkable level of performance ability. So-called armchair teaching has seldom produced great results. Students benefit far more from actual demonstrating of how a certain musical problem can be solved rather than merely discussing it. Teachers themselves find new challenges and receive new ideas and stimuli by being part of professional groups, such as the Music Teachers' National Association (MTNA). This is one of the finest organizations of its kind; its annual conventions, clinics, and meetings offer outstanding opportunities for discussion and finding new teaching materials and inventive ways of presenting ideas. Such meetings have attracted many newcomers to the teaching profession, who soon become convinced that opportunities are to be found in areas other than that of the professional concert artist. The art of accompaniment, of playing in orchestras, of participating in or directing choral groups, or of arranging musical scores can all be combined within the framework of a successful teaching career.

In a similar vein, our public schools have a rich history of offering a variety of musical training by highly qualified and motivated music teachers. A professional organization known as Music Educators' National Conference (MENC) has furnished the impetus for self-advancement to its teacher-members. After all, it is often the public school music teacher who is responsible for discovering and nurturing an exceptional young talent, especially in areas where little or no outside stimulation is available. Many artists today credit a teacher with awakening them to the beauties of music.

The private sector in America offers unique ways in which to aid young people of proven talent to reach a professional goal in music. For example, private foundations have come to the aid of deserving young musicians in many different and often highly inventive ways.

Another incentive exists in the form of contests and competitions designed to reward the winners with public acclaim and performance opportunities. Here the National Federation of Music Clubs has led the way for many years.

MUSICAL PERFORMANCES:
OPERA, BALLET, AND MUSIC FESTIVALS

Opera companies now exist in dozens of cities, their accomplishments being of far more importance than local pride. Among them – in addition to the major organizations mentioned earlier in this chapter – are opera companies in Cleveland, Houston, Hartford, Baltimore, Dallas, San Diego, Miami, Philadelphia, Seattle, St. Louis.

During the early part of the twentieth century it appeared that the few established opera companies met whatever need existed for this medium by staging performances of the conventional repertoire, presented by artists whose European fame had preceded them to these shores. The Depression years threatened their existence. Indeed, the Chicago Civic Opera Association was forced to close, while the Metropolitan Opera of New York was saved by public gifts, many of which were, and continue to be, prompted by the Met's weekly radio broadcasts and the more recent television presentations.

From its modest beginnings in 1943 as part of the New York City Center of Music and Drama, the New York City Opera has grown into a major organization. The first artistic director was László Halasz, and his successors have included, in recent times, conductor Julius Rudel and acclaimed soprano Beverly Sills. One of the most exciting aspects of the organization's purpose is giving young singers the opportunity to learn roles and gain valuable experience that can ultimately pave the way for advancement among world-class opera houses.

The Metropolitan Opera Company of New York celebrated its centennial anniversary in the fall of 1983. With the exceptionally gifted conductor James Levine as its artistic director, the Met has gained new stature among the world's leading opera houses.

American operas as a creative art form have been in short supply compared with the number of symphonic, choral, and chamber music works written in this country. As mentioned earlier, Gershwin's *Porgy and Bess* stands out as a high point. Few other operas dating from the same period – 1935 and the ensuing years – have survived.

Walter Damrosch (1862–1950), conductor of both the New York Philharmonic and the New York Symphony, was also a composer of operas. When he was seventy-five, Damrosch conducted his own work, *The Man Without a Country* (1937). Other notable operas he created include *The Scarlet Letter* (1896); *Cyrano de Bergerac* (1913); and *The Opera Cloak* (1942).

Deems Taylor (1885–1966), best known for his orchestral suite *Through the Looking Glass*, wrote an opera called *Peter Ibbetson*, based on Constance Collier's play after a novel by George du Maurier. First staged in 1931 at the Metropolitan Opera House, it had a record number of sixteen performances in four seasons.

Louis Gruenberg (1884–1964) enjoyed a certain success with his opera *The Emperor Jones*, first heard at the Metropolitan Opera in 1933. Based on a Eugene O'Neill play, it starred Lawrence Tibbett in the title role. Virgil Thomson's *Four Saints in Three Acts*, based on a text by Gertrude Stein, was first heard in 1934 in Hartford, Connecticut, with an all-black cast. It had forty-eight performances that year in New York's Forty-fourth Street Theater. It was revived on Broadway in 1952, and was later successfully produced in Paris.

The politically oriented opera *The Cradle Will Rock* by Marc Blitzstein (1905–64) premiered in New York in 1937 at the Mercury Theatre and was revived in the 1940s.

The cause of American opera has been greatly served by the Italian-born Gian Carlo Menotti (b. 1911), who was educated at the Curtis Institute in Philadelphia. It was in that city's Academy of Music that his comic opera *Amelia Goes to the Ball* was first presented in 1937. Its performance at the Metropolitan Opera in 1938 set Menotti on his way to operatic fame. *The Old Maid and the Thief* (1939) was commissioned by the National Broadcasting Company. *The Telephone* (1946) was staged by the Ballet Society as a curtain raiser for *The Medium* (1946), one of Menotti's most successful tragic operas. *The Consul* (1950) has enjoyed remarkable success both in the United States and abroad. Other notable lyrical dramatic operas include *Amahl and the Night Visitors*, written for television performance on Christmas Eve 1951; *The Saint of Bleecker Street*, which premiered in 1954; *The Last Savage* (1963); *Martin's Lie* (1964); and *Help, Help, the Globolinks!* (1968).

Schools and workshops have been both producers and recipients of operatic efforts. In addition to Aaron Copland's *The Second Hurricane* (1937), written for students from eight to eighteen years of age, Kurt Weill (1900–1950) created a folk opera designed for school performance entitled *Down in the Valley,* which was first staged at Indiana University in 1948. Opera workshops devoted to the propagation of American opera are found in many of our schools. They also represent a consumer market, as it were, for short works that can be produced and staged more economically than in major houses. Among the leading workshops are the ones at Indiana University, the University of Southern California, and those attached to various music schools like the Juilliard Institute in New York, the Peabody Institute in Baltimore, and the Cleveland Institute of Music.

Ballet in America has definitely come of age in the twentieth century, spearheaded in the 1930s by Lucia Chase and Richard Pleasant, Eugene Loring (who choreographed and danced in Ballet Caravan's 1938 production of *Billy the Kid*), and Anton Dolin. The establishment of the New York City Ballet in 1948 by Lincoln Kirstein and George Balanchine led to the formation of ballet companies in other American cities. A special debt of gratitude is owed to Lincoln Kirstein, who singled out American dancers for performances of American ballets enhanced by American music. Balanchine, a former associate of the renowned Serge Diaghilev, helped establish a generation of American choreographers, such as Todd Bolender, Ruthanna Boris, and Jerome Robbins. Without his immense contributions, the American ballet scene would be literally unthinkable. Robbins, in turn, created his own masterpiece in 1944, *Fancy Free,* for which Leonard Bernstein wrote a scintillating score.

Agnes de Mille, one of the original members of Chase and Pleasant's Ballet Theater, created a ballet typical of America's Southwest,

Rodeo (1942) with a brilliant score by Aaron Copland. She also conceived the dances for *Oklahoma!, Carousel,* and *Brigadoon,* as well as the choreography for *Fall River Legend* (1948), with music by Morton Gould.

One of the greatest forces on the American dance scene is Martha Graham, a pioneer of modern dance. Hers are not storytelling ballets; rather, they utilize body and limb movements for their own sake and for the conveyance of thoughts and emotions. In this manner she was greatly successful in bringing vividly to life the characters of Joan of Arc, Medea, and Judith. The three-dimensional scenery of the sculptor Isamu Noguchi enhanced her remarkable conceptions, lending an air of reality and immediacy to her dancing and that of her associates.

Graham's rich artistic imagination prompted her to commission significant musical scores by composers living in America. These include *Hérodiade* (1944) by Paul Hindemith; *Appalachian Spring* (1944), one of Aaron Copland's most important works; *The Serpent Heart* (1946; subsequently revised and renamed *Cave of the Heart*) by Samuel Barber; *Night Journey* (1947) by William Schuman; *Wilderness Stair* (1948) by Norman Dello Joio; and *Errand into the Maze* (1947) by Gian Carlo Menotti. The fact that so many of these ballet and dance scores also enjoy concert performances attests to their enrichment of American music.

The 1950s and 1960s new American dance groups emerged, among them the Joffrey Ballet, which has traveled widely for both performance and demonstration purposes. The originality and inventiveness of these highly gifted artists and their associates have brought additional riches to the musical scene. By now many American cities have their own ballet companies, thus reaffirming the consistent trend of decentralization of our cultural activities.

An American institution that has grown tremendously during the twentieth century is the music festival, which can be held either indoors or outdoors. Festivities of this sort began in America in the mid-1800s: Boston and Worcester, Massachusetts, initiated them in 1858, Cincinnati in 1871. Bethlehem, Pennsylvania, started its now-famous Bach Festival in 1900, and it still continues to this day. Baldwin-Wallace College in Berea, Ohio, has an equally renowned Bach Festival. The May Festival in Ann Arbor, Michigan, now over one hundred years old, features a single orchestra, until recently the Philadelphia Orchestra, as the main attraction, plus additional soloists. The Spoleto Festival of Two Worlds in Charleston, South Carolina, is an event that began in the 1970s.

The Berkshire Festivals in Pittsfield, Massachusetts, were devoted to chamber music until 1931, when Mrs. Elizabeth Sprague Coolidge, one of music's greatest patronesses, transferred them from her Berkshire estate to the Library of Congress in Washington, D.C. These chamber music festivals served, and still serve, as the vehicle for the performances of new works, many having been commissioned by Mrs. Coolidge.

Tanglewood, near Lenox, Massachusetts, has been the summer home of the Boston Symphony Orchestra since 1937. Some of its members also serve as faculty of the associated Berkshire Music Center at Tanglewood. Over the years many great musicians, performing artists, and composers have become alumni of this magnificent institution. The founder of the festival, Serge Koussevitzky, started an ongoing tradition of inviting to Tanglewood visiting composers, performers, and lecturers that has, in effect, made the festival an institution of higher musical learning in one of the most beautiful settings for the performance of outstanding music during the summer months.

The combination of concerts and educational programs has become a popular formula, one that is used successfully by other orchestra's "summer homes." Many symphonic organizations, however, have evolved summer festivals in outdoor settings near their home base; these are chiefly devoted to concerts. The most prominent are: the Hollywood Bowl concerts, near Los Angeles, with the Los Angeles Philharmonic; the Philadelphia Orchestra at Robin Hood Dell, near Philadelphia, and in Saratoga, New York; the Blossom Music Festival of the Cleveland Orchestra, near Akron, Ohio; the Detroit Symphony Orchestra's Meadowbrook Festival in Rochester, Michigan; and the Chicago Symphony's Ravinia Park Festival.

In addition, there are also important musical summer sessions devoted primarily to instrumental and vocal instruction of a high caliber; they function as a sort of graduate school, with faculty and students joining forces for orchestral and chamber music performances. The leading "festivals" of this type are held in Tanglewood, Massachusetts, in Chautauqua, New York, and in Aspen, Colorado.

Altogether unique is the position of the Marlboro Music Festival, often called "Music at Marlboro," in Vermont. Its original function was a completely private one, namely, a summer get-together for members of the legendary Busch family of artists. Adolf Busch, the violinist, and his son-in-law Rudolf Serkin, the pianist; Fritz Busch, the conductor, and his son-in-law Martial Singher, the baritone, as well as his son Hans Busch, the opera producer; Hermann Busch, cellist; and some of their closest musician friends assembled in Marlboro for music making, chamber music sessions, plus reading and rereading of new and old scores.

The death of some of the family members prompted Rudolf Serkin to perpetuate the sessions as a memorial to his kin. Soon he surrounded himself with his students and with other musicians, young and old, to continue the original purpose of making music together. Interested visitors began to come to Marlboro to "listen in"; soon their numbers grew. The facilities of Marlboro College, a small school, were made available for rehearsals and performances. Famed cellist Pablo Casals was a regular visiting artist.

The number of musicians from all parts of America and Europe wishing to participate in the Marlboro Music Festival increased, and a process of selection had to be instituted. Marlboro is not a school; there are no lessons. It is devoted solely to studying and performing ensemble music, a "republic of equals" in the words of its director, Rudolf Serkin.

In America today a great variety of musical offerings is available to the general public, affording satisfaction of a considerably high level for every possible taste. Opportunities for gifted and persevering musicians are greater here than in most other countries. Audiences have become more sophisticated in their musical tastes, their knowledge of musical subjects and backgrounds, and in their choice of musical interests. Music in all its forms, even in isolated areas, is as near as your radio or television dial or the switch on your stereo.

From symphony orchestras to chamber music groups, ballet ensembles, and opera companies, and from free public concerts in the parks to musical institutions of higher learning, we can witness the accomplishments of years of continuous musical progress in America, from a land of undaunted pioneers of modest musical sophistication to a nation of leadership, promise, and hope in the future achievements of music.

POSTSCRIPT

To terminate at any given point a discussion of music in relation to history and to other arts is to deny its lifeblood, which is in a constant state of flux, and man's infinite ability to create and recreate. Any movement or period of music must be considered as a link in that endless flow of inspiration. Only in this manner can we begin to understand the importance of individual efforts, goals, and achievements along the way. Though we are prone to attach special importance to one span of time over another, each is conditioned by that which precedes and by that which follows.

Music in all its shapes and manifestations is an essential part of life itself, not an isolated form of entertainment. Whether we create, interpret, or simply listen to it, music can become an integral and indispensable part of our being if we only allow it to. History, in its inexorable course, has always bestowed final judgment upon the individual worth of a composer or a piece of music.

There are few of us who are able to judge in retrospect as history does. We therefore must be prepared to evaluate in our own time as best we can. If the reader, when he or she lays down this book, has been aided in some measure in the formation of a more knowledgeable judgment of the various phases of so elusive yet so thoroughly enjoyable, uplifting, and noble an art as music, I will gladly and contentedly rest my case.

APPENDIX

Suggestions for Building a Music Library

The following are some thoughts on how to proceed, step by step, in building a recorded music collection. Obviously there are some highly subjective factors involved, such as personal taste, the availability of a serviceable system composed of a record, cassette, or compact disc player and speakers, and a modest budget to allow for the gradual acquisition of disks, cassettes, or CDs. Although taste itself can be cultivated with devotion and effort, given an increasingly critical ear and improved judgment, it will in the end dictate the value of the playing equipment and the amount spent on recordings.

It is advisable to begin unpretentiously. Too elaborate a stereo system can limit your record budget at the outset. We all have only two ears with which to listen, and their performance is not appreciably altered by expensive components that claim to faithfully reproduce so-called true concert sound. Start realistically and stretch your recording allowance so as to be able to purchase one or two at a time, perhaps on a monthly basis. Neither Rome nor a music library was built in a day.

I would begin by alternating categories: a symphony, a concerto, a single-instrument recital, an operatic album, and a choral or song selection. Suggestions are listed for each category in what I believe to be an order of progressively more demanding listening, from the fairly easy or well-known selection to the more elaborate and somewhat less familiar one. It is, of course, for the reader to decide whether to follow this system of alternation or to stay within a single category for a given period.

Just a few words of explanation regarding multiple selections of performances of any given work listed here. I consider these to be of especially high levels, both from the standpoint of interpretation and of reproduction quality. However, at no time do they represent my personal choice of one artist or group over another, or of one label over another. The reader may prefer a totally different recording; indeed, additional choices will become available long after this book has gone to press. I strongly advise you to take the time to listen to different renditions of a work before making a purchase.

At the time of this writing, the compact disk has become a reality, making storage much easier. While it may be harder on the wallet, it does become more feasible to own more than one recording of the same composition. I have marked an asterisk beside LP selections available on CD, noting any change in recording companies. Here, then, are some of the categories from which to choose, including my personal suggestions. Selections from other categories of music for your listening pleasure may be found in Chapter Eight and in scattered references throughout this book.

SYMPHONIES

Mozart   Symphony No. 40, G Minor, K. 550

    Cleveland Orchestra, Szell (Columbia)
    Berlin Philharmonic, Karajan
    (Deutsche Grammophon)*
    English Chamber Orchestra,
    Barenboim (Angel)*

Haydn   Symphony No. 94 ("Surprise")

    Pittsburgh Symphony, Previn (Angel)
    London Philharmonic, Jochum
    (Deutsche Grammophon)*
    New York Philharmonic, Bernstein
    (Columbia)

Beethoven   Symphony No. 5, C Minor, Op. 67

    Vienna Philharmonic, Maazel (CBS)

New York Philharmonic, Bernstein
(CBS)
Boston Symphony, Kubelik (Deutsche
Grammophon)

Schubert   Symphony No. 8, B Minor ("Unfinished")

Chicago Symphony, Giulini (Deutsche
Grammophon)*
Amsterdam Concertgebouw, Haitink
(Philips)*
Israel Philharmonic, Mehta (London)

Tchaikovsky   Symphony No. 5, E Minor, Op. 64

Philadelphia Orchestra, Ormandy (RCA)
(Delos)*
Chicago Symphony, Solti (London)
(Decca)*
London Symphony, Abbado (Deutsche
Grammophon)

Dvořák   Symphony No. 9, E Minor ("New World")

New York Philharmonic, Bernstein
(Columbia)
St. Louis Symphony, Slatkin (Telarc)
Chicago Symphony, Levine (RCA)

Bizet   Symphony No. 1, C Major

New York Philharmonic, Bernstein
(CBS)
Amsterdam Concertgebouw, Haitink
(Philips)
French National Orchestra, Munch
(Nonesuch)

Mendelssohn   Symphony No. 4, A Major ("Italian")

New York Philharmonic, Bernstein
(Columbia)

Boston Symphony, Davis (Philips)*
Cleveland Orchestra, Szell (Columbia)

Schumann | Symphony No. 3, E-Flat Major ("Rhenish")

Berlin Philharmonic, Kubelik
(Deutsche Grammophon)
Philadelphia Orchestra, Muti (Angel)
New Philharmonia Orchestra,
Klemperer (Angel)

Beethoven | Symphony No. 3, E-Flat Major, Op. 55
("Eroica")

Cleveland Orchestra, Szell (CBS)
Los Angeles Philharmonic, Giulini
(Deutsche Grammophon)
Berlin Philharmonic, Böhm (Deutsche
Grammophon)

Schubert | Symphony No. 9, C Major ("The Great")

Berlin Philharmonic, Karajan (Angel)
(EMI)*
Philadelphia Orchestra, Ormandy
(Columbia)
Cleveland Orchestra, Szell (CBS)

Sibelius | Symphony No. 2, D Major, Op. 43

Philadelphia Orchestra, Ormandy
(RCA)
New York Philharmonic, Bernstein
(Columbia) (Deutsche Grammophon)*
Royal Philharmonic, Barbirolli
(Quintessence)

Brahms | Symphony No. 1, C Minor, Op. 68

Vienna Philharmonic, Karajan
(London)
Chicago Symphony, Solti (London)
(Decca)*
Vienna Philharmonic, Mehta (London)

Mahler   Symphony No. 1, D Major

       Columbia Symphony, Walter (Odyssey)*
       New York Philharmonic, Bernstein
         (Columbia)*
       Israel Philharmonic, Mehta (London)*

Beethoven   Symphony No. 9, Op. 125 ("Choral")

       Cleveland Orchestra, Szell (Odyssey)*
       Amsterdam Concertgebouw, Haitink
         (Philips)*
       London Symphony, Giulini (Angel)

CONCERTOS – PIANO

Tchaikovsky   Concerto No. 1, B-Flat Minor, Op. 23

       Ashkenazy – London Symphony,
         Maazel (London) (Decca)*
       Gilels – New York Philharmonic,
         Mehta (CBS)*
       Richter – Vienna Symphony, Karajan
         (Deutsche Grammophon)

Beethoven   Concerto No. 5, E-Flat Major, Op. 73
         ("Emperor")

       Serkin – New York Philharmonic,
         Bernstein (Columbia)
       Rubinstein – Boston Symphony,
         Leinsdorf (RCA)*
       Weissenberg – Berlin Philharmonic,
         Karajan (Angel)

Grieg   Concerto, A Minor, Op. 16

       Rubinstein – RCA Symphony,
         Wallenstein (RCA)
       Fleisher – Cleveland Orchestra, Szell
         (Odyssey)

| | Zimerman – Berlin Philharmonic, Karajan (Deutsche Grammophon)* |

Rachmaninoff   Concerto No. 2, C Minor, Op. 18

Ashkenazy – Moscow Philharmonic, Kondrashin (London)

Anievas – New Philharmonia, Atzmon (Angel)

Graffman – New York Philharmonic, Bernstein (Columbia)

Rachmaninoff   Concerto No. 3, D Minor, Op. 30

Horowitz – New York Philharmonic, Ormandy (RCA)*

Janis – Boston Symphony, Munch (RCA)

Berman – London Symphony, Abbado (Columbia)*

Chopin   Concerto No. 2, F Minor, Op. 21

Argerich – National Symphony, Rostropovich (Deutsche Grammophon)*

Rubinstein – Philadelphia Orchestra, Ormandy (RCA)

Ax – Philadelphia Orchestra, Ormandy (RCA)*

Chopin   Concerto No. 1, E Minor, Op. 11

Perahia – New York Philharmonic, Mehta (CBS)*

Rubinstein – New Symphony London, Skrowaczewski (RCA)*

Ohlsson – Polish Radio National Symphony, Maksymiuk (Angel) (EMI)*

Liszt   Concerto No. 1, E-Flat Major

Watts – New York Philharmonic, Bernstein (Columbia)

Wild – Columbia Symphony, Kostelanetz (Odyssey)

Argerich – London Symphony, Abbado
(Deutsche Grammophon)*

Mozart   Concerto No. 21, C Major, K. 467

Perahia – English Chamber Orches-
tra, Perahia (Columbia)*
Barenboim – English Chamber
Orchestra, Barenboim (Angel)
Bishop – London Symphony, Davis
(Philips)

Mozart   Concerto No. 20, D Minor, K. 466

Perahia – English Chamber Orchestra,
Perahia (Columbia) (CBS)*
Serkin – Cleveland Orchestra, Szell
(Columbia)
Barenboim – English Chamber
Orchestra, Barenboim (Angel)
(His Master's Voice)*

Mozart   Concerto No. 27, B-Flat Major, K. 595

Perahia – English Chamber Orchestra,
Perahia (CBS)*
Serkin – Philadelphia Orchestra,
Ormandy (Columbia)
Casadesus – Cleveland Orchestra, Szell
(Columbia)

Mendelssohn   Concerto No. 1, G Minor, Op. 25

Serkin – Philadelphia Orchestra,
Ormandy (Columbia)
Firkusny – Luxembourg Radio,
Froment (Turnabout)
Perahia – Academy of St.
Martin-in-the-Fields, Marriner
(Columbia) (CBS)*

Beethoven   Concerto No. 4, G Major, Op. 58

Lupu – Israel Philharmonic, Mehta
(London)

Pollini – Vienna Philharmonic, Böhm
(Deutsche Grammophon)*

Serkin – Boston Symphony, Ozawa
(Telarc)*

Beethoven   Concerto No. 3, C Minor, Op. 37

Gilels – Cleveland Orchestra, Szell
(Angel) (EMI)*

Lupu – Israel Philharmonic, Mehta
(London)

Pollini – Vienna Philharmonic, Böhm
(Deutsche Grammophon)*

Beethoven   Concerto No. 1, C Major, Op. 15

Lupu – Israel Philharmonic, Mehta
(London)

Eschenbach – Berlin Philharmonic,
Karajan (Deutsche Grammophon)

Brendel – Stuttgart Philharmonic,
Boettcher (Turnabout) (Vox)*

Beethoven   Concerto No. 2, B-Flat Major, Op. 19

Lupu – Israel Philharmonic, Mehta
(London)

Brendel – Vienna Symphony, Wallberg
(Turnabout)

Kempff – Berlin Philharmonic, Leitner
(Deutsche Grammophon)*

Schumann   Concerto A Minor, Op. 54

Serkin – Philadelphia Orchestra,
Ormandy (Columbia)

Fleisher – Cleveland Orchestra, Szell
(Odyssey)

Argerich – National Symphony,
Rostropovich (Deutsche
Grammophon)

Brahms   Concerto No. 2, B-Flat Major, Op. 83

Serkin – Cleveland Orchestra, Szell
(CBS)

Fleisher – Cleveland Orchestra, Szell
(Odyssey)
Barenboim – New York Philharmonic,
Mehta (CBS)

CONCERTOS – VIOLIN

Tchaikovsky Concerto D Major, Op. 35

Heifetz – Chicago Symphony, Reiner
(RCA)*
Milstein – Vienna Philharmonic,
Abbado (Deutsche Grammophon)*
Perlman – Philadelphia Orchestra,
Ormandy (Angel) (His Master's
Voice)*

Mendelssohn Concerto E Minor, Op. 64

Heifetz – Boston Symphony, Munch
(RCA)*
Stern – Philadelphia Orchestra,
Ormandy (Columbia)*
Szeryng – Amsterdam Concertgebouw,
Haitink (Philips)

Bruch Concerto No. 1, G Minor, Op. 26

Stern – Philadelphia Orchestra,
Ormandy (Columbia)*
Perlman – London Symphony, Previn
(Angel)
Zukerman – Los Angeles
Philharmonic, Mehta (Columbia)*

Wieniawski Concerto No. 2, D Minor, Op. 22

Perlman – London Philharmonic,
Ozawa (Angel) (His Master's Voice)*
Zukerman – Royal Philharmonic,
Foster (Columbia)

Rabin – Philharmonia Orchestra,
Goosens (Seraphim)

Beethoven | Concerto D Major, Op. 61

Milstein – Philharmonia Orchestra,
Leinsdorf (Angel)
Stern – New York Philharmonic,
Bernstein (Columbia)
Perlman – Philharmonia Orchestra,
Giulini (Angel) (His Master's Voice)*

Bach | Concerto No. 1, A Minor

Szeryng – Academy of St. Martin-in-the-
Fields, Marriner (Philips)
Perlman – English Chamber
Orchestra, Barenboim (Angel)
Kremer – Vienna Symphony, Kremer
(Eurodisc)

Bach | Concerto No. 2, E Major

Szeryng – Academy of St. Martin-in-the-
Fields, Marriner (Philips)
Perlman – English Chamber
Orchestra, Barenboim (Angel)
(His Master's Voice)*
Menuhin – London Symphony,
Menuhin (Angel)*

Bach | Concerto D Minor for Two Violins

Grumiaux, Krebbers – Solistes Ro-
mands, Gerecz (Philips)
Stern, Zukerman – St. Paul Chamber
Orchestra (CBS)*
Perlman, Stern – New York Philhar-
monic, Mehta (CBS)

Paganini | Concerto No. 1, D Major, Op. 6

Rabin – Philharmonia Orchestra,
Goosens (Seraphim)
Szeryng – London Symphony, Gibson
(Philips)

Perlman – Royal Philharmonic, Foster
(Angel) (His Master's Voice)*

Mozart   Concerto No. 3, G Major, K. 216

Stern – Cleveland Orchestra, Szell
(CBS)

Szeryng – New Philharmonia, Gibson
(Philips)*

Zukerman – English Chamber Orchestra, Barenboim (Columbia)*

Mozart   Concerto No. 4, D Major, K. 218

Stern – English Chamber Orchestra,
Schneider (Columbia)

Szeryng – New Philharmonia, Gibson
(Philips)*

Mutter – Philadelphia Orchestra, Muti
(Angel) (His Master's Voice)*

Mozart   Concerto No. 5, A Major, K. 219

Grumiaux – London Symphony, Davis
(Philips)*

Szeryng – New Philharmonia, Gibson
(Philips)*

Mutter – Berlin Philharmonic,
Karajan (Deutsche Grammophon)*

Lalo   Symphonie Espagnole, Op. 21

Perlman – Orchestre de Paris,
Barenboim (Deutsche
Grammophon)*

Stern – Philadelphia Orchestra,
Ormandy (Columbia)

Grumiaux – Lamoureux Orchestra,
Rosenthal (Philips)

Brahms   Concerto D Major, Op. 77

Heifetz – Chicago Symphony, Reiner
(RCA)*

Milstein – Philharmonia Orchestra,
Fistoulari (Seraphim)

Oistrakh – Cleveland Orchestra, Szell
(Angel)

Sibelius   Concerto D Minor, Op. 47

Heifetz – Chicago Symphony, Hendl
(RCA)*

Stern – Philadelphia Orchestra,
Ormandy (Columbia)

Perlman – Boston Symphony,
Leinsdorf (Angel) (RCA)*

Prokofiev   Concerto No. 2, G Minor, Op. 63

Heifetz – Boston Symphony, Munch
(RCA)*

Szeryng – London Symphony,
Rozhdestvensky (Quintessence)

Perlman – Boston Symphony,
Leinsdorf (RCA)

CONCERTOS – CELLO

Haydn   Concerto D Major, Op. 101

Starker – Philharmonia Orchestra,
Giulini (Angel)

Rostropovich – Academy of St.
Martin-in-the-Fields, Rostropovich
(Angel) (His Master's Voice)*

Ma – English Chamber Orchestra,
Garcia (CBS)*

Boccherini   Concerto B-Flat Major

Starker – Philharmonia Orchestra,
Giulini (Angel)

Du Pré – Chicago Symphony,
Barenboim (Angel)

Fournier – Lucerne Festival Strings,
Baumgartner (Deutsche Grammophon)

Lalo	Concerto D Minor
	Rose – Philadelphia Orchestra, Ormandy (Columbia)
	Ma – Orchestre National, Maazel (CBS)*
	Fournier – Lamoureux Orchestra, Martinon (Deutsche Grammophon)
Saint-Saëns	Concerto No. 1, A Minor, Op. 33
	Rostropovich – London Philharmonic, Giulini (Angel) (EMI)*
	Starker – Philharmonia Orchestra, Giulini (Seraphim)
	Rose – Philadelphia Orchestra, Ormandy (Columbia)
Dvořák	Concerto, B Minor, Op. 104
	Rostropovich – Berlin Philharmonic, Karajan (Deutsche Grammophon)*
	Starker – London Symphony, Dorati (Mercury)
	Rose – Philadelphia Orchestra, Ormandy (Columbia)
Schumann	Concerto, A Minor, Op. 129
	Rostropovich – French National Radio Orchestra, Bernstein (Angel) (His Master's Voice)*
	Starker – Philharmonia Orchestra, Giulini (Seraphim)
	Du Pré – New Philharmonia, Barenboim (Angel)
Bloch	Schelomo – Hebrew Rhapsody
	Starker – Israel Philharmonic, Mehta (London) (Decca)*
	Rostropovich – French National Radio Orchestra, Bernstein (Angel) (His Master's Voice)*
	Piatigorsky – Boston Symphony, Munch (RCA)

CONCERTOS – VIOLA

Vanhall   Concerto C Major

> Wallfisch – Württemberg Chamber Orchestra, Faerber (Turnabout)

C. Stamitz   2 Concertos

> Zukerman – English Chamber Orchestra, Zukerman (Columbia)

Handel   Concerto, B Minor

> Zukerman – English Chamber Orchestra, Zukerman (Columbia)

Telemann   Concerto G Major

> Shingles – Academy of St. Martin-in-the-Fields, Marriner (Argo)

Walton   Concerto

> Menuhin – New Philharmonia, Walton (EMI)

CONCERTO – DOUBLE BASS

Koussevitzky   Concerto

> Karr – Oslo Philharmonic, Antonini (CRI)

CONCERTOS – FLUTE

Mozart   Concertos K. 313, 314

> Rampal – Vienna Symphony, Guschlbauer (RCA)
>
> Baker – Solisti di Zagreb, Janigro (Vanguard)
>
> Galway – Lucerne Festival Strings, Baumgartner (RCA) (Eurodisc)*

C. Stamitz	Concerto G Major, Op. 29

Rampal – Saar Chamber Orchestra,
Ristenpart (RCA)

Galway – New Irish Chamber
Orchestra, Prieur (RCA)

E. Zukerman – English Chamber
Orchestra, P. Zukerman (CBS)

CONCERTOS – OBOE

Mozart	Concerto C Major, K. 314

Black – Academy of St. Martin-in-the-
Fields, Marriner (Philips)

Holliger – Munich Chamber Orchestra,
Stadlmair (Deutsche Grammophon)

Koch – Berlin Philharmonic, Karajan
(Angel)

Marcello	Concerto

Holliger – Dresden State Orchestra
(Philips)

Pierlot – Solisti Veneti, Scimone (RCA)

Zanfini – Virtuosi di Roma, Fasano
(Angel)

Cimarosa	Concerto

Holliger – Bamberg Symphony, Maag
(Deutsche Grammophon)

Pierlot – Paillard Chamber Orchestra,
Paillard (RCA)

Lardrot – Vienna State Opera
Chamber Orchestra, Prohaska
(Vanguard)

R. Strauss	Concerto D Major

Black – English Chamber Orchestra,
Barenboim (CBS)

Holliger – New Philharmonia,
De Waart (Philips)

CONCERTOS – CLARINET

Mozart   Concerto A Major, K. 622

> Stoltzman – English Chamber Orchestra, Schneider (RCA)*
>
> Leister – Berlin Philharmonic, Karajan (Angel)
>
> De Peyer – London Symphony, Maag (London)

Weber   Concerto No. 1, F Minor, Op. 73

> Leister – Berlin Philharmonic, Kubelik (Deutsche Grammophon)
>
> De Peyer – New Philharmonia Orchestra, Frühbeck de Burgos (Angel)
>
> Glazer – Württemberg Chamber Orchestra, Faerber (Turnabout)

CONCERTOS – BASSOON

Mozart   Concerto B-Flat Major, K. 191

> Piesk – Berlin Philharmonic, Karajan (Angel) (His Master's Voice)*
>
> Walt – Boston Symphony, Ozawa (Deutsche Grammophon)*
>
> Zeman – Vienna Philharmonic, Böhm (Deutsche Grammophon)

Weber   Concerto F Major, Op. 75

> Miller – Copenhagen Chamber Orchestra, Farberman (Cambridge)
>
> Turkovic – Bamberg Symphony, Schneidt (Deutsche Grammophon)

CONCERTOS – HORN

Mozart
Concertos K. 412, 417, 447, 495
Tuckwell – London Symphony, Maag (London) (Decca)*
Seifert – Berlin Philharmonic, Karajan (Deutsche Grammophon)*
Högner – Vienna Philharmonic, Böhm (Deutsche Grammophon)*

R. Strauss
Concerto No. 1, E-Flat Major, Op. 11
Bloom – Cleveland Orchestra, Szell (Odyssey)

CONCERTOS – TRUMPET

Telemann
Concerto D Major
André – English Chamber Orchestra, Mackerras (Deutsche Grammophon)

Hummel
Concerto E-Flat Major
Dokschitser – Moscow Chamber Orchestra, Barshai (Quintessence)
André – Berlin Philharmonic, Karajan (Angel)
Berinbaum – English Chamber Orchestra, Somary (Vanguard)

CONCERTOS – SAXOPHONE

Glazunov
Concerto
Abato – New York Studio Orchestra, Henderson (Odyssey)

Ibert
Concertino da Camera
Rousseau – Kuentz Chamber Orchestra, Kuentz (Deutsche Grammophon)

CONCERTO – HARPSICHORD

Haydn   Concerto D Major, Op. 21

       Malcolm – Academy of St. Martin-in-
         the-Fields, Marriner (London)
       Kipnis – London Strings, Marriner
         (Odyssey)

CONCERTOS – HARP

Handel   Concerto B-Flat Major, Op. 4, No. 5

       Zabaleta – Kuentz Chamber Orchestra,
         Kuentz (Deutsche Grammophon)*
       Robles – Academy of St.
         Martin-in-the-Fields, Brown (Argo)

Dittersdorf Concerto A Major

       Zabaleta – Kuentz Chamber Orchestra,
         Kuentz (Deutsche Grammophon)
       Robles – Academy of St.
         Martin-in-the-Fields, Brown (Argo)

Boieldieu Concerto C Major

       Robles – Academy of St. Martin-in-the-
         Fields, Brown (Argo)
       Michel – Monte Carlo Opera
         Orchestra, Almeida (Philips)

CONCERTOS – GUITAR

Giuliani   Concerto A Major, Op. 30

       Williams – English Chamber Orchestra
         (Columbia)
       Bream – Melos Ensemble (RCA)
       Yepes – English Chamber Orchestra
         (Deutsche Grammophon)

Castelnuovo-
Tedesco   Concerto D Major, Op. 99
> Williams – English Chamber Orchestra,
> Groves (CBS)*
> Romero – English Chamber Orchestra
> (Angel)
> Diaz – Solisti di Zagreb, Janigro
> (Vanguard)

Villa-Lobos   Concerto
> Williams – English Chamber Orchestra,
> Barenboim (Columbia) (CBS)*
> Bream – London Symphony, Previn
> (RCA)*

CONCERTOS – ORGAN

Handel   16 Concertos
> Chorzempa – Concerto Amsterdam,
> Schröder (Philips)

Rheinberger   2 Concertos, F Major, Op. 137; G Minor,
Op. 177
> Biggs – Columbia Orchestra, Peress
> (Columbia)

Poulenc   Concerto G Minor
> Alain – ORTF Orchestra, Martinon
> (Erato)
> Preston – London Symphony, Previn
> (Angel)
> Duruflé – National Radio Orchestra,
> Prêtre (Angel) (His Master's Voice)*

CONCERTOS – MULTIPLE INSTRUMENTS

Bach   Concertos for 2, 3, and 4 Harpsichords

             Gerlin, Dreyfus, Verlet, Douatte (Nonesuch)

             Richter, Bilgram, Fütterer, Schott – Munich Bach Orchestra (Deutsche Grammophon)

Bach   6 Brandenburg Concertos

             Berlin Philharmonic, Karajan (Deutsche Grammophon)*

             I Musici (Philips)*

             Stuttgart Chamber Orchestra, Münchinger (London) (Decca)*

Dittersdorf   Sinfonia Concertante for Double Bass and Viola

             Hörtnagel, Lemmen – Württemberg Chamber Orchestra, Faerber (Turnabout)

Beethoven   Concerto C Major for Violin, Cello, Piano, Op. 56

             Oistrakh, Rostropovich, Richter – Berlin Philharmonic, Karajan (Angel) (His Master's Voice)*

             Beaux Arts Trio – London Philharmonic, Haitink (Philips)*

             Mutter, Ma, Zeltser – Berlin Philharmonic, Karajan (Deutsche Grammophon)*

Brahms   Concerto A Minor for Violin and Cello, Op. 102

             Oistrakh, Rostropovich – Cleveland Orchestra, Szell (Angel)

             Szeryng, Starker – Amsterdam Concertgebouw, Haitink (Philips)

Stern, Rose – Philadelphia Orchestra,
Ormandy (Columbia)

Mozart   Concerto E-Flat Major for 2 Pianos, K. 365

Firkusny, Weiss – Rochester Symphony,
Zinman (Vox)

Emil & Elena Gilels – Vienna Philharmonic, Böhm (Deutsche Grammophon)*

Ashkenazy, Barenboim – English
Chamber Orchestra (London)

Mozart   Concerto C Major for Flute and Harp, K. 299

Rampal, Nordmann – English Chamber
Orchestra (CBS)*

Galway, Robles – London Symphony,
Mata (RCA)*

Baker, Jellinek – Solisti di Zagreb,
Janigro (Bach Guild)

Mozart   Sinfonia Concertante E-Flat Major for Violin and Viola, K. 364

Stern, Zukerman – English Chamber
Orchestra, Barenboim (Columbia)

Druian, Skernick – Cleveland Orchestra, Szell (Columbia)

D. & I. Oistrakh – Moscow Philharmonic, Kondrashin (London)

Mozart   Sinfonia Concertante E-Flat Major for Oboe,
Clarinet, Bassoon, Horn, and Strings,
K. 297b

Berlin Philharmonic, Karajan (Angel)
(Deutsche Grammophon)*

Vienna Philharmonic, Böhm
(Deutsche Grammophon)*

Saar Orchestra, Ristenpart (Nonesuch)

Vivaldi   Concertos for 4 Violins and Orchestra

Zukerman, Sillito, Garcia, Tunnell –
English Chamber Orchestra
(Columbia)

Poulenc   Concerto for 2 Pianos and Orchestra
Gold & Fizdale – New York Philharmonic, Bernstein (Columbia)

SONATAS FOR PIANO

Haydn   Sonatas Nos. 20, 49
Brendel (Philips)*

Clementi   Sonata, Op. 40, No. 2
Berman (CBS)

Mozart   Sonata A Minor, K. 310
De Larrocha (London)

Mozart   Sonata A Major, K. 331
Brendel (Philips)

Beethoven   Sonata C-Sharp Minor, Op. 27, No. 2
("Moonlight")
Serkin (Columbia)

Beethoven   Sonata C Minor, Op. 13 ("Pathétique")
Horowitz (Columbia)
Serkin (Columbia)

Beethoven   Sonata C Major, Op. 53 ("Waldstein")
Ashkenazy (London) (Decca)*

Beethoven   Sonata F Minor, Op. 57 ("Appassionata")
Serkin (Columbia)
Horowitz (Columbia)
Kempff (Deutsche Grammophon)*

Chopin   Sonata No. 2, B-Flat Minor, Op. 35 ("Funeral
March")
Rubinstein (RCA)*
Perahia (Columbia) (CBS)*
Argerich (Deutsche Grammophon)*

Chopin   Sonata B Minor, Op. 58
                Rubinstein (RCA)
                Ashkenazy (London)
                Argerich (Deutsche Grammophon)

Schubert   Sonata D Major, Op. 53
                Curzon (London)

Schubert   Sonata A Major, Op. 120
                De Larrocha (London)

Schubert   Sonata B-Flat Major, Op. Posth.
                Serkin (Columbia)
                Curzon (London) (RCA)*
                Barenboim (Deutsche Grammophon)*

Brahms   Sonatas Nos. 1 & 2 in C Major and F-Sharp Minor
                Zimerman (Deutsche Grammophon)*

OPERAS

Bizet   *Carmen*
                Horne, Maliponte, McCracken, Krause
                   Bernstein – Metropolitan Opera
                   (Deutsche Grammophon)

Verdi   *Aida*
                Price, Bumbry, Domingo, Milnes, Raimondi
                   Leinsdorf – London Symphony (RCA)*
                Price, Gorr, Tozzi, Merrill, Vickers
                   Solti – Rome Opera (London) (Decca)*

Puccini   *La Bohème*
                Freni, Pavarotti, Ghiaurov
                   Karajan – Berlin Philharmonic
                   (London) (Decca)*

Puccini   *Madama Butterfly*
                Freni, Ludwig, Pavarotti, Kerns
                Karajan – Vienna Philharmonic
                (London) (Decca)*

Puccini   *Tosca*
                Price, Domingo, Milnes
                Mehta – New Philharmonia, Alldis
                Choir (RCA)

Mozart   *The Marriage of Figaro*
                Te Kanawa, Popp, Von Stade, Ramey,
                Allen, Moll
                Solti – London Philharmonic
                (London) (Decca)*

Mozart   *Don Giovanni*
                Moser, Te Kanawa, Berganza, Riegel,
                Raimondi, Van Dam, Macurdy
                Maazel – Paris Opéra (CBS)*

Mozart   *The Magic Flute*
                Lear, Peters, Otto, Wunderlich,
                Fischer-Dieskau
                Böhm – Berlin Philharmonic
                (Deutsche Grammophon)*

Verdi   *La Traviata*
                Sills, Gedda, Panerai
                Ceccato – Royal Philharmonic,
                Alldis Choir (Angel)

Verdi   *Il Trovatore*
                Price, Cossoto, Domingo, Milnes,
                Giaiotti
                Mehta – New Philharmonia (RCA)*

Mascagni   *Cavalleria Rusticana*
                De los Angeles, Corelli
                Santini – Rome Opera (Angel)

Leoncavallo *I Pagliacci*
> Freni, Pavarotti, Wixell
> Patané – National Philharmonic
> (London) (Decca)*

Saint-Saëns *Samson et Dalila*
> Vickers, Gorr, Diakov, Blanc
> Prêtre – Paris Opéra (Angel) (EMI)*

Wagner *Die Meistersinger von Nürnberg*
> Donath, Kollo, Schreier, Evans, Adam, Ridderbusch
> Karajan – Dresden State Opera (Angel)

Beethoven *Fidelio*
> Janowitz, Popp, Kollo, Dallapozza, Fischer-Dieskau, Sotin, Jungwirth
> Bernstein – Vienna Philharmonic & State Opera Chorus (Deutsche Grammophon)*

Oratorios, Masses, Lieder Cycles

Handel *Messiah*
> Ameling, Reynolds, Langridge, Howell – Academy of St. Martin-in-the-Fields & Chorus, Marriner (Argo)*
> Donath, Reynolds, Burrows, McIntyre – Alldis Choir, London Philharmonic, Richter (Deutsche Grammophon)
> Harper, Watts, Wakefield, Shirley-Quirk – London Symphony & Chorus, Davis (Philips)*

Mendelssohn *Elijah*
> Jones, Baker, Gedda, Fischer-Dieskau – New Philharmonia & Chorus, Frühbeck de Burgos (Angel)

> Marsh, Verrett, Lewis, Krause – Colum-
> bus Boychoir, Chorus, Philadelphia
> Orchestra, Ormandy (RCA)

Walton   *Belshazzar's Feast*

> Luxon – London Philharmonic &
> Chorus, Solti (London)
> Shirley-Quirk – London Symphony &
> Chorus, Previn (Angel) (His Master's
> Voice)*

Haydn   *The Creation*

> Janowitz, Ludwig, Wunderlich, Fischer-
> Dieskau – Vienna Singverein, Berlin
> Philharmonic, Karajan (Deutsche
> Grammophon)*
> Donath, Tear, Van Dam –
> Philharmonia Orchestra & Chorus,
> Frühbeck de Burgos (Angel)*
> Harper, Tear, Shirley-Quirk – King's
> College Choir, Academy of St. Martin-
> in-the-Fields, Willcocks (Arabesque)
> (His Master's Voice)*

Bach   *Mass in B Minor*

> Ameling, Minton, Watts, Krenn,
> Krause – Singakademie, Stuttgart
> Chamber Orchestra, Münchinger
> (London) (Decca)*
> Janowitz, Ludwig, Schreier, Kerns,
> Ridderbusch – Vienna Singverein,
> Berlin Philharmonic, Karajan
> (Deutsche Grammophon)
> Marshall, Baker, Tear, Ramey –
> Academy of St. Martin-in-the-Fields,
> Marriner (Philips)*

Beethoven   *Missa Solemnis*

> Janowitz, Baltsa, Schreier, Van Dam –

Vienna Singverein, Berlin Philharmonic, Karajan (Angel) (His Master's
Voice)*

Giebel, Höffgen, Haefliger, Ridderbusch
– Netherlands Radio Choir, Amster-
dam Concertgebouw, Jochum
(Philips)

Harper, Baker, Tear, Sotin – London
Philharmonic Choir, New Philharmonia, Giulini (Angel)

Mozart   *Mass in C Minor, K. 427* ("The Great")

Donath, Harper, Davies, Dean – London
Symphony & Chorus, Davis (Philips)

Hendricks, Perry, Schreier, Luxon –
Vienna Singverein, Berlin Philharmonic, Karajan (Deutsche Grammophon)*

Cotrubas, Kanawa, Krenn, Sotin –
Alldis Choir, New Philharmonia,
Leppard (Seraphim)*

Fauré   *Requiem, Op. 48*

Armstrong, Fischer-Dieskau – Orchestre de Paris & Chorus, Barenboim
(Angel)

Ameling, Kruysen – Netherlands Radio
Choir, Rotterdam Philharmonic
Orchestra, Fournet (Philips)

Verdi   *Requiem Mass*

Arroyo, Veasey, Domingo, Raimondi –
London Symphony & Chorus,
Bernstein (London)

Price, Baker, Luchetti, Van Dam –
Chicago Symphony & Chorus, Solti
(RCA)

Freni, Ludwig, Cossutta, Ghiaurov –
Vienna Singverein, Vienna Philhar-

monic, Karajan (Deutsche Grammophon)*

Berlioz   *Requiem, Op. 5* ("Grande Messe des Morts")

Domingo – Orchestre de Paris &
Chorus, Barenboim (Deutsche
Grammophon)

Dowd – London Symphony & Chorus,
Davis (Philips)*

Burrows – French National Radio
Orchestra & Chorus, Bernstein
(Columbia)

Brahms   *Ein Deutsches Requiem*

Cotrubas, Prey – New Philharmonia &
Chorus, Maazel (Columbia)

Kanawa, Weikl – Chicago Symphony
& Chorus, Solti (London) (Decca)*

Janowitz, Krause – Vienna State
Opera Chorus, Vienna
Philharmonic, Haitink (Philips)*

Schubert   *Die Schöne Müllerin* (Song Cycle)

Fischer-Dieskau, Moore (Deutsche
Grammophon)*

Schumann   *Dichterliebe* (Song Cycle)

Fischer-Dieskau, Eschenbach (Deutsche
Grammophon)*

Schumann   *Frauenliebe und -leben* (Song Cycle)

Baker, Barenboim (Angel)
Ameling, Baldwin (Philips)

Glossary

Tempos and Interpretive Markings:

Accelerando   Becoming faster in tempo

Adagietto   Somewhat faster than adagio

Adagio   Slow. This term is frequently used as the heading of a composition or a portion thereof (e.g., a movement of a symphony or sonata).

Affettuoso   Affectionate, with tender expression

Agitato   Agitated, restless

Allargando   Broadening or slowing the tempo

Allegretto   Fairly fast, but slower than allegro

Allegro   Quite fast, lit. lively; frequently used in association with adjectives, such as allegro moderato (moderately fast) or allegro ma non troppo (fast, but not too fast)

Andante   Fairly slow, between allegretto and adagio; a leisurely, walking tempo

Andantino   A little faster than andante

Appassionato   With passion or pathos

Arioso   With songlike interpretation

A Tempo   Resumption of original tempo after temporary deviation

Attacca   Designation to start an ensuing part or movement without the customary break or wait

Calando   Gradually diminishing in intensity or speed

Cantabile   In a singable manner; mostly applied to instrumental interpretation

Crescendo   Increasing in volume, getting louder. As a rule, the abbreviation "cresc." is used.

Diminuendo (or Decrescendo)   Getting softer. Abbreviated "dim." or "decresc."

Dolce   Sweet, gentle tone

Doppio Movimento   Lit. double movement. An indication to play twice as fast

Forte   Loud; varies in volume according to adjacent grades of force (ff – fortissimo; mf – mezzo forte)

Largo   Very slow

Legato   Smooth; smoothly connected playing of tones

Leggiero   Light

Leise   Soft and gentle

L'istesso Tempo   The same tempo as before

Luftpause   A rest to facilitate breathing

Meno Mosso   With less motion, less fast

Mezzo   Half. Mezzo forte (mf) – half or moderately loud. Mezzo piano (mp) – half or moderately soft. Mezzo-soprano – a vocal range halfway between soprano and contralto

Moderato   Moderate in tempo

Molto   Very. Allegro molto – very fast

Mordent   Ornament, or extra notes (also called grace notes), played before a main note, extending to neighboring tones above or below

Notes and Rests

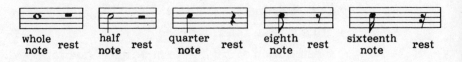

| whole note | rest | half note | rest | quarter note | rest | eighth note | rest | sixteenth note | rest |

Pianissimo   Very soft (pp)

Piano   Soft (p)

Più More. Più forte – a little louder. Più allegro – a little faster

Pizzicato Plucked. Direction for plucking the strings with the fingers rather than by playing with a bow

Presto Fast, faster than allegro

Ritardando Gradually slower (rit.)

Ritenuto Lit. to hold back in tempo; equivalent of ritardando

Rubato Lit. robbed. A word denoting a flexible but tastefully controlled style of performance, allowing for borrowing part of one note value to add to another

Spiccato Well articulated. String playing with the middle of the bow, a loose wrist bouncing on the strings in light staccato fashion

Spirito To be performed in a spirited manner

Staccato Lit. detached. Notes are to be played as short as possible.

Stretto Drawing together of fugal entrances of subjects, or heightening the tempo at the final section of a piece

Tenuto Lit. held. A marking indicating that the note is to be held for its full value – at times even longer – rather than releasing it sooner

Tranquillo To be performed in a calm manner

Tremolo Rapid repetition of a single note or rapid alternation of two or more notes

Trill An embellishment or ornamentation of a note achieved by rapid alternation of a tone with a neighboring one

Tutti Lit. all. The term indicates the entrance of the full orchestra after a period of playing by either a solo instrument or a small group of instruments.

Una Corde Lit. one string. A direction for the use of the soft pedal on the piano

Unison Simultaneous sound of two or more notes played or sung in the same pitch

Vibrato A continual slight fluctuation of pitch achieved by rapid motion of the hand and/or finger upon the strings of an instrument

General:

Absolute Music   Music for its own sake, without any association with or influence from outside or extramusical sources. Opposite of program music

Absolute or Perfect Pitch   The ability to sing or recognize any note without any help from instruments or from other voices. The presence of this skill does not, however, necessarily imply extraordinary musical ability.

A Capella   Choral music without accompaniment by an orchestra or individual instruments

Acoustics   Science dealing with the physical basis and properties of music

Ad Libitum   Lit. at pleasure; often abbreviated "ad lib."; generally referring to a certain freedom of interpretation, such as a gradual change in speed

Agréments   Ornaments or embellishments of individual notes

Antiphonal   Singing in alternating sections or choruses

Appoggiatura   An ornamental note dependent upon the following main note, usually accented so as to emphasize its ornamental nature

Arco   Bow of stringed instruments. The term is used to indicate the resumption of the bow after a pizzicato section.

Aria   A song for solo voice

Arpeggio   The notes of a chord played in fast succession rather than simultaneously; broken rather than solid chords

Bar Line   A vertical line across the horizontal staff lines denoting the end of a metric unit

Beat   A basic unit by which the measurement of musical time can be perceived. The beat can be felt by the pulse that pervades a composition – at times exaggerated by percussion instruments, as in jazz or popular music – or it can be observed in orchestral or choral works by means of the conductor's baton motions.

Bel Canto   Lit. beautiful singing or song. The term is derived from eighteenth-century Italian vocal technique and is applied to the production of beautifully sustained vocal lines rather than dramatically expressed emotions. Composers such as Bellini and Donizetti are frequently associated with bel canto writing.

Bridge   A wooden attachment to the body of stringed instruments that supports the strings as they are drawn across the pegs near the scroll to the string holder at the bottom of the instrument

A connecting passage between two major thematic sections of a composition. The bridge often accommodates a modulation between the keys or tonalities of such sections.

Cadence   A melodic or harmonic pattern with which to end a phrase, section, or an entire composition. According to the harmonies employed, the ending can be temporary or conclusive.

Cadenza   Traditional with most concertos, the cadenza is a section generally occurring just before the end of a movement, in which the solo instrument is featured without the orchestra, performing in a brilliant, often improvisational style. Thematically the cadenza is usually built upon passages of the movement just concluded.

Capriccio   A composition of a capricious or humorous character

Chaconne   A stately dance of Spanish origin, written in triple time, in which a set of variations is based on a recurring harmonic progression in the bass

Chorale Prelude   An organ composition whose musical texture is woven around a Protestant hymn. Its original purpose was that of an introduction to the congregational singing of the hymn. At the hands of Bach and subsequent composers (e.g., Reger, Mendelssohn) the chorale prelude became an important individual category for the organ.

Chord   A structure of tones sounded simultaneously

Clef   A sign placed at the beginning of the staff to determine the pitch of the notes to follow

Coda   Lit. tail. An extension at the end of a piece or section, often extraneous to its structure. Its purpose is to add emphasis or a sense of finality.

Contrapuntal   An adjective denoting the use of elements of counterpoint

Corda   Lit. string. Una corda in piano music refers to the use of the soft (left) pedal, which moves the keyboard to a position where the hammers strike only one of the three strings apportioned to them for softer effect.

Diatonic   The generally accepted natural scale, starting on any of its constituent tones and consisting of five whole tones and two half tones

Entr'acte   Music designed to be performed between the acts of an opera or play

Fermata   Pause of assigned duration, depending upon the note value to which it is applied

Finale   Last movement of a large-scale work, or the last part of a composition

Fret   A thin crossbar fitted to the fingerboard of a stringed instrument to assist the player in stopping the string. Frets are used on guitars, lutes, viols, and related instruments, but not on violins, violas, or cellos.

Giocoso   Jocular, merry

Glissando   Lit. sliding. On the piano, a rapid sliding up or down on the keys, with one or more fingers turned to the nail. On the harp, a rapid sliding of one or more fingers across the strings. On stringed instruments of the violin family, a rapid sliding of the finger up or down the string. On the trombone, the slide attachment produces the glissando.

Harmonics   A soft, almost flutelike sound produced by touching a string lightly and without pressure to achieve upper partials of any given pitch

Idée fixe   A recurring theme characterizing the appearance of an extramusical idea. For example, the clarinet theme in Berlioz's *Symphonie Fantastique* depicts the protagonist's beloved in various situations in each of the work's five movements.

432

Interval   The distance between any two notes of the scale, measured by the number of intervening notes (e.g., a third from C to E, a fifth from C to G, a seventh from C to B). The number of tones and half tones qualifies such adjectives as major, minor, augmented, or diminished intervals.

K.   The letter *K,* followed by a number, which is found after every Mozart composition, represents the name of Ritter von Köchel, the Austrian musical bibliographer who published a "Chronological Thematic Catalogue of Mozart's Complete Works."

Key   The pitch upon which the scale is built that forms the basis for a composition's harmonic structure. We speak of a work being in the key of C when the scale of C underlies its tonal identity, when it begins and/or ends with C or a chord based on C.

Leading Motif (Leitmotiv)   See Idée Fixe.

Libretto   Lit. booklet. Text or story of an opera, operetta, or oratorio. The creator or arranger of such a story is known as a librettist.

Major   Designation for the tonal character of a piece or a section thereof, based upon the use of a major scale

Measure   A space in which the total values of a group of notes recur in regular intervals, thus assuring a rhythmically proportioned profile of a composition

Meter   An order of recurring accents in regular intervals governed by a time signature (e.g., $\frac{2}{4}$, $\frac{3}{4}$, $\frac{4}{4}$, $\frac{6}{8}$)

Minor   Designation for the tonal character of a piece or section thereof, based upon the use of a minor scale

Modulation   The process of transition from one key to another, or from one tonality to another, according to established harmonic progressions

Movement   A section of a large-scale work, such as a sonata, symphony, concerto, trio, quartet, etc. A movement can be thematically independent or it can be associated with another movement by common thematic material.

Mute   An attachment to strings or instruments to soften the tone produced by such instruments, and with it the timbre of the tone

Nocturne   Lit. night piece. A composition of a quiet, melodious character. The name was first used by the Irish-born composer John Field and was later adopted and elaborated upon by Chopin.

Obbligato   An instrumental part essential to the performance of a work; hence it is "obligatory" that it not be left out at the discretion of performers. The opposite designation would be "ad libitum," meaning "at pleasure."

Op.   Abbreviation used in music printing for the Latin word "opus," meaning "work." Numbers affixed to compositions are so designated (e.g., Op. 59 meaning work No. 59). It can also be modified to read Op. 59, No. 1, denoting that the composer wishes to have "work No. 59" known as a collective opus containing more than one work.

Ostinato   A musical pattern that occurs persistently, usually in the bass part of a composition (frequently referred to as basso ostinato or ground bass)

Partita   Lit. division. The word is used to denote a series of pieces, often composed of dances of a given period. Divertimento, serenade, and suite are closely related concepts.

Passing Note   A note that appears in succession from one scale note to the next; it may constitute a dissonance with the prevailing harmonies when taken out of context.

Phrasing   Musical articulation of a work or of parts thereof. It is governed by various signs in the score, as well as by the performer's taste and thorough knowledge of the style involved.

Pitch   The height of sound as determined by the vibrations per second of the sound-issuing body or instrument

Polyphonic   Lit. many-voiced. A composition consisting of many voices used alternately or simultaneously. Among prominent examples are rounds, canons, and fugues.

Register   A category of organ pipes controlled by one stop or knob

A portion of the complete range of an instrument or a voice (e.g., middle register)

Relative   Pertaining to the relationship between two scales of the same key signature (e.g., C major and A minor are relative keys, both having no sharps or flats)

Rhapsody   A term taken from Greek poetry, denoting a composition of epic, rhetorical, at times national character (e.g., Liszt's Hungarian Rhapsodies)

Ricercar   Lit. to seek out. The term is used for a contrapuntal or polyphonic composition using intricate combinations of themes and subjects or phrases.

Scherzo   Lit. joke. A separate piece or movement of a larger work (e.g., a symphony) of a jocular or light character, mostly in a brisk tempo

Score   Full notation of a composition. The word is used primarily to comprise all individual instrumental and vocal parts of an elaborate work, such as a symphony. In the latter case each instrumental notation is listed in a traditional sequence.

Setting   Order of notation for any given category of composition or for any given instrument

Staff   A term designating the five lines and four spaces between them, upon each of which notes are written whose pitch is determined by their position on the staff

Stop   Organ – a handle that admits wind to a particular row of pipes

Stringed instruments – a certain position of the finger on the fingerboard activating a partial of the string to produce a desired pitch

Horn – the insertion of the player's hand into the bell of the instrument to achieve both a certain pitch and a varied tone

Tangent   A blade of brass used in the clavichord. Set in motion by the key, the tangent is pressed against the string and divides it into two parts. One is left free to vibrate; the other is dampened with a tiny cloth.

435

Toccata   From the Italian verb *toccare*, "to touch." A composition for a keyboard instrument, primarily the organ, harpsichord, or piano. The toccata is generally in the nature of a brilliant display piece.

Tonality   The key in which a composition is written and to which it returns even after distant modulations. Tonality implies a loyalty to the home key.

Transposition   The transferring of a composition from its original key to another key

Bibliography

Apel, Willi. *Harvard Dictionary of Music.* Cambridge: Harvard University Press (Belknap Press), 1969.

Bazin, Germain. *The Baroque.* Trans. Pat Wardroper. Greenwich: New York Graphic Society, 1968.

Blume, Friedrich. *Die Musik in Geschichte und Gegenwart.* Kassel: Bärenreiter, 1958.

Blunden, Maria and Godfrey. *Impressionists and Impressionism.* Geneva: Skira, n.d.

Borris, Siegfried. *Die Grossen Orchester.* Hamburg: Claassen, 1969.

Bücken, Dr. Ernst. *Handbuch der Musik – Wissenschaft.* Potsdam: Athenaion, 1931.

Canaday, John. *Mainstreams of Modern Art.* New York: Simon & Schuster, 1959.

Carse, Adam. *The Orchestra from Beethoven to Berlioz.* New York: Broude Bros., 1949.

Chase, Gilbert. *America's Music.* New York: McGraw-Hill, 1955.

Dolge, Alfred. *Pianos and Their Makers.* New York: Dover, 1972.

Einstein, Alfred. *Mozart, His Character, His Work.* Trans. A. Mendel and N. Broder. New York: Oxford University Press, 1945.

————. *Music in the Romantic Era*. New York: Norton, 1947.

Ewen, David. *The Complete Book of Classical Music*. Englewood Cliffs, N.J.: Prentice-Hall, 1965.

————. *The World of Twentieth-Century Music*. Englewood Cliffs, N.J.: Prentice-Hall, 1968.

Farga, Franz. *Violins and Violinists*. New York: Macmillan, 1950.

Fleming, William. *Art, Music, and Ideas*. New York: Holt, Rinehart and Winston, 1975.

Fletcher, Sir Banister. *A History of Architecture*. New York: Scribner, 1958.

Forsyth, Cecil. *Orchestration*. London: Macmillan, 1929.

Garland, Henry and Mary. *The Oxford Companion to German Literature*. Oxford: Oxford University Press (Clarendon Press), 1976.

Grove, Sir George, and Eric Blom. *Grove's Dictionary of Music and Musicians*. Fifth Edition. New York: St. Martin's Press, 1954.

Harvey, Sir Paul. *The Oxford Companion to English Literature*. Oxford: Oxford University Press (Clarendon Press), 1958.

————, and J. E. Heseltine. *The Oxford Companion to French Literature*. Oxford: Oxford University Press (Clarendon Press), 1959.

Howard, John T., and George K. Bellows. *Music in America*. New York: Crowell, 1967.

Láng, Paul Henry. *Music in Western Civilization*. New York: Norton, 1941.

Marek, George R. *Beethoven, Biography of a Genius*. New York: Funk & Wagnalls, 1969.

Michel, François, ed. *Encyclopédie de la Musique*. Paris: Fasquelle, 1958.

Osborne, Harold. *The Oxford Companion to Art*. Oxford: Oxford University Press (Clarendon Press), 1970.

Raynor, Henry. *The Orchestra*. New York: Scribner, 1978.

Riemann, Hugo. *Riemann Musik Lexikon*. Mainz: B. Schott, 1959.

Sartori, Claudio, ed. *Enciclopedia della Musica*. Milan: Ricordi, 1963.

Scholes, Percy A. *The Oxford Companion to Music*. Oxford University Press, 1970.

Summer, William L. *The Pianoforte*. London: MacDonald, 1966.

Westrup, Sir J. A., and F. Ll. Harrison. *The New College Encyclopedia of Music*. New York: Norton, 1960.

Young, Percy M. *The Concert Tradition*. New York: Roy Publishers, 1965.

Index

441

About the Author

KARL HAAS, in his daily radio broadcasts "Adventures in Good Music," is heard by millions of music lovers throughout the world. His network stretches from Alaska to Florida, across Australia, and throughout Europe and Canada. It is the only program in the history of broadcasting to be so widely acclaimed, and to continue for an uninterrupted run of thirty years.

Haas has been decorated with the Officier d'Académie; the Chevalier d'Ordre des Arts et Lettres, an order established by André Malraux; and the First Class Order of Merit from West Germany. Recently he was honored with his second George Foster Peabody Award for excellence in broadcasting. He has received the National Telemedia Award, and in 1988 was chosen Person of the Year by Boston's classical music station WGBH, resulting in his conducting the Boston Pops Orchestra.

Renowned as a pianist-conductor and a student of the legendary Artur Schnabel, Karl Haas has served as Distinguished Visiting Professor at many leading universities; he has received eight honorary doctorates, and several scholarships have been established in his name.

In New York City, Haas hosts an annual spring and fall series of "Recitals with Commentary" at the Metropolitan Museum of Art. Mr. Haas appears regularly throughout the country on radio and television as recitalist and conductor.